The Timelessness of God

John C. Yates

UNIVERSITY
PRESS OF
AMERICA

Lanham • New York • London

Copyright © 1990 by
University Press of America®, Inc.
4720 Boston Way
Lanham, Maryland 20706

3 Henrietta Street
London WC2E 8LU England

Library of Congress Cataloging-in-Publication Data

Yates, John C., 1951-
The timelessness of God / John C. Yates.
p.   cm.
Includes bibliographical references and index.
1. Time. 2. Eternity. 3. God. I. Title.
BD638.Y37   1990   231'.4—dc20   90–39956 CIP

ISBN 0–8191–7937-X (alk. paper)

 The paper used in this publication meets the minimum requirements of
American National Standard for Information Sciences—Permanence
of Paper for Printed Library Materials, ANSI Z39.48–1984.

ACKNOWLEDGEMENTS

I should like to thank Dr. Philip Almond who advised this project when it was a doctoral dissertation at Queensland University and who was always available to give clear directions at times of need. I also want to thank my wife Donna for her unfailing patience during the years which were given to this book's production.

Excerpts from *The Theological Tractates and The Consolation of Philosophy* by Boethius, translated and edited by H.F. Stewart, E.K. Rand, S.J. Tester, reprinted by permission of the Harvard University Press and the Loeb Classical Library, Cambridge, Mass.: 1973;

Excerpts from *Summa Contra Gentiles,* by Thomas Aquinas, translated by A.C. Pegis, reprinted by permission of Doubleday Press, a division of Bantam, Doubleday, Dell Publishig Group, Inc;

Excerpts from *Summa Theologica*, by Thomas Aquinas, reprinted by permission of Eyre and Spottiswoode Pty Ltd;

Excerpts from *Church Dogmatics* by Karl Barth, 1956-75, and *The Christian Faith* by F.D. Schleiermacher, 1960, reprinted by permission of T. and T. Clark Pty. Ltd.;

Extracts from *The Enneads*, by Plotinus, translated by Stephen Mackenna and revised by B.J. Page, reprinted by permission of Faber and Faber Limited.

CONTENTS

CONTENTS

Preface

We live in the midst of a climate of philosophical opinion which is strongly set against natural theology in general and the claims of the classical Christian concepts of God in particular. One of the convictions behind this book is that much of this criticism has not sufficiently familiarised itself with the larger framework in which the traditonal doctrine of God was worked out. Within the limits of space the present work is an attempt to systematically articulate the attribute of divine timelessness in such a way as to show how it fits into such a framework. Although the book is primarily an extended argument the alerted reader will discern throughout a personal commitment that the ancient Christian doctrine of God is religiously satisfying. It is my hope that both the logical and existential implication of the argued position on divine timelessness will be given greater consideration by philosophers of religion because of this publication.

CHAPTER ONE

INTRODUCTION

> Men of our European culture do not talk at all of eternity in
> the metaphysical sense unless they have been subject to the
> influence of a certain tradition (which I have tried to
> sketch) ... the doctrine of timeless eternity is a dubious
> partner for theology ... If anyone thinks he can
> nevertheless make use of the old phraseology, he must
> explain it afresh.[1]

So writes William Kneale at the conclusion of a paper which
heralded the commencement of the contemporary onslaught against the
predominant received concept of the "eternity of God",[2] and which in
many ways provides a suitable preface to the intention of this book.
Contra Kneale, and many others, I will be contending in this work
that the said metaphysical tradition possesses the resources adequately
to explicate and defend its own position, and that "the doctrine of the
timeless eternity" is a vital component of a coherent theological
position.

With respect to the parameters of the discussion my thesis arises
out of that metaphysic\al system which has become known as
"classical theism". Historically, a clearly recognisable concept of God
has been forged in Western thought through a self-conscious synthesis
of rational and putative revelational elements,[3] that is, through the
fusion of Hellenistic philosophy and the Bible.[4] A "classical theist"
could fairly be expected to accept the following description of God
offered by Richard Swinburne: "a person without a body (i.e. a
spirit), present everywhere, the creator and sustainer of the universe, a

---

[1] W. Kneale, "Time and Eternity in Theology", *Proceedings of the Aristotelian
Society*, 61, 1960-61 p.107.

[2] At this early stage of the book I do not wish to consider the exact character of
this notion, but rather to note only its place in a larger system of thought, and to
outline the projected character of the book itself.

[3] See, C. Pinnock, "The Need For a Scriptural, and Therefore a Neo-Classical
Theism", in *Perspectives on Evangelical Theology*, K. S. Kantzer and S.W. Gundy
(eds), Grand Rapids: Baker, 1979, p.38.

[4] Though this statement strictly refers to Christianity, it is also fundamentally
true of Judaism.

free agent, able to do everything (i.e. omnipotent), knowing all things, perfectly good, a source of moral obligation, immutable, eternal, a necessary being, holy, and worthy of worship."[5] Such a description lists the attributes of God,[6] amongst which is the property of eternity.

The importance of the concept of the "divine eternity" for classical theism becomes apparent once it is recognized that for this type of theism the attributes of God are predicated of God "essentially", that is, the predicate terms commonly used to designate qualities of God express an identity relation.[7] As Augustine says: "For whatever seems to be said there according to qualities is to be understood according to substance or essence."[8] Or, to put it at its simplest, God "is" what he "has".[9] Given this as a pre- understanding for what is to follow, it is immediately recognisable that in discussing the "divine eternity" I will be investigat-ing a question of central importance to philosophical theology, viz. what sort of being God is (or might be).[10] For classical theists additionally, the tension in any discussion of the divine attributes is heightened by an adherence to the idea of the

---

[5] R.G. Swinburne, *The Coherence of Theism*, Clarendon: Oxford, 1977, p.2.

[6] It is recognised that some of the terms in this list, e.g. "the creator and sustainer of the universe" are better understood as relational predicates rather than as referring to God **in se**. Cf. R.H. Nash, *The Concept of God*, Grand Rapids: Eerdmans, 1983, p.16. "Eternity" however is uniformly recognized as a necessary and formal attribute by all classical theists. "Eternity is the very substance of God Himself" St. Augustine, *Enarr in Ps.101, Sermo* 2, 10 cited in W. Gundersdorf von Jess, "Divine Eternity in the Doctrine of Saint Augustine", *Augustinian Studies*, 6, 1975, p.75. Cf. R. Garrigou-Lagrange, *God: His Existence and His Nature*, tr. B. Rose, St. Louis: Herder, vol II, 1949, p.33.

[7] Rather than a logical or semantical connection.

[8] St. Augustine, *On the Trinity*, 15, 5,8. tr. S. McKenna, Washington: Catholic University of America, 1963. Cf. St. Thomas Aquinas, *Summa Theologiae*, 1a. 3, 2 and 7., Oxford: Blackfriars, 1964-1981. Henceforth, S.Th. (All subsequent quotations are from the Blackfriars translation unless otherwise indicated).

[9] It is not to be supposed that the personal pronoun "he" carries any implications concerning gender identity, it is merely used throughout the book for convenience and as a way of avoiding the impersonal implications of some other ways of referring.

[10] I am here deliberately omitting a discussion of those views emanating from a more radical apophatic theology exemplified in the writings of many Eastern Orthodox Christians, for whom a logical distinction can be made between the essence and attributes ("energies") of the Godhead, e.g. V. Lossky, *The Vision of God*, tr. A. Moorhouse, London: Faith Press, 1963, pp.124-137.

2

simplicity of God, that all his attributes perfectly coincide in a supereminent manner incomprehensible to the human intellect.[11] This means that should our discussion lead to any substantive re-conception of the "divine eternity" the whole structure of classical theism, if true to its own principles, would become questionable. To make the same point from a more external perspective, if the qualities predicated of God in this metaphysical system form logically a mutually entailing cluster, then the redefinition or deletion of one property will have critical implications for the system as a whole.[12] That the "divine eternity" is not an exception to this rule will become apparent as the discussion proceeds.

There are a number of outstanding features of classical Christian theism which will dominate the form of the remainder of the book. First and foremost amongst these is the Anselmian emphasis on defining God as the "greatest conceivable being".[13] For my purposes, that God is such a being, that is, a maximally perfect being, will be given the status of an analytic truth grasped intuitively by all who accept that "God" has the logical status of a definite description.[14] On these terms the debate concerning God's attributes becomes one centred upon which particular properties are indeed the greatest "great making" properties conceivable and which array of such properties is self- consistently exemplifiable in such a manner as to be unsurpassable in value. Against this background this book can be identified as an exercise in what has recently been described as "perfect being theology".[15] Taking up its stand very much from within an already established theological and philosophical tradition, it does not attempt to establish its conclusions from first principles, that is, no attempt will be made to demonstrate that the Being described

[11] See St. Thomas Aquinas, *Summa Contra Gentiles*, 1, 31; N.Y.: Doubleday, 1955-56. Henceforth, *S.C.G.*, *S.Th.* 1a. 3, 7. (All subsequent quotations are from Doubleday volumes unless otherwise indicated).

[12] One of the foremost virtues of Nelson Pike's important book *God and Timelessness*, London: Routledge and Kegan Paul, 1970, is the clear grasp of how the divine attributes are placed with respect to one another in classical Christian thought (see especially pages 39- 52).

[13] Anselm, *Proslogion* 2. tr. M. J. Charlesworth, Oxford: Clarendon, 1965.

[14] Cf. Pike, *Timelessness*, pp.28 ff.

[15] T.V. Morris, "Perfect Being Theology", *Nous*, 21, 1987, pp.19-30.

3

actually exists, and dialogue is thereby primarily with other contending forms of theism.[16]

Such a task is delineated and made more exacting for classical Christian theism by its insistence that conclusions reached by reason alone may not contradict what has been received as central elements of revelation. A number of such elements are of outstanding importance for the purposes of this work. The first of these is the personal nature of God. That God is personal would seem to be a foundational truth for all recognizable forms of Christian thought and devotion.[17] Brunner speaks for much more that a biblical neo-orthodoxy when he says: "Thus everything that theology avers must remain within this basic structure and everything that contradicts this fundamental presupposition must be rejected and fought against as an un-Biblical and even anti- Biblical error of speculation and doctrinal distortion. We call this basic formal relation personal correspondence."[18] One major undertaking of this essay will be to show that this basic personalist presupposition is not incompat-ible with the understanding of the timelessness of God found in classical Christian theism.[19]

A second element which places a limit on possible speculation is the tenet of God as Creator and preserver of all finite being. "Maker of heaven and earth" is so central to Christian confession that it occupies a place next to the head of each of its major creeds. Subsequent discussion of the "divine eternity" would be enormously, though impossibly, simplified if it could be limited to a discussion of deity **ad intra**. Again, the attribute of the "divine eternity" must cohere with God as creator-preserver or the very framework of our discussion will be shattered.

---

[16] I am not here or elsewhere appealing to orthodoxy as an argument for the existence of a certain type of deity but only seeking to stay within and argue for the consistency of this orthodoxy. Cf. D.R. Griffin, "Divine Causality, Evil and Philosophical Theology: A Critique of James Ross", *International Journal for Philosophy of Religion*, 4, 1973, pp.181-182.

[17] J.J.C. Webb, *God and Personality*, London: Allen & Unwin, 1919, pp.81-84 would seem to be on firm ground when he claims that Christianity is the best example of belief in a "personal God". Cf. G. Jantzen, *God's World God's Body*, London: D.L.T., 1984, pp.12-20.

[18] E. Brunner, *Divine-Human Encounter*, tr. A.W. Loos London: S.C.M., 1944, pp.46-47.

[19] For a clearly reasoned argument that classical theism is **on its own terms** not truly personalist see G.A. Cole, "Towards a New Metaphysics of the Exodus", *Reformed Theological Review*, 42, 1983, pp.75-84.

4

Finally, we must reckon with the fact that Christianity is the historical religion **par excellence**.[20] Judaeo-Christian influence is largely responsible for the now deeply embedded Western consciousness of history's linear and non-repetitive character.[21] This successive view of time and history is necessarily presupposed in this book.[22] Any characterisation of "timeless eternity" incompatible with such an understanding would therefore have to be abandoned.[23] Of critical importance here lies the consideration of the Christian doctrine of the Incarnation in its classical expression. The postulation of this "becoming" of God in human form will place one of the severest strains on the discussion as a whole.

Prima facie we would seem to be faced with an almost all-embracing inner tension between the two component poles of classical theism. On the one hand it's **a priori** emphasis on perfect being would seem to lead us towards a wholly transcendent deity detached from the world, whereas its adherence to putative revelation draws us to an undeniable imminence or action in the world. That the one being could be both timeless/eternal and personal-creative-incarnate seems acutely unlikely. It is the primary aim of this thesis to argue that such a compatibility is in fact reasonable.

Since I have alluded to the relationship between revelation and reason in what I have said above it is necessary at this point to make clear how the present study relates to the use of the Bible. Although it has been traditional for classical theists since patristic times to produce proof texts to support their philosophical argumentation concerning God's timelessness, this approach is hardly legitimate.[24] On the one hand it has been argued that the biblical view of time and eternity is **opposed** to that of Hellenistic philosophy and its intellectual heirs. Oscar Cullman has been the chief disputant here: "there can be no real

---

[20] Argued at length by S.G.F. Brandon, *History, Time and Deity*, Manchester: Manchester University Press, 1965, pp.148-205.

[21] Cf. J.T. Fraser, *Of Time, Passion and Knowledge*, N.Y.: Braziller, 1975, p.23.

[22] Though different logically possible forms of "succession" will be fully discussed in Chapter 3 on the nature of time.

[23] "A God who in no sense acts in or on history would be a very different God from that of Western religion and philosophy." J. Cobb, "Natural Causality and Divine Action", *Idealistic Studies*, 3, 1973, p.207

[24] Among the very few **recent** commentators who seriously argue that a concept of God as atemporal can be found in the Bible, is John Marsh, *The Fulness of Time*, London: Nisbet, 1952, pp.142, 144-145, 147-149, 154, 181.

reconciliation when the two positions are so radically different. Peaceful companionship is possible only when either Hellenism is Christianised on the basis of the fundamental Biblical position or Christianity is Hellenised on the basis of the fundamental Greek position."[25] Cullman argues that Christian thought must be purged of Greek influence. I believe that there is a basic methodological error underlying the asserted antithesis, the neglect of the fact that by its very nature the Bible is metaphysically underdetermined. That is, the Bible is not a philosophical treatise, it does not set itself the task of answering nuanced metaphysical problems, and so cannot fairly be taken as opposing those systems which do. With respect to the content of this study I concur with James Barr: "if such a thing as a Christian doctrine of time has to be developed, the work of discussing and developing it must belong not to biblical but to philosophical theology ... We cannot take seriously Cullman's insistence that all philosophical considerations be excluded, for the question he asks, namely, 'What is the nature of time and eternity in biblical thought?' is a question for which the Bible itself gives no precedent."[26] For this reason no reference will be made to the Bible throughout this essay.

Before embarking on this programme however it is important to take note of some particular difficulties that confront us. The first and most general of these concerns religious language. The problems of "God-talk" are too well known and expansive to be rehearsed, and it is not unlikely that many of the conclusions of this thesis could be attacked on linguistic grounds. I only wish to claim here that whilst **all** language about **God** may be, indeed, must be, inadequate,[27] it

---

[25] O. Cullman, *Christ and Time*, tr. F.V. Filson, London: S.C.M., 1951, p.58 and passim. Cf. K. Barth, *Church Dogmatics*, ed. G.W. Bromiley and T.F. Torrance Edinburugh: T and T Clark, 1956-1975, II/1, p.610; J. Kleinig, "Anthropomorphism", *Tyndale Paper*, 17, 1973, p.9; Pike, *Timelessness*, p.184; Pinnock, "Neo- Classical", p.41.

[26] J. Barr, *Biblical Words for Time*, London: S.C.M., 1967, pp.156-157. Cf. R. Aldwinckle, *Death in the Secular City*, Grand Rapids: Eerdmans, 1972, pp.152-153; G. Jantzen, "Time, Timelessness", in *A New Dictionary of Christian Theology*, A. Richardson and J. Macquarrie (eds), London: S.C.M., 1983, p.571; E.A. Nida, "The Implications of Contemporary Linguistics for Biblical Scholarship", *Journal of Biblical Literature*, 91, 1972, p.83.

[27] "**Whatever** is said about God must be stated in improper terms and be subject to a sort of logical discount." A. Farrer, *Faith and Speculation*, N.Y.: New York University. Press, 1967, p.105. On the importance of adhering to this negative principle see the discussion by David Burrell, Aquinas: *God and Action*, Notre Dame: Notre Dame University Press, 1979, pp.68-69.

can nevertheless be meaningful. The orbit of thought within which I shall be working is one which makes final appeal to the real utility of analogical predication.[28] In the course of discussion it will also become apparent how a consideration of the particular property of "eternity" lends itself to the use of the classical **triplex via** - causality, negation, intensification.[29]

More specifically, any essay involving the philosophy of time cannot avoid the problem that its key term is indefinable. As Richard Gale puts it: "Any definition that we might propose will suffer from circularity, since it will have to employ some temporal expression in the **definiens**."[30] Gale's point is that since temporal notions are implicitly involved in all of the basic concepts by means of which we think and talk about the world they are practically unavoidable. This has important implications for any attempt to excogitate a concept of "timelessness", for our minds are so constituted and habituated to a temporal way of thinking that it is only by rigorous and persistent discipline that any justice can be conceivably done to this proposed property of God.

Finally, we will need to keep in mind constantly the distinction between what can be imagined and what can be conceived. To accept that it is impossible to have even a weak and inadequate conception of the "divine eternity" would be to vitiate this project from the beginning. Such is Kevin Ward's opinion: "It is tempting to think that one can make affirmative statements about the real nature of God. But, if God is beyond time, the sort of being he may possess just cannot be expressed in tensed language."[31] This line of reason, I think, denies that it is possible to have a finite grasp of an infinite

---

[28] For classical discussions of analogy, reference may be made to Aquinas, *S.C.G.* 1, 32-35; *S.Th.* 1a. 13, 2, 3 and 6, for neo-Thomism E.L. Mascall, *Existence and Analogy*, Hamden: Archon, 1966, for an attractive existentialist presentation John Macquarrie, *God-Talk*, London: S.C.M., 1967, pp.212-230, and for a vigorous defense and re-working James Ross, *Portraying Analogy*, Cambridge University Press, 1981.

[29] See Gundersdorf von Jess, "Augustine", p.75.

[30] R. Gale, *The Language of Time*, London: Routledge KP, 1968, p.4. Cf. G.H. Clarke, "The Theory of Time in Plotinus", *The Philosophical Review*, 53, 1944, p.352.

[31] Keith Ward, *The Concept of God*, Oxford: Blackwell 1974, p.218. Cf. J. S. McKenzie, "Eternity", in *The Encyclopedia of Religion and Ethics*, J. Hastings (ed), Edinburgh: T and T Clarke, 1912, vol 5, pp.401-405; J. N. D. Findlay, "Time and Eternity", *Review of Metaphysics*, 32, 1978, p.3.

which, as infinite, infinitely exceeds this grasp. My position is that one can have a real grasp that there is an "eternity" in God with certain positive qualities, **and** that its extension is such to be incomprehensible.[32] Even if only God can adequately conceive his own eternity[33]

this does not deny us **any** conception of it. On the other hand, to claim that "timelessness" is imaginable seems, at least to me, patently false. To confuse intelligibility with imaginability is a logical blunder that commits one to a form of positivism which lacks the possibility of ever being established philosophically.[34] When put together all this amounts to a real knowledge and intelligibility of the "divine eternity", but not without a heavy dose of mystery. I am therefore in agreement with Eric Mascall's position:

> And since temporal existence is the only existence that creatures have, God's activity towards them is necessarily experienced by them in terms of time. But the fact that we can experience and speak of God only in temporal terms does not mean that we cannot speak of him accurately; it means that when we speak of him accurately we have to speak of him in temporal terms. It does of course mean that there is a great deal about God which we cannot speak, except perhaps in the most obscure way, but that is a different matter. God is supremely mysterious and transcendent ... the final alternative is not between mystery and clarity, but between mystery and absurdity. And it is not absurd, though it may sound paradoxical, to say that it is only in temporal language that we can talk about God's timelessness[35]

---

[32] Cf. S. Charnocke, *Discourses Upon the Existence and Attributes of God*, London: Henry G. Bohn, vol 1, 1860, pp.343, 374.

[33] So, G.F. Stout, *God and Nature*, Cambridge: Cambridge University Press, 1952, p.223; W. Temple, *Christus Veritas*, London: Macmillan, 1954, p.93.

[34] Just how are we to judge what is imaginable; surely not by consensus. To consider matters of imagination is first the domain of psychology, not philosophy. Cf. M. Westphal, "Temporality and Finitism in Hartshorne's Theism", *Review of Metaphysics*, 19, 1966, p.556; R.H. Teske, "Omniscience, Immutability and Divine Transcendence", *The New Scholasticism*, 53, 1979, p.293.

[35] E.L. Mascall, *The Openness of Being*, London: Darton, Longman and Todd, 1971, p.167. Cf. C.G. Daly, "Metaphysics and the Limits of Language", in

Given all of these qualifications the sort of intelligibility aimed at in this book is that of consistency and coherence. I have already remarked upon the need for consistency between the two poles out of which classical Christian theism is synthesized.[36] This matter aside, the argument within these parameters must not only be non-contradictory but must also agree with certain undenied and undeniable facts.[37] As alluded to earlier the principle one of concern is the reality of time. That time and "timelessness" are compatible, each in their own mode, is a central burden of the book.

The first stage of the argument proper, chapters two and three, seeks to clarify what is at issue in the time - "eternity" question by outlining the classical concept of the "divine eternity" and examining a number of relevant issues in the philosophy of time. In the fourth chapter I shall argue that various contemporary attempts to solve the time - "eternity" problem are inadequate. Chapter five argues for an intelligible concept of timelessness in terms of a model of one sided continuous creation. Chapter six dwells on the question of the compatibility of eternity and personhood in the divine life. The seventh chapter endeavours to demonstrate how God's foreknowledge may be understood in terms of concept of timeless causation, and seeks to specify exactly what it is that God knows. In the eighth chapter of this book I try to reply to the allegation that the sort of casual model with which I am working leaves no room for finite freedom. Then, in chapter nine, I turn to develop some positive reasons for believing that the supreme being must be timeless - providence, necessary being and perfection all require the divine simultaneity. Finally, I seek to draw out some of the implications of the argument, particularly with respect to further investigation that

---

Prospect for Metaphysics, I.T. Ramsey (ed). London, Allen and Unwin, 1961, pp.204-205.

[36] For a lengthy discussion on this type of consistency see D. Pailin, "Authenticity in the Interpretation of Christianity", in *The Cardinal Meaning*, R. Morgan and M. Pye (eds), The Hague: Mouton, 1973, pp.127-159.

[37] I concur with Langford's understanding. M.J. Langford, *Providence*, London: S.C.M., 1981, p.147. "I am using the word `rational' in a particular and rather narrow sense. By a rational position I mean one that is capable of satisfying two basic criteria, first, internal consistency, and second, consistency with the most obvious facts of experience. One could describe this as a demand for both 'internal' and `external' coherence." Cf. A. Flew, *God and Philosophy*, London: Hutchinson, 1966, p.30.

needs to be undertaken in more closely defining the nature and implications of the divine eternity.[38]

---

[38] The very broad sweep of the book can be defended on the grounds that a proper consideration of the attribute of "eternity" **as** the fulness of the divine Being in all its relations demands a thorough treatment of a number of diverse topics involved in the God-world relationship. This should become manifest as the argument develops from stage to stage.

CHAPTER TWO

THE CLASSICAL CONCEPT OF DIVINE ETERNITY

The purpose of this chapter is three fold:[1] first, to examine the teaching of the major figures involved in the construction of the classical doctrine of the divine eternity up to the twentieth century;[2] second, to consider whether the attribute is uniformly defined in this literature, as is frequently supposed;[3] finally, to establish a base from which contemporary criticisms may be evaluated.

A. Parmenides to Neo Platonism

I begin with the pre-Socratics, and the Eleatic philosopher Parmenides.[4] Of interest here is fragment 8 line 5 of his poem "The Way of Truth".[5]

> oude pot' en oud' estai, epei nun estin homou pan hen suneches

---

[1] The very succinct nature of this chapter is due to the fact that the real matters of interest are philosophical and not historical. I here present in summary form conclusions of my research. The substance behind these conclusions can be found in the works cited in the footnotes.

[2] The most adequate historical discussion of God's timelessness known to me is Richard Sorabji's, *Time, Creation and the Continuum: Theories in Antiquity and the Early Middle Ages*, London: Duckworth, 1984. Sorabji however only takes us up to the fourteenth century.

[3] Despite having the status of a Gifford lecturer, F.H. Brabant could be so bold as to say: "the conception of eternity was neither the subject of conciliar decisions nor of heretical attacks. It was taken by St. Augustine from Plotinus and Christianised; Boethius gave it its most famous formula and Aquinas gave it its final definitions." *Time and Eternity in Christian Thought*, London: Longmans, 1937, p.45.

[4] Born c. 515 B.C.

[5] Cited in G.S. Kirk, J.E. Raven, M. Schofield, *The Presocratic Philosophers*, Cambridge: Cambridge University Press 2nd ed., 1983, p.249.

"It never was nor will be, since it is now, all together, one, continuous."

The denial of "was" and "will be" express a denial of normal temporal duration and hence some concept of eternity. Unfortunately it is not clear which.[6] Opinions divide into two main groups. A minority viewpoint interprets the statements about the subject as ascribing to it immutable everlasting duration.[7] A majority view sees the emphasis of the second part of the line as a denial of all temporal distinctions. The subject of the sentence, "it",[8] does not exist from stage to stage but in unextended all- togetherness.[9] The latter interpretation is probably correct, though there is relatively little to go on.[10]

When we turn to our next major figure, Plato,[11] the situation is only a little less confusing. In an extended passage in the *Timaeus* 37 C6-38 C3, Plato describes how the **Demiurge**, having brought the universe into being, sought to make it more perfect by the generation of time, modelled upon the eternity of the ideal Forms:

---

[6] Sorabji, Time, Chapter 8, lists eight different interpretations of Parmenides' words. Since this is not primarily an historical essay I shall not pause over the complex textual and contextual questions involved. So too for the rest of the discussion below.

[7] See for example J. Owens, "The Physical World of Parmenides", in *Essays in Honour of Anton C. Pegis*, J.R. O'Donnell (ed), Toronto: Pontifical Institute of Medieval Studies, 1974, pp.390,394; M. Schofield, "Did Parmenides Discover Eternity", *Archiv Fur Geschichte Der Philosophie*, 52, 1970, pp.113-135; L. Taran, *Parmenides*, Princeton: Princeton University Press, 1965, pp.175-181.

[8] Probably anything which can be spoken and thought of; so, G.E.L. Owen, "Eleatic Questions", *Classical Quarterly*, 10, 1960, pp.84-102.

[9] So, K. Graham, *Religious Views of Time and History*, LaTrobe University, Unpublished M.A. thesis, 1983, p.158; W. Jaeger, *The Theology of the Early Greek Philosophers*, tr. E.S. Robinson, Oxford: Clarendon, 1947, p.106; Kirk, Raven and Schofield, *Presocratic*, p.250; W. Kneale, "Eternity" pp.87-92; McKenzie, "Eternity", p.402; Owen, "Eleatic", pp.97 ff; Sorabji, *Time*, pp.101, 128-130., F. von Hugel, *Eternal Life*, Edinburgh: T and T Clark, 1913, p.32.

[10] J. Hintikka, *Time and Necessity*, Oxford: Clarendon, 1973, p.84, shows good historical sense when he says; "Surely such a sophisticated idea (as atemporal existence) must in any case have developed by stages from something more concrete, such as the idea of omnitemporal existence."

[11] c. 427-384 B.C.

When the father and creator saw the creature which he had made moving and living, the created image of the eternal (**aidioi**) gods, he rejoiced, and determined to make the model still more like the original; and as this was eternal (**aidios**) he sought to make the universe eternal (**aiōnios**), so far as might be. Now the nature of the ideal being was everlasting (**aiōnios**), but to bestow this attribute in its fulness upon a creature was impossible. Wherefore he resolved to have a moving image of eternity (**aiōn**), and when he set in order the heaven, he made this image eternal (**aiōnios**) but moving according to number, while eternity (**aiōn**) itself rests in unity, and this image we call time ... the past and the future are created species of time, which we unconsciously but wrongly transfer to the eternal (**aidios**) essence; for we say that he `was', he `is', he `will be', but the truth is that `is' above is properly attributed to him, and that `was' and `will be' are only to be spoken of according of becoming in time, for they are motions, but that which is immovably the same cannot become older or younger by time, nor ever did or has become, or hereafter will be, older or younger, nor is subject to any of those states which affect moving and sensible things and of which generation is the course. These are the forms of time, which imitates eternity (**aiōn**) and revolves according to a law of number ...[12]

Three main positions concerning the temporal status of the Forms can be discerned amongst Plato scholars. A minority position argues that Plato ascribes eternity to his Forms only in the sense of everlasting duration.[13] By tracing the main terms **aei, aidios, aiōn,** throughout Plato's works it is argued that since they are used both for

---

[12] B. Jowett, *The Works of Plato*, 3rd ed, Oxford: Oxford University Press, Vol 3, 1892, p.456.

[13] See for example: F.M. Cornford, *Plato's Cosmology*, London: Routledge and Kegan Paul, 1937, pp.98, 102; Hintikka, *Time*, p.83; W. von Leyden, "Time, Number and Eternity in Plato and Aristotle", *Philosophical Quarterly*, 14, 1964, pp.35-44, 52; J. Whittaker, "The Eternity of the Platonic Forms", *Phronesis*, 13, 1968, pp.131-144.

the Forms, and temporal entities, (e.g. in the above passage even time is said to be **aiōnios**), it cannot be that the Forms transcend all duration, they must be unchanging and everlasting. A majority of scholars however, noting how Plato insists that "is" alone is a truly proper way of thinking about the eternal, and noting how he denies of it the possibility of any becoming (**genesis**) or age, insist that in the *Timaeus* at least the Forms exist above succession.[14] Sorabji seemed to have resolved the conflict by strongly arguing that when all the material is given due consideration: "Plato allowed implications of timelessness and of duration to stand side by side in his account of eternity without offering a resolution."[15] More recently however the debate has been redirected with R.D. Mohr's argument.[16] Mohr attempts to bring together the diverse material by reasoning that for Plato both the Forms and time are eternal in the same **sense**. They both fall outside the category of things of which it is intelligible to make temporal judgments about dates and duration. Since they are standards (ontologically) of measurement, they cannot be subject to measurement.[17] The thesis is well argued and seems to make better sense of the data, in the *Timaeus* at least, than do other views. One gains the impression that a final judgment on this matter is heavily dependent upon how a philosopher conceives of the overall consistency of the Platonic system. I cautiously conclude that it has not been demonstrated beyond reasonable doubt that a full blown

---

[14] E. Caird, *The Evolution of Theology in the Greek Philosophers*, Glasgow: James MacLehose, vol 1, 1904, p.231; H.F. Cherniss, "Timaeus 38A-B5" in *Selected Papers*, L. Taran (ed), Leiden: Brill, 1977, p.344; J.F. Callahan, *Four Views of Time in Ancient Philosophy*, Cambridge Mass: Harvard University Press, 1948, p.190; Graham, *Religious*, pp.167, 173-4; D.A. Kolb, "Time and Timelessness in Greek Thought", *Philosophy East and West*, 24, 1974, pp.137-138; McKenzie, "Eternity", p.402, Taran, *Parmenides*, pp.166, 183-187.

[15] Sorabji, *Time*, p.111. Cf. Those who seen unable to make up their minds on the matter: Kneale, "Eternity", pp.93-94; G.E.L. Owen, "Plato and Parmenides On The Timeless Present", *The Monist*, 50, 1966, pp.317-340.

[16] R.D. Mohr, *The Platonic Cosmology*, Leiden: Brill, 1985.

[17] Mohr, *Platonic*, pp.70-71. The Forms of course fall outside of the category of things which may or may not alter.

doctrine of timelessness (as complete simultaneous existence) is to be found in Plato.[18]

However, despite this conclusion, the importance of Plato for the development of such a doctrine cannot be over-estimated. In the first place the ingredients for a **theological** doctrine of eternity would seem to make there first appearance for Western thought in this Greek thinker. Whether or not Plato intended it, the concept of total existence without succession is not difficult to read into the *Timaeus*. The other vital ingredient is that this non-durational entity be conceived of as living. The language of the *Timaeus*[19] easily lends itself to such a development the **zōon aidion** of 37D1 could easily be taken as a living being, though in context it is clearly a member of the world of Forms. More important than these specifics is the shape of the Platonic world view itself. It is Plato who raises for Western philosophy and theology,[20] what John Passmore has celled "the two worlds argument".[21] Passmore raises the problem that, having divided the totality of existence up into two modes of being, a supraphenomenal mode of ideal patterns and a phenomenal mode of process and temporal change, how does one bring the two back together again? The problem is not primarily epistemological, though this is real enough, but ontological. How is it possible to bridge a real ontological gap, that is, a divide between two essentially different modes of being? It is to doubted that Platonic systems can resolve this problem and still remain dualistic.[22] The insuperable obstacle would seem to be that the Forms **qua** Forms (above the mode of change) lack the possibility of causal action.[23] It will become increasingly evident

---

[18] "One sort of timeless eternity which Platonic Ideas do not possess is an eternity **totum simul,** an eternity, that is, in which an eternal object ... contains within any `moment' of its existence the entire history of the world." Mohr, *Platonic*, p.68, footnote 22.

[19] And see Whittaker, "Platonic Forms", p.143 for further references in Plato.

[20] The pre-Socratics, Empedocles, Anaxagoras and the Atomists were monists, so for them there could be no essentially divided world.

[21] J. Passmore, *Philosophical Reasoning*, London: Gerald Duckworth, 1961, pp.38-57.

[22] The *Demiurge* of course is only a source of order, and the emanationism of neo-Platonic cosmology can be interpreted as a sidestepping of the problem under discussion.

[23] Mohr, *Platonic*, pp.79-80.

during our discussion that the question of the logical possibility of a causal relationship between the "two worlds" is a central difficulty for any theistic system which would maintain that God is timeless **and** that he acts in some way in the world.[24]

In moving on to Aristotle[25] we consider a philosopher who is usually passed over quickly in reviews of the history of the doctrine of the divine eternity.[26] In my judgment this is an error, not only because of the importance of Aristotle's philosophy for Western thought in general, but in this matter because of his influence on the Latin Middle Ages in particular.

First we must notice that Aristotle does not predicate timelessness of any entity, though he speaks of a number of things (e.g. the stars) as not being **in** time.[27] By this he means, given his definition of time as "that in respect of whichtime is numerable",[28] things that are not subject to process or beginning, that which is not bounded by time. In the *De Caelo*, however, there is an important, though ambiguous passage where Aristotle discusses the condition "outside of heaven":

> It is therefore evident that there is also no place or void or time outside the heaven ... in the absence of natural body there is no movement, and outside the heaven, as we have shown, body neither exists nor can come to exist. Hence whatever is there (**ta'kei**), is of such a nature as not to occupy any place, nor does time age it; nor is there any change in any of the things which lie beyond the outermost motion, they continue for their entire duration (**aiōn**) unalterable and unmodified, living the best and most self-sufficient of lives (**zōē**). As a matter of fact, this word duration (**aiōn**) possessed a divine significance for the

---

[24] Classical theism is clearly a "two-worlds"system in that it ascribes reallity both to the temporal world of flux known in everyday experiences and to the atemporal and abiding life of God.

[25] c. 384-322 B.C.

[26] Kneale for example, "Eternity", p.94 brushes him aside in less than two lines: "Aristotle rejected Plato's account of time and eternity together with much else of his master's teaching."

[27] Aristotle, *Physics*, 4, 12, 220b32-222a9; 4, 13-14, 222b16 -223a15, 43.

[28] Aristotle, *Physics*, 4, 11, 219b2. W.D. Ross translation, Oxford: Clarendon, 1936, p.386.

16

ancients, for the fulfilment which included (**periechòn**) the period of life of any creature, outside of which no development can fall, has been called its duration (**aiōn**). On the same principle the fulfilment of the whole heaven, the fulfilment which includes (**periechòn**) all time and infinity, is 'duration' (**aiōn**) - a name based upon the fact that it 'is always' (**aei einai**) - duration - immortal and divine.[29]

The identity of "whatever is there" is uncertain, it means either God or the outermost sphere of the fixed stars or both. W. von Leyden[30] has drawn attention to two particular elements of this passage. First there is a sense in which **aiōn** stands for something different from everlastingness. Aristotle defines at as an encompassing term (**to periechòn telos**), even when it is applied to the world's duration. Thus **aion** is a container and infinite time the contained. In the second place he attaches to **aiōn** a divine significance, for from it the life of all other things is derived, the expression used to denote this derivation (**exērtētai** 279a29) has affinity to that used in the *Metaphysics* (**ērtētai** 12.7, 1072 b14) where heaven and the earth are said to depend on the "prime mover" (God) as the initiator of motion. Can we therefore say that for Aristotle it "practically means" that the prime mover exists in an all embracing timeless mode?[31] It would seem not. Firstly, we cannot overlook the etymology given for **aiōn**, viz; its connection with "always". Secondly, as noted above, Aristotle considers that there exist a class of entities not **in time**, in virtue of not being bounded **by** time. Many of the things said about **aiōn** in the *De Caelo* passage fit this category. Finally, in the *Metaphysics* God is described as having everlasting duration:

> It is a way of life like the best we ever have for a short time. For he is always (**aei**) in that state, which for us is impossible ... If, then, God is always (**aei**) in that good state in which we are sometimes (**pote**) ... God's self-

---

[29] Aristotle, *De Caelo*, 1. 9. 279a12-b3, tr. J.L. Stocks in *The Works of Aristotle Translated into English*, W.D. Ross (ed), Oxford: Clarendon, vol 3, 1930.

[30] von Leyden, "Number", pp.45 ff.

[31] von Leyden, "Number", p.47.

dependent actuality is a life most good and everlasting (**aidios**). We say then that God is a living being, everlasting (**aidios**) and most good, so that life and continuous, everlasting (**suneches, aidios**) **aiōn** belong to him. For that is what God is.[32]

It seems best to regard Aristotle's God as not timeless but the possessor of a special sort of omnitemporality.[33] Yet it can be argued that Aristotle moves our discussion beyond the principles of Platonism. With respect to the deity it has been well said, "What is supreme here is not a principle from which the forms can be generated, but an actual perfect substance whose complete `timeless' reality furnishes a teleological capstone for the world."[34] Aristotle's God may be wholly impassible and immutable[35] but it is nevertheless a concrete individual being that is the final cause for the whole finite order and its ultimate principle of regulation.[36] Aristotle is more conscious than Plato of what this involves: "there is not only an activity of movement, but also one void of movement."[37] The importance of the introduction of causality as Aristotle understood it, as over against the Platonic stress on participation, will have important implications for our attempted solution of the "two worlds" problem.

Finally, note should be taken of the significance of "now" in Aristotle's philosophy of time. Throughout his discussion in the tenth to twelfth chapter of book four of the *Physics*, much is said about the property of "now" to unite and divide, to be both the same and different. In the development of one of these poles lies the seed for a "now" that could stand unchangeably.[38] Philo Judaeus[39] deserves a place in our catalogue for a number of reasons. In terms of the history

---

[32] Aristotle, *Metaphysics*, 12, 7, 1072b13-1073a13, cited in Sorabji, *Time*, p.127.

[33] Hintikka, *Time*, p.83; Sorabji, *Time*, p.127.

[34] Kolb, "Greek Thought", p.139, my inner quotes.

[35] Aristotle, *Metaphysics*, 12. 1244b1-9; 1245b, 14-19, etc.

[36] Aristotle, *Physics*, 4, 267b8; *Metaphysics*, 12. 1074b3.

[37] Aristotle, *Nichomachean Ethics*, 7. 1154b, W.D. Ross translation, Oxford: Clarendon, 1925.

[38] Viz. the **nunc stans** of Scholasticism. Cf. Graham, *Religious*, p.183.

[39] c. 30 B.C. - 45 A.D.

of doctrine there is much to be said for Henry Chadwick's remark that the history of Christian philosophy begins with Philo.[40] More directly, however, it is in the syncretistic Hellenistic Judaism of Philo that we find the first attribution of timelessness to the God of the Bible.

> God is withdrawn from both ends of time. For His life is not so much Time as Eternity (**aiōn**), the archetype and pattern of time. And in Eternity there is nothing past and nothing future, but only present. [41] The one who alone is eternal and the Father of all things visible and invisible.[42]

Although Philo's thought is not always consistent,[43] it seems clear that we have arrived here at an ascription to deity of timeless eternity.[44] Philo, however, has nothing concrete to contribute towards a solution of our basic "two worlds problem", for he never pauses to consider how time and eternity might be related.[45]

That Philo is part of the cultural milieu which developed Plato's teaching into what has become known as "Middle Platonism" becomes evident when we consider the words of Plutarch:

> Wherefore it is irreverent in the case of that which is to say even that it was or shall be; for these are certain deviations, transitions, and alterations, belonging to that which by nature has no permanence in Being. But God (if there be need to say so), and He exists for no fixed time, but for

---

[40] In *The Cambridge History of Later Greek and Early Medieval Philosophy*, A.H. Armstrong (ed), Cambridge: Cambridge University Press, 1967, p.137.

[41] Philo, *Quod Deus Immutabilis Sit* 6. 32, L. Cohn and P. Wendland edition of Philo, 1896, vol 2, p.63, cited in von Hugel, *Eternal Life*, p.51.

[42] Philo, *De Virtutibus*, 39. 214, cited in H.A. Wolfson, *Philo*, Cambridge, Mass: Harvard University Press, vol 1, 1947, p.172.

[43] Wolfson, *Philo*, p.317; Sorabji, *Time*, pp.121-122.

[44] So Sorabji, *Time*, p.121, footnote 102, **contra** J. Whittaker, *God, Being, Time*, Oslo: Universitels-forlaget, 1971, pp.36-40.

[45] On the vagaries of his views of creation see W. Foerster, **"ktidzo"**, in G. Kittel (ed), *Theological Dictionary of the New Testament*, tr. G.W. Bromiley, Grand Rapids: Eerdmans 1965, vol 3, pp.1026-1027, and E.F. Osborn, *Clement of Alexandria*, Cambridge: Cambridge University Press, 1957, p.34f.

the everlasting ages (**kat'aiōna**) which are immovable, timeless (**achronos**), and undeviating, in which there is no earlier nor later, no future nor past, no older nor younger; but He, being One, has with only one `Now' completely filled `For ever'; and only when Being is after His pattern is it in reality Being, not having been nor about to be, nor has it had a beginning nor is it destined to come to an end. Under these conditions, therefore, we ought, as we pay Him reverence to greet Him and address Him with the words, `thou art'; or even, I vow, as did some of the men of old, `Thou art One'.[46]

These fine sounding words possess a clarity lacking in our earlier references. All the essential elements of a full blown doctrine of the divine eternity are present here **in nuce**. Without temporal extension, the whole of the divine being is telescoped together into a single life-filled `Now'. It is this conception which. through Plotinus, was to later pervade Christian thought. Plutarch however offers us no more than a statement of what the divine eternity might be.

There is little development of the doctrine of divine eternity in the first century and a half of Christian thought. God's timelessness is spoken of in both the Apostolic Fathers[47] and early Apologists[48] but never in a detailed or controversial manner.[49] Clement of Alexandria gives us no more than a definition: "Eternity (**aiōn**) holds together the future, the present and indeed the past of time in a hair's breath."[50],

---

[46] Plutarch, *On The E at Delphi*, 393 A-B, in Plutarch's *Moralia*, tr. F.C. Babbitt, London: Heinmann, vol 5, 1957, p.245.

[47] Ignatius, *Polycarp*, 3,2.

[48] Justin, *Apology* 1, 13, 4; *Dialogue* 3. 5; Tatian, *Ad Graecos*, 4. 1, 2; Athenagoras, *Supplicatio* 10. 1.

[49] The material is scattered, but see G.L. Prestige *God in Patristic Thought*, London: S.P.C.K., 1959, pp. 1-24. On early rabbinic material one may consult A. Marmorstein, *The Old Rabbinic Doctrine of God*, London: Oxford University Press, 1927, pp.176-179. Given limits of space the essay shall not discuss the work of Jewish and Islamic thinkers who would have otherwise been considered. Details may be found in Sorabji, *Time*, **passim**.

[50] Clement, *Stromateis* 1.13, cited in Sorabji, *Time*, p.122.

and the important African Father Tertullian speaks of eternity in only a fleeting fashion.[51]

B. Plotinus and the Influence of Neo-Platonism.

Plotinus[52] is one of the greatest figures in the development of the doctrine of the divine timelessness.[53] The complicated Plotinian metaphysics is geared around the idea of a descending system of emanating or suffused beings, an ontological hierarchy from higher to lower in which the direction of dependence is always one way. At the head of all is the attributeless One from whom all things flow through a complex series of subordinate hypostases.[54]

Temporality is explicitly excluded from this generation.[55] Sub-ordinate to the One and corresponding to Plato's world of Forms, is the second hypostasis, Intellect. Plotinus describes the emanation of the Intellect from the One as movement from a pure centre to the differentiated centre-and- circumference of a circle.[56] Timeless patterns of order for our world are generated through the activity of Intellect. Temporal beings are in turn born from a further act of contemplation, that of the third hypostasis, Soul.[57]

In the seventh tractate of the third book of the, *Enneads*, Plotinus discusses the origin and nature of time and eternity. After rejecting various definitions of eternity in the first and second paragraphs, in the third he arrives at his first definition of the eternity of the divine realm:

> That which neither has been nor will be, but simply possesses being; that which enjoys stable existence as neither in process of change nor having ever changed - that is Eternity. Thus we come to the definition: the Life -

---

[51] Tertullian, *Against Marcion*, 1. 25, 3.

[52] 205-270 A.D.

[53] For a helpful treatment of time and eternity in Plotinus see Callahan, *Four Views*, chapter 3., and, more generally, W.R. Inge, *The Philosophy of Plotinus*, London: Longmans Green, 2 vols, 1918.

[54] Plotinus, *Enneads*, 5. 2, 1.,; tr. S.K. McKenna, London: Faber and Faber, 1956.

[55] Plotinus, *Enneads*, 5. 2, 6.

[56] Plotinus, *Enneads*, 3. 8, 2.

[57] Plotinus, *Enneads*, 3. 8, 3.

> instantaneously entire, complete, at no point broken into
> period or part - which belongs to the Authentic Existent by
> its very existence, this is the thing we were probing for -
> this is Eternity.[58]

In the fourth paragraph he emphasises that Eternity is not accidental
to the intellectual essence, but in union with it, lacking nothing it is
ever-being (aei on). Then he presses on to describe the
self-contemplating life of the Intellect which cannot possibly suffer
change:

> Eternity, thus, is of the order of the supremely great;
> intuition identifies it with God: It may fitly be described as
> God made manifest, as God declaring what He is, as
> existence without jolt or change, and therefore also as the
> firmly living ... Thus a close enough definition of eternity
> would be that it is a life which, knowing nothing of past or
> future to shatter its completeness, possess itself intact for
> ever. To the notion of a Life (a Living-Principle) all-
> comprehensive add that it never spends itself, and we have
> the statement of a Life instantaneously infinite.[59]

Plotinus concludes his discussion of eternity in the sixth paragraph
of the *Enneads*, 3.7 first by transferring Plato's description of unity in
Timaeus 37D to his One, and then by describing how the Intellect, in
its relationship with the One, can have life we call eternity. Repeatedly
in this section Plotinus makes it clear that the eternal has no temporal
qualities:[60]

> such words as always, never, sometimes' must be taken
> as mere conveniences of exposition ... We must take this
> `Everlasting' as expressing no more than Authentic Being
> ... the conception of Eternity demands something which is
> in its nature complete without sequence ... Being does not
> depend upon any quality (such as instalments of time) but

---

[58] Plotinus, *Enneads*, 3. 7, 3. 45-50. in McKenna, *Enneads*, p.225.

[59] Plotinus, *Enneads*, 3. 7, 3. 24ff, in McKenns, *Enneads*, pp.226-227.

[60] For a collection of such protestations found throughout the *Enneads* see
Sorabji, *Time*, pp.112-113.

subsists before all Quality. Itself having no quality, it can have no contact with anything quantitative since its life cannot be made a thing of fragments ... The phrase `He was good' (used by Plato of Demiurge) refers to the idea of the All; and its very indefiniteness signifies the utter absence of the relation to Time.[61]

Without doubt Plotinus provides us with the fullest, clearest and most personalized definition of the divine eternity in the philosophy of non-Christian antiquity. It is unmistakable that, for this thinker, God possesses his being in a complete and undivided plenitude that is absolutely incompatible even with contact with temporality. It must be doubted however that Plotinian metaphysics provides us with a possible solution to our "two worlds" problem. Indeed the ascending hierarchy seems to generate a "many worlds" problem. In any system, emanationist or otherwise, which accepts the reality both of eternity, as a temporality, and time, the ontological problem remains. Though interpretations may differ,[62] it is the third hypostasis of Plotinus, Soul, which as a sort of "bridge Being" between the intelligible and phenomenal worlds is supposed to solve the problem.[63]

It is clear however that in a hierarchical arrangement two problems remain. Firstly, it is logically impossible to divide up the time-eternity barrier by a series of steps so that it somehow becomes easier to cross. As Plotinus' own remarks above make clear we are not dealing with a **quantitative** problem but with an infinite qualitative difference. Secondly, any Being in the hierarchical order supposed to "bridge" this problem only generates another difficulty for, in doing so, it comes to possess the mutually contradict-ory properties of time **and** timelessness.

Not withstanding these remarks Plotinus' own powerful expression of the totality of the divine eternity is a fine example of "perfect being"

---

[61] Plotinus, *Enneads* 3. 7, 6. in McKenna, *Enneads*, pp.227- 228.

[62] See Clark, "Plotinus", pp.352-354.

[63] Cf. Callahan, *Four Views*, pp.118-129; Graham, *Religious*, pp.197-200; R.T. Wallis, *Neoplatonism*, London: Duckworth, 1972, p.53.

theology many of whose elements will manifestly reappear in our subsequent discussion.[64]

In subsequent Neoplatonism from Porphyry (third century) to Simplicius (mid-sixth century) there is little in the way of important new developments in the philosophy of eternity, although the successors of Plotinus were careful to distinguish temporal and non-temporal senses of words in their discussions on numerous occasions.[65] By now the atemporality of the divine existence has become commonplace. A more interesting phenomenon is the tendency to hypostasise eternity, to make it another intermediary in the celestial hierarchy.[66] This is most fully worked out in Proclus.[67]

> The rank of eternity in relation to the Living Creature is therefore clear; it is superior and immediately superior, and is cause to the intelligibles of unchanging permanency - So there are three things in succession: the One-that-Is as monad of beings, eternity as dyad possessing the quality of everlastingness along with beings, and the eternity which participates both in being and in everlastingness, but is not the primary ever-existent as eternity is ...[68]

This tendency to multiply intermediaries, as exemplified by the citation from Proclus, is a clear example of the way in which such a

---

[64] Though for reasons which will become obvious I find S. Hatano's evaluation exaggerated: "his thought has dominated the entire field of philosophy since the Middle Ages ... We can safely say without exaggeration that after Plotinus no really new thought has been developed on eternity up to now". *Time and Eternity*, tr. I. Suzuki, Ministry of Edn, Japan, 1963, p.86.

[65] Sorabji, *Time*, p.115.

[66] So Porphyry, *Sentences* 44; *Simplicius, In Physics* 792. 20ff. See also Proclus *In Platonis Timaeun*, 3, p.51, 15-21 and Olympiodorus, *In Meteor.* 146, 15-23 on the "eternal now".

[67] c. 411-485 A.D. Proclus has importance for classical theism principally through his influence on Pseudo-Dionysius. See E.R. Dodds, *Proclus 'Elementa Theologiae'*, Oxford: Clarendon, 1933, pp.26-28.

[68] Proclus, *In Platonis Timaeum*, 3, p.15, 28ff, cited in W. O'Neill, "Time and Eternity in Proclus", *Phronesis*, 7, 1962, p.163. Cf. *Elementa Theologiae*, prop. 52-53.

method is essentially unable to solve our basic ontological problem, for it leads to the predication of mutual incompatibles to the one entity.

It is now possible to cross to those Christian thinkers heavily indebted to Neoplatonism. Origen,[69] the first of these, describes the Trinitarian relations in the following manner:

> Of course, the words we use, `always' and `was' and any other such word with a temporal meaning that we appropriate must be understood in an elastic way as an artless expression. For the meaning of these words are temporal, whereas the things of which we are speaking, although described in a temporal way for handling our discussion, go by their nature beyond any understanding in a temporal sense.[70]

Although important as a source of theological ideas, Origen's system as a whole was soon labelled as heterodox[71] and discarded by creedal Christianity. This was not so with the influential contemporary fourth century theologians Hilary of Poitiers, Athanasius, Basil of Caesarea and Gregory of Nyssa. Hilary, anticipating much later discussion, denies that the creation of the heavens involved a preparation on God's part:

> The things that shall be, although they are yet to be in so far as they must be created, have already been made in so far as God is concerned, for whom there is nothing new and unexpected in things to be created, since it belongs to the dispensation of time for them to be created, and they have **already been created in the activity of the divine power that forsees the future** ... The preparation of things to be created is uninterrupted and eternal. The body of this universe has not been brought into being by thoughts that follow one another ... there is

---

69 185-254 A.D. Perhaps, most accurately, one should say that Origen is influenced by Middle Platonism. See J.N.D. Kelly, *Early Christian Doctrines*, N.Y.: Harper and Row, 1978, p.128.

70 Origen, *De Principii* 1. 3, 4. Cited in Sorabji, *Time*, p.115.

71 E.g. on his doctrine of "eternal creation" see R.A. Norris, *God and World in Early Christian Theology*, N.Y.: Seabury, 1965, p.154f.

not even a moment of time discernible in the work of creating the heavens.[72]

Cosmological discussion becomes much more extended in Basil for whom time comes into being **with** the creation by God of Nature.[73] Athanasius and Gregory, through the Arian controversy, were forced to consider in some detail the relation of temporality to the life of God. In his **Orations Against the Arians** the former held that it is impossible to apply temporal attributes to God. As eternal, he is perfect and excluded from succession, and in God various properties diverse for ourselves, such as will and action, coincide.[74] In his dogmatic treatise against the Arians, **Contra Eunomium**, Basil many times denies duration to the divine being.[75]

As we turn to the great period of Western Latin philosophical theology beginning with Augustine,[76] it becomes evident that, by the middle of the fourth century, the doctrine of an atemporal life in God is a firmly established element in Christian orthodoxy. Even by this early stage, many of the problems that would continue to arise out of this dogma had reached the notice of thoughtful monotheists.

Augustine's indebtedness to neo-Platonism is explicit,[77] and he uses Platonic language in speaking of the divine timelessness in many places.[78] On the other hand, because he always desired to be faithful

---

[72] Hilary, *On The Trinity* 12.39-40 tr. S. McKenna, Washington: Catholic University Press of America, 1963, pp.528-529. (my emphasis).

[73] Basil, *Homily in Hexaemeron* 2.3, 32A-B. Cf. Gregory, *Apologia in Hexaemeron* 770.

[74] For details see E.P. Meijering, *God Being History: Studies in Patristic Thought*, Amsterdam: North Holland, 1975, pp.82-87.

[75] Basil, *Contra Eunomium*, 1.359-364, 370-371, 685-689, 2.459; 8.5; 9.2. See H.A. Wolfson, "Negative Attributes in the Church Fathers", *Harvard Theological Review*, 50, 1957, pp.148-149.

[76] 354-430 A.D. It is unclear to what extent the writings of the above Fathers were known to Augustine. P. Courcelle, *Late Latin Writers and Their Greek Sources*, tr. H.E. Wedeck, Cambridge, Mass: Harvard University Press, 1969, ch 4.

[77] Augustine, *Confessions*, 7. 2-5, tr. R.S. Pine-Coffin, Harmondsworth: Penguin, 1961; *Contra Academicos*, 13, 18.

[78] See Gundersdorf Von Jess, "Augustine". Since a portion of Augustine's thought is relevant to later discussion I here concentrate only upon sketching the framework of his system and his understanding of the divine eternity **per se**.

26

to Sacred Scripture, he found himself in conflict with the prevailing Hellenistic view of perpetual cycles of time.[79] Two questions arose out of this debate. The first was the problem of the incommensurability of the immutable eternity of God and the purported new act by which he created the world. Second, there was the allied Manichean challenge, "What was God doing before he created the world?" These matters are taken up at length in the eleventh book of the *Confessions* and in books eleven and twelve of the *City of God*. In answer to the first question Augustine replies ad hominem that we must not think of God anthropomorphically,[80] and, more seriously, that the problem is simply a mistaken one.

> As for us, we are forbidden to suppose that God is in a different condition when he is at rest than when he is at work. In fact it is improper to speak of God's `condition' which would imply that some novel element might come into his nature, something that was not there before. God knows how to be active while at rest, and at rest in his activity. He can apply to a new work not a new design but an eternal plan; and it is not because he repented of his previous inactivity that he began to do something he had not done before. Even if he rested first and started work later (and I do not know how man can understand this) this `first' and `later' refer, without doubt, to things which first did not exist and later came into existence. But in God there was no new decision which altered or cancelled a previous intention; instead, it was with one and the same eternal and unchanging design that he effected his creation.[81]

The creation of the world in time by God involves no new act of God for the plan of God is an eternal one. `Before' and `after' exist only in the effects of His act and not in the divine activity itself.

With regard to the question "What was God doing before he created?", Augustine clarifies the meaning of time and eternity and

---

[79] See T. Mommsen, "St. Augustine and the Christian idea of Progress". *Journal of the History of Ideas*, 12, 1951, pp.346- 374.

[80] Augustine, *City of God* 12.18, tr. H. Bettenson, Harmondsworth: Penguin.

[81] Augustine, *City of God* 12.18, in Bettenson, *City of God*, pp.495-496.

their interrelationship. For Augustine time, as a **distentio anima**, is above all a creature: "before God made heaven and earth, he made not anything. For ... no creature was made before any creature was made ... How could ages pass by if they had never been ... At no time, therefore, hadst Thou not made anything, because Thou hadst made time itself."[82] Without changeable things to pass away or become, there can be no future or past time and, without the existence of anything, no present time; hence the original query is misjudged. But if the "now" of time possess such an ephemeral character, the Eternal Now of the immutable God must be vastly different.

> But in eternity nothing moves into the past: all is present (**totum praesens**) ... It is in eternity which is supreme above time because it is a never-ending present, that you are at once before all past time and after all future time. For what is now the future once it comes, will become the past, whereas 'you are unchanging, your years can never fail' (Psalm 101:28). Your years are completely present to you all at one (**anni tui omnes simul stans**) because they are at a permanent standstill. They do not move on, forced to give way before the advance of others, because they never pass at all. Your years are one day, yet your day does not come daily, but is always today, because your today does not give place to any tomorrow nor does it take the place of any yesterday. Your today is eternity.[83]

The importance of Augustine's contribution to the philosophy of eternity[84] depends largely upon the evaluation of his relationship to Platonism. One element of his thought which certainly cannot be attributed to anything but attachment to received Christian orthodoxy is the origin of time **ex nihilo**. He does not pause to develop this idea at length, and, upon first consideration, it may seem to make the "two

---

[82] Augustine, *Confessions* 11.11, 11.13; 12.12 cited in Gundersdorf Von Jess, "Augustine", pp.86-87. Cf. *City of God*, 11. 5-6.

[83] Augustine, *Confessions* 11.11; 11.13, in Pine-Coffin, *Confessions*, pp.261, 263.

[84] The enormous historical **influence** of the Augustinian position is not in question, we are rather searching for new ideas and sustainable concepts.

worlds" association even more unintelligible than for systems where time has no beginning. (Subsequently I shall argue that the very opposite is the case) It is not unlikely that Augustine left this element of his thought undeveloped because for him the time-eternity relationship partook of what in Platonic terms is known as "participation".[85] Just as for Platonism the phenomenal world exhibits qualities through participating in the absolute Forms so for Augustine: "But what are the higher things if not those where the highest unchangeable undisturbed and eternal quality resides? Where there is no time, because there is no change, and **from where times are made and ordered** and changed, **imitating** as they do when the turn of the heavens comes back to the same state." ...[86] This conceptualization explains the character of the divine present: because eternity is to time as exemplar to image, it embraces and transcends time by sustaining it in a transcendent Now.[87] We seem to be left with two sides to Augustine's thought, not contradictory, but lacking a final synthesis: on the one side, the distinctiveness of the Judaeo-Christian Creator, on the other the use of the Platonic idea of participation.[88] If Augustine could have worked out the relationship of these different ideas in full he conceivably would have arrived at a solution to the "two world" problem much like that which will be offered later in this thesis.

At this point [89] we turn to consider what is arguably the classic definition of eternity, that of Boethius.[90] Boethius speaks of the

---

[85] We have already encountered this mode of thinking in both Plato's and Plotinus' understanding of time as an "image" of eternity. (*Timaeus* 37D, *Enneads* 3.7 respectively).

[86] Augustine, *On Music*, 6, 11, 29 tr. R.J. Deferrari, *The Fathers of the Church*, N.Y.: Fathers of the Church Inc, 1947, Vol 4, p.355 (my emphasis).

[87] So M.E. Ravicz, "St. Augustine: Time and Eternity", *Thomist*, 22, 1959, p.551.

[88] It would be erroneous and anachronistic to suggest that the mode of participation for Augustine is in the same manner as it is in Plato. Cf. Brabant, *Time*, pp.61-62.

[89] I pass by a consideration of Pseudo-Dionysius (c. 500 A.D.) whose philosophy confirms what we have observed so far (rather than generating anything new for discussion). On his thought and influence see I.P. Sheldon-Williams' article in Armstrong (ed), *Cambridge*, pp.457-472. For specific references to the

divine eternity in two of his works, the first of these being *De Trinitate*. In this publication he is concerned with the applicability of the Aristotelian categories to God. What does it **mean** to say that God always exists?[91]

> But what is said of God, `ever is', (**Semper**) signifies only one thing, that he was, as it were, in all the past, is in all the present - however that term be used - and will be in all the future. According to the philosophers this may be said of the heavens and of other immortal bodies, but of God it is said in a different way. He is ever, because 'ever' is with him a term of present time, and there is this great difference between the present of our affairs, which is now, and the divine present: our `now' connotes changing time and sempiternity (**sempiternitas**); but God's `now' abiding, unmoved, and immovable, connotes eternity (**aeternitas**). If you add semper to eternity, you will get the flowing, incessant and thereby perpetual course of our present time, that is to say, sempiternity.[92]

Several things attract our attention here. There is the classic distinction between temporal and eternal `now', and the first certain distinct separation of the words **sempiternus**, for everlastingness, and **aeternus**, for eternity.[93] This introduces a new clarity into the discussion. For Boethius it is clear that the divine life is, as it were, folded up into a single undifferentiated experience. A more important passage is that found in *De Consolatione*, where Boethius struggles to

---

divine eternity see *On The Divine Names* 10.2-3 in C.E. Rolt tr. London: S.P.C.K., 1920, pp.170-173.

[90] c. 480-c. 525 A.D. It is universally agreed that he is the most important transmitter of the Neoplatonic concept of eternity to the Christian Middle Ages.

[91] The focus of interest is logical rather than ontological.

[92] Boethius, *De Trinitate* 4. 65-77 in *Boethius: The Theological Tractates and the Consolation of Philosophy*, tr. and ed. H.F. Stewart, E.K. Rand, J.S. Tester, London: Heinemann, 1973, pp.21, 23.

[93] Although the distinction between the two **concepts** is found many times in Augustine, Boethius seems to be the first person to develop this word usage. So, Sor-abji, *Time*, p.116, Stewart et al, *Tractates*, p.22.

show that God's certain fore-knowledge and human freedom are not incompatible.

> That God is eternal, then, is the common judgment of all who live by reason. Let us therefore consider what eternity is, for this makes plain to us both the divine nature and knowledge. Eternity, then, is the complete possession all at once of illimitable life (**Aeternitas igitur est interminabilis vitae tota simul et perfecta possessio**). This becomes clearer by comparison with temporal things. For whatever lives in time proceeds as something present from the past into the future, and there is nothing placed in time that can embrace the whole extent of its life equally. Indeed, on the contrary, it does not yet grasp tomorrow but yesterday it has already lost; and even in the life of today you live no more fully than in a mobile, transitory moment. ... Therefore, whatever includes and possesses the whole fulness of illimitable life at one and is such that nothing future is absent from it and nothing past has flowed away, this is rightly judged to be eternal, and of this it is necessary both that being in full possession of itself it be always present to itself and that it have the infinity of mobile time present (to it).[94]

I wish to call attention to three ingredients in the definition.[95] The first of these is that eternity involves life.[96] The Boethian definition therefore excludes things like numbers or truths from eternity. Eternity then is something more than mere atemporality. Secondly, the life of an eternal being is illimitable. This certainly excludes both a beginning and an end from eternity. But does it exclude duration **per**

---

94 Boethius, *Consolation* 5.6, cited in Stewart et al, *Tractates*, pp.422, 424. (my emphasis)

95 Cf. E. Stump and N. Kretzmann, "Eternity" *Journal of Philosophy*, 78, 1981, pp.431ff. I follow the order of their analysis, but with some major departures in interpretation.

96 There are many points of contact here between Boethius and Plotinus (*Enneads* 3.7).

se? Various commentators[97] have argued that it does not. There are however good reasons for rejecting this interpretation. An acceptable definition of duration is "to exist at each moment in a temporally extended interval".[98] Yet temporal extension, which is inseparable from duration, is utterly incompatible with the **totum simul** of another part of the definition. The life of an everlasting entity is limited to events at the time it exists.[99] Illimitability, for Boethius, excludes temporal succession,[100] and so, since extension involves persistence through successive moments of time, it also excludes temporal extension and location. Illimitability must be taken to connote "boundlessness".

The third ingredient is of greatest importance: "complete possession all at once". The quality of an eternal life is unlike that of any being subject to time, whose sequential character necessarily imposes fragmentariness or incompleteness upon such a life. In eternity, division of any sort is impossible. The punctiliar character of eternity seems clear enough, but at the end of the passage quoted above Boethius makes it clear that the indivisible life of God does not exist in isolation from time but encompasses the latter. This seeming contradiction, which is for him the solution to the problem of foreknowledge and freedom. How does eternity include or contain time?[101] The first possibility seems to be that Boethius is working with a model of "inclusive simplicity". This is the interpretation of Lewis Ford.[102] Ford claims that eternity may be said to possess the temporal in the way in which an "inclusive simplicity" possesses a multiplicity. An "inclusive" simplicity contains and preserves subordinate multiplicity whilst "exclusive" simplicity exists in

---

[97] For example R.D. Jordan, *The Temple of Eternity*, Port Washington: Kennikat, 1972, p.22; Stump and Kretzmann, "Eternity", pp.432-433; F.R. Tennant, *Philosophical Theology*, Cambridge: Cambridge University Press, 1930, vol 2, p.130.

[98] Pike, *Timelessness*, p.12.

[99] Cf. Aristotle, *Physics*, 4.11, 219a21-b1; 4.14, 223a29- b1; Aquinas, *S.Th.* 1a. 10, 1.

[100] Cf. Duns Scotus' observation, *Quodlibetal Questions*, 6.14. tr. F. Alluntis and A.B. Wolter, Princeton: Princeton University Press, 1975, p.142.

[101] Once again we confront the "two-worlds" problem.

[102] L.S. Ford, "Boethius and Whitehead on Time and Eternity", *International Philosophical Quarterly*, 8, 1968, pp.38-67.

transcendent aloneness. In an inclusive simplicity, the underlying diversity is retained and functions as "the necessary basis for the higher unity". Since this underlying diversity retains its "extensiveness" in the inclusive simplicity, it is "available for analysis and becomes our best means for indirectly understanding the simplicity itself".[103] For Ford, the **totum simul** of the definition designates the simplicity of eternity and the **possessio** signifies its inclusivity, its retention of the diverse moments of time.[104] Ford finds an essential similarity between Boethius' position and that of process thought, of which he is a major exponent. Ford's claims have however been subject to careful criticism by Thomas P. McTighe:[105]

> But **how** does it include or contain time? That is the hub of the issue. ... But how can eternity embrace all moments of time at once and yet leave the diversity of these moments `available for analysis'? Surely analysis entails distinction, discrimination and differentiation. How then, can the many of time be in the unicity of the eternal all the while retaining its manyness?[106]

As philosophical questions, we will be concerned with these issues at length later, but McTighe's interest is to demonstrate that, for Boethius, eternity is not an inclusive simplicity. McTighe notices that in *Consolation* 4.6 Boethius teaches that being, eternity, intuition and the centre of the circle stand to becoming, time, discursive thinking and the circle as Providence to fate. Herein fate is described as the terminus of a "procession" from providence (**progressio, procedit**); and in the Neo-Platonic tradition to which most commentators assign Boethius, procession never means efficient causality.[107] Providence, in the divine mind, is a pure undifferentiated unity; fate, its finite manifestations in the world, is a multiplicity. McTighe concludes: "we are, therefore, before a version

---

[103] Ford, "Boethius", p.42.

[104] Ford, "Boethius", pp.49-50.

[105] T.P. McTighe, "Eternity and Time in Boethius" in *History of Philosophy in the Making*, L.J. Thro (ed), Washington: Uni. Press of America, 1982, pp.35-62.

[106] McTighe, "Eternity", p.37.

[107] McTighe, "Eternity". p.39.

of Neo-Platonic metaphysics in which the many emerge from the One because they are already present in the One ... Providence is said to enfold (**complectitur**) all things equally (**pariter**), however diverse. however endless they are."[108]   The basic metaphysical model[109] is **complicatio - explicatio**, enfolding - unfolding, in which opposites sink out of sight in the enfolding pure identity of God.

There are many places in which Boethius stresses the absolute unity of God.[110]   "The fixed order of nature would not proceed forth (**procederet**), nor would it unfold (**explicaret**) ... unless there were One who, by remaining himself (**maneas ipse**) disposes the variety of these changes ..."[111]   The language and movement of thought of Boethius is heavily indebted to Neoplatonism. The notion of a higher unity that envelopes a multiplicity without passing over into the latter is also found in Proclus,[112] whilst the Neoplatonic tradition is rich in texts which turn upon the enfolding - unfolding correlation and the metaphor of the circle and its centre.[113] McTighe sums up the Neoplatonic/Boethian metaphysics of containment: "An enfolding unity is not a synthesis built up from its components. It is not a whole subsequent to its parts. Enfolding unities such as centre, science or **nous** itself are prior to their multiplicities. They envelop their multiplicities in indistinction."[114] Applying this framework to the **possessio** of the time-eternity relationship, we find a self enfolding of the divine existence in a manner which includes past, present and future. Boethius' theory of time and eternity is in accordance with his theory of reality as a whole.[115] As McTighe says: "For him, the temporal is, indeed, truly present in the eternal. All temporal moments are present there, not divided off from each other, but identical to the other in the encompassing (**complectens**) identity of eternity ... time

---

[108] McTighe, "Eternity", p.39.

[109] That is, for all the relations between God and the world.

[110] Boethius, *Consolation* 3.10, 3.11, 3.12.

[111] Boethius, *Consolation* 3.12, cited in McTighe, "Eternity", p.42.

[112] Proclus, *In Platonis Timaeum* 2: 243.

[113] Plotinus, *Enneads* 6.8, 18, 1-25; Proclus, *Elementa Theologiae*, Prop. 93, etc.

[114] McTighe, "Eternity", p.47. Cf. Courcelle, *Greek Sources*, pp.306-307.

[115] See Callahan, *Four Views*, p.189.

is an unfolding ... It is the divine unity unfolded into plurality."[116] If we accept this interpretation of Boethius, and the evidence seems compelling, how are we to evaluate this definition of eternity? Various problems at one arise. Given it's Neoplatonic milieu,[117] can it be made to fit other metaphysical schema ta, based not on **complicatio - explicatio** but on cause and effect?[118] Can time qua time (past, present and future) be both ontologically present, and epistemologically distinguished in terms of tense, after the manner of unfolding proposed by Boethius? These are the questions which he poses for us, and they raise more sharply than before the character of the "two-worlds" problem. We are faced not only with the conceptual difficulty of crossing an ontological barrier, but in doing so in such a manner that the two poles somehow retain their distinctive but antithetical character, viz. the **totum simul** of eternity **and** the flowing of time. However we might subsequently tackle this paradox, it will and must be in terms compatible with the language of the Boethian definition, not simply because it established itself historically as the definition **par excellence** of the classical doctrine of the divine eternity, but even more because it presents us with the concept of the highest life conceivable by the human intellect.[119]

C. The Medieval Consolidation[120]

---

[116] McTighe, "Eternity", p.53.

[117] I am not implying here that Boethius was not a Christian philosopher at all, but rather that his metaphysics cannot but be described as Neoplatonic. On theological differences between Boethius and Neoplatonism see H.M. Barrett, *Boethius*, Cambridge: Cambridge University Press, 1940, pp.105, 133.

[118] I do not intend to defend the Boethian definition within its native metaphysical nexus, not only because I believe that such a metaphysics is indefensible, but more importantly because what became the classical doctrine of the divine eternity was not attached to Neoplatonism.

[119] This assertion will be defended at length later in the book. Cf. Inge, *Plotinus*, vol 2, p.100.

[120] Lest the impression be given that every Christian Father adopted a notion of timeless eternity it should be noted that several influential Eastern Fathers understood God's eternity as a sort of time. John Philoponus, an antagonist of Neoplatonism, produced his major work *de Aeternitate Mundi Contra Proclum* in 529 A.D. Eternity for Philoponus is a sort of unsegmented time: "eternity is some single, uniform extension (**paratasis**), not cut by any differentiation, but

I have titled this section the medieval consolidation simply because it seems that there was very little genuine dissent from the Boethian position amongst the Schoolmen. It is therefore sufficient to consider only a few major representatives.

St. Anselm[121] is a model of clarity. The divine timelessness is referred to in many places in his works, but at length in *Proslogion* 19 and 20 and *Monologion* 18 to 24. In the latter he not only expounds the concept but gives a number of positive reasons why God cannot be contained in time. In chapters eighteen and nineteen, he argues that the Supreme Nature and Supreme Truth, viz. God, could neither have precedent or antecedent. This however establishes only everlastingness. In chapters twenty and twenty one, he generates a deliberate antinomy: the Supreme Being must exist at all times and at no time. At all times either no thing would exist, and at no time else it would be composite. In chapter twenty two the doctrine of timelessness is invoked to resolve this contradiction.

> For only those things which exist in space and time in such a way that they do not transcend spatial extension or temporal duration are bound by the law of space and time ... if something's size or duration has no spatial or temporal limitation, then no place or time is truly ascribed to it ... no law of space or time in any way restricts a nature which space and time do no confine by any

---

staying always (**aei**) the same, and remaining without change in itself". *Aet.* 116.1, cited in Sorabji, *Time*, p.118. Maximus Confessor (c. 580-662 A.D.) seems to equate eternity with immutability: "To put it in a nutshell, eternity equals time without change, and time equals eternity being measured by change". *Ambiguorum Liber*, 6.31 cited in J.R. Lucas, *A Treatise on Space and Time*, London: Methuen, 1973, p.303. St John of Damascus (c. 675-749 A.D.) seems to identify God's eternity with sempiternity (ever-lastingness): "Before the framing of the world, when there was no sun to separate day from night, there was no measurable age, but only an age co- extensive with eternal things after the fashion of some sort of temporal period and interval". *The Orthodox Faith*, 2.1, tr. F.H. Charles, *The Fathers of the Church*, N.Y.: The Fathers of the Church, 1958, vol 37, p.204.

[121] c. 1033-1109 A.D.

limitation ... the Supreme Truth does not at all undergo increase or decrease of spatial or temporal extension ... (it) is not prevented from being present as a whole at the same time in many places or times ... in the case of the Supreme Being only one thing is understood, viz., that the Supreme Being is present - not in addition, that it is constrained.[122] ... it would seem more appropriate to say that (the Supreme Being) is with a place or a time than to say that it is in a place or a time. For saying that a thing is in another signifies that it is contained ... Nevertheless ... temporal modes can in a sense be predicated of the Supreme Being, in as much as it is present to all finite and mutable beings just as if it ... were changed during the same times (as they).[123]

The doctrine is summarized with precision in the twenty fourth chapter:

Hence, if the Supreme Being is said to always exist, then since for it to exist is the same as for it to live, nothing better is understood (by `always existing') than eternally existing, or eternally living - i.e. having an unending life which at once is completely whole. For its eternity is seen to be an unending life existing as a complete whole at once.[124]

On the negative side these chapters provide us with a comprehensive denial of temporality - the divine nature is not subject to temporal composition, containment or change. Positively, eternity is the simultaneous and complete possession of life. Here, we have advanced no further than Boethius.[125] However, the nature of the relationship between time and eternity is more easily discernible in Anselm than in Boethius:

---

[122] Anselm is here repeating an idea of Augustine, *Confessions*, 5.2.

[123] Anselm, *Monologion*, 22. tr. J. Hopkins and H. Richardson, *Anselm of Canterbury*, London: S.C.M. 1974, vol 1, pp.35-38.

[124] Hopkins and Richardson, *Anselm*, vol 1, p.39.

[125] This is a direct appropriation of the Boethian definition. *Consolation* 5.6.

> For as an age of time contains temporal things, so Your eternity contains also the very ages of time.[126] Even though nothing exists within eternity except the present, nevertheless this is not a temporal present as we know it but an eternal present in which the whole of time is contained. Just as the temporal present encompasses every place and everything whatsoever that is occurring in these places, so too does the eternal present contain the whole of time and everything which is in time ... Eternity has its own "simultaneity" and encompassed all of the things that occur at the same time and place and that occur at different times and places.[127]

This seems to amount to an explicit doctrine of metaphysical co-presence, i.e. that eternity exists together with every time.[128] This means that the life of God is to be thought of as containing not only the present time but also past times and future times, viz. the seemingly non-existent. Anselm, with Boethius, would seem to be logically committed to such a position, otherwise God cannot possibly be **totum simul**. Here we face again the same yawning ontological chasm that we noticed in Boethius. How can it be bridged? Anselm provides us with no answers for he shows no awareness of the problem.[129] In considering the philosophy of St. Thomas Aquinas [130] I wish again to restrict the scope of my analysis to certain salient points in Thomas' doctrine of God. I do this not only because a comprehensive consideration of his concept of eternity would be a full length book in itself, but also since I shall return to him many times in the course of the subsequent discussion. In due time I hope to show

---

[126] Anselm, *Proslogion* 21, tr. M.J. Charlesworth, Oxford: Clarendon, 1965, p.143.

[127] Anselm, *On the Harmony of the Foreknowledge, the Predestination and Grace of God with Free Choice*, qn 1, ch 5: Hopkins and Richardson, *Anselm*, vol 2 1976, p.162. Cf. *De Casu Diaboli*, 21.

[128] Cf. R.G. Swinburne, "The Timelessness of God,1", *Church Quarterly Review*, 96, 1965, p.327.

[129] I cannot here follow Jordan, *Temple*, p.23, who thinks that time is an element of eternity for Anselm. The texts cited above do not bear this out. That is precisely why we seem to be faced with ongoing confusion.

[130] c. 1225-79 A.D.

that it is in Aquinas that the resources are to be found for a logically coherent solution to the ontological problem that plagues the time-eternity question.

The most lengthy discussions on eternity are found in the *Summa Contra Gentiles* 1, 15 and in the *Summa Theologiae* 1a.10, 1-4. Notably Aquinas shows little interest in the time-eternity relationship as a matter of independent concern, and in both works he is discussing the attributes of God. Additionally one finds that in each case the deliberations are preceded by an article on immutability. This sequence is not accidental for at the beginning of our *Contra Gentiles* passage we read: "From the foregoing it is also clear that God is eternal. For whatever begins or ceases to be, suffers this through movement or change. Now it has been shown that God is altogether unchangeable. **Therefore** he is eternal, having neither beginning nor end."[131] Then in the *Summa Theologiae*: "We have shown already that the notion of eternity derives (**consequitur**) from unchangeableness in the same way that the notion of time derives from change."[132] Aquinas is clearly wrong at this point, for while any eternal entity, as **totum simul**, is necessarily immutable, it is logically possible for a temporal entity to exist unchangeably through time.[133]

The importance of the way in which Aquinas links immutability and eternity is that it introduces us to the rather negative character of his treatment of the latter. In large measure this is doubtless due to his acceptance of a doctrine of negative attributes,[134] and is a reflection of his programmatic statement at the beginning of the *Summa Theologiae*: "since we cannot know that God is, but rather that he is not, we cannot consider how he is but how he is not ... We can show how God is not by denying of Him whatever is opposed to the idea of

---

[131] Aquinas, *S.C.G.* 1,15. (my emphasis).

[132] Aquinas, *S.Th.* 1a.10,2.

[133] I am thinking here of a universe made up of a plurality of objects, one or more of which, but not all, is unchanging. In such a situation one would have to exclude relational change, what has become known as "Cambridge change", from what counts as "real change". Without the former condition there would be an immutable entity, but not time, without the latter condition the entity could, wrongly, be thought to change.

[134] See I. Frank, "Maimonides and Aquinas on Man's Knowledge of God: A Twentieth Century Perspective", *Review of Metaphysics*, 38, 1985, pp.591-615.

Him."[135]   In speaking in this way St. Thomas denies that we can know the essence of God, but a real knowledge of God is possible through negation. It we take this statement seriously,[136] then we are in a position to appreciate how Aquinas differs in his understanding of eternity from the Boethian emphasis.

He begins article one of the tenth question of the *Summa Theologiae* with the Boethian definition, and then in "reply" reasons that the Aristotelian notion of time, as numbered motion, cannot be applied to an eternal entity lacking beg inning, end and succession. He interprets Boethius in the following manner: "To deny that eternity is time Boethius uses `instantane-ously whole':  to deny temporal instanteity the word `perfect'."[137]   By this Aquinas understands Boethius to be saying that which is "instantaneously Whole" must be without succession, and so non-temporal, similarly, anything which is "perfect" must be fully actual, but no temporal thing is ever fully actual.   The eternal therefore, as whole and perfect, cannot be temporal.

In searching out the question "is God eternal?" we are presented with a typical statement of essential predication. "God is his own eternity, whereas other things, not being their own existence, are not their own duration. God however, is his own invariable existence, and so is identical with his own eternity just as he is identical with his own nature."[138]   The time-eternity antithesis is picked up again [139] when he says,

> For just as we become aware of time by becoming aware
> of the flowing instant, so we grasp the idea of eternity by
> grasping the idea of an abiding instant (**nunc stans**) ...
> Eternity and God are the same thing. So calling him
> eternal does not imply his being measured by something
> extrinsic; the notion of measurement only arises in our

---

[135] Aquinas, *S.Th.* 1a.3. cited in Frank, *Aquinas*, p.601.

[136] It is a major claim of David Burrell's, *Aquinas*, pp.13ff, that this emphasis in Aquinas underlies his whole treatment of the divine attributes.

[137] Aquinas, *S.Th.* 1a.10,1 and 5.

[138] Aquinas, *S.Th.* 1a.10,2.

[139] This is particularly obvious when we recall the Aristotelian concept of "now" and the relation of time to measurement.

way of conceiving of the situation ...[140] eternity is an instantaneous whole while time is not, eternity measuring abiding existence and time measuring change ... The 'now' remains unchanged in substance throughout time, but takes on different forms ... But eternity remains unchanged both in substance and form ... as eternity is the measure of existence as such, so time is properly the measure of change.[141]

The impression given by these texts is that Aquinas' predominant view of eternity is essentially a negative one; eternity is that which **lacks** time, it is atemporality.[142] On these grounds we seem driven to accept the conclusion that for Aquinas eternity is reached by thinking away time rather than by fulfilling it.[143] Thomas McTighe believes that the real heirs of Boethius' philosophy of time and eternity are the medieval and renaissance exponents of Neoplatonism, and not Aquinas,[144] whose philosophical light is Aristotle rather than Plato. Must we then accept a position like Ford's, that the eternity of Aquinas' God, and so most of classical Christian theology, is one of exclusive simplicity,[145] and that God remains the being that he is only by sheerly transcending,[146] rather than encompassing, time?

Such an assessment would be both hasty and unfair; firstly because there are other passages in Aquinas where time and eternity are more positively related, and secondly, because he puts the doctrine of timelessness to work in solving various theological and philosophical problems. In consideration of the first point the following can be marshalled:

---

[140] Aquinas, *S.Th.* 1a.10,2 *ad* 1, 3.

[141] Aquinas, *S.Th.* 1a.10,4 *ad* 2, 3.

[142] Cf. La croix, "Aquinas on God's Omnipresence and Timelessness", *Philosophy and Phenomenological Research*, 42, 1982, pp.392ff.

[143] So I.T. Ramsey, "The Concept of the Eternal", in *The Christian Hope*, G.B. Caird (ed), London: S.P.C.K., 1970, p.42.

[144] McTighe, "Eternity", p.55.

[145] Ford, "Boethius", pp.42-43.

[146] So J.A. Gunn, *The Problem of Time*, London: Allen and Unwin, 1930, pp.39-40. Cf. Jordan, *Temple*, p.23.

> Verbs of different tenses are used of God, not as though he varied from present to past to future, but because his eternity **comprehends** all phases of time.[147] Verbs and participles which signify time, are applied to Him because His eternity **includes** all time.[148] Again, since the being of the eternal never fails, eternity synchronizes with every time or instant of time. Somewhat of an example of this may be seen in the circle: for a given point in the circumference, although indivisible, does not coincide in its position with any other point, since the order of position results in the continuity of the circumference; while the centre which is outside the circumference is directly opposite any given point in the circumference. Accordingly whatever exists in any part if time, is **coexistent with** the eternal as though present thereto, although in relation to another part of time it is present or future.[149]

These texts reveal a more positive side to the Thomist doctrine of the divine eternity. As for his predecessors the timelessness of God is not that which excludes time but it embraces it all at once without itself becoming temporal. Here too it is all of time, past and future as well as present, that is in the eternal embrace. This raises once more both the problems of the metaphysical co-pres ence of apparent antitheticals, viz. time and timelessness, and also the difficulty in conceiving how the apparent non-existent, viz. past and future, can co-exist with the plenitude of existence, viz. eternity. This brings me to my second point made above, that timelessness is a doctrine that does much metaphysical work in Aquinas. As the essay proceeds towards a proposed solution of the "two worlds" problem, I shall have recourse frequently to the Thomist metaphysical scheme, for unlike his predecessors Aquinas seems much more aware of how acute this problem truly is and has much to say about it.

I leave St. Thomas at this point drawing attention to the two-fold, negative and positive, characteriza-tion of eternity found in him.

---

[147] Aquinas, *S.Th.* 1a.10,2 and 4. (my emphasis).

[148] Aquinas, *S.Th.* 1a.13,1 and 3, in Dominican Fathers Translation, N.Y.: Benziger, 1947, p.151. (my emphasis).

[149] Aquinas, *S.C.G.*, 1. 66, 6. (my emphasis).

Unlike others,[150] I shall subsequently argue that this dialectic, even if not completely worked out in Aquinas, is a sign not of inconsistency, but of a grasp of the truly paradoxical nature of the time-eternity relationship.

An important deviation from the line of development noted above is that of John Duns Scotus.[151] The Scotist material is inconsistent but penetrating, and anticipates various modern objections to the classical doctrine of timelessness. In one place, Scotus seems to approve without qualification the Boethian definition, for he merely repeats it and seeks to draw out its meaning:

> Eternity then includes `life' as part of its connotation, because life is the quasi-subject or foundation for eternity. Now it is certain that life, like perfect existence, is in God extramentally. But the other three components of the Boethius definition, namely `endless' (which excludes cessation), `all at once' (which excludes succession) and `possessed perfectly' (which excludes dependence and participation), only add to life a positive or negative relation it seems.[152]

But elsewhere Scotus attacks the **totum simul**, as presented from Boethius to Aquinas, as incoherent, for he denies that both our present and our future can be present to God. If it be said that the future Antichrist is now present to eternity he must in that case have already been brought into existence by God: "But the very fact that Antichrist is yet to come means that at a certain time God is about to produce him. Therefore the same thing would have been brought into being twice, which is absurd even to think."[153] It is impossible, according to Scotus, that eternity can encompass the future, for the future does not exist: "eternity ... has infinite sufficiency to encompass all of time, if time exist all at once ... On account of the boundlessness of one

---

[150] Swinburne, "Timelessness 1", p.327, goes so far as to claim that Aquinas "adds nothing" to the Boethian position.

[151] c. 1265-1308 A.D.

[152] Duns Scotus, *God and Creatures, The Quodlibetal Questions*, tr. F. Alluntis and A.B. Wolter, Princeton: Princeton University Press, 1975, p.142.

[153] Scotus, *Opus Oxon*, 1.d 3a n8 cited in Swinburne, "Timelessness 1", p.327.

relatum coexistence with another cannot be inferred, but only coexistence with whatever exists of the other relation. And what is required for the relation cannot be non-entity, such as is every time besides the present."[154] Scotus therefore seems to prefer a position whereby eternity is understood as immutable everlasting duration: "The eternal is what has not beginning and no end and is not subject to change."[155] To complicate matters further Scotus wishes to affirm that God has "true intuitive cognition" of all things past, present, and future, such that although God knows that some of them have been accomplished, he cognizes all of them "just as occurring".[156] Just how this is possible we are not told, but I shall subse-quently be arguing that such suppositions are no less ridiculous than the ones Scotus has himself rejected.

At this point I leave the medieval period, noting that the problems for metaphysics generated out of the time-eternity relationship have surfaced with added vigour and clarity, without however being attacked **en masse** in this context by any of the thinkers I have reviewed.

D. From the Reformation to the Twentieth Century.

Concerning this period Richard Swinburne has said: "The only new contribution to the issue for the last five hundred years[157] seems to be that of the German post-Kantian tradition of Protestant theology." Although Swinburne's remark is some thing of an exaggeration, it is nevertheless true that despite enormous philosophical developments in general during this period, work on the concept of eternity, from a classical theistic perspective, fell into relative desuetude.

The Reformer's interests were directed towards matters other than the doctrine of God. There is no discussion of the timelessness of

---

[154] Scotus, *Ordinatio* 1 *Senentiarum* dist 39, q5, a2. In Johannes Duns Scotus *Opera Omnia*, L. Wadding (ed), 16 vols, Hildesheim: George Olms Verlagsbuchhandlung, 1969, 5. 2: 1316.

[155] Scotus, 2 *De Trinitate* 4, cited in Swinburne, "Timelessness 1", p.327.

[156] Scotus, *Ordinatio* 1 *Senentiarum* dist 39, q5, a35 in *Opera Omnia*, 5. 2: 1317.

[157] Swinburne, "Timelessness 1", p.329. Swinburne has in mind twentieth-century Protestant theology.

God in Calvin's *Institutes* and Luther avoids such speculation as part
of his rejection of Aristotelian schola sticism. Any examination of
later major Reformed philosopher-theologians shows that the Boethian
position is strictly adhered to.[158]
On the other hand the seventeenth century witnesses, in England at
least,[159] a reaction against the Scholastic view of eternity, in favour of
unending time. Variations within this theme can be found in Thomas
Jackson, Hobbes, Thomas Traherne, John Locke and Henry More.[160]
The thinking of the period was strongly influenced by the development
of classical physics. Barrow, Newton and Clarke all took the infinity

---

[158] See, for example, H. Bavinck, *The Doctrine of God*, tr. W. Hendriksen,
Grand Rapids: Baker, 1951, pp.155-156; L. Berkhof, *Systematic Theology*,
Edinburgh: Banner of Truth, 1974, p.60; J. Edwards, "Freedom of the Will" 4.8 in
The Works of Jonathan Edwards, Edinburgh: Banner of Truth, 1974, vol 1, p.72;
H. Heppe, *Reformed Dogmatics*, tr. G.R. Thompson, Grand Rapids: Baker, 1978,
p.65; W.G.T. Shedd, *Dogmatic Theology*, Nashville: Nelson, 1980, vol 1,
pp.342-350. For an important exception to this general rule see R. Hooker, *On
The Laws of Ecclesiastical Policy*, 5.69, London: Dent, 1907, p.349. Hooker was
an influential sixteenth century Anglican divine, for him eternity is equated with
sempiternity; "So likewise his continuance is from everlasting to everlasting and
knoweth not beginning nor end".
[159] On the continent Spinoza gives an essentialist definition of eternity: "By
eternity I understand existence itself, so far as it is conceived necessarily to follow
from the definition alone of eternal truth. For such existence, like the essence of
the things, is conceived as an eternal truth. It cannot therefore be explained by
duration or time, even if the duration be conceived without beginning or end".
Ethics, 1, Def. 8. tr. W.H. White, London: Oxford University Press, 1910, p.2.
Cf. Prop. 19, *Ethics*, p.23; *Cogitata Metaphysica*, I. 4; II.1 cited in H.A. Wolfson,
The Philosophy of Spinoza, Cambridge, Mass: Harvard University Press, 1934,
vol 1, pp.367-368. Spinoza's conception is part of his pantheist metaphysics, in
relating God's eternity to the atemporality of truth, and in the neglect of the **vitae
tota simul**, he stands outside the classical understanding of the divine eternity.
[160] T. Hobbes, *Leviathan* 4.46, London: Dent, 1914, p.370; T. Traherne,
Christian Ethics, C.L. Marks, G.R. Guffey (eds), Ithaca: Cornell University Press,
1968, pp.67, 68-69, 111, 184; J. Locke, *Essays Concerning Human Understanding*
2. 15, 12; ed. P.H. Nidditch, Oxford: Clarendon, 1975, p. 204; H. More, *Divine
Dialogues*, London: vol 1, 1668, pp.60-61: "Continuity of Duration is also
compatible to the Divine Existence, as well as *Eternity* or *Life eternall* ... ", cited
in Jordan, *Temple*, p.26.

of absolute time to be an attribute of God.[161] At the same time the classical view was rigorously defended and expounded by others, but without originality.[162] The eighteenth century is also a period of relative neglect. British empiricism of course could not on its own epistemological grounds entertain the concept,[163] whilst for Kantian Idealism knowledge of such transcendent things was impossible for human reason.[164] In coming to Hegel we recognize a source for much later theological and philosophical speculation,[165] but; as Swinburne says, "he does not seemed to have touched directly upon the doctrine of the timelessness of God."[166] His basic metaphysical principle, dialectic (thesis, antithesis, synthesis) implies some sort of movement in the divine. But where he speaks of eternity, little light is thrown on the matter.[167] It would seem to be an oversimplification of

---

[161] See, M. Capek, **The Philosophical Impact of Contemporary Physics**, Princeton: Van Nostrand, 1961, p.40 and discussion in the chapter to follow.

[162] See, S. Charnocke (1628-1680), *Discourses upon the Existence and Attributes of God*, London: Henry G. Bohn, 1860, vol 1, pp.339-383 (perhaps the major work of "Protestant- Scholasticism" on the subject); J. Bramhall, *Works*, Dublin: 1676, p.873. R. Cudworth, *The True Intellectual System of the Universe*, London: Thomas Tegg, 1845, p.529 (1st Ed. 1678).

[163] For empirically minded theists such as W. Paley, proponents of a "new look" natural theology, eternity is broken down into everlastingness. "'Eternity' is a negative idea, clothed with a positive name. It supposes, in that to which it is applied, a present existence; and is the negation of a beginning or an end of that existence". *Natural Theology*, 24, Edinburgh: Oliver and Boyd, 1817, p.384.

[164] So I. Kant. *Critique of Pure Reason*, tr. N. Kemp-Smith, London: Macmillan 1929. (Transcendental Aesthetic 2.4.2: 2.6) See also Jantzen, *God's World*, pp.42-43.

[165] See, Brabant, *Time*, pp.110-123 for the God-time relationship in Hegel's philosophical descendants.

[166] Swinburne, "Timelessness 1", p.329.

[167] "Eternity is not before or after time, it is not prior to the creation of the world, nor is it the sequel to its disappearance; it is absolute present, the now, and has no before or after ... the true universal is the Idea, which is eternal ... but infinite time, if it is still regarded as time, and not as transcended time, is still to be distinguished from eternity, and if thought cannot resolve the finite into the eternal, it can never be this time; it is perhaps another time, or another, and always another". G.W.F. Hegel, *Introduction to the*

Hegel's complex thought to interpret the Absolute as possessing sheer timelessness[168] or mere omni-temporality.[169] Roberts seems closer to the mark when he says: "In the dialectic Hegel subsumed all objects of reality, including those in a state of permanent contradiction, such as time and eternity, into a single over- all process of noetic realization, that is in absolute thought."[170] I take it that for Hegel the divine eternity involves **non-temporal** movement as an ultimate principle.[171] At any rate Hegel cannot be considered to either adhere to or attack the classical understanding of the timelessness of God. To consider him further would take us beyond the scope of the book.

Before bringing this chapter to a conclusion our treatment will receive insight from a quarter hardly expected to be found allied with the philosophical interests of classical theism, Friedrich Schleiermacher.[172] The foundation of Schleiermacher's dogmatics is "the feeling of absolute dependence", "the consciousness that the whole of our spontaneous activity comes from a source outside of us."[173] The metaphysical basis for this feeling is to be sought beyond the limited character of the natural order, its basis is "God".[174] It is entirely comprehensible therefore that his treatment of the divine attributes is subsumed under a concept dialectically related to dependence, namely, causality.[175]

Philosophy of Nature 247. 15-18, 24, 31-34, tr. M.J. Petry, London: Allen and Unwin, 1970, vol 1, p.207.

[168] As Gunn, *Problem*, p.129, does.

[169] So, R. Gale, "Omniscience-Immutability Arguments", *American Philosophical Quarterly*, 23, 1986, p.319.

[170] Roberts, "Barth", p.93.

[171] On this basis Paul Tillich, *Systematic Theology*, London: S.C.M., 1978, vol 1, p.277-278, is right to defend Hegel on the grounds that his eternity does not **include** time.

[172] 1768-1834 A.D. All quotations of *The Christian Faith*, hereafter *CF*, are from the translation by H.R. Macintosh and J.S. Stewart, Edinburgh: T and T Clarke, 1960.

[173] Schleiermacher, *CF*, 4.3, in Mackintosh, p.16.

[174] Schleiermacher, *CF*, 4.4.

[175] On Schleiermacher's methodology as it relates to our discussion see J.E. Thiel, "Schleiermacher's Doctrines of Creation and Preservation: Some Epistemological Considerations", *Heythrop Journal*, 22, 1981, pp.32-48.

> The ground of our feeling of absolute dependence, i.e. the divine causality, extends as widely as the order of nature and the finite causality contained in it; consequently the divine causality is posited as equal in compass to finite causality ... The divine causality as equivalent in compass to the sum-total of the natural order is expressed in the term, the divine **omnipotence**; this puts the whole of finite being under the divine causality. The divine causality as opposed to the finite and the natural is expressed in the term, the divine **eternity.** That is, the interrelationship of partial causality and passivity makes the natural order a sphere of reciprocal action, and thus of change as such, in that all change and all alteration can be traced back to this antithesis. It is therefore just in the relationship in which the natural causality is set over against the divine, that the essence of the former is to be temporal; and consequently, so far as eternal is the opposite of temporal, the eternity of God will be the expression of that antithesis.[176]

The casual action of God considered as to scope is omnipotence, considered as to character it is eternity. What marks the divine causality from natural causality is its unconditioned and active nature. Whereas every finite cause is also, **qua** finite, effect, and therefore mutable and temporal, the one sided character of the divine action excludes all change and so is eternal. Given this foundation Schleiermacher moves on to a consideration of eternity proper. We find here little more than what has been laid down thus far:

> By the eternity of God we understand the absolutely timeless causality of God, which conditions not only all that is temporal, but time itself as well ... If the eternity of God be separated from his omnipotence ... it becomes a so-called `in active' attribute ... The religious consciousness, however ... becomes actual only as consciousness of His **eternal power** ... the divine causality, since time itself is conditioned by it, must be so much the more thought of as utterly timeless ... We must

---

[176] Schleiermacher, *CF*, 5.1.1, in Mackintosh, p.201

therefore reject as inadequate all those explanations which abrogate for God only the limits of time and not time itself, and would form eternity from time by the removal of limits, while in fact these are limits.[177]

He emphasises his conviction that eternity, as omnipotence looked at from a particular angle, is an active property of God. It is not therefore to be confused with bare atemporality. Nevertheless, it is atemporal, for it conditions all things, even time. How is all this possible? Schleiermacher first admits a difficulty, then appeals to analogy:

> For, in that a divine activity is posited, something may be posited, unknown indeed and perhaps not clearly conceivable, but by no means simply nothing. Indeed, finite being offers us some real help in conceiving the idea of eternity, since to a great degree time is merely an adjunct to finite being in so far as it is caused, and to a less degree in so far as it is cause. But in so far as finite being produces time- series with their content, thus remaining the same and identical with itself (as, e.g. the Ego, as the enduring ground of all changing spiritual states, especially of resolves, each of which again as a moment of the Ego produced a concrete time-series), then, as the enduring casual ground relatively to the changing caused, it is posited as timeless. And with some such kind of analogy we must rest content.[178]

Just as the divine-all conditioning activity generates time by conditioning finite changeable entities, without itself being temporal, so in their order finite entities can through causation produce temporal changes whilst themselves remaining unchanged. I am not certain how far this analogy takes us. It certainly gives us a picture, couched somewhat in the anthropology of Schleiermacher's own day, of how the mutable can arise from the immutable, but whilst this is certainly part of what would be required for timeless causality, it does not seem to be identical with it. The weakness of the illustration is hidden in the

---

[177] Schleiermacher, *CF*, 52.1.2, in Mackintosh, pp.203, 204, 205.
[178] Schleiermacher, *CF*, 52.2, in Mackintosh, pp.205, 206.

words "it is **posited** as timeless." It would seem to me, even in the light of Schleiermacher's own metaphysics, where the finite sphere is characterized by passivity and reciprocity, that at most we might posit **immutability** in time of the entities (such as transcendental egos?) of which he is talking. Once this is done however we seem left with an analogy that does not help us to understand the nature of **timelessness**.

Wider doubts have been raised concerning Schleiermacher's position. Nelson Pike comments:

> Schleiermacher seems to have been aware of a logical tension between the idea that God is timeless and the standard interpretation of divine creation. Schleiermacher also seems to have been alert to the internal friction involved in the claim that a timeless being is omnipotent. It is not at all obvious that a timeless individual can be consistently characterized as having any creative power let alone creative power that is unlimited or infinite.[179]

Pike is of the opinion that the absolute dependence of the universe upon God, considered in Schleiermacher to be identical with what Christianity had traditionally meant by both creation and preservation,[180] is incompatible with a timeless relation.[181] The basic problem according to Pike is that, "This way of talking surely suggests that God's sustaining activity is **temporally co-extensive** with the duration of the universe."[182]

Prima facie Schleiermacher's language seems to support Pike's assertion:

> "If we think of the creation of the world as a single divine act and **including the whole system of nature**, then this conception may be a complete expression of the feeling of absolute dependence, so long as we **do not**

---

179 Pike, *Timelessness*, p.173.

180 Schleiermacher, *CF*, 36.1, 38.1.

181 Pike, *Timelessness*, pp.108-115.

182 Pike, *Timelessness*, p.114 (my emphasis). We need to keep in mind in this discussion that for Schleiermacher the causal preserving activity of God **is** his eternity.

conceive of the act as having ceased, and consequently imagine on the one side, in God, an alteration of activity and rest relatively to the world ... In the same way if we regard Preservation as a continuous[183] divine activity exerted on the **whole course of the world,** covering the first beginning no less than each subsequent state then this is a complete expression of the self-consciousness in question, provided we do not think of the origin of the world as conditioned by something else before and after that activity."[184]

It has recently been argued that to accept this approach would be to misinterpret Schleiermacher. Bruce Boyer maintains:

> The world, as the whole of natural order, is such that although there is an entity, that causally affects it, the world does not causally affect God. This being the case, the world, taken as a unit including the whole of its history, that is including all of its `internal' temporal relations, is itself non-temporal ... We no longer have a picture of a non-temporal being sustaining a temporal being, but a non- temporal sustaining a non-temporal.[185]

Boyer's point here is that if temporality is defined in terms of change and reciprocity, as we earlier saw Schleiermacher do, then the world taken as a unit throughout all space-time cannot, since indivisible, be subject to these fluxes, and so must be non-temporal. Yet is it reasonable to think of the world in this way? In answering this question Boyer basically repeats what he has said already:

> But the world is a temporal thing, isn't it? In a sense it is and in a sense it is not, depending on how you look at it. The world is a natural order of cause and effect, and so is conditioned by time with respect to the relations within it. Taken as a whole, however, it is only the product of the

---

[183] "Continuous" is lacking in the German.

[184] Schleiermacher, *CF*, 38.2 (my emphasis), in Mackintosh, p.147.

[185] B.L. Boyer, "Schleiermacher On The Divine Causality", *Religious Studies*, 22, 1986, pp.120-121.

divine eternity, not involved in a relation of partial causes and effects, but is wholly effect. The world itself, taken as a whole, does not satisfy the conditions to be temporal.[186]

This however will not do, for to my mind it subjugates the ontological question to an epistemological one. It is one thing to abstract out in thought the perpetual flux of the world for the sake of clarity of conceptualization, it is another thing to treat this mental construct as an ontic reality. It does not seem to me that the world with its perpetual motion and with the apparently real distinctions of past, present and future can be "frozen" in the way suggested. It is one thing to say it is this way **sub specie aeternitatis**, it is another thing to say it **exists** this way **sub specie temporalis**, and it is this existent that God creates and preserves. **Contra** Boyer's interpretation of Scleiermacher,[187] we need a concept of timeless activity that can deal with **particular** finite effects in the natural order both synchronically and diachronically. I conclude that Schleiermacher's position as presented is incomplete; later however we will find his identification of the divine eternity with timeless causality very useful.

E. Summary and Conclusions

Looking back over the material of this chapter it is possible to discern two broad historical approaches to the nature of the time-eternity relation.[188]

The first of these I shall call the "Platonic" model. Its chief representative are Plato, Plutarch, Plotinus, Neoplatonists, Augustine, Boethius and Anselm. The key mechanism here is "projection", and the link between time and eternity is thought of in terms of participation. Eternity is the exemplar, the pattern, and time its mirrored image. The idea is that time as an essential ingredient in the

---

[186] Boyer, "Schleiermacher", p.121.

[187] I am not sure that Schleiermacher was aware of the depths of the problems associated with the notion of an "active" atemporal relation between God and the world.

[188] It is to taken that the comments below apply variously to the different authors named.

ordering of the finite "unrolls"[189] or descends out of a transcendent order which is perfectly structured. On this basis eternity "grasps" or holds together the contents of time in an illimitable now.[190] The second model may be broadly titled "Aristotelian". Its representatives are Aristotle, Aquinas and Schleiermacher. The key mechanism here is causation and this provides the link between time and eternity.[191] Time is related to eternity as effect to cause or in a ratio of measured to unmeasured. On this basis eternity produces or creates time as its distinctive action.[192] Since this approach is more empirical[193] or existential (Cf. essentialist)[194] than the former, that is, it stresses the concrete reality of the world, the question of the time-eternity gap is raised more overtly and more sharply for this model.[195] At this point in the essay two matters have become plain. The first is that the "classical doctrine of the divine eternity", or, more broadly, the time-eternity relationship[196] as conceived in classical theism, is not as uniform as is usually supposed. In other words we are not dealing at this point with a single metaphysical system. Boethius' understanding of eternity, for example, is not the same as Aquinas' because of the differences of their metaphysical worlds. There may be formal identity in the definition of the divine eternity accepted by classical Christian theism generally, but this does not ensure a material identity. That is, the appearance of the same words does not guarantee that they possess the same meaning. How then are we to decide between the two

---

[189] P. Weiss puts it well for Plotinus: "The picture of a
thread unrolling from a ball might be useful if only the ball representing the One could be imagined dimensionless". *Modes of Being*, Carbondale: Southern Illinois University Press, 1958, p.238.

[190] Cf. I.T. Ramsey, "Concept", pp.42-43.

[191] Sempiternity for Aristotle.

[192] I am thinking particularly of the doctrine of creation in Aquinas and Schleiermacher. Cf. "God is the **esse** of all things, not the essential (**esse**) but the causal". Aquinas *I. Sent* 8. 1,2 cited in J.F. Anderson, "The Creative Ubiquity of God", *New Scholasticism*, 25, 1957, p.157.

[193] Callahan, *Four Views*, pp.126-129.

[194] Mascall, Existence and Analogy, ch. 2 and 4.

[195] Jordan, *Temple*, p.24.

[196] Arguably however, the divine eternity is absolutely determinative of the nature of time, so that the distinction here made is only one of importance in the order of knowing.

contending models? I have already intimated my preference for the Scholastic position. The reasons for this preference will become obvious in the course of my discussion of relevant issues in the contemporary philosophy of time in the chapter to follow, and will be worked out more fully in the fifth chapter of the book.

When one considers the explicit theological motives for a doctrine of timelessness provided by the major contributors, a variety of factors appear. Perhaps foremost amongst these is that eternity considered as **totum simul** ensures that the deity possesses a complete, unfragmented and so perfect life. This is explicit in Plutarch, Plotinus, Boethius and Anselm.[197] Second, there is a reconciliation of God's immutability or immutable action, especially in creating, in terms of a concept of timelessness. This feature is most important in Au gustine and Aquinas. Thirdly, the concept of eternity is put to work in removing the apparent contradiction between God's certain foreknowledge and man's freedom, and in such a way that the divine sovereignty is preserved. Boethius generates the solution and is followed by the classical tradition generally.[198]

These motives are of diverse character, and reflect the fact that there has been a failure to draw together the various strands of ideas associated with the classical concept of eternity. One of the major aims of this book, and in particular its second half, is to show how these different motivations adhere once the character of the divine timelessness is explicated in some detail.

Throughout the remainder of this essay I will be struggling with what I have termed at different places in this chapter "the two worlds problem" and which is deeply acute over the particular matter of the time-eternity relationship. This is so because here the basic

---

[197] For example: "if this Nature were made to exist as a whole distinctly and successively at different time ... then this Nature would properly be said to have existed, to exist, and to be going to exist. Therefore its lifetime - which is nothing other than its eternity - would not exist as a whole at once but would be extended by parts throughout the parts of time. Now its eternity is nothing other than itself. Hence, the Supreme Being would be divided into parts according to the divisions of time". Anselm, *Monologion*, 21, in Hopkins and Richardson, *Anselm*, vol 1, p.34.

[198] Boethius is not the first to derive the concept of timeless knowledge but the first to use it to solve the supposed deterministic implications of foreknowledge. Sorabji, *Time*, p.125.

ontological difficulty seems two fold - how can atemporality relate to temporality, a "vertical" or transcendental problem, and how can eternity, as **totum simul**, embrace equally past, present and future given that only the middle temporal term seems to have reality, a "horizontal" problem? Since we are dealing with some sort of relationship, both terms involved must be considered carefully.

CHAPTER THREE

THE NATURE OF TIME

Given, that for the non-monistic systems of thought, like classical theism, the time-eternity question is a relational one, it is surprising that philosophers of religion concerned with this subject have given so little space to considerin g the nature of time.[1] So far in this book I have spoken of time in a rather naive uncritical fashion, it is now appropriate to investigate what time "is", for only in this way can clarity be brought to questions about the relationship between time and eternity.

A. Is Time Ideal or Real?

The first great divide between philosophers of time concerns the epistemological status of time, is it something that is dependent for its form upon the existence of a cognitive subject or is it an objective feature of the world?[2]

The most important exponent of the former view is Kant.[3] In the "Transcendental Aesthetic II" of the *Critique of Pure Reason* Kant argues that time is an **a priori** condition of perception, that is, it is a presupposition of knowing. As such it cannot be said to inhere in things themselves, for it precedes them: "Time is nothing but the form of inner sense, that is, of the intuition of ourselves and our inner state."[4] Apart from the knowing subject we cannot speak of time at all: "It is no longer objective, if we abstract from the sensibility of our intuition, that is, from the mode of representation which is peculiar to us, and speak of **things in general**. Time is therefore a purely

---

[1] Nelson Pike's *God and Timelessness*, despite being the most influential recent treatment of the topic, devoted no space at all to a separate consideration of the philosophy of time.

[2] On the various ways in which philosophies of time may be divided up on ontological and epistemological questions see R. Bunge, "Physical Time: The Objective and Relational Theories", *Phillosophy of Science*, 35, 1968, p.355.

[3] For an exposition of Kant see Gunn, *Problem*, pp.87-192.

[4] Kant, *Pure Reason*, in Kemp-Smith translation, p.77.

subjective condition of our (human) intuition ... and, in itself, apart from the subject, nothing."[5] For Kant, time is purely an aspect of the world as we perceive it, the phenomenal world, but whether it is also an aspect of the world as it really is, the noumenal world, we have no way of knowing for we cannot shake off time, or space; they are a sort of grid we necessarily impose upon our knowledge of the world.

If Kant's analysis of time was acceptable we would be left in a position of necessary agnosticism as far as **any** relationship between God and the world goes.[6] God belongs to the noumenal realm, and as such cannot be subject to the forms of time and space, but we would seem to be able to say nothing positive about him. To ask how his Being could relate to "time", where time is understood in Kantian terms as a pre-perceptual condition, is an em pty question. We must therefore leave the idealist position at this point.[7]

B. Is Time Absolute or Relational?

Our second great divide in the philosophy of time concerns a matter of ontological status. Does time exist in itself, is it absolute, or is it a feature of other ultimate realities in the world, is it relational? If time is somehow an ultimate datum it seems that God must be temporal, but if it is relative the question is left open for further discussion.[8]

---

[5] Kant, *Pure Reason*, in Kemp-Smith translation, pp.77-78.

[6] That Kant found a place for God as a necessary postulate for ethics is well known. But on certain difficulties even here see G.E. Michalson, "The Non-Moral Element in Kant's 'Moral Proof' Of the Existence of God", *Scottish Journal of Theology*, 39, 1986, pp.501-515.

[7] Cogent philosophical objections have been raised against the Kantian viewpoint. See: C.D. Broad, "Time", in *Encyclopedia of Religion and Ethics*, J. Hastings (ed), Edinburgh: T and T Clark, 1921, vol 12, p.344; A.C. Ewing, *Value and Reality*, London: Allen and Unwin, 1973, pp.279-280; N. Kemp-Smith, *A Commentary to Kant's Critique of Pure Reason*, N.Y: Humanities Press, 1963, p.139; A. Plantinga, *Does God Have a Nature?*, Milwaukee: Marquette University Press, 1980, pp.24-26.

[8] It is common in the literature to overlook the difference between relational and relative theories of time. Strictly speaking classical relational theories assume that succession involves absolute relations between events whilst relative theories hold that relations between events are relative, being subject to extra-temporal circumstances (reference frame, velocity, etc.). It is unessential for me to separate the perspectives at this point in the book. For details see H. Mehlberg, *Time,*

In opposition to the dominant Aristotelian tradition, which in different ways associates time with change, proponents of absolute time understand time in a substantivalist sense. Instants of time are thought of as substances, things which exist independently of other things. The classical statement is Newton's: "Absolute, true and mathematical time, of itself, and from its own nature flows equably without regard to anything external, and by another name is called duration: relative, apparent and common time, is some sensible and external ... measure of duration by the means of motion."[9] In other words absolute time perdures of itself, though it may only be **measured** because of the existence of physical objects.[10] Time has independent ontological status. As Sklar puts it: "there would still be those ordered pairs of places in space and instants in time which constituted event locations even if there were no events at all."[11] Although the universe may or may not be temporally unbounded, or may or may not have a beginning and an end, time is logically boundless: before and after every moment of time there must be another. In Schopenhauer's pithy language: "Time cannot be thought away, but everything can be thought away from it."[12] Newton-Smith puts the point in theological terms - "if it had not pleased the Creator to produce world history the time system would none the less have existed."[13] This view has important theological consequences, at least it did for its classical exponents. If time and space are in some final sense receptacles in which events may occur, and they are this everlastingly, it is only a short step to Newton's statement: "God, by

---

Causality, and the Quantum Theory, R.S. Cohen (ed), Dordrecht: Reidel, Vol 1, 1980, pp.43-45, 226- 229.

[9] I. Newton, *Principia Mathematica, Scholium* 1, N.Y: Philosophical Library, 1964, p.17. Newton's views are largely a development of those of his tutor, Isaac Barrow, *Lectiones Geometrica*, in *The Concepts of Space and Time*, M. Capek (ed), Dordrecht: Reidel, 1976, pp.203-208.

[10] R.G. Swinburne, *Space and Time*, London: Macmillan, 1968, p.207.

[11] L. Sklar, *Space, Time and Spacetime*, Berkeley: University of California Press, 1974, p.161.

[12] A. Schopenhauer, *Praedicibilia "A Priori"*, 3 cited in Capek, *Concepts*, p.227.

[13] W.H. Newton-Smith, *The Structure of Time*, London: Routledge and Kegan Paul, 1980, p.9. Cf. Locke, *Essay*, 2.15, 7.

existing everywhere and always, constitutes duration and space."[14] This is not quite the same as saying that time is an "attribute of God"[15], but rather that there is thought to be some necessary connection between the existence of time and the nature of God. On this sort of view God's eternity is construed as omnitemporality. It is his very "presence" which constitutes time in an absolute way.

Prominent theists were not slow to recognize the theological implications of such a view. Leibniz was swift to reply: "If the reality of time and space is necessary to the immensity and eternity of God ... he will in some measure depend up on time and space and stand in need of them."[16] To leave the matter there however would be just special pleading, a theological **petitio principii**. A number of good reasons exist for questioning whether time can be correctly thought of as possessing a self-subsistent status. Before examining these however, it is useful to briefly consider what is meant by the relational view of time.

Relationalism is a reductionist programme which seeks to eliminate problems about time (and space) by dropping all references to time from the ontological order. "Time" is to be regarded as a theoretical construct, one which is built up on the basis of primitive terms which are more clearly and directly understood than is "time" itself.[17] This is not the same as saying that time is merely subjective or unreal, for in Hackett's words: "Time is ... a relation among objects that are apprehended in an order of succession or that objectively exist in such an order: time is a **form** of perceptual experience and of objective processes in the external world."[18] Time understood as a relation between events both in the mind and outside of it is real, but apart from events it can be given no meaning or existence. To think otherwise about time is to be misled by both common and scientific

---

[14] Newton, *Principia*, 1713 edition, p.311, cited in Gunn, *Problem*, p.61.

[15] **Contra** Capek, *Philosophical Impact*, p.40.

[16] G.W. Leibniz, *5th Letter to Clarke*, 50, in *Leibniz's Philosophical Papers and Letters*, L.E. Loemker (ed), Dordrecht: Reidel, 1969, p.705.

[17] On references to the literature of developmental psychology to support this precept, see K.G. Denbigh, *Three Concepts of Time*, Berlin: Springer-Verlag, 1981, p.10.

[18] S. Hackett, *Theism*, p.263, cited in W.L. Craig, "God, Time and Eternity", *Religious Studies*, 14, 1978, p.500. Cf. E.E. Harris, "Time and Eternity": *Review of Metaphysics*, 29, 1976, p.465.

language use,[19] and to make numerous unnecessary complication for the philosophy of time.[20]

The first of the major objections to the absolute view of time begins with a denial of the distinction between absolute and measured time. If the latter is sufficient for all practical purposes we have no need to posit another and distinct time. If this is so then absolute time must be considered as nothing more than a reification,[21] an assumption that an entity must exist because we have words for it. The next step is to make appeal to the principle of parsimony, "Ockham's razor". If we do not need absolute time then it should be excluded.[22] This objection is however not substantive. Applying "Ockham's razor" is only valid in cases where it has been established that some entity is not necessary, viz. that it has no explanatory power. This can hardly be claimed to be the case with respect to absolute time outside of a full consideration of its place in a wider metaphysics and the sufficiency of the notion of relative time as a principle of explanation.

More frequently it is argued that the notion of empty time, that is, time devoid of events, is vague or meaningless. Van Fraasen puts it well:

> For any theory of time in the Aristotelian tradition, according to which time does not exist independently of motion, there can be no such thing as empty time. If nothing happens no time elapses. And if we try to imagine an interval of time d uring which nothing happens, we can succeed only by cheating. We can cheat in one of two ways: we can draw an invalid analogy to something picturable (a box with nothing in it, a road with no one on it) or we can imagine ourselves living through the interval

---

[19] Sklar, *Space*, p.167.

[20] "One of the greatest sources of philosophical bewilderment" occurs when "a substantive makes us look for a thing that corresponds to it". When this is recognized, the question "What is time"? is seen to be "an utterance of unclarity". L. Wittgenstein, *The Blue Book*, Oxford: Basil Blackwell, 1964, pp.1, 26.

[21] See, Denbigh, *Three Concepts*, p.3; G.J. Whitrow, *A Natural Philosophy of Time*, London: Nelson, 1961, p.33.

[22] See, Zwart, *About Time*, p.25.

(in which case the `clock' is the succession of our thoughts and feelings).[23]

As to the standard objection of relationalists that the concept of empty time is vacuous there have been attempts to tell stories showing that under logically possible circumstances the concept of time without events is meaningful. Sydney Shoemaker[24] describes a universe which is divided into three parts, each part periodically undergoes a freeze on New Year's day, in which all change is arrested. The freezes are detectable from other parts of the universe through the use of extra-sensory perception, not involving the travel of light. In one part the freeze occurs every third year, and lasts three minutes, being preceded and followed by a three minute period of sluggishness. In a second part of the universe, the freeze occurs every fourth year, and the period both of the freeze and of the sluggishness is four minutes. In the third part of the universe the frequency of the freeze is five years, and the period of the freeze and the sluggishness is five minutes. There occurs a simultaneous total freeze over the whole universe every sixty years, a three minute period in which no change occurs anywhere. Such a changeless period is not undetectable because the preceding regularities provide evidence for its occurrence.

On first appearances Shoemaker's story is a useful demonstration of the logical possibility of time without change, that is, absolute time. The first, partial freeze conditions, present no problem for the relationalists, for changes are occurring in other parts of the universe - the duration of the freeze is measured by the clocks in those regions where change is still occurring. In these situations we are not compelled to believe that this is an example of empty time at all. But why then should we believe that time continues when the whole universe is frozen, the situation is completely compatible with the supposition that no time is passing at all. It is easy to see how the

---

[23] Van Fraasen, *Introduction*, p.28. Cf. B.P. Bowne, *Metaphysics*, N.Y: Harper and Row, 1882, p.220; Gale, *Language*, p.156; Harris, "Time", p.466; W. James, *The Principles of Psychology*, London: Macmillan, vol 1, 1890, pp.619-620; A.E. Taylor, *Elements of Metaphysics*, London: Methuen, 1903, p.249. For Aristotle on this matter see *Physics*, 4.11, 218b21-219a1, and on "imaginary time" Aquinas, *S.Th.* 1a.1. *ad* 4.

[24] S. Shoemaker, "Time Without Change", *The Journal of Philosophy*, 66, 1969, pp.363-381.

regularities preceding the "freeze" could be taken as evidence for a changeless period, but just how is this "changeless period of time" supposed to be different from no time at all? It is at this point that "Ockham's razor" may be applied. There seems to be no need to postulate a substantial entity above change in order to explain the circumstances described. Richard Sorabji attempts to support Shoemaker's position by arguing for the possibility of a universal freeze of observation, including the freezing of the observers own mind. To the objection: "no one can observe that his own mind has become frozen ... the answer is that when the observers' minds become frozen, they are not imagined as observing this change, but simply as observing the subsequent changelessness."[25] Sorabji's reply to the objection seems to imply, by the use of the word "subsequent", that a temporal passage was observed during the period of changelessness. But how does one observe changelessness? There is nothing to observe; phenomenologically, if Sorabji's conditions were fulfilled there could be no consciousness that a freeze had ever occurred.

Shoemaker and Ian Hinckfuss[26] have attempted to strengthen the case for the logical possibility of changeless time by appeal to the concept of "mnemic causation". This type of causation occurs across a gap between changes, making possible the recommencement of events after "freezes". Whilst such a form of causation is not logica lly absurd, there would seem to be little evidence that it is an important part of the universe with which we are familiar. I take it that the necessity to appeal to additional concepts such as this, over and above our normal working ideas of the world, whilst not making it logically **impossible** that absolute time exists, nevertheless makes it increasingly implausible. Additionally, given that this essay is concerned with an eternal God's relationship with the **actual** world, the preceding arguments have little force in showing that God must somehow exist **vis a vis** absolute time.

---

25 Sorabji, *Time*, pp.76-77.
26 I. Hinckfuss, *The Existence of Space and Time*, Oxford: Clarendon, 1975, p.72ff.

A rather different argument against absolute time makes use of the principles of the identity of indiscernibles[27] and of sufficient reason. Leibniz states this as follows:

> To suppose two things indiscernible is to suppose the same thing under two names. And therefore to suppose that the universe could have at first another position of time and place than which it actually had, and yet all the parts of the universe should have had the same situation among themselves as that which they actually had - such a supposition, I say is impossible fiction.[28]

Leibniz takes up an indubitable posit of the absolute time theory, that considered in themselves, as subsisting entities, the various moments of absolute time must be identical. Leibniz' point is that if all the moments of time are identical, no reason can be given why the universe did not have a beginning at a time earlier than it did; or at any other time for that matter. God's action in creating at a particular time becomes inexplicable, for all times are indiscernible.

There are a number of ways of attempting to countermand Leibniz. Hinckfuss says that instants in absolute time need not be reckoned as identical for: "t_2 has the property of **being later** than t_1 whereas instant t_1 hasn't the property of being later than t_2."[29] This contention is however highly dubious. It seems to depend on the notion of temporal anisotropy. Yet such a feature of time cannot be separated from appeal to various events (entropy, wave radiation, etc), and this is excluded for absolute time.[30] Newton-Smith wants us to abandon the principle of sufficient reason: "If it were necessarily true that everything is in principle capable of explanation, we might have an argument to support the thesis that there could not be time before change. As this is not a necessary truth we do not have such an

---

[27] If A and B are indiscernible, that is, have all their properties in common, then A is identical to B.

[28] Leibniz, *4th Letter to Clarke*, 6. in Loemker, *Leibniz*, p.687.

[29] Hinckfuss, *Existence of Space and Time*, p.77.

[30] Cf. Capek, *Philosophical Impact*, pp.125ff. That is, Hinckfuss has not given any content to "later" but presupposed its meaningfulness in the context of absolute time theory.

argument."[31] Whilst the question "Why?" must indeed stop somewhere it seems rather strange that it should stop with such a vague entity as absolute time. A little later Newton-Smith argues that the world and time may have begun together. Yet this is surely to move to a relational framework in which there is no need to employ the principle of sufficient reason about the timing of the beginning of time (for there was no time in which time began).

To the theistically inclined, Leibniz's argument as applied to God's timing of creation is a very strong one. I do not see how the absolutist can give a reply concerning why God created at the time that he did. The relational view of time however is fully consonant with the notion of time beginning with the first event, that is, at creation.

Finally, objections have been raised against the notion of absolute time based on modern physics. The absolute theory of space and time treats these two entities as going to make up a rigid invariable framework in which events occur. Absolute theories of time have no room within them for the assignment of different time coordinates to the same event.[32] But this is exactly what becomes possible within the framework of the Special Theory of Relativity.[33] Even if one overlooks this more radical implication of Relativity Theory it is widely accepted that there is no way of establishing that any two spatially separated events are temporally simultaneous. This is because it is impossible to simultaneously synchronize any two clocks across the separate systems, for instantaneous coordination between them is impossible. We are left with no recourse to absolute time, no meaning can be given to a time value outside of its particular (i.e. relative) frame of reference.[34] Whilst this is not a final argument against absolute time, for the contradiction is generated by contingent empirical data,[35] nevertheless, as Broad long ago put it: "it helps to render the notions of absolute space and time still more spectral and remote from all possible experience than before."[36] On various grounds therefore it seems that we must conclude that time is

---

[31] Newton-Smith, *Structure*, p.23.

[32] See, Newton-Smith, *Structure*, p.23.

[33] I will discuss this in some detail in the next section of this chapter.

[34] Cf. Jantzen, "Time", p.573; Swinburne, *Space and Time*, p.244.

[35] Cf. Swinburne, *Space and Time*, chapter 11.

[36] Broad, "Time", p.342.

relational. It is important at this stage to make clear what this means for this essay.

The upshot of our discussion on the ontological status of time is a denial of the assertion that tie is an entity in its own right. In terms of general theological implications, this means that the possibility of a timeless God cannot be immediately ruled out via the necessary existence of an absolute time in which God would have to be found. More specifically it gives the time-eternity question greater precision. With respect to this question it will be necessary to investigate the relation between an atemporal entity, God, and the order of events ("time") in the world. However, before we can do this it is necessary to examine the nature of this temporal ordering in some detail, for it represents another great divide amongst th ephilosophers of time.

C. Tensed or Tenseless Time?

In 1908, J.M.E. McTaggart wrote a paper which has proved to be a water-shed in the modern philosophy of time.[37] In the process of developing an argument against the reality of time McTaggart made the distinction between two ways in which events can be ordered. He gave the name A-series to positions which run from the "past" through the "present" and into the "future" and in the name B-series to the ordering of events from earlier to later. As McTaggart noticed, the distinctions of the B-series are fixed, if M is ever earlier than N it is always earlier, but the distinctions of the A- series are not permanent - an event which is now present was future and will be past. McTaggart accepted that the A-series was a necessary feature for time, since without it, that is with only a B-series, there would be no change, and time necessarily involves change. From this point he asserted that since past, present and future are incompatible determinations (no event can compatibly be more than one of them), and yet with the passage of time all events come to possess each of them, a contradiction is generated. **Ergo**, the A-series must be rejected, and with it the reality of time.

---

[37] J.M.E. McTaggart, "The Unreality of Time", *Mind*, 17, 1908, pp.457-474; revised in *The Nature of Existence*, Cambridge: Cambridge University Press, 1927, vol 2, ch. 33, and reprinted in R. Gale (ed) *The Philosophy of Time*, N.Y: Humanities, 1978, pp.86-97.

Whilst it is not necessary at this point to engage the form of McTaggart's argument[38] it is readily evident that two ways of escaping his conundrum present themselves. On the one hand it is possible that the supposed contradiction can be avoided by eliminating the A-series from talking and thinking about time, B-theories, or "tenseless" concepts of time seek to argue, **contra** McTaggart, that all the properties of temporality can be explained in terms of the invariable relations "earlier than", "simultaneous with", "later than". A-theories, or "tensed" concepts of time, seek to show that B predications are parasitic upon A-relations and that only a theory of time which embraces the notion of temporal change is adequate to all the known facts. The debate between the "tensers" and "detensers" is an on-going one, and is certainly not likely to be settled in the foreseeable future. Nevertheless, it will become obvious in the course of the coming analysis that the consequences of this debate are of so great an importance theologically that the course of the dispute must be reviewed in some detail.[39] If it is decided that time is tenseless the logical problem of reconciling eternity and time will be considerably simplified, it the tensed theory is accepted all the old objections will remain to be tackled.

The first important question to be decided is whether the A- series is reducible to the B-series. I put the question in this way because, given the place of tense in ordinary language use, the onus must be on the reductionist to demonstrate that his alternative programme is a viable one.[40]

---

[38] For a recent supporter of McTaggart see H. Mellor, *Real Time*, Cambridge: Cambridge University Press, 1981, pp.89-103; and for replies to McTaggart, C.D. Broad, *Scientific Thought*, London: Routledge and Kegan Paul, 1923, pp.79-82; R. Gale, *Language*, pp.23-31; Sorabji, *Time*, pp.65-69; Whitrow, *Natural Philosophy*, pp.290-292, etc., and to Mellor, A.B. Levison, "Events and Time's Flow", *Mind*, 96, 1987, pp.348-350.

[39] For convenience the order of treatment follows that of Gale's *Language of Time*.

[40] Gale, *Language*, chapter 6 attempts to reduce B relations to A determinations, whilst this may be possible I do not think it is necessary (at least for the purposes of this work) in order to demonstrate the indispensible reality of tense. Cf. also, L.N. Oaklander, "The `Timelessness of Time'", *Philosophy and Phenomenological Research*, 38, 1977, pp.228-233.

Is it possible to reduce A-statements to B-statements without a loss of temporal information? Attempts at such linguistic reduction usually make use of dates or token-reflexive words.[41] An early attempt was made by Nelson Goodman: "Time t was future, is now present, and will be past" is equivalent in meaning to "This utterance is at t, is later than some earlier time, and earlier than some later time."[42] It will be noted how the tenses in the first quote have been replaced by invariable B-relations in the second.[43] If it be objected that the first sentence has illicitly imparted a reference to a speaker, the relations of future, present and past in a time sense can be expressed by: "Time t is later than some time x, identical with some time later than x, and earlier than some still later time." Dates also provide a means of saying when events occur that is independent of tense usage. For example, consider the following tensed statements:

(1) The sun is shining in Brisbane today.
(2) The sun was shining in Brisbane yesterday.
(3) The sun will be shining in Brisbane tomorrow.

These can easily be replaced by tenseless statement using dates and the tenseless "is":

(1') The sun shines in Brisbane on June 30th, 1987.
(2') The sun shines in Brisbane on June 29th, 1987.
(3') The sun shines in Brisbane on July 1st, 1987.

The characteristic difference between (1), (2) and (3) and their replacement is that the latter possess stability with respect to their specifications, that is (1'), (2') and (3') are timelessly true. The fixed

---

[41] On the logic of token-reflexives, words which when used in sentences necessarily refer back to the location of the speaker ("I", "you", "here", "now", "this") see H. Reichenbach, *Elements of Symbolic Logic*, N.Y: Macmillan, 1948, p.284.

[42] N. Goodman, *The Structure of Appearance*, 3rd ed. Dordrecht: Reidel, 1977, p.207. (1st ed. 1951).

[43] Cf. N. Rescher and A. Urquhart, *Temporal Logic*, Vienna: Springer-Verlag, 1971, ch 3. The "is" of these expressions is used tenselessly, see F.D. Miller, "Aristotle on the Reality of Time", *Archiv Fur Geschichte der Philosophie*, 56, 1974, pp.135-141.

feature of dates makes their logic considerably simpler than that of tenses, but it is at this point that serious objections are raised. It becomes doubtful whether the relations expressed in B-series sentences can perform all the functions of A-determinations.

The first difficulty that arise can be seen by comparing (1) and (1') above. It makes good sense to ask the basis of (1') whether the sun is **now** shining in Brisbane, but it makes no sense to ask this of (1) where the information is already contained in the expression. From this it seems to follow that (1') is not a true translation of (1) viz. not logically equivalent, therefore A-sentences cannot be reduced to B-sentences.[44] A second objection is raised by A.N. Prior who appeals to the apparently unique emotional connotations attached to tensed language:

> One says, e.g. `Thank goodness that's over!' and not only is this, when said, quite clear without any date appended, but it says something which it is impossible that any use of a tenseless copula with a date should convey. It certainly doesn't mean the same as, e.g. `Thank goodness the date of the conclusion of that thing is Friday, June 15th, 1954'. even if it be said then. (Nor, for that matter, does it mean `Thank goodness the conclusion of that thing is contemporaneous with this utterance'. Why should anyone thank goodness for that?).[45]

Prior's point is that there seems to be an inextricable relationship between the **passage** of certain events and our attitudes and feelings, the inflexible nature of the B-series cannot explain such evocations.

A third objection, and that usually taken by A-theorists to be fatal to the tenseless position[46] is that B-series sentences cannot guide action. If, (while unaware that today is June 30th, 1987) I switch on my radio before driving to the university and hear: "The main entrance to

---

[44] So, R. Gale, "Is It Now Now?", *Mind*, 1973, pp.97-105 and for a reply to objections *Language*, pp.57-66. Cf. N. Wolterstorff, "God Everlasting", in *Comtemporary Philosophy of Religion*, S.M. Cahn and D. Shatz (eds), Oxford: Oxford University Press, 1982, pp.80-88.

[45] A.N. Prior, "Thank Goodness That's Over", *Philosophy*, 34, 1959, p.17.

[46] Gale, *Language*, chapter 4; C. Hartshorne, "The Meaning of `Is Going To Be'", *Mind*, 74, 1965, p.53; Sorabji, *Time*, pp.134-135.

Queensland University is (tenseless) blocked for road repairs on June 30th, 1987", I will be uncertain if I should take any action. If however the radio announcer says: "the main entrance to Queensland University is (tensed) blocked for road repairs", I am quite sure what action I should take. Tenseless theories, since they are committed to a timeless theory of truth cannot handle expressions which seem to change in truth value. As such they cannot perform many of the vital directing functions of language which we normally attribute to tensed talk.[47] On these grounds the logical equi-valence of the A and B series is denied, A-expression are not reducible to B-relations.

Recently however a reply has been put forward by Hugh Mellor which seeks to undercut all the above objections by distinguishing between **A-words** and **A-judgments**, and **A-facts** (past, present, future).[48] The former, including their associating with emotion and action are accepted as basic, but reality is denied to the latter. To make a judgment about one's experience is to make a judgment about something which is immediately given. If I make a temporal judgment about my experience, that judgment, because it is about my experience, will infallibly be true. According to Mellor, any token which says an event is present will be true if and only if the event occurs at the same B-series time as the token does. But in this case the events to which presence is attributed are themselves picked out by the use of the present tense. Not all our experiences, past, present and to come, are alleged to have the A-series property, only the experience we are having now. But these, by the same take n- reflexive definition of the present tense, are among the events which **do** have the property now ascribed to them: i.e. events occurring just when the judgment itself is made. So these judgments are always true. Their token-reflexive truth conditions are such that they cannot but be true; in tenseless terms they are tautologies. The tenseless fact is that

---

[47] There are a number of variations of this argument. Q. Smith, "The Mind Independence of Temporal Becoming", *Philosophical Studies*, 47, 1985, pp.116-117, for example, points out that tenseless statements cannot supply us with the practical information about which events can or cannot be prevented.

[48] D.H. Mellor, "The Self From Time to Time", *Analysis*, 40, 1980, pp.59-62, *Real Time*, pp.47-57; "History Without the Flow of Time", *Neue Zeitschrift Fur Systematische Theologie and Religions Philosophie*, 28, 1986, pp.71-72, Cf. W. Charlton, "Review of 'Time, Creation and the Continuum'", *Philosophy*, 60, 1985, p.137.

experiences themselves are neither past, present and future, but we can make past, present and future judgments about them.

Any question of the form "Is it now now?" is itself a token and so datable. The truth as to whether the tenseless token inquired of by the questioner is "now" is dependent upon the date of the question relative to the token referred to. It the date of the question and that of the token are the same then it is true that the token statement is being made "now". This question and all like it, the truth or falsity of every tensed judgment, can therefore be settled without recourse to tensed facts. John Delmas Lewis[49] has attempted to reply to Mellor in the following way. Mellor's reduction of the peculiar ontological status of present guiding judgments to truth-at- a-time overlooks the fact that for a tenseless view of reality there is no unique moment for our existence, but only a series of many earlier/later moments, none of which can be picked out distinctly:

> Having deprived tense judgments of any tense content, the tenseless view of time can make no sense of the way such judgments are needed and used to guide and direct our actions ... On the tenseless view, time is like a sheer wall of rock on w hich a climber can find no foothold; it is utterly mysterious on this view that we often take the right steps to act at the right times.[50]

I am not persuaded that Mellor's position has been overthrown. The "peculiar ontological status" which Lewis, with all A-theorists, attributes to the present, is replaced in Mellor's thought by a particular association between judgments and events in time. If this association holds, as Mellor argues that it does, then the guiding force of present tensed statements can be explained without recourse to a notion of the present. In terms of language use there seems to be no way in which Lewis' "peculiar ontology" can be made to stick, for it is just such an ontology that Mellor's position is denying. I suspect that when these sort of arguments are directed against the B-theory, they are little more than masked phenomenological assertions, statements about how we

---

[49] Delmas Lewis, *God and Time: The Concept of Eternity and the Reality of Tense*, unpublished Ph.D. thesis, University of Winsconsin, Madigan, 1985, pp.114ff.

[50] Lewis, *God and Time*, pp.118, 120.

feel about time and action in time, and not rigorous logical refutations of the "de-tensers" position.[51] In order to settle the debate it seems necessary to go beyond the notoriously bedevilling arguments about language use and to consider the structure of "time" and the world.[52] This will occupy the remainder of the chapter.

> "Time like an ever-rolling stream bears all its sons away,
> they fly like forgotten as a dream dies at the opening day."

Isaac Watts' famous Christian hymn introduces us to the second major area of debate between the two theories of time - is temporal becoming objective, does time "flow", or is this just a subjective appearance?

Bertrand Russell seems to have opened the discussion by saying: "It will be seen that past, present and future arise from time relations of subject and object. In a world in which there was no experience there would be no past, present, or future, but there might be earlier and later."[53]

---

[51] L.J. Cohen, "A Brief Rejoinder to Professor Prior", *Philosophy*, 24, 1959, p.363 makes a useful point when he says, "I was not concerned with the relatively vague problem of `what we ordinarily mean' by expressions like `and' or `thank goodness that's over'. Instead I was concerned ... with the **logical** analysis of these expressions ..." In the debate between the two major theories of temporal relations there is a persistent danger that A-theorists will demand of B-theorists a full **translation** of tensed statements, whereas the B-theory, as a reductionist programme, need give only a satisfactory **explication** of these statements. If the B- theory is indeed true we would expect that an "ideal language" would omit a certain amount of talk that the `tenses' hold to indispensible.

[52] Hinckfuss, *Existence of Space and Time*, pp.93-99 and J.L. Plecha, "Tenselessness and the Absolute Present", *Philosophy*, 59, 1984, pp.529-534, have argued at length that the **logic** of tenses might be such as to be purely indexical but that it could be a **contingent** fact about the world that a real ontological difference exists between events described in the present tense and those described in the past and future tenses. On the other side, even if on linguistic grounds the A-theory seems preferable, this does not entail the ontological differences just referred to. An additional step is needed, it must be shown that the information provided by the A-theory of tense over and above that of the B-series is explicitly ontological. So, T.D. Vaughan, *The Divine Eternality*, unpublished B.A. (Hons) thesis, University of Queensland, 1985, p.62.

[53] B. Russell, "On the Experience of Time", *The Monist*, 25, 1915, p.212.

What Russell is denying is that events somehow "come into being"
there is a "becoming" that cannot be described simply in series
terms.[54] Whilst some of the early replies to this objection seem to be
heavily phenomenological, and so to miss the centre of Russell's
objection,[55] later attempts refer much more directly to the nature of
time itself.

C.D. Broad for instance wants to argue in the following way:

> Let us call the third kind of change **Becoming**. It ... is of
> so peculiar a character that it is misleading to call it a
> change. When we say a thing changes in quality, or that
> an event changes in pastness, we are talking of entities that
> exist both before and after the moment at which the change
> takes place. But, when an event becomes, it is; and it was
> not anything at all until it had become.[56]

This "pure becoming" of Broad's is thought of as something: "over
and above the sheer spread of events ... along the time axis, which is
analogous enough to the spread of space, there is something extra,
something active and dynamic, which is often and best described as
'passage'."[57]

Before returning to Russell, an initial argument to be examined
which is directed against objective temporal becoming is that it
generates an infinite series of times. As the early Broad said: "Time
cannot be said to flow, for this seems to imply time changes and this
would make time consist of a series of events in time."[58] Or, in the
pithy phrases of Harris, then Goodman, "Time itself does not take
time,"[59] "No time is at another time."[60] Donald Williams argues that
if flow of time is understood as a rate of change in time then we
immediately invoke a higher time dimension and so on: "we have no

---

[54] Cf. Denbigh, *Three Concepts*, p.59.

[55] E.g. W. Carr, "The Moment of Experience", *Proceedings of the Aristotelian
Society*, 16, 1915-1916, pp.1-32.

[56] C.D. Broad, *Scientific Thought*, p.67.

[57] D.C. Williams, "The Myth of Passage", reprinted in Gale, *Philosophy*,
p.102.

[58] Broad, "Time", p.339.

[59] Harris, "Time", p.464.

[60] Goodman, *Structure*, p.375.

recourse but to suppose that this movement in turn takes time of a special sort: time 1 moves in a certain rate in time 2 ... which cries to be vitalized by a new level of passage, and so on forever."[61] In reply it needs only to be remarked that talk of the passage or flow of time is not to be interpreted in the same way as we would speak of the flow of objects in a stream or movement in space, the language is figurative, but intended to capture a **sui generis** truth about time.[62] More seriously, a feasible answer to the logic ofthe objection is put by Zwart: "in the relational view of time the concept of a hyper-time is completely without meaning because the flow of time is, in this view, the flow of **all** events."[63] That is, on this view, there is nothing left over to constitute a hyper-time. Allied to this reply is an answer to the frequently raised objection concerning the meaning of the **rate** of time flow. The rate of flow of any process is equal to the number of process events per time interval. What constitutes a time interval is decided by convention in terms of a standardized clock measuring "true" duration. On earth our standardized clock is based on subdivisions of the sidereal year. Zwart again: "The rate of time flow is the proportion of the total number of events in the whole universe in a certain period to the number of standard clock events in the same period."[64] Whilst an actual result is indeterminable, because we can never know the total number of events in the universe, the concept so described is meaningful, and enables us to conclude that the rate of time flow is constant.[65] I take it that these initial objections to the notion of objective becoming have been satisfactorily resolved.

The subjective theory of becoming, referred to in association with Russell earlier, has a number of components.[66] It denies to temporal becoming, or successiveness as it is usually thought of, objective ontological status. Succession in our experience is on a par with other

---

[61] Williams, "Myth", p.106. Cf. J.J.C. Smart, "The River of Time", *Mind*, 1949, p.484.

[62] A.N. Prior, "Time after Time", *Mind*, 67, 1958, p.244.

[63] Zwart, *About Time*, p.67.

[64] Zwart, *About Time*, p.73.

[65] Since "all events" would necessarily have to change proportionally.

[66] The programme is subjectivist and not idealist for it does not attempt to deny that there are objective conditions in the "real world" which give rise to the impression of time flow. Cf. C. Hoy, "Becoming and Persons", *Philosophical Studies*, 34, 1978, p.271.

secondary qualities. We experience one after the other what are physically in space-time not successive. In one way I have already referred to a stratum of the subjectivist's programme in discussing the use of token-reflexive language. There it was pointed out how this was an attempt to consistently remove tensed language from discourse. A further extension of this analysis moves on to draw supposed ontological implications from the linguistic reduction. If "now" can be defined in terms of "this", where "this" is an object of attention or a sense-datum, "now" means "simultaneous with this". That is, there is no more to the present, to the supposed locus of temporal becoming, than an association with subjective experience.[67]

That A expressions are uniformly associated with subjective conditions does not entail that they have no objective referent. It just so happens that they possess the peculiar logical status of only being true if uttered simultaneously with (later than, earlier than) the event reported by the statement made. I can only truly say, "It is (tensed) the 1st July, 1987" if the token is stated at the time referred to, but from this I cannot draw any conclusions about the ontological status of the present one way or other.[68] (Even if the meaning of A statements in **ordinary** temporal discourse seems to be committed to a realistic view of becoming).[69] Adolf Grundbaum is one philosopher who has argued seriously, particularly from the side of science, that becoming is mind-dependent:

What qualifies a physical event at time **t** as belonging to the present or as now is not some physical attribute to the event or some relation it sustains to other **purely**

---

[67] See Russell, "Experience", pp.220-221; R.M. Blake, "On Mr. Broad's Theory of Time", *Mind*, 34, 1925, pp.418-435; J.J.C. Smart, "Time and Becoming", in *Time and Cause*, P. Van Inwagen (ed), Dordrecht: Reidel, 1980, p.6; Williams, "Myth", p.105.

[68] Cf. Gale, *Language*, chapter 10; E.P. Brandon, "What's Become of Becoming", *Philosophie*, 16, 1986, pp.71-77.

[69] It is fair however for the advocate of temporal becoming to appeal to the apparently unique character of the "now" in ordinary language use as something which must be seriously reckoned with in any philosophy of time. Unlike the "here" or "this" of space the "now" or "present" of time seems, in terms of usage, all embracing, that is, non-selective. This is something which an adequate metaphysics of time must explain, and not just explain away.

physical events. Instead, what so qualifies the event is that at least one human or other **mind-possessing** organism **M** experiences the event at the time **t** such that at **t, M** is conceptually aware of the following complex fact: that his having his experience of the event **coincides temporally** with an awareness of the fact that he has it at all.[70]

He cites H. Bergson with approval "'Now' is the temporal mode of the experiencing ego."[71] Where A-theorists go wrong is that they confuse epistemic precipitation, the determination of actualities out of possibilities in the experience of the knower, with existential coming into being. The perspectival character of the former need not be denied, but the assertion of the latter is unnecessary.[72] This is closely related to his second objection: "If there is becoming (independently of awareness) the physicist must know about it."[73] Since however physics gives no place to the notion of "becoming", because "the present" does not appear in its equations, assertions of presentness are trivial, and there is nothing above the physical events in question. Statements of experience should not be exported into the scientific ontology.

In reply to Grundbaum's second objection it is sufficient to note on empirical grounds that it is simply untrue that science makes no use of the concept of the present or "now". As Quenton Smith has pointed out: "One of the basic concepts in cosmological theory is of the present value of the Hubble age, the time elapsed between the beginning of the universe and now."[74] If, as per Grundbaum's

---

[70] A. Grundbaum, "The Status of Temporal Becoming", in Gale, *Philosophy*, p.333.

[71] A. Grundbaum, *Philosophical Problems of Time and Space*, Dordrecht: Reidel, 2nd ed, 1973, p.323.

[72] A. Grundbaum, *Philosophical Problems*, pp.324-325. Cf. "The Meaning of Time", in *Basic Issues in the Philosophy of Time*, E. Freeman and W. Sellars (eds) La Salle: Open Court, 1971, pp.195 -213.

[73] A. Grundbaum, *Modern Science and Zeno's Paradoxes*, Middletown: Wesleyan University Press, 1967, p.20. See also L.R. Baker, "Temporal Becoming: The Argument from Physics", *Philosophical Forum*, 6, 1974-75, pp.218-236.

[74] Smith, "Mind-Independence", p. 113.

interpretation, the Hubble age was tied to sentient observation its value would thereby be unalterably fixed, yet it does seem to be a contradiction to say that the actual value of the Hubble age is contingent. Grundbaum's thesis cannot be accepted as a reduction of temporal becoming because·it would, by legislation, deny the possibility of singularity, viz. an absolute beginning. In matters such as this it is illicit for philosophy to dictate to science what its theories **should be.**[75] Additionally, one should not expect to find values for "the present" or notions of absolute becoming woven into scientific calculations, just because, if reality is the present and if everything is in a constant flux of becoming, temporal flow is something that **is** presupposed by science in all possible worlds.[76]

If references to the present world were as trivial as Grundbaum suggests, then they could be neglected with impunity. Yet this is not the case. For we regard it as a serious matter, a matter of fact, when such judgments are false, and the use of falsity in this regard presumes that such statements can correspond to an objective reality. Furthermore, it is not difficult to conceptualize a situation in which the universe was bereft of conscious life, while further imagining that, if there **had** been an intelligent being present, he **would** have been able to say `so and so is earlier (or later) than this time'. This is not illegitimately to imagine conscious beings as both present and absent. As Sorabji argues: "It is rather to imagine a counterfactual situation within a counterfactual situation: having imagined that conscious being might have been absent, we further imagine what could have been said by one, if one had after all been present."[77] A strong case can be put forward for the argument that temporal pictures of the world are irreducibly "tensed" because irreducibly perspectival. Wilfred Sellars argues:

---

[75] See Smith, "Mind-Independence", pp.118-119 for a catalogue of references to the use of "the present" in contemporary cosmology. I am not here denying the possibility that the universe had no beginning, an empirical position compatible with Grundbaum's rejection of absolute becoming, but merely pointing out that his appeal to the way science works is in error.

[76] It is no more surprising that these concepts are not found in working theory than that the notion of "existence" or "reality" is not found there.

[77] Sorabji, *Time*, p.69.

only a primary picture of the world with its explicit `now' makes clear the non-fictional character of the statement, its rootedness in the real life activities of observation and inference ... The **existence** of the world as well as the `events' which make it up is irreducibly perspectival. The **structure** of the world as well as a **temporal** structure is irreducibly perspectival - though not ... `subjective' in any pejorative sense.[78]

If as Sellars believes, this perspectival attitude, represented in the temporal theory of becoming, is more basic than non-tensed modes of expression, such as earlier/later, then it is not possible to consistently unthink the tensed representation of reality. Earlier and later are as mind- dependent as past, present and future.[79] Or, in Capek's words: "They all require the presence of a mind endowed with memory. In denying that the physical world has a past and future one denies the reality of physical time as well ... Only of a completely unchanging system could it be said that it had no past."[80] At this point we are beginning to engage a question closely related to that of the objectivity of becoming -are all events equally real?[81] On an A-series

---

[78] W. Sellars, "Time and the World Order", in H. Feigl and G. Maxwell (eds), *Minnesota Studies in the Philosophy of Science vol 3. Scientific Explanation, Space and Time*, Minneapolis: University of Minnesota Press, 1962, pp.592, 593.

[79] Capek, *Concepts of Space and Time*, p.LI raises an important question. If, as per physicalism, the brain is as physical as the rest of reality (in which there is no counterpart to the "now" or transition) "where does Grundbaum then obtain the **illusion** of becoming?" His point is one often brought against the thesis for which time is purely subjective, viz. an illusion is itself a temporal, transitory phenomenon. Cf. J. Laird, *Theism and Cosmology*, London: Allen and Unwin, 1940, p.145, "`we must either admit the becoming of an unreal appearance of Becoming' (Lotze, *Metaphysics*, p.105) and without an implicit appeal to Becoming this is impossible. " Whitrow, *Natural Philosophy*, p.311. See also M. M. Schuster, "Is the Flow of Time Subjective?", *Review of Metaphysics*, 39, 1986, pp.704-710.

[80] Zwart, *About Time*, p.47.

[81] I have omitted here from discussion two types of positive attempt to specify objective means by which content can be given to the temporalist assertion that becoming is other than mind-dependent. The first consists of the generation of theoretical models descriptive of the actual state of the universe in a way that is independent of reference to an observer. Storrs McCall, "Objective Time Flow",

understanding of time it is possible to go on from an insistence on absolute becoming to what is sometimes called the "empty future theory".[82] According to this theory, or at least in the form it will be presented here, in Bunge's words: "Whatever exists at a given place is, metaphorically speaking, on the brink of two abysses: a past nothingness and a future nothingness. Consequently every space-time diagram is, right **now**, a purely mental aggregate of events. Time is not out there, by itself and ready-made ... time is in the making alongside happenings."[83] Only present things **do** exist, past things

---

Philosophy of Science, 43, 1976, pp.356-362, attempts to do this in terms of branching indeterministic universe structures. The past is represented as the base of the "tree" and future possibilities by the "branches". Smart, *Time and Becoming*, pp.8-10, objects that this way of approaching the question treats the future as real after all and in such a way as it becomes enormously "bloated". The second tack is to try to give an empirical base to the notion of becoming. Hans Reichenbach, *The Direction of Time*, Berkeley: University of California Press, 1956 and W.G. Pollard, *Chance and Providence*, London: Faber and Faber, 1958, pp.98-104, argued that the quantum uncertainity principle opened up an interpretation of time flow in terms of "becoming determined". This attempt fails because it does not provide a **unique** ontology for **the** present. It singles out infinitely many "presents" which can only be distinguished from our own present by reference to "us". Many others have tried to pin-point some thing or proce ss in the natural order which will function as an invariable indicator of a one way time flow, temporal anistropy. Favourite conditates have been the principle of entropy, the cause-effect relationship, wave radiation, knowledge and decision. For full discussion of these matters see Denbigh, *Three Concepts*, chapter 6; Hinckfuss, *Existence of Space and Time*, chapter 6; Mellor, *Real Time*, chapter 7, 9, 10; G.D. Yarnold, *The Moving Image*, London: Allen and Unwin, 1966, chapter 4. In the case of measurable variables it seems that all processes are probabilistic and as such cannot be appealed to for evidence of absolute irreversibility. For logical asymmetries, it is always possible to imagine situations in which conventional linguistic usage, say, for the order of cause and effect, is overthrown, or meaning can be given to the terms consonant with a tenseless view of time. None of this however settles the matter against a theory of absolute becoming, simply because there is no logical entailment between the concepts of "direction" and "becoming". Both "becoming" and flow may be meaning-fully said to take place in the absence of a normative direction. "Time simply has no direction, it is just the succession of events and states." Zwart, *About Time*, p.103.

[82] P. Fitzgerald, "Is the Future Partly Unreal?", *Review of Metaphysics*, 21, 1968, p.422.

[83] Bunge, "Physical Time", p.375.

have existed and future things **will** exist; the only real things in the world ate present things. The presentness of an event is, in a sense, just the event.[84] It will be immediately apparent that this is an ontological thesis of the first order.[85] In fact, it is the understanding of temporal reality which seems to have been tacitly assumed by all the important classical exponents of the idea of the divine eternity. It is this understanding of reality as confined to a single indivisible "now", a "wave of becoming", that generated the "two-worlds problem" in its most acute from, viz. how can all of the past, present and the future be metaphysically co-present with God if only the temporal present is real? Nothing I have discussed in terms of modern philosophy of time so far in this chapter has led me to reject this particular form of the time-eternity problem.[86] At this point, however, the dynamic view of time faces, to my mind, its severest test. Is it, or can it be made to be, compatible with the working principles of modern Relativity theory.

First we must recall what was said about the objections to absolute time based on the Special Theory of Relativity. There it was noted that since it seems impossible to instantaneously co-ordinate two positions in space, (an upper limit be ing set to velocity by the speed of light, which is finite) there is no way of establishing that for any given event in either of the two reference frames (or any other reference frame) that

---

[84] For various statements of "empty-future" theories see Broad, *Scientific Thought*, chapter 2; D.R. Griffin, "Bohm and Whitehead on Wholeness, Freedom and Causality", *Zygon*, 20, 1985, p.190; G.L. Kline, "`Past', `Present', and `Future' as Categorical Terms, and the `Fallacy of the Actual Future'", *Review of Metaphysics*, 40, 1986, pp.220-225; Laird, *Cosmology*, pp.151-152; A.N. Prior, *Past, Present and Future*, Oxford: Clarendon, 1967, chapter 8; J.E. Smith, "Existence, The Past and God", *Review of Metaphysics*, 6, 1952, pp.287- 295.

[85] I am in agreement with Wittgenstein's statement, *The Brown Book*, Oxford: Basil Blackwell, 1960, p.109, "If a philosopher says that propositions about the future are not real propositions, it is because he has been struck by the asymmetry in the grammar of temporal expressions. The danger is, however, that he thinks he has made a kind of scientific statement about `the nature of the future'." This recognition cuts both ways, it is dangerous to make inferences about the ontological reality **or** unreality of future events on the basis of an examination of language. On these sorts of issues, truth conditions and so forth, see Fitzgerald, "Future", pp.424-432, and the literature referred to in chapter 7 of this book.

[86] The necessity of rehearsing the B-theory objections to the tensed view of time earlier in this chapter arose out of a need to be clear about the ontological status of temporal relations.

this event is simultaneous with any particular event in another frame. Simultaneity relations are frame dependent. Time is tied to spatial position, so we find that simultaneity is relative.[87] This means that it is impossible to establish the verisimilitude of the ontological identity of the present across reference frames. Such an implication might simply be treated as a quirk of our finitude,[88] but when additional factors are considered from our context of the Special Theory the notion of a single universal present seems positively contradicted.

Consider the following example used by Paul Fitzgerald.[89] Max is wondering if tomorrow's sea fight will actually occur. It is assumed that whether or not it occurs depends on the "free" (i.e. uncaused) decision that one of the admirals will make tonight. According to any "empty future" theory the battle is "non-actual", a non-existent. Max predicts that a battle **will** occur. As Max makes his prediction, a man in a rocketship zooms past his at high velocity. As he passes Max he utters a statement that commits him to the occurrence of the sea fight. The situation can be pictured using a Minkowski diagram which shows a two-dimensional cross section of the relevant regions of space-time.

---

[87] For an extended discussion see A.A. Robb, *The Absolute Relations of Time and Space*, Cambridge: Cambridge University Press, 1921, pp.1-42.

[88] Denbigh's comments, *Three Concepts*, p.63, is correct but incomplete (unless the problem to be discussed below is dealt with): "The occurrence of events does not become illusory simply because distant observers may not agree on their simultaneity, or on the intervals between them, for these are problems to do with signalling."

[89] The argument is a standard one, for purposes of convenience I follow P. Fitzgerald, "The Truth About Tomorrow's Sea Fight", *Journal of Philosophy*, 66, 1969, pp.307-329. Fitzgerald is using as an example questions first posed by Aristotle (*De Interpretatione* 9. 18a 34-19b4) concerning the ontological status of a sea fight which takes place "tomorrow".

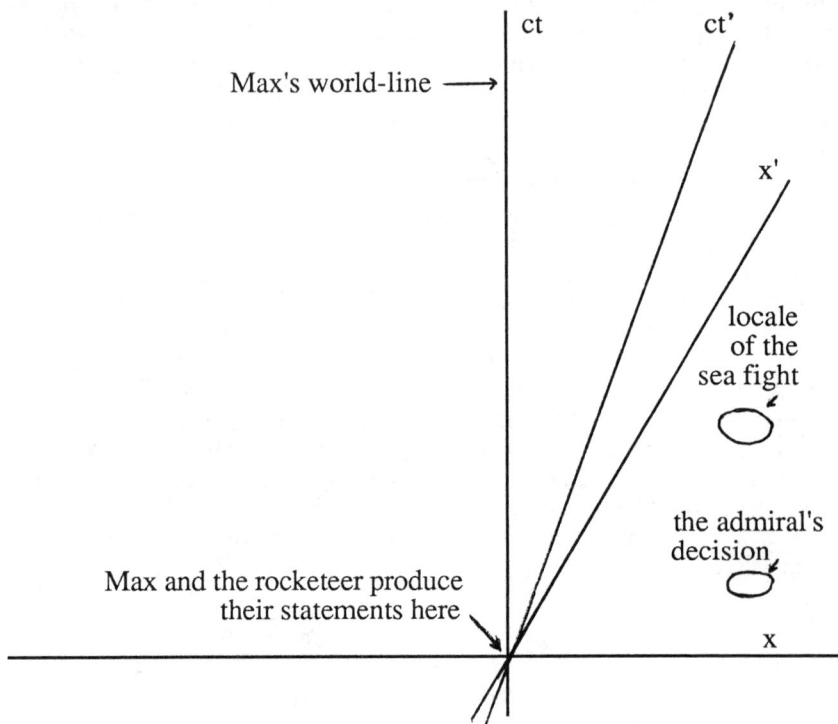

Max has the unprimed co-ordinate (c) system; the rocketeer's is primed. The ct-axis is Max's world line, the locus of place-times successively occupied by his body. The ct'-axis is the rocketeer's world line. The world lines serve essentially as time axes. Max's and the rocketeer's c- systems have a common place-time origin, where their statements are uttered, here $t = t' = 0$.[90] The x-axis is the line of simultaneity for Max's reference frame, the locus of events he judges to be simultaneous with his prediction of the sea fight. The rocketeer's line of simultaneity is represented by the x'-axis. He judges all events along this axis to be simultaneous with Max's utterance. As the diagram shows, for Max's reference frame both the

---

[90] For further conditions pertinent to this example see Fitzgerald, "Sea Fight", p.312, footnote 8.

admiral's decision and the sea fight lie in the future (above the x-axis) but for the rocketeer his judgment, and Max's occur such that the sea fight lies in the past (below the x'-axis). Since neither co-ordinate system can be treated as preferre d, the "empty future" theory is faced with an intractable problem: how can the same event be future (non-existent) in one reference frame and past in another reference frame for two observers, who, in terms of two-place simultaneity, are simultaneous with one another.[91] What illustrations such as this seem to overthrow is the A-theory thesis that only the present exists, viz. that simultaneity is absolute and not relative to frame of reference.[92] The posited alternative to the absolute present is to deny that "the present" possesses any unique ontological status. All events, regardless of their location in space-time are (tenseless) equally real. Before turning to examine this inference in detail, I wish to consider replies to the above objection to the tensed theory of the present.

One move is to attack the Special Theory of Relativity as being verificationist. Statements in Einstein seem to support this interpretation: "so we see that we cannot attach any absolute signification to the concept of simultaneity, but that two events which, when viewed from a system of co-ordinates are simultaneous, can no longer be looked upon as simultaneous events when envisaged from a system which is in motion relatively to that system."[93] So too Milton

---

[91] The example could be modified slightly so that when the rocketeer makes his judgment the battle is "present" for him (existing on "empty-future" terms) but future for Max (non- existent on "empty-future" terms). Cf. H. Putman, "Time and Physical Geometry", *Journal of Philosophy*, 64, 1967, pp.240- 247.

[92] "The argument (of tensed theories of time) runs as follows: the existence of an objective lapse of time means that reality consists of layers of `now' which come into existence successively. But if simultaneity is relative, reality cannot be split into layers in an objectively determined way. Each observer has his own set of nows." K. Godel, "A Remark about the Relationship Between Relativity Theory and Idealistic Philosophy", in *Albert-Einstein: Philosopher Scientist*, P.A. Schilpp (ed), N.Y: Harper, 1951, vol 2, p.558; Cf. W.B. Jones, "Physics and Metaphysics".

Henry Stapp on Time", in *Physics and the Ultimate Significance of Time*, D.R. Griffin (ed), Albany: S.U.N.Y., 1985, pp.278-288.

[93] A. Einstein, "On the Electrodynamics of Moving Bodies", in H.A. Lorenz **et al** (eds), *The Principle of Relativity*, London: 1923, pp.42f, cited in R.G.

Capek; "Which of these successive `nows' is declared to be simultaneous with my `here-now' depends on the frame of reference, i.e. ultimately, on convention ... the simultaneity of distant events **cannot be established**, not even retrospectively. This can only have one **meaning**: such simultaneity does not exist."[94] Some, like Delmas Lewis, have jumped to the conclusion that: "since there is no good reason to accept verification, there is no good reason to accept the argument from special relativity against the realistic notion of the present."[95] Such a decision is over- hasty, for the arguments from relativity are not simply verificationist in flavour but rooted in an apparently empirically supported theoretical structure. Swinburne[96] is on firmer ground when he defends the negative thesis that verificationist arguments cannot exclude claims for the absolute character of simultaneity based upon a certain undetectable preferred frame of reference. He argues in detail how, if certain cosmological facts are true, meaning can be given to absolute simultaneity. On these grounds the issue awaits final empirical clarification. That is, any conclusions regarding the reality of "absolute becoming" and the ontological status of the present based on the Special Theory of Relativity can only be treated as provisional in character.

More concretely, it is logically possible to remain within the framework of the findings of the Special Theory and avoid its apparent implications for the status of the present by denying the transivity of reality. In a rather different context to the above Swinburne has remarked:

> The counter-argument depends on the assumption that being temporally related is by logical necessity a transitive relation; that if event A is temporally related to event B, and event B is temporally related to event C, then event A is necessarily temporally related to event C ... The

---

Swinburne, "Verificationism and Theories of Space-Time", in *Space, Time and Causality*, R. Swinburne (ed), Dordrecht: Reidel, 1983, p.76, footnote 10.

[94] Capek, *Philosophical Impact*, p.218 (my emphasis) Cf. M. Born, *Einstein's Theory of Relativity*, N.Y: Dover, 1962, p.226: "the qualtitative physicist ... sees no meaning in the statement that an event A and an event B are simultaneous, since he has no means of deciding the truth or falsity of the assertion."

[95] Lewis, *God and Time*, p.108.

[96] Swinburne, *Space and Time*, pp.212-242; *Verificationism*, pp.71-74.

assumption is a natural one ... because the corresponding assumption about space is a necessary truth ... The assumption that being temporally related is of logical necessity a transitive relation needs proving ...[97]

The problem in the example above (with Max) disappears if it is denied that the simultaneity relations can be compared across reference frames.[98] This radical suggestion (but is it any stranger than the implications of the Special Theory?) can go on to make use of the fact that past, present and future are applicable to individual world lines. Wilfred Sellars remarks: "While the total set of co-present events (relative to S) is not the same set of events which are co- present for S', the temporal order of the events which belong to one and the same thing is ... frame invariant, as is the order in which these events become more or less future, then present, then more and more past."[99] It is illicit to extrapolate from the non-existence of a **universal** absolute reference frame to the non-existence of "a present" at each location.[100] There are as many "absolute presents" as there are reference frames. On this basis a believer in the reality of tense accepts both the special ontological status of "the" present and the findings of relativity theory if he combines both the relativity of simultaneity with a relativizing of the notion of reality.[101] Finally, it is possible to argue that a non-flowing conception of time is no less put in question by Relativity Theory than a flowing view. Godfrey-Smith emphasises this:

---

[97] R. Swinburne, "Times", *Analysis*, 25, 1965, pp.187-188.

[98] See, S. McCall, "Temporal Flux", *American Philosophical Quarterly*, 3, 1966, p.281.

[99] Sellars, "Time and the World Order", p.574. Cf. Findlay, "Time and Eternity", p.6.

[100] Cf. Denbigh, *Three Views*, p.54, **Contra** Hinckfuss, *Existence of Space and Time*, pp.106-115.

[101] See, Sklar, *Space*, p.275. This amounts to what Stein calls "a peculiarly extreme (but pluralistic!) form of solipsism", H. Stein, "On Einstein-Minkowski Space-Time" *Journal of Philosophy*, 65, 1968, p.18. It should be noticed at this point that this theory of "multiple presents" is not to be identified with the "block universe" position (described below) because it, unlike the latter, includes, in each coordinate system, real becoming.

It is curiously overlooked by most detensers that the special relativity problem which produces a conventionality about what is present leads to an exactly similar problem for a logic of tenseless dated propositions. One alleged advantage of the latter approach is that the resulting propositions are not subject to the exigencies of changing temporal reference. Tenseless dated propositions are claimed to have the merit of being freely repeatable. But `It is raining in Canberra' transformed into its tenseless counter-part `It **rains** (tenseless) in Canberra at **t**', is going to face comparable relativistic problems. For what date **t** is going to be will depend on the location and the inertial frame chosen from which the description is to be framed. According to the special theory of relativity the suggested tenseless translation will **not** be freely repeatable. Any system of dating depends on correlating events with one another, and which events are correlated with a time **t** depends on the frame of reference chose.[102]

I conclude this section with the conviction that the "tensed", or flowing view of time remains a viable conception. Since I began this discussion on the reality of tense I have been moving, as it were, progressively up the ontological scale - from discussions about language, to the reality of becoming, to the ontological status of the present. In drawing this review to a conclusion it is imperative to give proper consideration to the full blown metaphysical view of reality to which the tenseless theory of time leads, the "four-dimensional world" or the theory of the "block universe". As Donald Williams describes it:

> ... I wish to defend the view of the world, or the manner of speaking of it which treats the totality of being, of facts or of events as spread out eternally in the dimension of time as well as in the dimension of space. Future events and past events are by no means present events, but in a clear and important sense they do exist, now and forever,

---

[102] W. Godfrey-Smith, "Special Relativity and the Present", *Philosophical Studies*, 1978, pp.234-235: (Max and the rocketeer will give different dates for the sea battle.)

as rounded and definite articles of the world's furniture ... there 'exists' an eternal world total in which past, present and future are all alike determinately located, characterized, and truly describable ... past, present and future are ontologically on a level with one another and with west and south, are equally real.[103]

This theory of reality as a sort of **totum simul** owes its current popularity and influence to Relativistic views of time, and, in particular to the representations of Minkowski geometry.[104] Moritz Schlick explains the association clearly:

The meaning and scope of this proposition is most clearly demonstrated - according to Minkowski's method - by graphical representation in which time is introduced as the fourth-co- ordinate in addition to the other three spatial co-ordinates. The world thus described is a four-dimensional continuum traversed by world lines, each of which is the image of the motion of a point (material point, or packet of energy). Since the world lines represent motions, a deformation of a four-dimensional model denotes a change in the state of motion ... Now since ... a deformation never describes a genuine change, but only in a way of speaking, it follows that whether we ascribe a position of rest or some kind of motion to a particle, is also only change in the way of speaking ... The world-lines describe the motion of particles, but they must not be mistaken for the tracks of these particles ... For ... time is already represented within the model and cannot be introduced again from outside.[105]

---

[103] D.C. Williams, *Problems of Empirical Realism*, Springfield: C.C. Thomas, 1966, pp.262, 287-288.

[104] See, for examples Minkowski's own comments on the fusion of time and space in Capek, *Concepts of Space and Time*, p.253.

[105] M. Schlick, *Philosophy of Nature*, N.Y: Philosophical Library, 1949, pp.42-43. Cf. Yarnold, *Moving Image*, pp.132- 138.

This understanding of the world has been put to considerable use by philosophers. In particular it has been taken to resolve certain outstanding problems concerning personal identity. Persons are "mereological sums", that is, they are to be viewed as wholes having temporal parts in the 4-D manifold. The relation between these parts is one of "genidentity", of ordered stages in the continuum, rather than as continuity through time.[106] The theological implications of this metaphysical commitment, though slow in forth-coming, are of great significance for this book.

C.D. Broad seems to have been the first to notice how the theory of the manifold could come to the "aid" of theology. He reckoned that if the whole course of events is, in a certain sense, **totum simul**, free-will and God's foreknowledge become immediately compatible, for God will be able to be directly aware of every volition throughout time.[107] This follows providing that God does not share our limited epistemological ability of only being able to be aware of events simultaneous with our act of perception.[108] R.S. Laura accepts that our standard non-scientific ways of thinking and speaking are a function of the evolution of consciousness, so that our perspective on the true dimensionality on the world is limited:

> the intractable problems which beset the traditional articulation of the relation between space and time infect the ontological frame of reference to which that relation gives rise. It is true that within this frame of reference there is no `space' for the transcendence of God, but it is

---

[106] See, for example W.V.O. Quine, "Identity, Ostension, and Hypostasis", *Journal of Philosophy*, 47, 1950, pp.621-633; *Word and Object*, N.Y: Wiley, 1960, pp.170-172; G. Graham, "Person and Time", *Southern Journal of Philosophy*, 15, 1977, pp.309-315 and various articles in *The Identities of Persons*,
A.O. Rorty (ed), Berkeley: University of California Press, 1976.

[107] Broad, "Time", p.337.

[108] "Unless the block universe theory is logically incoherent, one can hardly rule out the idea of God seeing the future on the grounds that it makes no sense." P. McGrath, "Professor Geach and the Future", *New Blackfriars*, 54, 1973, p.501.

the frame of reference that needs to be jettisoned, not ...
the concept of God's transcendence.[109]

He goes on to identify time with the fourth dimension of space "or
Eternity as I should prefer to call it",[110] so giving a meaning to the
realm of God's transcendence. Hugh Mellor wants to argue that the
analytic philosophy of time can be of real service to theology.[111] As
he see it, if God is the Creator of a universe everlastingly spread out in
time, he, God, must be spread out in time too. Yet this is compatible
both with God's immutability and omniscience, for on the tenseless
view of time there are no changing facts. God is omnipresent with all
events in the space-time manifold **totum simul** because this is how
they exist and he is their Creator.

It is easy to see how accepting the "block universe" view of reality
would effectively dissolve the time-eternity problem as I have
presented it thus far. The ontological problem of the metaphysical
co-presence of God and the non-existent past and future simply does
not arise once we accept the ontic reality of the past and the future.
Omnitemporality takes on a new meaning, it is not God's presence at
each of the infinitely many successive slices ("nows") of time, but his
presence to the whole of time as it is "stretched out" in the manifold.
Such an understanding caters for the motives of the preservation, of
the fulness of the divine perfection, the assurance of God's sovereign
foreknowledge, and the explanation of the "time of creation" which
have been so influential in generating the classical concept of the
divine eternity. It is hardly surprising therefore, given the many
philosophical difficulties raised in the context of the classical form of
the theory, that some philosophers have maintained that **only** if a
tenseless view of time is correct can the traditional doctrine be
sustained.[112] I wish however to affirm both the reality of tense and
the classical concept of eternity in this essay. As a first step there are I

---

[109] R.S. Laura, "Towards a New Theology of Transcendence", *Sophia*, 25,
1986, p.36.

[110] Laura, "Transcendence", p.40.

[111] Mellor, "History Without the Flow of Time", p.75.

[112] This is a central contention of the recent post- graduate work of Lewis and
Vaughan (referred to earlier). Cf. B. Hebblethwaite, "Some Reflections on
Predestination, Providence and Divine Foreknowledge", *Religious Studies*, 15,
1979, pp.434-435.

believe a number of strong reasons against accepting the theory of the manifold.

Firstly, the 4-D picture is the result of an unnecessary concretization of a geometrical representation, and so involves an illicit spatialization of time. As Denbigh puts it, "let us ask with all seriousness how they (Minkowski world lines) can be drawn otherwise than schematically and with a flourish on the blackboard."[113] Psychologically, it is easy to understand how one can move from a fixed geometrical representation of space-time to a belief that everything exists **totum simul**, but this is hardly an argument that time can be thought of in spatial terms.[114] Relativity theory does not lead to a rejection of temporal (or spatial) properties, but only to a denial that they can be thought of in isolation.[115] One of the major formulae of Relativity Theory, the semi-Euclidean Minkowskian metric for spatial separations, gives a different sign to the time co-ordinate than to the three spatial co-ordinates $d = x + y + z - (ct)$. The minus sign indicates that time is not a fourth dimension of space. On account of it a signal cannot penetrate backwards through space-time. According to this formula the past is insulated from the present and nothing in the future can modify something now or in the past. The simultaneity and succession of isotopic (same place) events remains unchanged in the context of the Special Theory. The world lines, constituted by definition by a succession of isotopic events, have an order which is absolutely irreversible in all frames of reference.[116] In summing up this relative importance of space and time, Milton Capek says: "ontological priority of time over space could hardly have found a more convincing illustration."[117] Since a world line isn't a thing, but a recording of past occurrences, it is not valid to extrapolate a line into the observer's future and treat it in the same way

---

[113] Denbigh, *Three Views*, p.62.

[114] When other variables, e.g. force, temperature, are represented by spatial dimensions we do not infer that they have space-like properties. Cf. Mellor, *Real Time*, p.129; Zwart, *About Time*, p.182.

[115] So, W.B. Jones, "Physics and Metaphysics: Henry Stapp on Time", in Griffin, *Physics and Ultimate Significance*, p.281; Reichenbach, *Philosophy*, p.190.

[116] See, P.W. Atkins, *The Creation*, Oxford: W.H. Freeman, 1981, pp.57, 61, 63; Newton-Smith, *Structure of Time*, p.186.

[117] Capek, *Philosophical Impact*, p.168.

as the earlier completed portion of the line. To do so is simply speculative for it presumes that the future has a logical status comparable to that of, say, the conclusion of a syllogism from its premises. Unlike for timeless truths, we can have no absolute assurance that the future will ever exist.[118] For the "block universe" to function as a deduction of Relativity Theory it would need to be demonstrated, in the context of this theory, that all future events have the same sort of ontological reality as present events. This would mean that in principle, even if not in practice, all future events are predictable, whether or not determinism is true. Such a view would conflict with the current version of quantum mechanics according to which some events are in principle unpredictable. It would seem that such conclusions go well beyond what is warranted from within the Special Theory of Relativity itself.[119] Finally, if we take at all seriously the notion that "everything exists" (tenselessly), no room would seem to be left, meaningfully, for scientific **explanation.** If everything just "is", and the "block universe" is primitive, ultimate reality, lacking temporally dynamic parts and processes, then the notion of explanation is simply inapplicable. When viewed closely I believe that the theory of the manifold is nothing other than old-fashioned metaphysical Eleaticism of Parmenides masquerading behind the contemporary scientific respectability of modern Relativity Theory.[120] One way to avoid the accusation might be to try to explain how the use of "existence" in the theory of the continuum differs from that of its everyday use. I however fail to see how "existence" when applied to concrete objects like tables, chairs and people can have more than one meaning. It should also be noted that the four-dimensional view is no more empirically verifiable or falsifiable than the theory of the absolute present.[121] Since both make claims about the sum total of given existents (though they understand this differently) nothing could possibly count against them. At this stage of our review it must be apparent that the A and B theories of time are not merely theories of time but two rival **Weltanschauungen.** It is notoriously difficult to

---

[118] Cf. Denbigh, *Three Views*, p.63.

[119] See Stein, *"Einstein-Minkowski"*, *passim*, who is replying to arguments, purportedly derived from relativity theory, for a fully determinate future.

[120] Cf. Capek, *Philosophical Impact*, pp.161ff.

[121] Cf. P. Frank, "Is the Future Already Here", in Capek, *Concepts of Space and Time*, pp.387-395.

decide between two all encompassing rival positions. So far, it seems that there are no conclusive arguments against the flowing conception of time, even if some matters remain strange or inexplicable. There is however one matter which seems to stretch acceptance of the tenseless view of time beyond credibility; the unreality of change.

Pre-analytically, we understand change as involving an enduring substance possessing different qualities or relations at different times. For this to be so entails a movement of that substance through time.[122] Since, on a tenseless view of reality, movement through time does not occur, we must jettison the "unnecessary metaphysical assumption of permanence."[123] It is therefore necessary to redefine change. Smart seems to be consistent when he says: "we must not talk of our four-dimensional entities changing or not-changing",[124] for there is neither a hyper-space nor a hyper-time in which they could change. Later he is more specific: "In the 4-dimensional representation we do not talk of a thing changing but of a 4-dimensional solid having differing 3-dimensional cross-sections."[125] More recently Hugh Mellor has tried to give meaning to a continued use of the concept of change in the context of a tenseless view of time.[126] For Mellor, something may be said to change if it had different properties at different dates. This is not to be confused with spatial variation because the latter bears no relation to causation. Real changes must have effects. At the same time however Mellor insists that the facts about changes do not change.

Mellor's position is an implicit recognition of the difficulties that face the 4-dimensional theory concerning the reality of change. His view is however inadequate. If, as Mellor would seem to insist, objects are made up of four- dimensional worms in space-time, each successive spatio- temporal segment of the worm would have to be atomic and discrete. Nothing about these discrete entities changes, so it seems not to make sense that the summation of these states, which

[122] See, for example, Lewis, *God and Time*, p.121; A.N. Prior, *Papers on Time and Tense*, Oxford: Clarendon, 1968, pp.78-86.

[123] B. Russell, *Our Knowledge of the External World*, London: Allen and Unwin, 1926, p.111.

[124] J.J.C. Smart, "Spatializing Time", in Gale, *Language*, p.165.

[125] J.J C. Smart, "The Moving Now", *Australasian Journal of Philosophy*, 31, 1958, p.187.

[126] Mellor, *Real Time*, chapter 7.

goes to make up the worm, can be said to change. Heavy stress is laid upon causation as the distinguishing feature in spatio-temporal change, but Mellor gives the causation a purely statistical meaning: "causes make their effects more likely than in the circumstances they would otherwise have been."[127] But, unless a cause can be thought of as somehow moving across, or standing outside of, the fixed spatio-temporal continuum, as Mellor understands it, it does not seem to make sense to say that causes, by connecting with effects, constitute the four- dimensional worm "across" space-time. That is to say, if causes are not active entities, how can they meaningfully be said to perform a function like Mellor attributes to them. But if they are dynamic entities they fall outside the supposedly all inclusive continuum.[128] Neither do I believe that any sense can be made of the notion that things change but facts about them don't, least wise given the normal sense of "change" (which presupposes that things do **not** exist **totum simul**). I conclude that there seems to be no good reason to believe that there could be change in a four-dimensional world. Finally, on this sort of account temporal existence is an **essential** property of things. This means it makes no sense to talk of things starting to exist or ending their existence - they just are (tenselessly).[129] Philosophy might perhaps be constrained, if the evidence was otherwise compelling, to drop our ordinary language use in this way, but on other grounds such compulsion seems lacking.

Earlier I referred to the notion of personal identity in terms of "genidentity" and "mereological sums". According to this view a person is a temporally extended composite entity whose parts tenselessly and changelessly occupy certain temporal locations. This account contradicts common sense views of personal identity, such as put by Roderick Chisholm:

> Each of us with respect to himself knows that he now has properties he didn't have in the past, and that formerly he had properties he doesn't have now ... you are **now** such

---

[127] Mellor, *Real Time*, p.123.

[128] In saying "Time in short **is** the **causal** dimension of space-time", Mellor, "History Without the Flow of Time", p.70, seems to attribute efficiency to time. From a relationalist perspective this is simply to reify time unnecessarily.

[129] Cf. W. Godfrey-Smith, "Beginning and Ceasing to Exist", *Philosophical Studies*, 32, 1977, pp.393-402.

that you have these properties and lack those, whereas formerly you **were** such that you had those properties and lacked these. The `former you' **has** the same properties that the present you now has, and the `present you' **had** the same properties that the `former you' then had.[130]

On this sort of account of personal identity the alternative non-tensed view of reality simply does away with personhood altogether,[131] for a substantial unity is essential to personality.[132] Although it is inappropriate to take up these matters in detail two immediate repercussions of the changeless view of personhood readily emerge. The first of these is the indelible attachment we have to "our" past and future history. Memory and expectation seem to be genuine elements of our humanity, yet, if the tenseless view of the world is true we cannot remember events involving our past self nor anticipate experiences that might be had by ourselves in the future, this is simply because the self has not endured through the past into the present, neither will "it" persist into the future. These elements of (interpreted) human experiences may, conceivably, be delusory, but it would seem to be more parsimonious to deny the four-dimensional world than to reject our normal self-understanding with its myriad of associations. Allied to this problem, it seems that if persons are only genidentical entities the assignment of moral responsibility to person-stages lacks foundation. On what **moral** ground can a "presently existing" person-stage be held responsible for the actions of earlier person-stages? The type of enduring connection needed for the consistent assignment of moral responsibility simply seems to be lacking.[133] It is these sorts of "down to earth" considerations that, in my estimation, shift the balance of the argument against the B-theory of temporal relations. In order to accept a tenseless view of reality, one is required to jettison many concepts about the reliability of perception, the successiveness of consciousness, the perduring character of personal identity, and the objective assignment of moral

---

[130] R. Chisholm, *Person and Object*, La Salle: Open Court, 1976, pp.91-92.

[131] Prior, "Thank Goodness", p.16.

[132] R. Chisholm, "Problems of Identity", in *Identity and Individualism*, M. Munitz (ed), N.Y: New York University Press, 1971, pp.3-30.

[133] Cf. Delmas Lewis, "Persons, Morality and Tense- lessness", *Philosophy and Phenomenological Research*, 47, 1986, pp.305-309.

responsibility. The cost of doing this, in order to adhere to the perhaps neater four-dimensional view of the world, just seems too great. I conclude that the intuitive flowing view of time is to be favoured as a working hypothesis.[134]

D. Summary and Conclusion

Two major conclusions can be drawn from the material discussed in this chapter.

1. Time is real, but is not to be understood as a member of the entitative order. Rather, to speak of "time" is to speak of a relation existing among objects in that order. In this sense, but in this sense only, time is not ultimate but is parasitic upon the existence of things. The importance of this for the time-eternity relationship is that we are not required to think of God's relationship to some mysterious everlasting entity called "time", an absolute that would have to exist in all possible worlds, but rather of God's relationship to the ordering of events out of which time "arises". If things are more primitive than time, then the attention of the theist who would defend some intelligible relation between time and eternity is directed towards the most basic question that can be asked about enduring entities - how are they related to God as their origin? In the language of Christian theism this involves the doctrines of creation and preservation.

2. Our second major conclusion incorporates the findings of the third and largest part of the chapter. The order of temporal relations is not static but dynamic, time may meaningfully be said to "flow". Only the present or "now" is real, and change, temporal becoming, is part of the warp and woof of objective reality. This attachment to the tensed view of time means that the tension noted in Chapter two, the "two worlds problem" of a real relation between antitheticals, viz. the **totum simul** of eternity and the flux of temporality, and the conundrum of metaphysical co- presence, viz. between the successionless of timelessness and the successive reality of temporal

---

[134] Denbigh, *Three Ways*, p.170, wants to reduce the choice between the two rival theories to an attitude of mind or intuition. Though psychological factors are very important in such a decision, it would seem that the very broad implications of their different positions gives us a more objective basis for reasoned decision than simply a matter of preference.

existents, has not been dispelled. If anything, it has been made more visibly acute by the modern philosophy of time. To reconcile the classical concept of eternity, with its emphasis on the complete state of the divine being, and the dynamic nature of temporal relations will be a difficult philosophical task. Before going on to consider how the concepts of creation and preservation found in classical Christian theism might remove this tension, I propose to examine certain contemporary, and arguably unsatisfactory, models of the divine eternity.

CHAPTER FOUR

SOME CONTEMPORARY ATTEMPTS TO SOLVE
THE TIME-ETERNITY PROBLEM

The historical review of the second chapter of the book terminated with the nineteenth century. Here I wish to describe and critically evaluate a number of current models which attempt to resolve the time-eternity problem. The majority of these seek to remove apparent contradictions, not by a fresh understanding of temporality, a possibility examined and discarded in chapter three, but through redefining the divine eternality. This is hardly surprising, since from the Enlightenment there has been a progressive shift in the philosophy of religion away from, as Richmond puts it: "the static and timeless divine perfection" generally associated with Scholastic theology, towards: "the dynamic, outgoing, creative, volitional and participating aspects of the divine nature".[1] What is perhaps surprising is that the philosophical climate in relation to the paricular matter of God's timelessness took so long to become predominately anti-atemporality.[2] The following chapter attempts to demonstrate that the non-classical approaches to the central problem distinctly fail to address the question at hand; so that in order for philosophy to go forward with respect to the concept of God's eternity, a much more thorough consideration of past claims needs to be undertaken.

---

[1] J. Richmond, "God, Time and Process Philosophy", *Theology*, 68, 1965, p.237.

[2] As indicated in the first chapter of this book W. Kneale's 1961 paper seems to have been a distinct beginning of this trend, markedly accelerated by Pike's *God and Timelessness*, (1970). I cannot here enter into a discussion about the influence of non- conceptual factors in the rise of finitist theological models. But see J. Collins, *God in Modern Thought*, London: Routledge and Kegan Paul, 1960, Chapter 9; J.L. Tomkinson, "Divine Sempiternity and Atemporality", *Religious Studies*, 18, 1982, p.177.

A. Eternity as All-Embracing Temporality.

The various positions which can be grouped together under this heading can perhaps best be introduced by reference to certain results in experimental psychology involving our consciousness of duration.

Whereas for the older empiricism of Locke, Berkeley and especially Hume, time consciousness was reduced to succession of atomic impressions,[3] the findings of nineteenth century physiological psychology seemed to indicate that the perception of the present was not punctiliar but a "duration block" extending back into the past over a measurable period. William James took up some earlier speculation on this feature of temporal perceptions and used the term "specious present", which, unlike the abstract or "strict" present, which is by definition indivisible, is the content of our sensible experience of time. James states: "the practically cognized present is no knife-edge, but a saddle-back, with a certain breadth of its own on which we sit perched, and from which we look in two directions into time. The unit of composition of our perception of time is a **duration** ..."[4] The important point to note here is that **within** the one discrete "now" of the "specious present" we are aware of a number of successive events. This gives rise to an experience of what McGilvary has described as "division without disjunction".[5]

The existence of the "specious present" as defined above has been attacked on a number of grounds. Samuel Alexander felt it confused temporal with spatial extension.[6] Bertrand Russell thought it to be just an example of a particularly intense short-term or "immediate memory".[7] J.D.Mabbott finds the whole concept of "units" of temporal experience to be mistaken.[8] The tenseless view of time, by

---

[3] See J. Wild, "The New Empiricism and Human Time", *Review of Metaphysics*, 8, 1954, pp.537-557.

[4] James, *Principles*, p.609.

[5] E.B. McGilvary, "Time and Experience of Time", *Philosophical Review*, 23, 1914, p.140. Cf. J. Royce, *The World of the Individual*, N.Y.: Macmillan, 2nd series, 1901, pp.113-119.

[6] S. Alexander, *Space, Time and Deity*, N.Y.: Humanities, vol 1, 1950, p.122.

[7] B. Russell, *The Analysis of Mind*, London: Allen and Unwin, 1921, p.174.

[8] J.D. Mabbott, "Our Direct Experience of Time", *Mind*, 60, 1951, pp.153-167. He makes use of C.D. Broad's earlier work, *Scientific Thought*, pp.346-358, and

its very nature cannot accept the idea of an extended present **simpliciter**. As Hugh Mellor says: "It is present events that extend into the past and the future, not the present itself".[9]

The B-theory objection I have already dealt with in chapter three. For most other views the alternative to a "specious present" would seem to be a punctiliar perceptual present. Yet on this view we seem confronted with the inability to explain our consciousness of duration itself, for the experience of an infinite number of atomic presents could never produce in us the sensation of extension in time.[10] As for Russell's interpretation, it is feasible to think of the contents of the "specious present" as being too close to the leading edge of the "now" for memory to as yet be possible. If consciousness of successive past events has not yet had time to subside, so to speak, an act of explicit recollection is neither necessary, nor, as yet, possible.[11]

Whatever one makes of these empirical arguments about our actual experience I do not see that there is anything logically incoherent about the concept of a "specious present". The notion may therefore be allowed to stand for the purposes of subsequent discussion.

Given the patent difficulties associated with the classical doctrine of th divone eternity it is hardly surprising that philosohers unhappy with this position soon began to appeal to our experience of the "specious present" as an analogue to God's mode of temporality.[12] Josiah Royce expounds:

> the whole real content of this temporal order ... is **at once** known, i.e. is consciously experienced as a whole, by the

---

An Examination of McTaggart's Philosophy, Cambridge: Cambridge University Press, vol 2, 1938, Chapter 35.

[9] Mellor, *Real Time*, p.17. Cf. "History Without the Flow of Time", p.72.

[10] Cf. C.W.K. Mundle, "How Specious is the Specious Present?" *Mind*, 63, 1954, pp.26-48, and "Time, Consciousness Of", in *The Encyclopedia of Philosophy*, P. Edwards (ed), N.Y.: Macmillan, vol 8, 1967, pp.134- 138.

[11] See, P. Fitzgerald, "Relativity Theory and the God of Process Philosophy", *Process Studies*, 2, 1972, p.266. Cf. Gunn, *Problem*, pp.393-394.

[12] James does not seem to have taken up the idea and applied it to God, but he did make an important intermediate step by accepting Herbert Spencer's speculation that the span of the "specious present" varies enormously between different types of creatures. *Principles*, pp.638-639.

Absolute. And I use this expression **at once** in the very sense which we before used it when we pointed out that to your own consciousness, the whole musical phrase may be and often is known **at once, despite** the fact that each element of the musical succession when taken as a temporally present one, excludes from its own temporal instant the other members of the sequence, so that they are either **no longer** or **not yet,** at the instant **when** this element is temporally the present one. ... These same events ... in so far as they are viewed at once by the Absolute, are for such a view, all equally present. And their presence is a presence of all time, as a **totum simul,** to the Absolute. ... A consciousness related to the whole of the world's events, and to the whole of time, precisely as our human consciousness is related to a single melody or rhythm ... The difference is merely one of span. You now exemplify the eternal type of knowledge, even as you listen to any briefest sequence of my words. For you, too, know time even by sharing the image of the Eternal.[13]

Later philosophers were rather more aware than Royce how this concept of God's eternity would make his temporal experience different from ours. In particular it was recognized that the differentiation associated with our experience of time, succession and novelty, could not enter into divine experience.[14] More clearly it was seen that, as Carr says, the flowing order of "past, present and future would be excluded in God's duration, but not the invariable ordering of before and after".[15] For some authors, this entails that God is not to be thought of in time at all, at least he is not to be thought of in the

---

[13] Royce, *The World and the Individual*, pp.138, 142, 145, Cf. McGilvary, "Experience", pp.143-144; Carr, "Moment", pp.12, 13, 18; S. Pringle-Pattison, *The Idea of God in the Light of Recent Philosophy*, N.Y.: Oxford University Press, 1920, pp.347-365; F.J. McConnell, *Is God Limited?*, London: Williams and Norgate, 1924, pp.48-52.

[14] McGilvary, "Experience", pp.143-144.

[15] Carr, "Moment", p.9; W.R.Inge, *Mysticism in Religion*, Chicago: Chicago University Press, 1948, pp.58-60.

A- series, though if his temporal existence is **totum simul** this seems to be compatible with a B-series ordering of experience.[16]

Before passing on to evaluate these ideas I wish to mention another attempt to give some sort of meaning to the notion of the divine eternity in a manner which would avoid the many difficulties of the classical position. In two consecutive papers Richard Swinburne tried to work out a theory of timelessness by analogy with the laws of nature.[17] Universal scientific laws are ultimate principles governing nature and delimiting what is possible. As such they are determinative of all events in time. Controlled the pattern of events in time, forming the framework and not the content of the changing universe, they must be thought of as timeless. God, to whom these principles owe their ultimate origin, must likewise be a timeless ordering principle. In using this analogy to reply to various standard objections to the divine atemporality, Swinburne considers the problem of God's simultaneous awareness of events which happen at different times:

> If such a being is to be God, viewing all events of an infinte history in one view, what on the time scale of man or any other beings takes infinte time, must take for him a short finite period. An infinite scale of human time could be correlated with a finite scale of the time of God's experience, if he viewed things as happenings with infinite velocity ... God has only one experience ... all the events of history are grasped simultaneously in it ... Since there

---

[16] Ewing, *Value and Reality*, pp.281-283; V White, *The Fall of a Sparrow: a concept of special divine action*, Exeter: Paternoster, 1985, pp.148-159. At this juncture it is worth noting the unusual attempt of H.F. Saltmarsh, "Report on Cases of Apparent Precognition", *Journal of the Society for Psychical Research*, 134, 1934, pp.49-103, to use the "specious present" concept in the context of a "half-way theory of the future". That is, all determined (but no free- will) events already exist in the temporal order. On this account the "specious present" that surfaces in cases of precognition gives **bona fide** access to "future" events. Such an interpretation is incompatible with the major conclusions of the previous chapter of this book.

[17] R. Swinburne, "The Timelessness of God 1 and 2", *Church Quarterly Review*, 146, 1965, pp.323-337; 472- 486. Swinburne in his later works abandons the concept of the divine atemporality altogether.

is nothing before or after this one experience, it cannot be said to take place in time.[18]

The above models all appear to suffer from several basic flaws in their application of the principles of human temporal experience to the divine life, the first of these concerns the status of our grasp of events. In an illuminating paper on aesthetic phenomena, Ronald Hepburn discusses how successive elements in the awareness of a piece of music are built into larger unities by our mental apprehension. Then he adds: "This is transcendence, clearly, in an epistemological, not an ontological context ... it is from **time**, the temporally spread out, that the non- temporal structure emerges, it is because we remain aware of the temporally serial nature of the medium - never completely transcended - that we experience delight an astonishment at the partial transcendence".[19] That these sorts of experiences are ones of **partial** transcendence severely limits the use of the notion of the "specious present" as an analogue of the divine experience.[20] However God may be conceived, at least in the classical tradition, he eminently surpasses all our experiences in an **infinitely** superior qualitative manner. If this way of thinking is applied to the notion of a "specious present", for **God** the "specious present" dissolves in all but name.[21]

If, on the other hand, the consistent use of the **via eminentiae** is rejected, it does not seem that any form of the "specious present" can altogether extricate God from the inherent limits, the inner differentia,

---

[18] Swinburne, "Timelessness of God 2", pp.481-482.

[19] R.W. Hepburn, "Time Transcendence and Some Related Phenomena in the Arts", in *Contemporary British Philosophy*, H.D. Lewis (ed), London: Allen and Unwin, 1976, pp.152, 153, 157, 173.

[20] *Contra*, Brabant, *Time*, pp.160-162; S.F. Davenport, *Immanence and Incarnation*, Cambridge: Cambridge University Press, 1925, p.114; H. Meynell, "The Theology of Hartshorne", *Journal of Theological Studies*, 24, 1973, p.154; H.P. Owen, *The Christian Knowledge of God*, London: Athlone Press, 1969, p.240. It is interesting to note that long ago Augustine considered and rejected singing as one analogy to God's timeless grasp of changing things. "Far, far more wonderfully and in a far more hidden way do you know them", *Confessions*, 11.31.

[21] Cf. Taylor, *Elements of Metaphysics*, pp.263-264; and Gunn, *Problem*, p.361: "All such arguments aim at establishing a quantitative view of the Eternal, they attempt to grasp what they confess to be infinite in limits that are finite."

of the web of temporality.[22] As I see it, theories of an everlasting "specious present" are caught in a dilemma: if they stress the continuity between the human and divine modes of temporal duration, they become progressively less useful as explanatory models, but if they emphasise the distinction between the two modes of experience, they move ineluctably towards the **totum simul** of atemporality. That is to say, either God's temporality becomes altogether like ours, and so the notion of eternity is emptied of its characterisic significance, or God's temporality takes on properties incompatible with the very notion of temporality itself.

It may be felt that these vague speculations about degrees of transcendence are inconclusive. There is however one consideration which seems to settle the matter against the use of all "specious present" models of the divine eternity: how can a "specious **present**" give a direct knowledge of the (non-existent) future. A "specious present" **a parte ante** is unproblematical, but we have no grounds, analogical or logical, for extending the reach of the divine "specious presentiality" into the future.[23] Paul Fitzgerald, for example, draws out the consequences of the **a posteriori** character of the "specious present":

> a curious consequence arises if we construe God as experiencing the world in a single synoptic vision modelled on the specious present. God has an all-inclusive specious present. That seems to mean that he is infinitely `slow on the uptake', in that his fixing of a **now** literally takes forever! It appears that although perceptually no detail of world history escapes him, he does not **first** take explicit note of one detail and then another. He can forget nothing of what he notices, for his noticing of it takes forever, and there is no later time, after it has been noticed, at which God woud have forgotten it, that is, be unable to **recall** it to mind at will. This makes

---

[22] Cf. Laird, *Theism*, p.154; J.A. Leighton, *Man and the Cosmos*, N.Y: Appleton, 1922, p.516; F.R. Tennant, *Philosophical Theology*, Cambridge: Cambridge University Press, vol 2, 1930, pp.130-131.

[23] See: Gunn, *Problem*, pp.394-395; Laird, Theism, p.158 J. Ward *The Realm of Ends*, Cambridge: Cambridge University Press, 1912, p.473.

God out to be an infinitely sluggish observer of the passing scene.[24]

One suspects that the notion of a truly infinite "specious present" is simply a logical contradiction. It is difficult to conceive how any **temporal** duration could exist in a mode by definition non-extensible, and, as a mode of temporality, grasp **totum simul** the temporally boundless[25] history of the universe. I conclude that the concept of a divine "specious present", if developed in a manner consistent with its own premises, lacks the marks of true eternity and is not logically viable.

B. The Question of a Special Divine Eternity is Metaphysically Misplaced

In 1981, in a paper which seems to have drawn little attention, Dennis Holt picked up a line of thought in the philosophy of time, which, he argued, makes it unnecessary to predicate timelessness of God.[26] A.N. Prior, P.T. Geach, Wilfred Sellars, Nicholas Rescher and others[27] had previously argued that persons and things do not have either temporal extension or location in the way that processes and histories do.

"The question, `How long was it?', (temporally intended) is asked of last evening's performance of a play, but not of the actors or the props; it is not the waiter, but the wait in line that is long; and it is the life of a human being that measures three score and ten years, not the human being herself. To generalize: it is the length of processes, histories, and intervals between events, not the length of persons and things, which we measure with clocks and calendars. This is the

---

[24] Fitzgerald, "Relativity Theory", p.267.

[25] Sempiternity is at least a logical possibility for our universe.

[26] D. Holt, "Timelessness and the Metaphysics of Temporal Existence", *American Philosophical Quarterly*, 18, 1981, pp.147-156.

[27] Prior, *Papers*, pp.78-79; Geach, "Some Problems About Time" in *Logic Matters*, Berkeley: University of California Press, 1972, pp.295-301; Sellars, "Time and the World Order", pp.564-595; Rescher and Urquhart, *Temporal Logic*, pp.234ff.

fundamental meaning of the denial that persons and things have temporal extension."[28]

Holt goes on to argue that persons also lack temporal location. It is improper to assimilate the grammar of persons to that of other entities. The natural candidates for temporal locators - "now", "while", "at the same time". etc - do not function grammatically like their corresponding spatial indices - "here", "in front of", "at the same place" etc; and where they do serve such functions they do so with respect to names or descriptions of processes, histories and events, but not with respect to persons. It makes sense to ask, "Where is John?", but not "When (or while) is John". John is neither **before,** nor **after,** nor **at the same time as** Peter, nor is it correct to say that John is now or (even at five o'clock) that he is **at five o'clock.** Persons are not temporally composite, extended, located or related.[29] The upshot of all this with regard to the divine eternity is that composition, extension and location cannot be predicated of a personal God who exists everlastingly through time. Therefore there are not compelling metaphsyical reasons to regard God as timeless.

I think that Holt has confused the need to deny that persons have temporal parts with a denial of temporal extension. Graham is correct to say: "We usually assume, that at any time at which a person exists the whole or entire person exists at that time, and not just a temporal part or stage of him".[30] If the person can be thought of, **qua** person, as existng through time, i.e. successively, then it seems possible to consistently deny temporal length to an individual while affirming temporal extension. Extension through time, understood in terms of succession and not partition, may meaningfully be predicated of persons.

Is it also meaningful to say that persons exist at a time, viz. have temporal location? Whilst it is notoriously difficult to specify what is meant by "now" or "the present" in a temporal series, it seems no more inappropriate to say that "I exist at 11:20 a.m. on July 8th, 1987" than to say that my clock exists at that time.[31] This seems to be the case provided I understand such statements relationally, and this cannot be denied of "me" from Holt's side precisely because the

---

[28] Holt, "Timelessness", p.149.

[29] So, Holt, "Timelessness", pp.149-150.

[30] G. Graham, "Persons", p.309.

[31] Similar illustrations could be provided with respect to before and after.

appropriateness of temporal relations is one of the bones of contention. Of course, we do not usually, in reply to a question, say "John is **now**" or "John is **at five o'clock**", simply because, if the present is all that is, it is unnecessary to give such replies. If at any time we might ask about John meaningfully (not about his history but the enduring entity he is) then John exists at that time. Arguably one of the strongest impressions that we have is that our thoughts are successive, so that if anything exists in time our thoughts, and so arguably, our persons, do. I conclude that Holt has misread the implictions of tensed grammar and has sought to wring from it unwarranted metaphysical implications. He has not succeeded in showing that the concept of the divine atemporality need not be taken seriously.

C. The Synthesis of the Temporal and the Eternal

I intend to group a number of opinions under this heading, which, **prima facie,** have little in common. It will be observed however that they all share the conviction that there exists some sort of **essential** connection between God's eternity and the temporality of the world.

1. God as Timeless and in Time[32]

---

[32] An exhaustive discussion of this position, something beyond the scope of this book, would inlcude a comprehensive analysis of the association between mystical experience and the concept of eternity. On these matters see Findlay, "Time", pp.5, 10-13; Inge, *Plotinus*, vol 2, pp.98-101, Sorabji, *Time*, pp.163ff; W.T. Stace, *Time and Eternity*, Princeton: Princeton University Press, 1952, chapter 5 and *Mysticism and Philosophy*, Philadelphia: Lippincott, 1960, pp.73, 91, 99, 100, 191, 200, 269-270; J.L. Stocks, *Time, Cause and Eternity*, London: Macmillan, 1938, pp.141-143. It is my conviction that the nature of religious experience in general, and of mysticism in particular, forms an extremely dubious basis for assured philosophical reasoning. In regard to the argument of this book, I can attach no sense to the notion of experiencing God's timelessness. See, P. Bertocci, *The Person God Is*, London: Allen and Unwin, 1970, pp.161- 168; N. Frankenberry, "The Emergent Paradigm and Divine Causation", *Process Studies*, 13, 1983, pp.212- 213; Laird, *Theism*, p.159; D.A. Lane, *The Experience of God - An Invitation to do Theology*, N.Y.: Paulist Press, 1981, pp.29-30; E.L. Mascall, *He Who Is*, London: Longmans Green, 1943, Chapter 3; B. Russell, *Mysticism, Logic and Other Essays*, Harmondsworth: Penguin, 1954, p.17; Sorabji, *Time*, pp.172-173.

This view has different expressions. For example, Brabant says: "it is possible to believe without contradiction (through it is of course far beyond comprehension) that God's Being, while complete in Eternity, might also be `reflected' in a process of Becoming. The God who is eternally perfect is the same as the God who is growing perfect in Time; it is the same purpose or power viewed under two different aspects."[33] Whilst Brabant's position is equivocal, and seems to vacillate between epistemological and ontological assertions, others are more forthright; Hazelton comments: "Eternity is that mode of reality which includes time by transcending it."[34] Berdyaev echoes the idea: "In this interpretative structure, time can be related horizontally no less than vertically, to eternity, which is only to say that it is related **temporally** to eternity".[35] The enigmatic character of these ideas (which, if feasible, would dissolve at least the vertical aspect of the "two- worlds problem" of the time-eternity question) has not escaped the notice of their adherents. A.R. Peacocke visibly indicates this when he says:

> How can God be thought to act **in** time and yet be the creator **of** time? Recent analyses of this question show that a number of important traditional attributes of God ... lose coherence and meaning if God is regarded as being `timeless' in the sense of being `outside' time altogether in a way which means time cannot enter his nature at all, so that he can have no temporal succession in his experience. ... We must therefore posit **both** that God transcends space and time, for they owe their being to him, He is their Creator; **and** that space and time can exist `within' God in

---

[33] F.H. Brabant, "God and Time", in *Essays on the Trinity and the Incarnation*, A.E.J. Rawlinson (ed), London: Longmans Green, 1928, p.350.

[34] R. Hazelton, "Time, Eternity and History", *Journal of Religion*, 30, 1950, p.8.

[35] N. Berdyaev, *The Meaning of History*, London: Geoffrey Bles, 1936, p.67. Cf. Davenport, *Immanence*, pp.114-115; N.F.S. Ferre, *The Christian Understanding of God*, N.Y.: Harper, 1951, pp.71-74; J.S. McKenzie, "Eternity", in *The Encylopedia of Religion and Ethics*, J. Hastings (ed), Edinburgh: T. and T. Clark, vol 5, 1912, pp.401-405.

> such a way that he is not precluded from being present at
> all points in space and time...[36]

Others have gone on to make more explicit the asociation between
the being of God and the existence of time. For Paul Tillich, "If the
finite is posited within the processes of the divine life, the forms of
finitude (the categories) also are present in it," therefore, "The divine
eternity includes time and transcends it."[37] God's time, eternity, is
not existentially fragmented like ours, but "is the transcent unity of the
dissected moments of existential time."[38] Eternity is an eternal
present, but not one of a simultaneity which would abolish the modes
of time: "If eternity is conceived in terms of creativity the eternal
includes past and future without absorbing their special character as
modes of time."[39] The past is never completed for God, since he
takes it up in the present in creating the future, nor is the future hidden
from him since he is the limit of its openness and so can anticipate it
perfectly. For existential theologians the being of God exists in the
most intimate association with time.[40] Jung Young Lee puts the
matter carefully: "God is in time, because time is in the hand of God.
However, this does not mean that time controls God, but God controls
time ... He ... becomes voluntarily part of time ... `God in time' is
always subsequent to `time in God'".[41]

I am disposed to reject these strange amalgams out of hand, for, on
the surface, there seems to be an irresolvable contradiction between
time and any meaningful concept of eternity, that is to say, between
succession and simultaneity. It is not difficult to assemble citations

---

[36] A.R. Peacocke, *Creation and the World of Science*, Oxford: Clarendon, 1979,
footnote 53, pp.80-81. Cf. his "Cosmos and Creation", in *Cosmology, History
and Theology*, W. Yourgran and A.D. Breck (eds), London: Plenum, 1977, p.379.

[37] Tillich, *Systematic Theology*, vol 1, p.257.

[38] Tillich, *Systematic Theology*, vol 1, p.274.

[39] Tillich, *Systematic Theology*, vol 1, p.275.

[40] "Being takes time and history into itself": J. Macquarrie, *Principles of
Christian Theology*, London: S.C.M., 1977, p.191.

[41] Jung Young Lee, *God Suffers for Us: A Systematic Inquiry into a concept of
Divine Passibility*, The Hague: Martinus Nijhoff, 1974, pp.44. Cf. E. Brunner,
Dogmatics, tr. O. Wyon, London: Lutterworth, vol 3, 1952, p.378; L. Dewart,
The Future of Belief, N.Y.: Herder and Herder, 1966, p.195.

from the literature[42] which strain the limits of imaginability and conceivability beyond credibility, that is, they seem to be just plain contradictions, or else contentless. There are however a number of replies to this contention which deserve consideration.

One approach is to emphasis the limits of our understanding. Relton says: `What we have to do here as in other branches of knowledge is to hold truths as complementary and believe that ultimately they are reconcilable though to us they appear incompatible ... If the Christian admits of an element of paradox, contradiction and antinomy in this thought of God it is because the God he worships is too great for the finite mind to comprehend."[43] Nicholas Berdyaev is making the same point when he emphasises that the subject at issue, God, is beyond rational compre- hension and must be known mystically: "I believe that to assert that time does not exist in the divine life is to approach the question exoterically without reaching the ultimate depths of gnosis."[44]

With respect to Relton one quickly thinks of the complementarity theory of light, that the one phenomenon possesses properties of both waves and particles. Such empirical analogies as this are not however properly analogical to the time - eternity question; whereas waves and particles are not logical opposites, andit is only problematical how one phenomenon can possess both sets of properties, time and eternity (as usually taken) are antithetical. The theological problem, unlike all empirical problems, which could conceivably be resolved at a higher level (light, for example, might just be a "wavicle"), cannot be resolved in this way for nothing can conceivably transcend **God's** eternity. Additionally, it is unsatisfactory methodologically to accept complentarity models when less paradoxical alternatives are available. Paradox is never a satisfactory answer to a problem because it is no answer at all, and can be used as a mask for all sorts of genuine

---

[42] Consider statements like "Extension and Duration are not annihilated in simultaneity..." Davenport, *Immanence*, p.114; or, "The eternal order has a temporal quality but is not in time", Leighton, *Man*, p.516; or, the concept of God "Straddles the eternal and temporal", Ramsey, "Concept", p.45; or, "It includes at will change or fixity, movement or rest, succession or simultaneity ...", A.P. Shepherd, *The Eternity of Time*, London: Hodder and Stoughton, 1941, p.56.

[43] H.M. Relton, *Studies in Christian Doctrine*, London: Macmillan, 1960, pp.26-27.

[44] Berdyaev, *Meaning*, p.66.

contradictions. The purpose of this thesis is to show that the time-eternity relationship is neither paradoxical nor contradictory, but can be enunciated in a fully consistent way, as such it will have to be judged on its merits. As for Berdyaev, his statement is not an argument at all, but a bit of esoteric gnosticism. The presupposition of this book is that, following the classical Christian trdition, meaningful statements can be made about God's relationship to time whcih are fully open to rational scrutiny. A more satisfactory reply to the contradiction charge is J.L. Tomkinson: "But what is being denied of the divine eternity is univocal temporality. What is being asserted of it is something different from but analogous to temporal existence. In this there is no contradiction."[45] Trevor Vaughan has attempted to ground the notion of "approximate temporality" in an epistemological paradigm, one which avoids the more obvious problems associated with the idea of an eternal-temporal synthesis.[46] The illustration used is the familiar one of the inexplicability of a three- dimensional world to a two-dimensional organism. In this case however the organism is to be thought of as genuinely three-dimensional being would. A different three-dimensional being, not so limited, could interact with the organism by communicating in a two dimensional way, or in a fully three dimensional way. If the latter, the communication would be largely incomprehensible. Perhaps God's creatures share with him, to a very limited extent, aspects of his nature which they are unable to fully comprehend. Whereas before it was assumed that God was either fully temporal or atemporal, it is now feasible to hold that God is approximately temporal:

> ordinary temporal language is to be retained in characterisations of God, but with the recognition that is falls short of the reality is is intended to describe. Thus, it will be possible to retain the insights both of those who hold that God is essentially temporal, and of those who conceive of God a a **totum simul existens** - and this without any need to postulate a qualitative distinction within the divine nature.[47]

---

[45] Tomkinson, "Sempiternity", p.185.
[46] See: Vaughan, *Eternality*, pp.91-95.
[47] Vaughan, *Eternality*, p.95.

One problem with Vaughan's explanation is that it seems to move surreptitiously from a spatial analogy to a temporal application. The case of the two and three-dimensional organisms and their communication is readily acceptable because we already accept that space is multi-dimensional, but, we have no concrete reasons to believe that time is other than mono- dimensional. For the transition from the spatial example to the temporal application to work we would have to be able to make sense of the notion of a "vertical temporal series". On a relationist view of time this would mean an order of relations above an order of relations. Perhaps this higher order of relations is simply the thoughts or processes in the divine life. Yet, if, as Vaughan seems to argue, we share aspects of the divine nature, any partaking of this hyper-temporality could only be understood in terms of some sort of pantheism (for the "higher-time" **is** God's life). Not withstanding the problematic of giving sense to multiple temporal dimensions,[48] if Vaughan's proposal is followed through consistenly we are faced with an alternative theistic framework from that within which this book is operating, for classical Christian theism posits an infinite qualitative distinction between creature and Creator. Such matters therefore fall ouside our purview.

2. God as "Pure Duration"

I have kept apart for separate consideration an expression of the time-eternity relation which perhaps could have been incorporated above, that of the influential Protestant theologian Karl Barth.[49]

In the early Barth we find the theology of **krisis,** precipitated by the "'infinite qualitative distinction' betwen time and eternity."[50] By the time of the **Church Dogmatics** the absolute dichotomy and radical disjunction between the two concepts had been abandoned for a more Christological interpretation. As we could expect, for Barth there

---

[48] I shall return to this matter in further detail in Chapter seven.

[49] The role of the time-eternity relation inBarth's historical development is a large and complex question, here I am primarily concerned with the concept of eternity itself as it finds expression in the *Church Dogmatics.* For a brilliantly critical assessment of these concepts in Barth generally, see, R.H. Roberts, "Karl Barth's Doctrine of Time: Its Nature and Implications", in *Karl Barth*, S.W. Sykes (ed), Oxford: Clarendon, 1979, pp.88-146.

[50] K. Barth, *Romans*, tr. E.C. Hoskyns, Oxford: Oxford University Press, 1933, p.10.

is an important appeal to revelation, we must allow ourselves to be told what time is. "`God has time for us'.... The sufficient reason for rejecting the possibility of working here with a time comcept gained elsewhere, is contained in the basic subordiation of the investigation here instituted to the revelation attested in Holy Scripture."[51] For Barth, since God has time for us, time must be important for God: "But if we are to understand revelation time, time cannot be regarded merely as the product of man's existence interpreted as **distentio**; it must be regarded as a proper reality, as accessible to God as is human existence. A time concept which deies this cannot be of service to us."[52]

The ontological **fundamentum** for Barth is that God is not a thing, but an event, a happening, God is being- in-act. Barth sees this as the way of escaping the persistent Platonic threat of the dissolution of time into eternity. All of God's operations are a unified act, an act in which God freely chooses to be the sort of God that he is for man in Jesus Christ.[53] The integration of **Deus in se** and **Deus revelatus** is to be found in the act, being, love and person of God unified in Jesus Christ.[54] In him the categories or attributes of God find their proper synthesis. It is in the context of this framework that the divine perfections are discussed. Having denied the participation of eternity in the finite-infinite dialectic, a structure based on human reason,[55] and having based his conceptions on purely theological postulates, Barth says:

> eternity in itself and as such is to be understood as a determination of the divine freedom ... it primarily denotes the absolute sovereignity and majesty of God in itself and as such, as demonstrated in the inward and outward activity of his divine being and operative in this love as the eternal love. God's love requires and possesses eternity both inwards and outwards, for the sake of its divinity, its freedom. Correspondingly, it requires, creates and

---

[51] K. Barth, *Church Dogmatics*, G.W. Bromiley and T.F. Torrance (eds), Edinburgh: T. and T. Clark, 1956- 1975; I/2, p.45. Hereafter *CD*.

[52] Barth, *CD*, I/2, p.46.

[53] Barth, *CD*, II/1, pp.262-264.

[54] Barth, *CD*, II/1, pp.267-271, 281.

[55] Barth, *CD*, II/1, pp.188-189.

therefore possesses in its outward relation what we call
time. Time is the form of creation in virtue of which it is
definitely fitted to be the theatre for the acts of divine
freedom.[56]

This definition does little to help philosophical analysis, but it
introduces us to the deep enmeshing of time and eternity in Barth's
theology, - eternity is a sort of temporal **plenum** from which time
takes its reality. The soteriological interest of Barth is strongly at
work as he seeks to show how time and eternity "belong" together in a
new conjunction of transcendence and immanence: "The being is
eternal in whose duration beginning, succession and end are not three
but one .... Eternity is the simultaneity of beginning, middle and end,
and to that extend is pure duration."[57] Such an eternity: "is not an
infinte extension of time backwards and forwards. Time can have
nothing to do with God."[58] Barth can both affirm eternity as the
supreme principle of time[59] **and** deny the connection of time with God
because the time of God is "real time", not the time of the world. This
"theological time" is the time of humanity,:[60] "Temporality, as far as
our observation and understanding go, is of the universe is
humanity".[61] A correlation between human time and that of the rest
of the universe is explicitly denied.[62] At this point the self-enclosed
nature of the time-eternity relationship in Barth has become evident,
and we are dealing with a self-defined thought system lifted out of our
connections with natural reality.[63]

He cites the **possessio** of Boethius with approval,[64] but the divine
"now" is not to be thought of as excluding the past for the future. As
the Lord of time God is pre-temporal, supra-temporal and post-

---

[56] Barth, *CD*, II/1, pp.464-465.

[57] Barth, *CD*, II/1, p.608. Cf. III/2, p.437.

[58] Barth, *CD*, II/1, p.608.

[59] Barth, *CD*, II/1, p.465.

[60] Christologically defined and constituted in the image of God.

[61] Barth, *CD*, III/2, p.522.

[62] Barth, *CD*, III/2, p.521.

[63] This is consistent with the Barthian denial of any place to natural theology,
(*CD*, II/1, pp.10-16, 105).

[64] Barth, *CD*, II/1, p.611.

temporal, not in bare timelessness but with an eterntiy that affirms, fulfils and judges time.[65] God's eternity surrounds time on all sides and so includes its dimensions.[66] Time itself is in eterntiy.[67] "Eternity is really beginning, really middle and really end because it is really the living God ... before in Him does not imply `not yet'; after Him does not imply `no more'; and above all His present does not imply any fleetingness."[68]

The Bartian construction can be critically dealt with at a number of levels.[69] Most widely, Barth's habit of severely limiting the bounds of discussion by an appeal to the revelation of God in Christ alone immediately opens up a tension with what would seem to be the proper domain of natural philosophy, the nature of time. On what grounds, other than a **petitio principii**, are we to suppose that "real time" as over against cosmic time is as Barth supposes it to be. Empirical matters should bulk large here, but are altogether ignored by Barth in favour of a working out of the structure of time based **solely** on the content of human consciousness.

Where other sources seem to contradict those of his primal authority,[70] "This contradiction necessitates a complete reconstruction of reality on theological grounds. An ontology and epistemology of the world are produced in direct correlation with those of faith and its object Jesus Christ. Nature as such becomes wholly problematic in the face of this revelation".[71] In other words Barth's Christomonism removes the "two- worlds problem" by fiat; nature **in se** is simply denied or annihilated in favour of a stipulated theological circle. For those who cannot accept Barth's working principles his arguments can have no authority.

Even on its own terms the Barthian definition of eternity is not acceptable. As Colin Gunton puts it: "But what, conceivably, is

---

[65] Barth, *CD*, II/1, pp.621ff.

[66] Barth, *CD*, II/1, p.619.

[67] Barth, *CD*, II/1, p.623.

[68] Barth, *CD*, II/1, pp.639-640.

[69] For a positive evaluation of Barth on time and eternity see R. Jenson, *God after God: The God of the Past and the God of the Future, Seen in the Work of Karl Barth*, Indianapolis: Bobbs-Merrill, 1969, Chapter 8. Cf. H. Berkhof, *Christian Faith*, tr. S. Woudstra, Grand Rapids: Eerdmans, 1979, p.114.

[70] Barth, *CD*, I/2, p.45.

[71] Roberts, "Barth", p.123.

simultaneity that is pure duration".[72] If the key terms are used in the normal manner simultaneity and duration are opposites, being the denial of succession and the progress of succession respectively. Barth might reply that we are dealing here not with ordinary **time** but with "real Time", yet any sort of time which has, according to Barth, "the secondary quality which is its character as non-temporality"[73] is not time at all but a confused concept. Robert's point seems unanswerable:

> The `real contrast' between time and eternity is temporally expressed solely in the contrast between `contemporaneity' (in the fullsense Barth intends)[74] and `division' and `flux' respectively. Barth's equivocation regarding time ... relies upon a conceptual distinction, the separation of a `simultaneity' from a `successive' time order in which two logically interdependent aspects of the idea of time ... are distinguished and subsequently hypostasized into deceptively distinct categories of reality?[75]

I conclude that Barth's treatment of eternity is vague and internally contradictory. We must look in other directions if the "two-worlds problem" under the form of time and eternity is to be solved.

3. Process Thought

Although a proper analysis of process philosophy would take us beyond the limits of this book, the current influence of process thought and its self-conscious claim to be a "neo-classical theism" means that some discussion cannot be avoided.

Towards the close of his **magnum opus**, **Process and Reality**, Whitehead engages the question of the relationship between God and the world.[76] God, for Whitehead, is the chief exemplification of the

---

[72] C.E. Gunton, *Becoming and Being*, Oxford: Oxford University Press, 1978, p.180.

[73] Barth, *CD*, II/1, p.610.

[74] Viz. the simultaneity of beginning, middle and end in God.

[75] Roberts, "Barth", pp.135-136.

[76] A.N. Whitehead, *Process and Reality*, Cambridge: Cambridge University Press, 1939, pp.484-497. Henceforth *PR*.

metaphysical principles upon which all of reality is based.[77] This means that to understand the meaning of eternity in process thought, it is necesssary to give a brief outline of its complex metaphysics.[78]

The ultimate realities of which the world is made up are called by Whitehead "actual entities."[79] There are many such actual entities ranging from God down to the least existent. These are not however to be thought of as either instantaneous or as changeless substances but are in a constant state of becoming or "process".[80] This becoming is epochal and is the ultimate metaphysical feature of each actual entity. For each entity the epoch can be conceived as a changeless whole, but at its completion the entity necessarily "perishes".[81] The ultimate category for Whitehead is "creativity". This is a universal generic feature instantiated in all actual entities; it is a principle of self-creation inherent in the actual entities such that the universe is self- creating.[82] "Concrescence" is the name given to the coming together through perishing of a multiplicity of actual entities in such a way that their characters persist and go to make up a new "actual occasion".[83] Since the perishing actual entities "exist"as "elements" in the concrescing actualities they are said to be "objectively immortal".[84] To explain how the pure creativity of the actual entities leads to an ordered world, Whitehead refers to the category of "eternal objects".[85] These are not unlike Plato's Forms in that they are universal qualities. However they do not exist independently and are realized only in the concrescences of actual entities in the world- process. Their role is to

---

[77] Whitehead, *PR*, p.486.

[78] Such an outline is simply unavoidable, for the time-eternity discusssion in process theism is full of technical terms which can only be comprehended in the context of the system as a whole. The introduction here is largely based on I. Leclerc *Whitehead's Metaphysics*, Bloomington: Indiana University Press, 1958. It is appreciated here that process philosophy is a school of thought, but Whitehead's position largely exemplifies the characteristic strengths and weaknesses of the entire movement.

[79] Whitehead, *PR*, p.24.

[80] Whitehead, *PR*, p.48.

[81] Whitehead, *PR*, p.83.

[82] Whitehead, *PR*, pp.9, 302.

[83] Whitehead, *PR*, p.298.

[84] Whitehead, *PR*, p.40.

[85] Whitehead, *PR*, p.60.

"inform" the acutalities in the coming into being, so that temporal things arise out of eternal things. In themselves, eternal objects are nothing but pure potentialities.

Every actual entity is bipolar, having a mental (not necessarily conscious) and physical pole. An actual entity in the process of concrescence is a "subject" creating itself out of data, its "objects".[86] In the perishing of an actual entity it ceases to be a "subject" and becomes an "object" for superseding actual entities.[87] Actual entities involve one another and enter into relations, and it is this involvement that Whitehead designates by the important term "prehension": "the activity whereby an actual entitiy effects its own concreation of other things."[88] Considered "formally" the essence of an actual entity is that it is a prehending thing.[89] An inclusive act of prehension is considered to be a positive "feeling", whilst negative prehensions exclude objects from the subject's inner constitution.[90] In Whitehead's doctrine the ultimate nature of actuality is an activity of feeling, ie an activity of "transforming entities which are individually alien, into components of a complex which is concretely one."[91] Because the process of the objectification involves a "transference of feeling", the past does not perish with actual entities but is accumulated in the present.

In such a universe there is no activity without purpose. The fundamental purpose motivating an actual entity is its own self-creation; and through self- creation it achieves its "subjective aim".[92] The "conceptual" pole of the prehension of an actual entity is its "idea", a prehension the data for which is an eternal object. Even as "realized potentiality", eternal objects have the aspect of a "pure potentiality". That is, despite their **existing** as determining the definiteness of actualities, eternal objects are entities whose **nature** transcends the particular instances of their "realization": "as realized determinant it is imminent; as a capacity for determination it is

---

[86] Whitehead, *PR*, p.34.

[87] Whitehead, *PR*, p.40.

[88] Whitehead, *PR*, p.71.

[89] Whitehead, *PR*, pp.31, 56.

[90] Whitehead, *PR*, p.56.

[91] Whitehead, *PR*, p.300.

[92] Whitehead, *PR*, pp.313-314.

transcendent".[93] Mentality is potentiality above realization, physical polarity refers to the direct experience, "feeling", of other acutualities; here eternal objects enter into physical prehension as "realized determinants".[94]

In a manner reminiscent of Aristotle's "final cause" of all mundane motions, Whitehead introduces God as the source of the subjective aim of world events. God is a unique entity who is the primordial source of the aim at definiteness which other natures are unable to self-provide. God brings order to self-creativity where otherwise there would be chaos: "God is the principle of concretion ... He is that actual entity from which each temporal concrescence receives that initial aim from which self-creation starts."[95] This is not to say that God is the creator of creativity, for this is ultimate, but: "God is the basic instance of this creativity, and is therefore the fundamental condition which **qualifies** its action."[96]

God universally conditions creativity by conceiving or envisaging eternal objects in their relevances for actualisation by the actual entities constituting the world. The "existence" of all eternal objects is constituted by a primordial conceptual realization of them in God. This prehension of the sum of all possibility is God in his "primordial nature": "the primordial created fact is the unconditional conceptual valuation of the entire multiplicity of eternal objects. This is the `primordial nature' of God."[97] This unconditional conceptual pole of God as definer of possibles is indifferent to all actuality: "the **particularities** of the actual world presupposes **it**; while it merely presupposes the general metaphysical character of creative advance..."[98] This side of God's nature is conceived to be basic, timeless, unconscious and deficient of actuality.[99] The primordial nature must be non-temporal because it is the ideal (all inclusive) realization of potentialities. It is deficient in actuality because it is

---

[93] Whitehead, *PR*, p.339.

[94] Whitehead, *PR*, p.351.

[95] Whitehead, *PR*, p.345.

[96] See Leclerc, *Whitehead*, p.194.

[97] Whitehead, *PR*, p.42.

[98] Whitehead, *PR*, p.487.

[99] Whitehead, *PR*, p.489.

absracted from his interaction with "particulars"; it is God alone with himself.[100]

As with all actual entities, God must have a concrete or physical pole, this is his "consequent nature". The failure to recognize that God is dipolar, the failure to take congnisance of the "consequent nature", is reckoned by Whitehead to be the principle cause of classical theism's problems. It is in his physical experience that God prehends the totality of the actuality of the world's becoming. Here there is a reaction of the world on God: "he shares with every new creation its actual world; and the concrescent creature is objectified in God as a novel element in God's objectification of that actual world - his advance of the world ... It is determined, incomplete, consequent, `everlasting', fully actual and conscious ..."[101] Like all actual entities, God's "being" is constituted by a process of "becoming". His "primordial" nature is completed by his consequent nature as it objectively immortalises all the values in the world. It is this accumulation without loss which makes the concrete pole "everlasting".[102]

The most unusual and contentious part of process metaphysics is its existence that God, along with all other actual entities, must have two poles. The immediate question which springs to mind is how these two natures in God are related. This question is raised sharply for process theology because the "primordial" and "consequent" natures of God seem to possess contradictory properties, in particular, atemporality and temporality. One way of answering this question is that, for Whitehead, "nature" is simply an abstract way of talking about how something relates to the rest of reality, so that two natures can be different aspects of the one actual entity rather than two elements joined together.[103] This view seems correct in what it denies but wrong in what it affirms. It raises questions about how the "primordial" nature could remain simple if it is an aspect of a single entity which also involves the continuous ingression of the elements of concrescence, i.e. in the "consequent" nature. Secondly, it does not

---

[100] Whitehead, *PR*, pp.45-46.

[101] Whitehead, *PR*, pp.488-489.

[102] Whitehead, *PR*, p.491.

[103] So, R.B. Mellert, *What is Process Theology?* N.Y.: Paulist Press, 1975, pp.44-45.

seem to escape the principle of non-contradiction. D.R. Mason[104] has contended that, according to the metaphysics of process, we must understand the differences between the "primordial" and "consequent" natures in terms of existence and essence. **That** God exists is necessary, and in this way he is independent and immutable. **What** God **is** changes. The content of his being is relative to and contingent upon the multitude of beings in the changing world. Yet this does not get us any further, for as Joseph Donceel puts it:

> the traditional theist presses his charge. He inquires how we can distinguish two aspects in a being whom we call infinitely simple, of whom we say that he is Pure Act, supreme Unity. This seems to be the crux of the matter. For anybody who has decided to uphold in its totality the traditional Aristotelian-Thomistic logic and metaphysics, the case seems hopeless. If the supreme principle of our thinking and of all reality is the principle of identity or non-contradiction, we have reached a dead end.[105]

Process theists doubtless will interpret this as just another insoluble debate about ultimate categories. Yet that there is an "ontological tension" generated by dipolarity can hardly be denied. I agree with Baumer's thought: "It is still obscure, though, how Whitehead conceives of the relation between God's physical and conceptual prehensions, his consequent and primordial natures."[106] When process philosophy is evaluated as a complete metaphysical system this may well be its Achille's heel.

Consistent with this conviction, R.M. Martin has argued that, if consistent, Thomist metaphysics obviates the need for the bifurcation

---

[104] D.R. Mason, "An Examination of `Worship' as a Key for Re-examining the God Problem", *Journal of Religion*, 55, 1975, p.89.

[105] J. Donceel, "Second Thoughts on the Nature of God", Thought, 46, 1971, p.365. This is not where Donceel finishes, for he turns to Hegel in order to find help from a higher synthesis. I however do not believe that a **higher** synthesis is possible because the contradictory predicates are attributed to the one **God**.

[106] M.R. Baumer, "Whitehead and Aquinas on the Eternity of God", *The Modern Schoolman*, 62, 1984, p.40. Cf., on Hartshorne, K. Surin, "The Self-Existence of God: Hartshorne and Classical Theism", *Sophia*, 21, 1982, pp.26,33.

in God conceived necessary according to process thought.[107] He believes that the "consequent" nature of God can be elided without religious, metaphysical or theological loss. From one angle, to show that this is possible is what the present book is all about, so that, if it is apparently successful, Ockham's razor would require of us to abandon as unnecessary any talk of divine dipolarity. Using process language, God's nature would be "primordial" only, and so timeless.

Various process theists have sought to ease the tension discussed above by paying closer attention to the sort of temporality that God possesses as "consequent". If it is accepted that God is a single everlasting actual occasion, rather than a society of actual occasions, [108] then God must be thought of as prehending all actual occasions within his concrete nature. Now according to the epochal theory of becoming, the process undergone by actual entities is a changeless whole up until the point where the entity "perishes". But God, as everlasting, never perishes. His concrescence, in which there are no negative prehensions, is therefore a seamless whole which prehends all finite occasions as in a single moment. As Ford says; "Since his act of concrescing could never come to an end, there would be no transition from earlier to later moments in the divine life. There would be only the process of becoming, never change or transition. The simplicity of this present moment would include all occasions as they come into existence, even though it would take all time for this to occur."[109] There is morphological and genetic succession in God but not temporal succession.[110]

Can we make sense of becoming without change? This depends on whether we are willing to accept Whitehead's concept of time. He sets out his position succinctly in *Science and the Modern World*,

> we must not proceed to conceive of time as another form
> of extensiveness. Time is sheer succession of epochal

---

[107] R.M. Martin, "On God and Primordiality", *Review of Metaphysics*, 29, 1976, pp.497-522, and "Some Thomistic Properties of Primordiality", *Notre Dame Journal of Formal Logic*, 18, 1977, pp.567-582.

[108] I here follow the arguments of Baumer, "Whitehead", pp.36ff; Ford, "Boethius", pp.62ff; L.S. Ford, "The Non-Temporality of Whitehead's God", *International Philosophical Quarterly*, 13, 1973, pp.347-376.

[109] Ford, "Boethius", p.62.

[110] So, Baumer, "Whitehead", pp.33ff.

durations. But the entities which succeed each other in this account are durations ... the divisibility and extensiveness is within the given duration. The epochal duration is not realized **via** its **successive** divisible parts, but is given **with** its parts ... time and space is the extensive continuum ... time is the succession of elements in themselves divisible and continguous. A duration, in becoming temporal, thereby incurs realisation in respect to some enduring objects. Temporalisation is realisation. Temporalisation is not under continuous process. It is an atomic succession. Thus time is atomic (i.e. epochal), though what is temporalised is divisible ... temporalisation is the realisation of a complete organism.[111]

All this means is that while the contents of the "consequent" nature are divisible, the consequent nature is not in time because, as everlasting, it is not complete and so not temporalised.[112] (In some respects this is analogous to the "duration block" of the divine "specious present" discussed above, but without its radically incomplete character). This quantized theory of temporal becoming is in conflict with the philosophy of time accepted in chapter three. There I argued that time was indissolubly related to change, and that the theory of the "absolute present" entailed a universal (though not necessarily simultaneous) wave of becoming, which **is** the flow of time. Within such an understanding the notion of succession **within** time epochs, i.e. atemporal succession, is contradictory. If all duration is temporal succession, Whitehead's God must be, in his "consequent" nature, in time. If he is in time not only are we faced again with the "primordial"-"consequent" tension discussed above, but the "consequent" nature must be an infinite series of actual occasions, viz. an everlasting process of concretion of the many actual occasions in the history of the world. God's concrete nature becomes an enduring object composed of temporal entities which arise and perish.

---

[111] A.N. Whitehead, *Science and the Modern World*, Harmondsworth: Penguin, 1938, pp.149-152.

[112] This is essentially the "inclusive multiplicity" theory discussed in chapter two in association with L.S. Ford's interpretation of Boethius.

For such a God there could be no finality, no ultimate satisfaction,[113] and certainly no perfection in the classical sense.[114] Whilst such a God might be construed as personal,[115] it is difficult to see how we could be meaningfully identified as single.[116]

It is useful at this point, before concluding this discussion of process metaphysics, to pick up a problem raised by Relativity Theory. Arguably it represents a very serious **reductio** for any form of process thought. The problem for the process theist stems from the relativity of simultaneity (for further details refer back to Chapter 3). [117] According to relativity theory, there is no such thing as absolute simultaneity for spatially separated events. Certain pairs of events A and B are such that whether A is to be regarded as occurring before B, simultaneously with B, or after B, depends on the co-ordinate system with respect to which one judges. These event pairs, "contemporaries" in process language, are picked out by the fact that no light signal travelling from either could reach the other. This entails that what counts as "the past" or "the future" is also relative to coordinate systems. The question which process theology must answer is how this relativity of simultaneity and of the future can be fitted into a consistent doctrine of a God who is a temporal being and whose knowledge is growing.[118]

J.T. Wilcox posed the problem in terms of a privileged reference frame. If two observers disagree about the order of events in a series, with whom does God agree? He can hardly agree with either of the

---

[113] Cf. J. Cobb, *A Christian Natural Theology*, Philadelphia: Westminster, 1966, pp.188-189.

[114] This matter will be taken up further in Chapter 9.

[115] As in Charles Hartshorne's process philosophy, e.g. *The Divine Relativity*, New Haven: Yale University Press, 1948, pp.8ff.

[116] "Our God has no relevance for Abraham, for there was no such deity coexisting with Abraham"; Hartshorne, cited but not referenced, in Gunton, *Becoming*, p.168.

[117] This problem was first recognized by Hartshorne, *Divine Relativity*, p.98.

[118] See, Fitzgerald, "Relativity Physics", p.251. This problem is not a difficulty for classical theism for the eternity of God knows no division of past, present or future. See, B. Lonergan, "St. Thomas' Thought on **Gratia Operans**", *Theological Studies*, 3, 1942, p.542, for a catena of texts from St. Thomas concerning the possibility of multiple times.

relativistically bound observers. But if he chooses from some unique reference frame, what constitutes it as privileged, and what evidence do we have for it? It seems that temporalistic theism and the relativity of simultaneity cannot both be correct.[119]

One reply to this objection was put forward by Lewis Ford.[120] Ford's method is to treat God as a single actual entity, an approach rejected above, but which will here be allowed to stand for discussion. If God is single, he is exempt from either rest or motion, since these depend on relations between societies of actual occasions. Ford additionally accepts the relativistic thesis that simultaneity has no meaning apart from a particular reference frame. The next step is to argue that God prehends as actual all occasions which are part of the actual world for each spatio-temporal location (P), viz. occasions which are experienced at P (this excludes contemporaries). Ford writes: "by `God at P' or `God relative to P', we mean whatever prehensions of God which could possibly be objectified for P, and not necessarily God's prehension of P itself. These prehensions ... must share the standpoint of P under the conditions of P's cosmic epoch, and hence can be suitably described as God's prehension **at** P."[121] God prehends from every standpoint and is therefore available to every actual occasion for integration into its becoming, i.e. God is prehended by P from P's standpoint. Ford concludes that this approach is compatible with the relativity of simultaneity.

What Ford has done is to show that **actual occasions** in a relativistic world can be said meaningfully to objectify God in the process of becoming. But he has not demonstrated that **God's** experience **in se** can be meaningfully ordered.[122] The average occasion probably prehends several distinct occasions which are contemporaries of one another, and thus must belong to several different strands of occasions. Each "here- now" is the point of convergence of several causal sequences, which may perhaps have interacted with one another, i.e., strands of occasions are interlaced. This means that God-at-P is a member of several strands of occasions,

---

119 J.T. Wilcox, "A Question From Physics For Certain Theists", *Journal of Religion*, 40, 1961, pp.293-300.

120 L.S. Ford, "Is Process Theism Compatible with Relativity Theory?", *Journal of Religion*, 48, 1968, pp.124-135.

121 Ford, "Compatible", p.132.

122 Here I follow Fitzgerald, "Relativity Physics", pp.258ff.

or given the consciousness of the "consequent" nature, several streams of consciousness. At P this presents no problems for the occasions are unified. However, since there is no unique successor to P the consciousness of God (associated with the diverging occasion) will become multiple and unordered, phenomenologically equivalent to the simultaneous possession of multiple personalities in one individual. This chaotic condition might be overcome if we conceive of God possessing a higher order awareness of his physical prehensions, an awareness which must be timeless. As Fitzgerald says: "God knows what is happening in the world by perceiving it temporally, and he knows what is happening in himself, including his prehensions of the world, by prehending non temporally ... This single standpoint ... is in no reasonable sense a single Now ..."[123] Unfortunately for process thought such timeless knowledge of the world is incompatible with the characteristics of the "consequent" nature, and certainly cannot be equated with the primordial nature which is utterly detached from all actuality. It seems that process theologians must accept Fitzgerald's: "God of the Infinitely Interlaced Personalities".[124]

But is this **one** being? Fitzgerald argues that God may possess the constancy of character and purpose suggestive of a single personality, together with a temporal structure which suggests a multitude of streams of consciousness.[125] Yet if character and purpose are aspects of consciousness this seems to require a consciousness above the consciousnesses to ensure that each conscious occasion has the same character. But such a postulate is unavailable to process theists. Again, if God lacks such a hyper- consciousness, we are left with a plethora of interacting consciousnesses which take the character of their becoming, their "novelty" in process terms, from the actual occasions which they prehend. We seem to be left with diversity rather than unity. If personal identity is dependent upon some type of ontological endurance,[126] then we do not seem to be able to avoid the

---

[123] Fitzgerald, "Relativity Physics", p.270.

[124] Fitzgerald, "Relativity Physics", p.273. Nancy Frankenberry, *Emergent*, p.214, is content to do just this.

[125] Fitzgerald, "Relativity Physics", p.273.

[126] A controversial position defended in my unpublished M.A. Thesis, *The Intermediate State*, Deakin University, 1984. Cf. R. Purtill, "Disembodied Survival", *Sophia*, 12, 1973, pp.1-10. I am presuming here that it makes some sense to talk about the ontology of the individual streams of consciousness.

conclusion that process thought leads to an attenuated form of polytheism.[127]

I conclude that the nature of the time-eternity relationship as raised in the process theology seems to be confronted with a number of intractable difficulties. Whatever problems confront the classical theist in this situation, the way of dipolarity does not appear to be a viable one of escape.

D. The Stump-Kretzmann Hypothesis

In a paper published in 1981 Eleonore Stump and Norman Kretzmann attempted to expound the Boethian definition in a new form.[128] Their article is probably the most significant piece of writing from the pro-classical side in the last twenty years. For Stump and Kretzmann eternal existence is understood in terms of a duration without past or future, the sort of relation it has with temporal entities is one of simultaneity. Simultaneity in time and in eternity are distinguished, the latter being: "existence or occurrence at one and the same eternal present."[129] Stump-Kretzmann define a new species of simultaneity, "ET-simultaneity", as that which can obtain between what is temporal and what is eternal. Since time and eternity cannot be reduced to one another, or to some third mode of existence, there is no single mode of existence that can be referred to in defining a **relata** as ET-simultaneous. An analogy is drawn from the relativity of simultaneity, where the difference between reference frames makes it

---

[127] Charles Hartshorne, "Bell's Theorem and Stapp's Revised View of Space-Time", *Process Studies*, 7, 1977, pp.183-191 has appealed to certain views in quantum mechanics in order to overcome the problet the earlier of two events cannot effect the other if the distance between them is so great that a light signal can't traverse it during the time interval separating the two events. Closer analysis however reveals that the manner in which the theorem is used appeals to theoretically possible but empirically inaccessible data, so that we are left with no certain philosophical consequences. W.B. Jones, "Bell's Theorem, H.P. Stapp, and Process Theism", *Process Studies*, 7, 1977, pp.250-261. For recent critical analyses of such uses of Bell's Theorem, see W.B. Jones, "Physics and Metaphysics: Henry Stapp in Time", in Griffin (ed), *Physics*, pp.278-288; P. Miller, "On `Becoming' As a Fifth Dimension", in Griffin (ed), *Physics*, pp.291-292.

[128] E. Stump and N. Kretzmann, "Eternity", *Journal of Philosophy*, 78, 1981, pp.429-458.

[129] Stump-Kretzmann, "Eternity", p.435.

impossible to give a simple definition of temporal simultaneity. A relativized version of temporal simultaneity is offered: (RT) RT-simultaneity = existence or occurrence at the same time within the reference frame of a given observer.[130] Since in ET-simultaneity we are dealing with two equally real and irreducible modes of existence, (the temporal and the eternal), a definition must be constructed in terms of **two** reference frames and **two** observers. Let "x" and "y" range over entities and events then:

(ET) for every x and for every y, x and y are ET- simultaneous if;
(i)   either x is eternal and y is temporal, or vice-versa; and
(ii) for some observer, A, in the unique eternal reference frame, x and y are both present, i.e., either x is eternally present and y is observed as temporally present, or vice-versa; and
(iii) for some observer, B, in one of the infinitely many temporal reference frames, x and y are both present, i.e. either x is observed as eternally present and y is temporally present, or vice- versa.[131]

Condition (ii) provides that a temporal entity or event observed as temporally present by an external observer A is ET-simultaneous with every eternal entity or event; and condition (iii) provides that an eternal entity or event observed as eternally present (or simply as eternal) by some temporal observer B is ET-simultaneous with every temporal entity or event. If x and y are ET-simultaneous then x is neither earlier, later, nor past or future with respect to y. Further if x and y are ET-simultaneous they are not temporally simultaneous; since either x or y must be eternal, it cannot be the case that x and y exist **at one and the same time** within a given observer's reference frame. ET-simultaneity is symmetric, non- reflexive and non-transitive.[132]

---

[130] Stump-Kretzmann, "Eternity", p.438.

[131] Stump-Kretzmann, "Eternity", p.439.

[132] Stump-Kretzmann, "Eternity", pp.439-440. The non-transitive character of the simultaneity relationship is an effective rebuttal of Anthony Kenny's charge that the notion of **totum simul** generates as absurdity: "On St. Thomas' view, my typing of this book is simultaneous with the whole of eternity. Therefore, while I type these very words, Nero fiddles heartlessly on." "Divine Foreknowledge and Human Freedom", in *Aquinas*, A. Kenny (ed), London: Macmillan, 1969, p.264. For similar comments see Davenport, *Immanence*,

Several significant criticisms have been brought forward against this position. The first has to do with talk of "eternal duration". I have already argued in chapter two that this is a contradiction in terms, duration being nothing else but an entity's succession in time. If Stump and Kretzmann were found to be using "duration" in the ordinary sense their understanding of eternity would be hopefully confused.[133] A close examination of their paper however indicates that the use of duration as applied to eternity does not seem to infect their ET- simultaneity definition. This point may therefore be allowed to pass without further comment.[134]

It is to be doubted however whether the Stump- Kretzmann hypothesis helps us out of the ontological tangle of the "two-worlds problem". With respect to what I have termed the "vertical dimension" of the problem, viz. the bringing together of the antitheticals time and timelessness, we are offered an explanation in terms of observation. An observer in time is said to observe an eternal entity as eternally present. But how does one **observe** and eternal present? What is the particular **quale** of any of our temporal experiences which would enable us to conclude that the subject of the experience was non-temporal. That God is timeless or **totum simul** is surely a deduction of reason and not something that could conceivably be given in experience.[135] Then there is the problem of the eternal observation of entities as temporally present. Here "temporally present" must

p.115; Dewart, *Future*, p.194; M. Kneale, "Eternity and Sempiternity", *Proceedings of the Aristotelian Society*, 70, 1969-1970, p.227; R.G. Swinburne, *The Coherence of Theism*, Clarendon: Oxford, 1977, p.220; Wolterstorff, "Everlasting", p.192. Stump and Kretzmann's denial of transivity in the relation between temporal events and eternity was long ago anticipated by St. Bonaventure, 1 *Sent* 39, 2, 3, **conclusio**. For Bonaventure the **praesentialitas** of all things in the divine knowledge is to be understood in reference to God (**a parte cognoscentis**), not in reference to the things known (**a parte cognitorum**). Cited in F.C. Copleston, *A History of Philosophy vol 2. Medieval Philosophy: Augustine to Scotus*, London: Burns, Oates and Washbourne, 1950, p.262.

[133] Cf. P. Fitzgerald, "Stump and Kretzmann on Time and Eternity", *Journal of Philosophy*, 82, 1985, pp.262-264.

[134] It is interesting to note that talk about an "eternal duration" is not without precedent in the classical tradition, e.g. Aquinas *S.Th.* 1a. 46,3. Such speech is however to be taken as under the mode of our perception, **for us** God seems to endure.

[135] Cf. Fitzgerald, "Stump and Kretzmann", pp.267- 268.

mean present in the time series, not present in the eternal entity. We here face the problem of the non- successive observation of successive events as successive. This is a matter I will engage at some length in chapter seven, but for the time being it is adequate to note that Stump and Kretzmann offer no explanation.

Fitzgerald has argued that the problem of the metaphysical co-presence of time and eternity might be understood by analogy with the simultaneity between mental and physical particulars. Dualists must somehow temporally relate our mental states to physical events in space-time: "These non- relativistic temporal relations which span the physical and non-physical realms are analogous to Stump and Kretzmann's realm-spanning relation of ET- simultaneity."[136] I do not think the analogy is a true one. The tension between the dyad in question is between space and spacelessness, i.e., between not- mind and mind, and not between two types of time. Only if the dualist argued that the time of the mind and the time of matter were essentially different would we have a true analogy.

It has been argued that the observations of an eternal entity by a temporal entity **means** that the eternal entity must exist along with the temporal entity.[137] Yet Stump and Kretzmann deny that there is any single mode of existence for two **relata** of which one is eternal and the other temporal.[138] If, as seems to be true, the observations of temporal observers occurs in time, then the Stump-Kretzmann position needs radical revision. They simply offer us no concrete explanation of how time and timelessness can co-exist.

Turning to the horizontal aspect of the "two-worlds problem", i.e., how God can be present to the past and the future, we are no better served by Stump- Kretzmann: "the actual occasion of Nixon's death is present to an eternal entity. It is not that the future pre-exists somehow ... but rather that an eternal entity that is wholly ET-simultaneous with August 9, 1974, and with today, is wholly ET-simultaneous with August 9, 1990 as well."[139] What seems to have been done here is that appeal has been made to the ET-simultaneity definition to explain away the problem raised by that same definition.

---

[136] Fitzgerald, "Stump and Kretzmann", pp.268-269.

[137] J. Delmas Lewis, "Eternity Again": A Reply Stump and Kretzmann", *International Journal for the Philosophy of Religion*, 15, 1984, pp.75-76.

[138] Stump-Kretzmann, "Eternity", p.436.

[139] Stump-Kretzmann, "Eternity", p.442.

We are simply not given any content to go by, nothing to grasp in understanding how ET-simultaneity might be possible.[140]

I conclude that the Stump-Kretzmann hypothesis has not come to terms with the basic problem of the time- eternity relationship, and as such must be rejected as inadequate.

E. Summary and Conclusion

In different ways the various models examined in this chapter have tried both to preserve certain aspects of the classical concept of the divine eternity, and to present the basic concept in new ways so as to relieve apparent contradictions in the time-eternity relationship. I have argued that all of these models have been found to be deficient, either in terms of conceptual inadequacies and contradictions, or because they have so changed the notion of eternity as to make it improper to be predicated of the ultimate being. In particular, it seems that all contemporary models based on the analogy of perception are fundamentally inadequate to resolve the sharp ontological problems of our "two-worlds" conundrum. I wish now to go on and try to develop, from classical sources, a much more active model of the divine eternity, one based on the notion of "timeless causation".

---

[140] An appeal to the unique all inclusive reference frame of an eternal entity would be misplaced. The relativity of simultaneity explains how events judged future by one observer are judged simultaneous by another, but presumably there are some events which are future **simpliciter**, i.e., non-existent for all conceivable or actual **observers**.

CHAPTER FIVE

ETERNITY AS "CONTINUOUS CREATION"

So far I have sketched the time-eternity question as an example of the "two-worlds problem" - the difficulty in compatibly bringing together two orders of reality. The dimensions of the confronting problem has ontological and epistemological aspects. Later I shall take up the epistemological side in some detail. At this point however I wish to concentrate on what I have termed the "vertical" part of the time-eternity problem, how there can be any sort of relation between the timeless and the temporal. What we are searching for is a concept which can pair these antitheticals in some sort of meaningful way without denying the reality of either, or attempting to subsume them under some higher category. The concept which I am here putting forward as able to do this is that of a timeless cause of temporal effects.[1] If it can be established that the notion of a single universe - conditioning timeless cause is a coherent one, the "vertical" aspect of the time-eternity problem will have been solved.

A. The Concept of Timeless Causation

Does it make sense to speak of a cause without temporal location or extension? A timeless cause must not be in time, the cause itself must not take time neither must there be a delay in time between the cause and its effect.[2]

The notion of timeless causation is by no means new but requires much fuller treatment and defense before it can be accepted.[3] Thomas

---

[1] Not, strictly speaking a timeless cause of time, for time is not entitative, but a timeless cause of entities whose relations are temporal.

[2] This last feature may not be immediately self evident, but to speak of a temporal delay of a timeless cause suggests that the cause itself must be located at some earlier time than its effect.

[3] Aristotle, *Physics* 9.1, 251a8-b10; 8.7, 260a26-261a26; *De Generatione et Corruptione*, 2.10, 336a14-b17 could not conceive of a change without a prior motion. On a relationist view of the time this is the basic problem to be faced.

Aquinas used the notion to deny that the creation of the world places God in time: "we agree that an efficient cause which works through change must precede its effect in time, for the effect enters as the term of the action whereas the agent is its start. Yet in the event of the action being instantaneous and not successive, it is not required for the maker to be prior in duration to the thing made."[4] Aquinas denies temporal extension to the causal power of God, and his use of "instantaneous" (**instantanea**) must not be taken to mean at the same temporal instant as the cause, but without temporal lapse. At this point it is necessary to plunge briefly into the Thomist metaphysics in order to make some sense of the claim that efficient causality can occur without change.[5]

That efficient causation is a kind of "becoming" would seem to be a deliverance of common experience, for this kind of causality consists in the exercise of an action. Aquinas points out however that the agent as agent does not "become".[6] The becoming, the passage from potency to act, is in the "patient", not in the agent as such. The agent's action produces the change in the patient but is not itself a change. Efficient causality must communicate action, but this need not involve change in the cause, for action is an act not a potency. As he said: "It belongs to an act by its very nature to communicate itself so far as it can. Therefore every agent acts in so far as it exists in act. For to act is nothing else than to communicate that by which the agent is in act as far as possible."[7]

Abstracting from change, efficient causation can be understood as a relation, one of whose terms is the effect, the other the agent-in-act; this leaves us with a pure relation of dependence. Just as the act of existing is **intelligible** without change, so is action. This metaphysical truth however has actual application only for a being whose act does not presuppose the existence of patients, a being whose action of itself constitutes its subjects. Such a being would

---

[4] Aquinas, *S.Th.* 1a.46, 2 and 3.

[5] Cf. J.F. Anderson, "Creation as a Relation", *New Scholasticism*, 24, 1950, pp.271-273.

[6] Aquinas, *S.Th.* 1-2, 51, 2 *ad* 1.

[7] Aquinas, *De Potentia* 2, 1 cited in Anderson, "Creation", p.272. Thomas Gilby explains that causality is not a sequence of two changes, the only change is in the effect, the **existence** of the effect is the action of the cause. Appendix to *S.Th.* 2, pp.184-185.

have to be **actus purus**, fully actual. Norris Clarke takes up this theme in detail:

> If a cause possessed all the power required for the production of a given effect in total, completely available actuality, concentrated in a single indivisible point or centre, no successive phases would be required within the cause for unfolding its causal action, hence there would be no temporal process. This cause would then remain perfectly motionless and unchanging internally, though the effect on its part might be such that its emergence could or would have to occur in successive stages. In this case time would unroll within the effect, though not within the cause ... Now none of the causes accessible to our experience possess their active powers in such simple concentrated plentitude and totally available actuality ... Only an infinite, omnipotent, and omnipresent spirit could exhaust its relations to the whole rest of the universe in a single act ...[8]

Is it intelligible, even within the context of the stipulated metaphysical system enumerated above, to conceive a **cause** that is, as Rock puts it: "not **motio** ... but **creatio** ... not **pre** but simultaneous ...?"[9] If so we have come a very long way to filling out the meaning of **totum simul existens**, at least so far as its relation to its effects is concerned. However, an immediate objection springs to mind: to talk of causation in the manner presumed above is unacceptable, for it is at variance with the best contemporary understanding of the nature of a "cause". The literature on causation is enormous, and here is not the place to go beyond the portals of its labyrinthine structure.[10] It is necessary however to put our discussion on one side of the great divide in the philosophy of causation, that

---

[8] W. Norris Clarke, "Causing and Time", in *Experience, Existence and the Good*, I.C. Lieb (ed), Carbondale: Southern Illinois University Press, 1961, p.152.

[9] J.P. Rock, "St. Thomas on Divine Causality", *Philosophical Studies*, 5, 1955, p.42.

[10] On recent work in this area see P.A. French, T.E. Vehling and H.K. Wettstein (eds), *Mid Western Studies in Philosophy, 9, 1984: Causation and Causal Theories*, Minneapolis: University Minnesotta Press, 1984.

between the empiricists and the "productionists", between those who understand causation in terms of regularities and relations and those who see its essence in terms of some type of production or power to bring about an effect. The position taken up above is obviously metaphysical, and, so, "productionist", in matters of causation.

Hume's epoch making contribution to the debate[11] is too well known to be rehearsed here. His insight was that we have no empirical reasons for believing that there is some sort of necessary connection between a cause and its effects. Causation in the objects, as far as we know, is only regular succession. Any necessary association between causes and effects is in the mind, not in objects, though we tend to project it on to them. Modern regularity theories follow the negative side of Hume's thesis but analyse our statements and understanding of causation in conceptual rather than psychological terms. Causal sequences are to be regarded as instances of more general laws, or of the exemplification of sets of conditions which are either sufficient or necessary for their effects. Beauchamp summarizes: "Regularity exponents analyze laws as true, contingent, universal generalizations which are omnispatially and omnitemporally restricted in scope. Purported necessary connections between the antecedent and consequent events described in the law are regarded as gratuitous."[12]

Production theories of causation incorporate our unreflective intuition that a cause is in some immediate way responsible for the occurrence of an effect. As Richard Taylor remarks: "A cause has traditionally been thought of as that which produces something and in terms of which that which is produced, its effect, can be explained."[13]

---

[11] Hume, *An Enquiry Concerning Human Understanding*, 4-7; *Treatise of Human Nature*, 1, part 3.

[12] T.L. Beauchamp (ed), *Philosophical Problems of Causation*, Encino: Dickenson, 1974, p.36. For some instances of this type of theory see J.L. Mackie, *The Cement of The Universe*, Oxford: Clarendon, 1974; R. Martin, "The Sufficiency Thesis", *Philosophical Studies*, 23, 1972, pp.205- 211; M. Scriven, "The Logic of Cause", *Theory and Decision*, 2, 1971, pp.49-66. Of particular importance on this side of the debate is D. Davidson, "Causal Relations", *Journal of Philosophy*, 64, 1967, pp.691-703.

[13] R. Taylor, "Causation", in *The Encyclopedia of Philosophy*, P. Edwards (ed), N.Y.: Macmillan, vol 2,1967, p.56. Cf. K. Ward, *Fifty Key Words in Philosophy*, London: Lutterworth, 1968, p.13.

For convenience this grouping may be divided into two: those theories which emphasise the agent character of causation, and those which stress causal efficiency. In the former case, in Gale's words: "The paradigm cases of causality are those in which an agent intentionally intervenes into some situation and brings about a change in it."[14] It seems indubitable that the genesis of our concept of causation lies in our experience of our own voluntary actions, of being able to bring things about through an act of will.[15] Arguably, we know the nature of causation from our own most intimate actions; but it is notoriously difficult to step safely from epistemological data to conclusions about ontology. A more sophisticated modern rendition of this position is the "manipulability theory".[16] For this theory a "cause" means a state of affairs which human agents can control in order to produce or prevent another state of affairs, their "effect". Causes are conceived as means to ends. If it be objected that we ascribe causation to circumstances outside of or beyond the power of human agents it need only be replied that we could conceive of such action without logical contradiction.

According to the "productionist" view (in its emphasis on causal efficacy) there is something in natural causes which necessitates their effects. Causes will bring about their effects unless something, some interfering conditions, prevents this from happening. Causes are to be understood as dynamic entities which are in some sense intrinsically active and capable of expressing their dynamism externally so as to exert influence on things. On this view there need be no medium between the cause and the effect. Madden says: "The ineliminable but non mysterious powers and abilities of particular things, and not an ontological 'tie that binds' causes and effects together is what the

---

[14] Gale, *Language*, p.114.

[15] Cf. P.T. Geach, *Three Philosophers*, Oxford: Basil Blackwell, 1961, pp.108-109; M.J. Langford, *Providence*, London: S.C.M., 1981, p.69; Locke, *Essay*, Book 2, ch.21; H. Rashdall, *Philosophy of Religion*, London: Duckworth, 1909, pp.32-41; T. Reid, *Essays on the Intellectual Powers of Man*, 6.5, 6, 1785; M. Rieser, "Causation, Action and Creation", *Journal of Philosophy*, 37, 1940, pp.491-499.

[16] See Beauchamp, *Philosophical Problems*, pp.118-137 for a collection of articles by R.G. Collingwood, D. Gasking and Von Wright.

conceptual necessity of 'cause' reflects."[17] Effects presuppose their causes, and not vice-versa; from the side of the effect, causation can be understood as a specific type of dependence.[18]

The productionist model of causation is frequently considered to be pre-reflective, empirically unverifiable and mysterious. Such accusations however may not be a fair estimation of the nature of the subject under discussion. As Ernest Sosa says: "the view that a certain concept cannot be analyzed is difficult to refute except by producing an analysis. So far as I know no one has published a successful analysis of causation by reference to conditionality or lawfulness."[19] The charge that productionist notions are empirically unverifiable cannot entail that they are either false or meaningless, as the now abandoned forms of positivism would have it, for there may be necessary connections in the order of things beyond the power of the human mind to discern. Strict forms of empiricism are just a much **a priori** commitments to a certain way of seeing the world as are unashamedly metaphysical models. To my way of thinking the key question to be answered is whether causes

explain things in the strong sense of the word.[20] This is the question of the ultimate intelligibility of the order of nature, a quest which is denied by regularity theories. I doubt if such views can be overthrown on the basis of their own radical presuppositions, but

---

[17] E. H. Madden, "A Third View of Causality", in Beauchamp, *Problems*, p.180. Cf. Geach, *Three Philosophers*, pp. 101-103; B.S. Kogan, *Averroes and the Metaphysics of Causation*, Albany: S.U.N.Y., 1985, pp.1-4.

[18] L.O. Kattsoff, "Causality as Dependence", *Methodos*, 15, 1963, pp.17-24; B. Lonergan, "St. Thomas' Theory of Operation", *Theological Studies*, 3, 1942, pp.375-402.

[19] E. Sosa, cited in M.J. White, "Causes as Necessary Conditions", in *New Essays on Aristotle*, F.J. Pelletier and J. King-Farlow (eds), Guelph: University of Calgary Press, 1984, p.189.

[20] "Explanation involves an asymmetrical relation-ship that is not captured either by the concepts of necessary or sufficient conditions.... The main thing that explanation does, I take it, is to make coherent some set of beliefs. This means that the **explicans** is logically or ontologically prior to the thing it explains. An **explicans** makes the **explicandum** understandable". L. Zagzebski, "Divine Foreknowledge and Human Free Will", *Religious Studies*, 21, 1985, p.295. This understanding of explanation will be found ideally suited to the concept of divine causal creation to be developed below.

neither do they have the ability to persuasively dispel the common sense conviction about causal efficacy.

Theism, in its classical forms, is clearly committed to the productionist side of the debate.[21] It is impossible to think of divine causation in terms of either conditionality or lawfulness, for God as Creator is conceived as the one who supremely and absolutely brings things about. The appeal to human analogies of volition, emphasis on the dynamism of causation and the immediacy of causal influence are all part of that wider metaphysical milieu out of which classical theism emerged and in which it makes sense. Unless causality is understood against this background and accepted in this form as at least reasonable, if not true, then the remainder of this book must be considered as insubstantial.

Yet even if one accepts a non-regularity view of causation it may still be felt that a "timeless cause" is a confused concept. The objection is put with various degrees of forcefulness. John Hospers has argued that even if a timeless God relates to this universe he could not do so causally, for causal relation is a relation among temporal events.[22] This is put with greater clarity by Grace Jantzen: "The logic of the concept of an event requires that there must have been a `before' and `after' - this is not just a function of our psychology."[23] James Morreall draws out the consequences of this type of thinking: "Is it not analytically true that immutable timeless beings cannot **do** anything ... concepts like action logically require concepts like time, so that nothing could count as a timeless action any more than something could count as a square circle."[24] If it is analytical truth that causation must take place in time the concept of timeless "causation" is immediately ruled out of court.

---

[21] The cosmological argument, for example, is best understood in terms of causes explaining their effects. Cf. A.C. Ewing, "Two 'Proofs' of God's Existence", *Religious Studies*, 1, 1966, pp.30-32.

[22] J. Hospers, *Introduction to Philosophical Analysis*, Englewood Cliffs: Prentice-Hall, 1963, p.331.

[23] Jantzen, *Time*, p.572.

[24] J.S. Morreall, *Analogy and Talking About God*, Washington: University Press of America, 1978, p.3. Cf. J.B. Kozak, "Causality, Time, Eternity", *Communio Viatorum*, 14, 1971, pp.267-278; T.F. Tracy, *God, Action and Embodiment*, Grand Rapids: Eerdmans, 1984, p.130; Weiss, *Modes*, p.38.

There are many philosphers however who would deny that even in the case of non-divine causation we must make reference to temporal sequence. One might ask of an empiricist who would be likely to press the charge of contradiction how it could ever be established on the basis of the observation of **contingent** sequences of causes and effects in time that temporal sequence is a necessary **logical** condition for causation.[25] We may grant that it is a truth of language that by a "cause" is usually meant something that is temporally prior to its effect, but this gives us neither a truth about logic nor a truth of metaphysics.[26] If we examine even our ordinary thinking about causation we find that besides the temporal element there is a logical element. Numerous everyday examples can be given to show that invariable succession is not a sufficient condition for causation,[27] and unique historical events mean it can never be established that sequence is a necessary condition.[28] The logical element in the causal relationship therefore pertains to a non-temporal sufficiency and necessity of causes for effects,[29] thus we are able to make sense of non-temporal causation.

The argument for non-temporal causation is considerably strengthened from the fact that some causes and effects appear to be contemporaneous.[30] Kant's example of a lead ball sitting on and causing an indentation in a cushion is a well known example of simultaneous causation.[31] A locomotive's pulling of a caboose is another, gravitation is a third. Although the notion of simultaneous causation is not without controversy,[32] it does accord well with

---

[25] Cf. B. Brier, "An Atemporal View of Causality", *Journal of Critical Analysis*, 4, 1972, pp.8-16; Kattsoff, "Causality", p.23; Mackie, *Cement*, chapt. 7.

[26] Cf. Taylor, *Causation*, pp.59, 64-65.

[27] Night invariably follows day and the dawn a cock-crow but we do not suppose any causation is involved. Cf. J.B. Cobb, *Natural Causality*, pp.207ff.

[28] So, Whitrow, *Natural Philosophy*, p.277.

[29] See, Hinckfuss, *Existence of Space and Time*, pp.119-121.

[30] For a recent discussion and bibliography see M. Brand, "Simultaneous Causation", in *Time and Cause*, P. van Inwagen (ed), Dordrecht: Reidel, 1980, pp.137-153.

[31] Kant, *Critique of Pure Reason*, tr. N. Kemp-Smith, N.Y.: St. Martin's Press, 1965, pp.227-228.

[32] See for example, the arguments in D. Ehering, "Simultaneous Causation and Causal Chains", *Analysis*, 45, 1985, pp.98-100, "Non Simultaneous Causation",

everyday experience and has the great advantage of making the whole notion of causation more explicable. Norris Clarke comments:

> there is irremediable confusion if one attempts to maintain both the temporal succession of cause and effect and the objectivity of truly ontological causal influx or active efficacy of cause on effect ... No action which remains self-enclosed, which terminates in the agent **as** agent, can be properly causal ... The myth of some kind of entity which **passes** or **travels** through space and time from the cause to its effect must be exorcised uncompromisingly; it destroys the specific intelligibility of what is trying to explain.[33]

Although the simultaneity argued for here is temporal, the concept does create a background against which the notion of a timeless cause can be more easily comprehended.

Objectors to the enigmatic "timeless cause" do not however give in so easily. Stewart Sutherland finds the idea incomprehensible: "The point here is that we are not constrained to limit ourselves to the notion of non-corporeal action, but rather we are in pursuit of the wild goose of a non-tensed action, one that does not involve the possibility of temporal coordinates being given to it. Such is inconceivabe."[34]

There are a number of ways to answer this charge. In the first place it must be asked if Sutherland has not confused conceivability with imaginability. I certainly do not want to claim that I can imagine what a timeless cause is like, but if the arguments above are valid, and the reasoning to follow, there is a great deal to be said about the

---

Analysis, 47, 1987, pp.28-32; R.W. Field, "The Temporal Dimensions of Causal Relationships", *Dialogue*, 26, 1983, pp.17-26. For a different view, J.W. Wilkie, "The Problem of the Temporal Relation of Cause and Effect", *British Journal for the Philosophy of Science*, 1, 1950, pp.211-229.

[33] Norris Clarke, "Causality", pp.149-150. Clarke's article is explicitly metaphysical and on its own terms seems to answer contemporary criticism of simultaneous causation.

[34] S.R. Sutherland, "God, Time and Eternity", *Proceedings of the Aristotelian Society*, 79, 1978-1979, p.107. Cf. G.W. Shields, "Davies, eternity and the cosmological argument", *International Journal for Philosophy of Religion*, 21, 1987, p.22.

intelligibility of non-tensed action.[35]   At the very least timeless causation is not a **manifest**, contradiction, like the assertion that the Absolute is both temporal and timeless.[36] R.L. Sturch takes up the linguistic side of the argument: "part at least, and a central part, of the meaning of `X is producing Y' (where X is a person) is `If X wishes Y to be, Y is; and X wishes Y to be'... Now clearly, neither `X wishes Y to be' nor `If X wishes Y to be, Y is' has any temporal implications."[37]   Sturch's point is that if God wishes something to be or happen or come about, so it is, and linguistically we are not compelled to associate the becoming in question with any temporal extension. This concept will be taken up in much greater detail later in this chapter. Even at this early stage however I do not think that Sutherland's objection can be sustained.

Granted that God is timeless, the objector might go on, he must be essentially dissimilar to temporal things, and so lack a necessary condition for agent causation. As Stout says: "The real question is whether two existences can interact unless they are comprehended within a spatio- temporal whole or some such complex unity. Can there be an interaction without community? To me it seems evident that there cannot."[38]   If there is no community between time and eternity, if eternity is defined as the antithesis of time, how can there be any sort of relation between them?

The first part of the problem, the request for "community", is familiar from the debate between dualists and materialists about the possibility of mental causation of physical events. **Prima facie**, the

---

[35] W. Hasker, "Concerning the Intelligibility of `God is Timeless'", *New Scholasticism*, 57, 1983, pp.170-195, discusses this matter at some length. At this point I am in agreement with him, but not when he claims that we can make a ready transfer from the concept of non-spatial causality to a non-temporal causality.

[36] So, Owen, *Christian Knowledge*, p.246.

[37] R.L. Sturch, "The Problem of the Divine Eternity", *Religious Studies*, 10, 1974, p.488.

[38] G.F. Stout, *Mind and Matter*, p.123, cited in Passmore, *Philosophical*, p.52. Cf. E. Baltazar, "Evolutionary Perspectives and the Divine", in *Traces of God in a secular Culture*, G.F. McLean (ed), N.Y.: Alba House, 1973, pp.147- 148; E.S. Brightman, *The Problem of God*, N.Y.: Abingdon, 1930, pp.99; Caird, *Evolution*, vol 2, p.11; Chung-ying Cheng, "Greek and Chinese views on time and the timeless", *Philosophy East and West*, 24, 1974, p.156; McKenzie; "Eternity", p.401; Tennant, *Philosophical Theology*, vol 2, p.133.

conflict is sharper here, because at least in the debate about the nature of mind, the mental and physical have some things in common - they both exist in time and are finite. Traditional theism however has understood efficient causation to be the sort of concept which can be predicted analogically to both God and creatures. It applies properly and proportionately to every type of agency. I shall argue in detail below that creation is a type of efficient causation which does not require the usual sort of solidarity necessary for causal action, and that, whereas an actual relation exists between God and creatures, interaction, viz. the action of creatures on God, is impossible. It will also become clear during the course of the book that to understand eternity as bare atemporality is misleading. The **possessio** of Boethius must always be kept in mind.

A not unrelated difficulty moves the objection a stage further - if a timeless being could act in time it would cease to be timeless. The problem is not a new one. Plotinus took it to entail that there would be no contact between the eternal and the temporal.[39] One way of putting the question, as for example, Lovejoy does, is clearly unsatisfactory: "For the eternal to enter into relations with aught that becomes or changes is **ipso facto** to lose its reality, for the change in the temporal term of the relation makes the relation one of change; and since the proposition that a thing may change its relations while remaining absolutely unaffected by change is a plain contradition, the change must necessarily affect the other term of the relation also."[40] Lovejoy's argument fails to distinguish between "Cambridge change" and "real change". In the former case only one term in a relationship changes, in the latter both.[41] Change in the temporal term does not logically entail change in the timeless cause and so only a "Cambridge change" is involved.

Amongst contemporary philosophers Nelson Pike seems to have revived the objection:

---

[39] Plotinus, *Enneads* 3.7,6.

[40] A. Lovejoy, "The Obsolescence of the Eternal", *Philosophical Review*, 18, 1909, p.490.

[41] See, P.T. Geach, *God and the Soul*, London: Routledge, 1969; pp.71-72; T.P. Smith, "On the Applicability of a Criterion of Change", *Ratio*, 15, 1973, pp.325-333.

If something is produced, created or brought into being it begins to exist. To produce something is to effect its beginning. If something begins to exist it has position in time ... It would seem that if we can assign a temporal location to what one produced, by the logic of `produces', as revealed in the logic of the specialised verbs falling under this determinable, we can assign relative temporal position to the productive act itself ... If God were to create or produce an object having position in time, God's creative activity would then have to have occurred at some specific time.[42]

The fundamental flaw in the argument is the assumption that the time-eternity relationship is reflexive. If this is denied there is no longer any reason to believe that temporality in the effect entails temporality in the cause. To suggest otherwise is to confuse speaking of God by way of extrinsic denomination - the "x is created at t by God", with univocal predication - "God is t". The former is allowable when its proper form is recognized, the latter is a contradiction.[43] Aquinas long ago provided an adequate solution to the difficulty.

... an effect follows from the intellect and the will according to the determination of the intellect and the command of the will ... just as the intellect determines every other condition of the thing made, so does it prescribe the time of its making ... Nothing therefore prevents our saying that God's action existed from all eternity, whereas its effect was not present from eternity,

---

[42] Pike, *God and Timelessness*, pp.105-107. Pike's challenge was basically anticipated by B.P. Bowne, *Studies in Theism*, N.Y.: Phillips and Hunt, 1880, pp.184-185., and Laird, *Cosmology*, p.162. He is followed by Hebblethwaite, "Predestination", p.439, Plantinga, *Does God Have a Nature?*, p.46; Swinburne, *Coherence*, p.221; White, *Sparrow*, p.162.
[43] So, B. Lonergan, *Insight*, London: Longmans, 1961, p.661; J.F. Ross, "Creation 2", in *The Existence and Nature of God*, A.J. Fredosso (ed), Notre Dame: Notre Dame University Press, 1983, p.137.

but existed at the time when, from all eternity, He ordained it.[44]

As this book progresses it will become increasingly patent how the notion of creation is bound up with these ideas.

I conclude the introductory section of this chapter with the observation that the concept of "timeless causation" seems to be both meaningful and free from obvious objections. It now remains to put this concept to work in order to explicate the "vertical" dimension of the time-eternity problem.

B. A Model of the Divine Eternity

I wish now to construct by stages a coherent model of the divine eternity which will give positive content to the **totum simul** claim of classical theism. It is not to be supposed that these steps in any way reflect stages in an ontological order, they are merely put together as a heuristic aid. The first step is to consider what is meant by the Judaeo- Christian doctrine of **creatio ex nihilo**.

1. The Act of Creating

Peter Bertocci introduces our subject cautiously by stating: "By saying that God created `out of nothing' we are simply denying (a) that he made it out of something (b) that creation is to be identified with him. Frankly, we do not know what is actually involved in God's creation."[45] In examining the traditional Judaeo-Christian doctrine of **creatio ex nihilo**, it is important to recognize the parameters of our discussion.[46] Negatively, I do not intend to attempt to establish demonstratively that the world must have come into being **ex nihilo**, nor do I claim to comprehend what the creative act is.

---

[44] Aquinas, *S.C.G.* 2.36,4. Cf. Ewing, *Value and Reality*, p.284; Stump and Kretzmann, "Eternity", pp.449-451; W.E. Mann, "Simplicity and Immutability in God", *International Philosophical Quarterly* 23, 1983, p.271; J. Maritain, *Existence and the Existent*, tr. L. Galantiere and G.B. Phelan, N.Y.: Pantheon, 1948, p.115.

[45] P. Bertocci, *An Introduction to the Philosophy o Religion*, N.Y.: Prentice-Hall, 1951, p.451.

[46] For the history of the doctrine see, A. Erhardt, "**Creatio Ex Nihilo**", *Studia Theologica*, 4, 1950,pp.13-43.

However, it is both legitimate and necessary to show what it is not, and to stipulate what creation means from the side of its products, viz. creatures. In so doing, it should become apparent that we are dealing with a **sui generis** relation witout true intra-cosmic analogues and which must be conceived as a temporal event.

A useful point to begin with is Aquinas' treatment of creation. I follow the order in the forty-fifth question of the *Summa Theolgiae*. In the first article dealing with creation, Thomas denies that creation presupposes any finite being. This is so because creation is: "the issuing of the whole of being (**totius entis**) entire substance (**tota substantia rei**)." Even at this early stage it is apparent that we cannot truly conceive creation to involve either sequence or change, for both presuppose an alteration in an **already existing** subject. There is no **terminus a quo** for created being. Its starting point "is conceived as non-being utterly" and the **terminus ad quem** of creation is the created substance itself. This comes out explicitly in the **responsio** of the second article: "Creation is not a change, except merely according to our way of understanding ... creation, whereby the entire substance of things is produced, does not allow of some common subject now different from what it was before, except according to our way of understanding, which conceives an object at first not existing at all and afterwards as existng." In thinking about creation we must remember that the nothing of **ex nihilo** is not to be thought of in terms of a distinctive ontological entity, a not-something, but as an absolute null, the utter nothingness of not-being.[47] Only if this is kept in mind can we avoid thinking of creation as some sort of transition.

If creation is non-transitive, it must be the case that the coming into being of finite entities can only be conceived of as atomic: "What is being made at the moment is; by speaking of its becoming made we signify that it comes from another and previously did not exist. Hence, since there is no process of change in creation, a thing is simultanesouly being created and is created."[48] The `moment' of becoming and of being are identical through the act of creation.

---

[47] Cf. J. Donnelly, "**Creatio Ex Nihilo**", in *Logical Analysis and Contemporary Theism*, J. Donnelly (ed), N.Y.: Fordham University Press, 1972, pp.200-217. On the logic of creation see P.T. Geach, "Causality and Creation", *Sophia*, 1, 1962, pp.1-8, 22-27.
[48] Aquinas, *S.Th.* 1a.45,2 - **responsio**.

Aquinas continues in the third article to discuss the concept of "passive creation", creation as considered from the side of the creature. The important thing to grasp here is that creation, in this context, **is** a relation.

> To be created is not to be produced through a motion of mutation which works on something that already exists ... take away motion from the acting-on acted-upon situation and only relation remains. Hence creation in the creature is left just as a relation to the creator as the origin of its existence ... taken in its passive sense creation is in the creature and is the creature. Nor does this demand a further creation for its creation, since being with reference to another, which is precisely what a relation is, explains itself without need for supervening relations.

Cf. "Creation is not a change or becoming, it is the very dependence of created being in relation to its principle."[49]

Creation is just the introduction of dependent reality into the nature of things. Since the production of the **totius esse** of anything and everything from the universal cause, God, excludes the motion characteristic of particularity, and since passion also presupposes an already existing entity, nothing is left to characterize creation but as a relation. The **ratio** of creation is not newness of being, for we are not to think of it in terms of alteration, but total dependence in being. If the creature **is** this relation of total dependence on God, then we must note that the relation of creation is not created, as though something other than creation, but **concreated**. As Anderson puts it: "To be created is nothing else than to receive existence from God and thus to be related to Him by a relation of total existential dependence."[50] So, too, Wilhelmsen: "Were creation as a relation a subsisting thing it could not simultaneously be in a creature, which, taking creation passively, is nothing other than the creature itself."[51] Creation is a relation in a result that has been reached without process of production and no real point of departure. If we follow the Thomist treatment

---

[49] Aquinas, *S.C.G.* 2.18.
[50] Anderson, "Creation as Relation", p.275.
[51] F. D. Wilhelmsen, "Creation as Relation in St. Thomas Aquinas", *Modern Schoolman*, 56, 1979, p.115.

above, there can be only one conclusion: creation is not a temporal event.

Before pushing on to discuss this however, it is clear that what we are required to embrace is a unique cause-effect relation. Created being alone depends upon its cause for its very being as such. The term "cause" is not to be taken as a kind of master concept applied in the same way to God and the creature. There is a genuine **analogia operationis** because, in both cases, a conditioning of another being is involved; but there is a great unlikeness, in that only the divine action is self grounded and self-causing.[52] One finite individual may cause another to come about but it does not cause its nature or conserve its being: a full cause is **agens aequivicum**, and the likeness between it and its effect is analogical.[53] The nature of this sort of causal activity has been partially clarified by the recent work of James Ross.[54]

Ross makes a distinction between what he calls "metaphysical" and "nomological" causation. Nomological explanations derive outcomes from antecedents by qualified laws. Such laws involve transaction, transformation, transmission or correlation. Among nomological causes the **concept** of the outcome, e.g. increased pressure, does not include the thing that is the cause, e.g. increased temperature. The effect is logically possible without the cause. Metaphysical causation does not involve transaction, transformation, transmission or correlation. It is constant and instantaneous causation. Metaphysical causation produces being, so that a logical relation of necessity exists between the effect and the cause. God's causing is one of a number of analogous examples of this type of causation.[55] Ross's treatment is helpful in bringing out the meaning of the sort of causation I will be dealing with in the remainder of the book. Perhaps however this terminology is misleading, for it suggests that some types of causation might not be metaphysical in character. For this reason I prefer to use the terminology of R.C. Neville: **"Cosmological causation is**

---

[52] So, Barth, *CD* III/3, pp.102-103.

[53] T. Gilby, *S.Th.* vol 2, p.199.

[54] J.R. Ross, *Philosophical Theology*, Indianapolis: Hackett, 2nd edition, 1980, "Creation", *Journal of Philosophy*, 77, 1980, pp.614-629, "Creation 2", inFredosso, *Existence*, pp.115-141.

[55] Among Ross's favourite examples are a song to a singer and a dream to a dreamer.

causation between determinate or partially determinate things in the world, whereas **ontological causation** is the causation of the world by what cannot itself be determinate."[56] Before proceeding to bring out more explicitly how the notion of ontological causation helps resolve the time-eternity tension, it is necessary to briefly defend the concept of creation **ex nihilo** against some objections. The first of these is that **creatio ex nihilo** is metaphysically impossible. If God is the supreme exemplification of the basic metaphysical principles, and we have no reason to believe that these include **fiat** creation, then to claim that God can create in an absolute way is simply a contradiction.[57] Closely tied to this theoretical position is that nothing could ever count as showing that the world has the sort of ontological dependence required by the creation doctrine. Ronald Hepburn finds a major problem here: "The second possibility is that the alleged relation of ontological dependence is no relation at all - that it is illusion. All the instabilities of state and situation are irrelevant to the question `Is there instability of **being?**' ... neither observation and experience nor strict rational argumentation seems able to show that the world has this sort of precariousness."[58] Given these sort of arguments it is not surprising that it has been claimed that **creatio ex nihilo** is, by intent, unintelligible. This is Le Roy Howe's conviction: "precisely because the doctrine is unthinkable, it cannot be taken as an assessable assertion. Its functions seem to be primarily to carry the enormous emotive and performative charges essential to on-going circles of Christian believers."[59]

If any of these objections successfully force an impasse at this point of my work its future course is obviously stymied. Replies however are at hand. How does one determine **a priori** what is and what is not metaphsycially possible? If it is claimed that **ex nihilo nihil fit** (out of nothing nothing is produced) is an inviolable metaphysical datum then one must face the counter-assertions: how can this dictum

[56] R.C. Neville, "From nothing to being: The notion of creation in Chinese and Western Thought", *Philosophy East and West*, 30, 1980, p.22 (my emphasis).
[57] L.S. Ford, "An Alternative to **Creatio Ex Nihilo**", *Religious Studies*, 19, 1983, pp.206-207.
[58] R.W. Hepburn, "The Religious Doctrine of Creation", in *The Encyclopedia of Philosophy*,P. Edwards (ed), N.Y.: Macmillan, vol 2, 1967, p.254.
[59] L.T. Howe, "Is the World **Ex Nihilo**?", *Sophia*, 7, 1967, p.29.

be established so that it is more than just a **petitio principii**,[60] and for **whose** metaphysical system is **creatio ex nihilo** impossible? Metaphysical principles are not given to us by some direct intuition; on these matters they are system dependent. Aristotle and Whitehead, for example, simply don't see matters in the same way as, say, Augustine and Aquinas. To deny the metaphysical possibility of creation **ex nihilo**, it would be required to show that this peculiar ontological assertion entails a logical contradiction. This however is not apparent. Neither can the unavailability of empirical evidence which suggests the absolute dependence of the world on God be taken to count against the **ex nihilo** hypothesis.[61] It may be (see further on this below) that the world as created has been given just those sorts of phenomenologically accessible properties which would lead us to believe that it is self-inherent. But from this we can draw no immediate conclusions about its ontology. Anyway, to say that we find no traces of ontological **precariousness** is misleading. The world's existence would only be precarious if the upholding will of the Creator were capricious. Finally, to claim that creation is unthinkable is to overlook the distinction between **quod est** and **quid est**. It is not impossible to think of a universe containing only a single being who then wills that there be other beings which "appear",[62] the **that** of creation is imaginable. The what of creation is however not able to be conceptually grasped, its inner operation is utterly inconceivable.[63] As long, however, as we can make some sense of the concept of **ex nihilo** and show that it is free from contradictions, as I have argued, it is feasible to continue using the notion to build up a model of the divine eternity.

---

[60] Shedd, *Dogmatic Theology*, vol 1, p.469.

[61] For a reply to positivism see: T.V. Morris, "Creation **Ex Nihilo**: Some Considerations", *International Journal for Philosophy of Religion*, 14, 1984, pp.233-239.

[62] Cf. Morreall, *Talking*, p.39.

[63] Strictly speaking it is inappropriate to claim **ex nihilo** creation as a violation of the **ex nihil nihil fit** principle, for God precedes his creation (logically not temporally). Some objections to the concept of absolute creation seem to try to imagine a situation in which **nothing at all existed**, then entities. This may perhaps be unthinkable, but it is not what theists are arguing for. See, Shields, "Davies", pp.31-32.

Having given some consideration to the form and defensibility of the concept of **creatio ex nihilo**, it now remains to give it concrete application to the question of temporal beginnings.

One might jump in at this point and put together a simple argument:

1. Both relativity physics and the philosophy of time have demonstrated that time must be interpreted in terms of the relations between physical objects.
2. God is the creator of the material world.
3. God is therefore the creator of time.
4. Therefore God must be outside of time, i.e. timeless.[64]

Such a shortcut is neither valid nor felicitous. That God is the creator of all physical objects and their relations does entail that God is incorporeal, but it does not entail that God is outside of time, for conceivably the act of creating, by analogy with the succession of mental events in our lives, could take time. The creator of the world's time could therefore precede it in (his) time. It is therefore necessary to return and examine the concept of creation to see that it by no means requires time in God.

Augustine argued that: "there could be no time had not a creature been made whose movement would effect some change."[65] This does not take us very far however, since it seems to presuppose the immutability of God. The Thomist contribution is much more satisfactory. We have already seen how Aquinas expounded creation in terms of a coming into being which does not involve either change or process, creation is intransitive and must be conceived as a pure relation of absolute dependence. Given this view of creation without

---

[64] For various forms of this argument see B. Britton, "Evolution by Blind Chance", *Scottish Journal of Theology*, 39, 1986, pp.350-351; B. Davies, *Introduction to the Philosophy of Religion*, Oxford: Oxford University Press, 1982, pp.77-84; Langford, *Providence*, p.479, R.C. Neville, *God the Creator*, Chicago: University of Chicago Press, 1968, pp.104-105; Peacocke, *Creation and the World of Science*, p.80; G.F. Stout, *God and Nature*, Cambridge: Cambridge University Press, 1952, p.222; Sturch, "Problem", p.492; T.F. Torrance, *Space, Time and Incarnation*, London: Oxford University Press, 1969, p.60.

[65] Augustine, *City of God*, 11.6. He was anticipted by Philo, *De Opificio Mundi*, 7.26 and Basil of Caesarea, *Homily in Hexaemeron*, 1.6, 16C; 9.2, 189B. Cf. Also the important later, and possibly independent contribution, of John Philoponus, in Simplicius', *In Physics*, 8.1, p.1141-1142, 1163.

passage, and the relationist concept of time, **creatio ex nihilo** must specify a timeless event. We have no reason therefore to think that the cause of this event, any more than the event itself, was temporal.[66] Unless it can be somehow established that ontological dependence requires temporality in **both** terms of the pure relation of becoming (God as well as the creature) then the concept of timeless creation must be allowed to stand.[67]

Many of the objections to this sort of reasoning have already been anticipated. A few comments at this point however are necessary. The Barthians insist that creation must be in time, elsewise the nexus is cut between God and man and the gracious action of God in history, "God has time for us, is abandoned.[68] This however is to make an illegitimate deductive leap from a theological value judgment to a metaphysical condition. Nothing, logically, requires us to abandon either of the two assertions - a gracious **and** eternal God. Lewis Ford postulates a difficulty: "A Divine willing which wholly takes place at no time whatever cannot enter into any temporal connection."[69] Yet I have earlier argued that a non-temporal connection between God and the world is meaningful. A number of philosophers think that creative action presupposes temporal extension. Farnell, for example, writes:

---

[66] To conclude otherwise would be to suppose either that time existed before the material world, or that time existed in God before creation, or that action necessarily requires time. The first and last of these assumptions have been questioned and rejected earlier, the middle factor is what is at issue here.

[67] So far in this chapter I have argued a basically negative thesis, that timelessness and **creatio ex nihilo** are not incompatible. Thomist metaphysics however goes beyond this point and argues that the creative act **cannot** be temporal. As God is **ipsum esse**, all of his actions, even those which posit extrinsic effects, are immanent, as the creative action occurs within the agent it implies no mutability and so no temporal succession. For details see J.F. Anderson, "The Creative Ubiquity of God", *New Schalasticism*, 25, 1951, p.158; Aquinas, *S.C.G.* 2.23, *De potentia*, 3.15; W.J. Hill, "Does the World Make a Difference to God?", *Thomist*, 38, 1974, pp.155-156; Ross, "Creation", pp.624-629. Ross emphasises that creation means a "Cambridge change" for God and a real "change" for the world.

[68] Barth, *CD* III/1, pp.67-71; Berkhof, *Systematic Theology*, p.114; T.E. Hosinski, "Creation and the Origin of the Universe: 1", *Thought*, 48, 1973, pp.225-226.

[69] L.S. Ford, "The Eternity of God and the Tempor-ality of the World", *Encounter*, 36, 1975, p.119.

150

"one cannot timelessly create; for to create is to make something new, something which at least in that shape did not exist before; and `now' and `before' are time determinations."[70] The use of "before" here is however just what is being denied by the classical theist. Neither does "newness" necessarily denote a beginning **in** time, rather than simply a beginning. One final protest, this time from J.Wolfe: "To cause the first event would require acting in time, for the occurrence of the first event is datable. But a timeless being would be one to whom temporal predicates would be applicable."[71] Nothing however can be inferred about the temporal character of the cause of the first event from the fact that this event is datable. The datability of the first event only means that it must be a part of a temporal series, at the head of which **it** is located retrospectively. This tells us nothing about the temporality of its cause.

It is one thing however to hold to the coherence of a timeless act of creation, it is quite another to establish the compatibility of relation between a timeless God and a temporally extended world. This brings us to the problem of timeless preservation.

2. Timelessness and Preservation

A good number of contemporary theists consider that even if Gods timelessness is compatible with his act of creating it cannot be reconciled with preservation. Grace Jantzen sums up the objection:

> Unfortunately, however, the doctrine of preservation cannot escape temporal implications any more than the doctrine of creation. It is true that a doctrine of preservation avoids the need to postulate a temporal beginning. Still, preservation means that things are **kept**, they are sustained in being over time. Thus any relation of causality interpreted as preservation requires that the preserver is involved in a temporal relationship with that which he preserves, so that it continues to exist. But the

---

[70] L.R. Farnell, *The Attributes of God*, Oxford: Clarendon, 1925, p.257. Cf. McTaggart, *Nature of Existence*, vol 2, p.179; R. Puccetti, "Before Creation", *Sophia*, 3, 1964, pp.24-36; J.H. Thomas, "The Idea of Creation", *Hibbert Journal*, 50, 1951, p.158.

[71] J. Wolfe, "On the Impossibility of An Infinite Past: A Reply to Craig", *International Journal for Philosophy of Religion*, 18, 1985, p.91.

notion of continuity is as temporal a notion as that of beginning or end. Even if creation could be reinterpreted as preservation, therefore, preservation itself could not dispense with the temporal notion of continuity.[72]

(a) Strong **creatio continua**

One way of replying to the above problem is by what I have termed the "strong **creatio continua**" doctrine. This really removes the problem by interpreting preservation in terms of an infinite number of repeated acts of creation. The idea seems to be present in Descartes:

> For the whole duration of my life is divisible into countless parts, all mutually independent; so from my having existed a little while ago it does not follow that I need exist now, unless some cause creates me anew at this very moment, in other words preserves me. For it is clear, when one considers the nature of time, that just the same power and agency is needed to preserve any object at the various moments of its duration, as would be needed to create it anew if it did not yet exist: there is thus only a conceptual distinction between preservation and creation, and this is one of the things that is obvious by the light of nature.[73]

The notion is certainly present in Jonathon Edwards, who frames it with deliberation in the context of his doctrine of original sin:

---

[72] Jantzen, *God's World*, p.50. Jantzen is replying to Schleiermacher, whose position I discussed in Chapter three; the central problem enunciated must however be faced by all forms of theism for which God is timeless. For similar criticisms see: R.La Croix, "Aquinas on God's Omnipresence and Timelessness", *Philosophy and Phenomenological Research*, 42, 1982, pp.391-399; Lewis, *God and Time*, pp.151-153; Morreall, *Talking*, pp.42-43, Pike, *God and Timelessness*, pp.97-118.
[73] From the *Third Meditation*, cited in R. Descartes, *Philosophical Writings*, tr. and ed., E. Anscombe and P.T. Geach, Edinburgh: Nelson, 1954, p.88. Cf. *Principles*, I, 21. On the atomic theory of time which lies behind Descartes' statement see Capek, *Philosophical Impact*, p.162; Whitrow, *Natural Philosophy*, pp.154-157.

God's upholding created substance, or causing its existence in each successive moment, is altogether equivalent to an immediate production out of nothing, at each moment, because its existence at this moment is not merely in part from God, but wholly from him; and not in any part, or degree, from its antecedent existence ... If the existence of created substance, in each successive moment be wholly the effect of God's immediate power, in that moment, without any dependence on prior existence, as much as the first creation out of nothing, then what exists at this moment, by this power, is a new effect; and simply and absolutely considered, not the same wih any past existence ...[74]

According to the strong **creatio continua** doctrine, the universe does not really have a history. What we take to be extension in time is really an infinite number of occasions of coming into being and going out of being. Since **creatio ex nihilo**, and with it the concreation of each temporal instant, does not require a temporal act, and since, presumably, neither does annihilation, God is able to preserve the universe atemporally.

Although I think that such a view succeeds in defending the divine eternity, its associated costs are too high to be entertained. Aquinas rejected the view for it implied that nature has been given a potentiality for non-being, rather than being, and, by denying the reality of secondary causes, it undermines the integrity of the Creator.[75] More directly, the identity of creatures as real self-determining centres of action would be destroyed. If it is no more than a piece of linguistic

---

[74] Cited in P.L. Quinn, "Divine Conservation, ContinuousCreation, and Human Action", in Fredosso, *Existence*, pp.63- 64. Quinn also, pp.56-57, gives quotations from Berkeley and Leibniz, but I am not persuaded that they are expressing the same view as either Descartes or Edwards. Barth, *CD*, III/3, pp.68-70 has references to Goethe and Cocceius which do seem to parallel Edwards' position.

[75] Aquinas, *S.C.G.* 3.65, 10; *S.Th.* 1a.45,3 *responsio* 3; 1a.46, 2; 1a.104, 1; 1a.104, 2; *De Potentia* 5.3. Eric Mascall makes an acute point when he reminds us that to talk about a tendency to non-being is to reify nothingness. *Existence and Analogy*, p.147. Cf. E. Gilson, *The Elements of Christian Philosophy*, N.Y.: Mentor-Omega, 1960, pp.215ff; G.C. Berkower, *The Providence of God*, tr. L. Smedes, Grand Rapids: Eerdmans, 1952, pp.67- 70.

(or even divine) legislation to say that an individual endures through time every basis for moral accountability is destroyed.[76] It is impossible to attach moral responsibility to any single one of the infinitely many existent-moments which go to make up an action for which we would normally attribute moral praise or blame.[77] Once these implications are enumerated, the strong **creatio continua** scheme must be abandoned.

(b) The traditional doctrine of **creatio continua**

To anyone unfamiliar with the classical tradition of Christian theism the nature of the relationship between the doctrines of creation and preservation must come as a surprise. Historically, the tight separation between the two concepts that is characteristic of most of contemporary, especially Protestant theology, is a relatively late development and must be held at least partially responsible for what I take to be the rather misplaced criticism of the idea of timeless conservation referred to above.[78] In discussing this matter we need to be reminded that, for classical theistic thought, the idea of a plurality of self- existing beings is impossible. All created being, that is all being other than God, is absolutely dependent for its coming into being and continued being upon the divine causal power. Substance is not a **causa su**˙ Augustine stresses this point: "to govern things is to create them an˙ to create them is to govern ... What is contingent and subject to becoming cannot give itself what it does not possess ... it must therefore be admitted that every contingent thing receives its form from God ... to say that God is the immutable form by which all that is contingent subsists and develops according to the rhythm and law of its form, is to say that God is its providence. Things would not exist if God did not exist."[79] Aquinas expresses the same conviction, but more metaphysically:

---

[76] Barth, *CD* III/3 pp.68-69; L. Berkhof, *Systematic Theology*, p.171

[77] Quinn, "Divine Conservation", pp.64-65.

[78] On the historical relationship between the two concepts see J. Pelikan, "Creation and Causality in the History of Christian Thought", *Pastoral Psychology*, 10, 1960, pp.11-20.

[79] Augustine, *De. Libero arbitrio* 2, 17.25 in E. Gilson, *The Spirit of Medieval Philosophy*, tr. A.H.C. Downes, London: Sheed and Ward, 1936, p.155.

just as the coming to be of an effect cannot continue once the action of the agent causes its coming to be ceases, so too the **esse** of an effect cannot continue once the action of an agent causing not only its coming to be but also its **esse** ceases ... God alone is being by his essence, which is **esse**, while every creature is being participatively, i.e. its essence is not its **esse** ... There is no more possibility of God's conferring on any creature that it be sustained in **esse** on the cessation of his action than of his conferring on it that its **esse** be uncaused by him. For the need of the creature to be upheld in being by God is equivalent to the dependence of the **esse** of an effect upon the cause of the **esse**.[80]

Since it is being as being, being as to its **esse**, that is the proper objective of the divine causality, all that is, whether in its beginning or continuance, is dependent upon God. To put it a little differently, finite beings are **entia ab alio**, they have their being "from another".[81] They are metaphysically dependent on a being other than themselves; they are the subjects of ontological causation.[82] Antony Flew has grasped the situation well when he sums up the thrust of Aquinas' first "Three Ways": "What this argument requires is an order which, if temporal at all and not purely hierarchical, is of simultaneous conditions. The causal chains needed here have to hang, as it were, at right angles to, and also to be additional to, those

---

[80] Aquinas, *S.Th.* 1a.104, 1. Cf. *S.C.G.*, 3. 64-67; 76-76 etc.

[81] Ross, "Creation 2", pp.123-125. Cf. Also Chisholm, *Person and Object*, pp.50-51, 104.

[82] Contra Robert Oakes, "Classical Theism and Pantheism, A Victory for Process Theism", *Religious Studies*, 13, 1977, pp.167-173; this does not mean that finite beings are modifications of God's being. As Philip Quinn, "Divine Conservation and Spinozistic Pantheism", *Religious Studies*, 15, 1979, pp.289-302, pointed out Oakes has failed to demonstrate that all truths which make reference to contingent beings can be analysed into truths that refer only to God. Ross, "Creation", 1980, pp.622-623 gives an example which seemingly cannot be so analysed: "Ross is making some mistakes about God." See also the articles by Michael Levine, "Why Traditional Theism Does Not Entail Pantheism", *Sophia*, 23, 1984, pp.13-35, "More On 'Does Traditional Theism Entail Pantheism'", *International Journal for Philsophy of Religion*, 20, 1986, pp.31-35.

stretching backwards into the past and forward into the future. But they have to be not originating causes but standing conditions."[83]

Given the above, what is the precise relationship between creation **ex nihilo** and conservation? Aquinas says: "God does not maintain things in existence by any new action, but by the continuation of the act whereby he bestows **esse**; an act subject neither to change nor to time."[84] In Thomist thought, as James Anderson puts it, the distinction between beginning and remaining is nominal and conceptual: "`conservation' - the continuous upholding of the thing in existence - is in the finite thing the very same relation as that whereby it is a creature. The term `creation' signifies this dependence from the standpoint of origination, whether eternal or temporal, whereas `conservation' denotes the same dependence from the angle of its continuance in being ... Conservation thus `follows from' creation not really but only logically."[85] From God's side there is no difference at all between the act of creation and that of preservation, from the side of the individual creature there is a vital difference, the difference between coming into being, or newness of being, and continuation in being. The absolute dependence or pure relation that the creature bears to God is however identical in both cases, it cannot be otherwise, for this is what it means to be a creature. If the metaphysical scheme outlined above is accepted it becomes plain that conservation can no more be considered to require a temporal cause than can creation. This is because considered in themselves they are not two causes but one. To speak of a multiplicity of timeless causes is both unnecessary and does not permit of independent characterization. We must consider that in one indivisible timeless act of will, God willed both that the world would come into being and that it would continue in being in

---

[83] Flew, *God and Philsophy*, p.888.

[84] Aquinas, *S.Th.*1a, 104, 1.*ad*4. The use of continuation (**continuationem**) here should not mislead us, as the context indicates, and as Aquinas explicitly states elsewhere (*S.C.G.* 2.35) by the continuous activity of God it is not implied that God is in time. This point is missed by Delmas Lewis, "Timelessness and Divine Agency", *International Journal of Philsophy of Religion*, 21, 1987, p.157, who finds fault with Aquinas for speaking as if timeless activity could begin or cease.

[85] Anderson, "Creation as Relation", p.283. Cf. Scotus: "even though the (real) relation implied by both terms is absolutely identical, still the (conceptual) relation is not the same as that implied by conservation." *Quodlibetal Questions*, 12.35.

time. Only the failure to take seriously what is meant by a **timeless** cause could lead us to deduce from the extended character of finite effects that their ultimate origin must lie in a likewise extended cause.

Even if the argument so far is granted, an objector may raise what seem to be a number of unacceptable corollaries. The first of these has to do with the eternity of the world. In this context "eternal", as applied to the world, means sempiternal or everlasting in time. An argument of the following form was put seriously by the Islamic philosopher Avicenna.[86] God preceded the world either in nature only, or also in duration. There is no third possibility. Now a cause in act is simultaneous with its effect. Therefore, if God is only ontologically prior to the world, and existed from eternity, does it not follow that creatures also will have existed from eternity? Creation is God's action. Whatever is "in" God is God. Hence God's action is himself. But God is eternal. Therefore his action is eternal. The effect of his action, the world, is then likewise eternal. There are a number of possible ways of replying to this problem. Firstly, we might consider that the conclusion is just a logical impossibility, that an infinite series in time is a contradiction of some sorts. I do not intend to consider this opinion both because it would take us too far afield from our course and because, as our continuing discussion will make clear, it is unnecessary.[87] A second way out, popular with contemporary theologians influenced by existentialism, is to set aside the question as being of no religious interest. Such matters are the

---

[86] See Kogan, *Averroes*, Chapter 5. Cf. Also the lateNeoplatonist Simplicius in G. Verbeke, "Some Later Neoplatonic Views on Divine Creation and the Eternity of the World", in *Neoplatonism and Christian Thought*, D.J. O'Meara (ed), Albany: S.U.N.Y., 1982, pp.45-53; and for a contemporary opinion: Kozak, "Causality", p. 276.

[87] The most notable theist who has insisted that the world must have had a temporal beginning was St. Bonaventure see Copleston, *History of Philosophy*, vol 2, pp.265-266. Recently Pamela Huby has put forward a very strong argument that the universe must be finite in both space and time. "Kant or Cantor? That the Universe, if Real, Must be Finite in Both Space and Time." *Philosphy*, 46, 1971, pp.121-132. See also W.L. Craig, "**Creatio Ex Nihilo**", in *Process Theology*, R.H. Nash (ed), Grand Rapids: Baker, 1987, pp.145- 173, who summarises a number of arguments to this end.

proper concern of empirical science, not of theology.[88] A short cut like this is neither feasible nor satisfactory for a book of this nature.

The first step in a reply is to accept that God wills himself and all other things in one timeless act of will.[89] To deny this would not only introduce multiplicity in to the Godhead but also contradict the very nature of timeless causation. The nature of the temporal duration of the world will therefore depend on the way in which God wills it to be. Now it is logically possible that God could have willed that the world exist everlastingly, that something could always have existed in time. Augustine was not troubled by the apparently everlasting existence of angels,[90] and Boethius and other Christians influenced by Neoplatonism embraced the eternity of the world.[91] Aquinas also held that it was an article of faith and not reason that the world had a beginning.[92] The chief reason he gives why such a position **could** be embraced with equanimity is that it has no bearing on either the **ratio** of creation or the status of the Creator. As Richard Taylor says: "it is no answer to the question, why a thing exists, to state **how long** it has existed ... it can be asked why there is a world, why indeed there is a beginningless world, why perhaps there should always have been something rather than nothing."[93] The point is that the everlastingness of the world would leave its ontological dependence on God unchanged. Extension in time cannot change its metaphysical structure. Long ago Boethius pointed out that a sempiternal world would pose no threat to the status of the Christian God: "For it is one thing for existence to be interminably prolonged, as Plato thought the

---

[88] See, L. Gilkey, *Maker of Heaven and Earth*, Garden City: Doubleday, 1959, pp.310-318; Macquarrie, *Principles*, p.199; J.W. Thomas, "The Idea of Creation", *Hibbert Journal*, 50, 1951, pp.153-161; Tillich, *Systematic Theology*, vol 1, p.252; C.H. Wagers, "Creation and Providence", *College Bible Quarterly*, 38, 1961, pp.36-50.

[89] Cf. Aquinas, *S.C.G.* 1.72-79.

[90] Augustine, *City of God*, 12.16.

[91] See, Verbeke, "Neoplatonic", pp.45ff., J. Whittaker, *Studies in Platonism and Patristic Thought*, London: Variorum, 1984, pp.58-61.

[92] Aquinas, *S.Th.* 1a.46,2. For a full discussion on Aquinas see J.F. Anderson, "Time and the Possibility of an Eternal World", *Thomist*, 15, 1952, pp.136-161; W.A. Wallace, "Aquinas on Creation: Science, Theology and Matters of Fact", *Thomist*, 38, 1974, pp.485-523.

[93] R. Taylor, *Metaphysics*, N.J.: Prentice-Hall, 2nd ed., 1973, pp.106-107.

world was, another to grasp simultaneously the world of endless life in the present, which is clearly a property peculiar to the mind of God."[94] The ontological priority of the Creator over the creature has nothing at all to do with temporal precedent but is a matter of essential superiority.[95]

This reply might no be counted as sufficient to counter the argument, for it seems that if God is eternal the world **must** have existed always, not just possibly so, and we might have good reasons on other ground, i.e. cosmology, for believing that the world is not everlasting. If so, the concept of timeless creation would be thrown into question.

An answer to this difficulty was anticipated by Augustine: "In the eternal Word you (God) speak eternally all that you speak, and yet not all exists at once and from eternity that you effect in speaking."[96] This however was not given satisfactory form until Aquinas:

> it does not follow, if the action of the first agent is eternal, that His effect is eternal ... For ... in producing things God acts voluntarily ... Now the effect follows from the intellect and the will according to the determintion of the intellect and the command of the will. And just as every other condition of the thing made is determined by the intellect, so is the time appointed to it ... But just as the will ... wills this thing to be such and such, so does it will it to be at such and such a time. Wherefore, for the will to be a sufficient cause, it is not necessary for the effect to be when the will is, but when the will has appointed the effect to be ... the effect of the divine will was not delayed ... because the object of the divine will is not only the existence of the effect, but also the time of its existence ...

---

[94] Boethius, *Consolation*, 5.6. Cf. Augustine, *Confessions*, 11.30; Charnocke, *Attributes*, p.762; Schleiermacher, *CF*, 52.1.

[95] See K.L. Schmitz, "Weiss and Creation", *Review of Metaphysics*, 18, 1964, pp.147-169 for an extended treatment on this subject.

[96] Augustine, *Confessions*, 11.7. Cf. Albert the Great, *Commentary on the Celestial Hierarchy* 4.

the creature began to exist at the time appointed by God from eternity.[97]

Creation is the perfectly free action of God. God can therefore will it to be either everlasting or with a temporal beginning, and it appears that he has willed the latter. There is nothing paradoxical about this matter, for the notion of a delay in the effectiveness of a non-successive cause is a mistaken one. A cause above time cannot be measured in any way by time as to the coming into being of its effect.[98] There is therefore no contradiction between the temporally limited nature of the world and the timeless action of God.

The line of objection however is pressed one degree further by Keith Ward:

> If God is really a necessary and immutable being, how can he ever have a free choice, surely all he does will have to be done of necessity and without any possibility of alteration? ... In Aquinas free creation is at once asserted and qualified out of existence by the demands of the concepts of necessity, simplicity and eternity in the divine nature. It is impossible to see how the doctrine that God must know and will the world simply in the same act of knowing and willing himself, as a necessary eternal being, can be reconciled with the assertion of genuine contingency in the world.[99]

Although the question is not often put in this fashion, it is important to consider in what sense a timeless and eternal being may be said to freely produce temporal and contingent effects.[100] Besides the

---

[97] Aquinas, *S.C.G.* 2.35. Cf. *S.Th.* 1a, 46.1 and 10; *De Potentia*, q3.a17. Cf. Scotus: "The operation is in eternity, and the production of **esse existentiae** is in time." *Opus Oxoniense* 1.39, 21.

[98] Cf. R. Garrigou-Lagrange, *God: His Existence and His Nature*, tr. B. Rose, St. Lousi: Herder, vol 2, 1949, p.53.

[99] Keith Ward, *Rational Theology and the Creativity of God*, Oxford: Basil Blackwell, 1982, pp.73, 77, 78.

[100] George Mavrodes, "Aristotelian Necessity and Freedom", *Mid-West Studies in Philosophy*, 1, 1976, pp.17-21, mentions the problem in passing. For related formulations of the problem based on God's necessary and immutable nature see:

philosophical significance of the matter, it is of religious importance for classical theists, since only if creation is freely willed by God can it be understood as the gratuitous exercise of love.

As a first step it is helpful to distinguish between "conditional necessity" and "absolute necessity". Supposing that God freely created, it is now necessary that he be creating, and that creatures exist. This sort of necessity is conditional on the creative act as really occurring. "Absolute necessity" however is to be predicated of God alone. It could not be that God not exist. This is quite independent of the world of creatures.[101] Given that God does will creatures, he cannot not will them, because this will cannot change.[102] In this conditional sense only can it be said that he creative act is as eternal and immutable as God himself.[103] But, as Copelston remarks, that God so wills is not necessary: "That God's will is free in regard to finite objects other than Himself follows from the infinity of the divine will, which can have as its necessary object only an infinite object, God himself."[104] We may suppose that divine intellect formulates and contemplates an infinite number of possible worlds atemporally,[105] but since no sense can be given to unsurpassibly good finite world, and since no finite array could ever be sufficient to receive or express the infinite good[106] we cannot suppose that God's will to create is

---

Hartshorne, *Divine Relativity*, pp.12-15, 117-118; C. Hartshorne and W.L. Reese (eds), *Philosophers Speak of God*, Chicago: Chicago University Press, 1953, p.133; L.T. Howe, "The Necessity of Creation", *International Journal for Philosophy of Religion*, 2, 1971, pp.96-112; T. Kapitan, "Can God Make Up His Mind?" *International Journal for the Philosophy of Religion*, 15, 1984, pp.43-45; Kogan, *Averroes*, pp.221ff; W. Pannenberg, "The Appropriation of the Philosophical Concept of God as a Dogmatic Problem of Early Christian Theolgoy", in *Basic Questions in Theology*, London: S.C.M., vol 2, 1971, p.144; G.W. Shields, "God, Modality and Incoherence", *Encounter*, 44, 1983, pp.29-32; Swinburne, *Coherence*, p.214.
[101] So, Dom Mark Pontifex, *Providence and Freedom*, London: Burns and Oates, 1960, pp.25-37., R.A. Redlon, "St. Thomas and the Freedom of the Creative Act", *Fransciscan Studies*, 20, 1960, pp.13-14.
[102] See, Aquinas, *S.Th.* 1a.19, 3.
[103] See, T. Mourien, *The Creation*, London: Burns and Oates, 1962, p.103.
[104] Copleston, *History of Philosophy*, vol 2, p.532.
[105] See, Leibniz, *Theodicy*, 2, 225.
[106] So, Aquinas, *S.Th.* 1a.25, 5. Cf. Mascall, *He Who Is*, pp.104-105.

caused by his goodness.[107] This does not mean that creation is not motivated, but it does preserve the absolute divine transcendence. At this point we come to the nub of the issue. Given that God is not compelled to create by either external conditions or by his own nature, how are we yet to make sense of a free atemporal decision to create when timelessness seems to leave no "room" for choice? I quote from Delmas Lewis whose answer I believe is satisfactory:

> Although the notion of a timeless decision smacks of incoherence because of the temporal connotations of decision making, the notion of a timeless choice is not obviously confused. It does not seem incoherent to assert that a timeless God **chooses** to sustain this universe (i.e. the actual physical universe...) instead of sustaining no universe at all and instead of sustaining a different possible universe (i.e. a universe with a different history, etc. ...) A timeless choice would be free just in case it is not causally or logically necessitated by God's nature or existence ... the theological problem seems to be generated by the attributes of omniscience, omnipotence and perfect goodness, independently of whatever stance is taken on God's relation to time.[108]

This reply may appear anticlimactical but it is nevertheless difficult to see how timelessness **per se** could be supposed to make what otherwise would be a free choice a necessary one. The concept of an unconditioned atemporal choosing of one out of an infinite number of possibles to be actual is indeed unimaginable, but it is not contradictory once we have granted that a timeless being can have positive content.[109]

---

[107] Aquinas, *S.Th.*1a.19.5: "Therefore he wills this to be in relation to that, but he does not will this to be because that." That is, the creature is willed in relation to the divine goodness, but not because of it. This is enough to ensure that creation is not arbitrary.

[108] Lewis, *God and Time*, p.157.

[109] For a rather different approach to the one which I have sketched above, yet still within the classical tradition, one should consult the work of Dom Illtyd Trethowan, *An Essay in Christian Philosophy*, London: Longmans, 1954,

C. Summary and Conclusion.

The express intention of the present chapter was to find a solution to the "vertical" dimension of the "two-worlds problem" in its time-eernity form. I have argued that the apparent antitheticals of time and eternity, or of becoming and **totum simul existens**, can be reconciled through the notion of the timeless causation of temporal effects. Once it is granted that timeless causation is a coherent concept it becomes apparent that a model of the divine eternity, in terms of God's relationship with the world, can be built up from this idea as it applied to the doctrine of creation **ex nihilo** and the preservation of the mundane world. Such a model, at least in the context of classical, and particularly Thomist metaphysics, seems compatible with both the freedom of the Creator and the contingency of a finite world.

At this point however serious questions may be raised about the characteristics of a being whose whole relationship to the universe can seemingly be subsumed under the category of a temporally non-extended action which brings creatures into being and sustains them. It may readily be felt that such a deity must be rather mechanical and that it can hardly possess the properties of personhood so intimately associated with Christian theism. The next chapter will address these concerns.

---

pp.93-102, "A Changing God", *Downside Review*, 1966, pp.247-261, "The Significance of Process Theology", *Religious Studies*, 19, 1983, pp.311-322.

CHAPTER SIX

THE PERSONAL REDEEMER

In the introduction to this book I mentioned that one of the major areas of apparent tension within classical theism lay in its joint insistence on the timelessness **and** personhood of the devine being.[1] Many philosophers, especially in the contemporary literature, have felt that it is a contradiction to maintain that both of these concepts can be combined in a single being. Adherence to the doctrine of the Incarnation, a matter shared by all classical theists, brings the question of the relationship between an atemporal God and personhood into especially sharp relief. In this chapter I will be arguing that the concept of **totum simul existens** is by no means incompatible with personhood, but, if anything, leads us in that direction.

A. The Necessity of a Personal God

Before embarking on the argument proper it needs to be set out in brief why Christianity should consider that the category of personhood as attributed to God is indispensable.

1. The first reason that an ordinary non- philosophical Christian is likely to give for belief in a personal God is that the God who reveals himself in the personal Christ must be personal. The Incarnation is claimed to be the adequate and final revelation of the personality of

---

[1] It is recognized that to claim that God is a person is not identical with the claim that he is either personal or possesses personality, and that the terms involved are historically fluid ones. For the purposes of discussion I will ignore the nuances involved, so that whenever any of these terms appear below it may be assumed that what is at issue is the strong claim that God is not exempt from the modern metaphysical category of "person". On these distinctions see G. Aulen, *The Faith of the Christian Church*, London: S.C.M., 1954, pp.159-160; H. Bavinck, *The Doctrine of God*, tr. W. Hendriksen, Grand Rapids: Baker, pp.124-127; P. Bertocci, *The Person God Is*, London: Allen and Unwin, 1970, p.67; P. Ramsey, "A Personal God" in *Prospect for Theology*, E.G. Healey (ed), London: 1966, p.56; A. Thatcher, "The Personal God and the God Who Is a Person", *Religious Studies*, 21, 1985, pp.61-73.

God.[2] Or, in Barth's well known words: "this personalising of the concept of God's Word (is not) a case of anthropomorphism. The doubtful thing is not whether God is a person but whether we are..."[3]

2. A second factor that would be put forward is that the Christian scriptures consistently speak of God in a personal way.[4] John Hick is one who has argued this way. "The conviction that God is personal. He rather than It, has always been plainly implied in the biblical writings ... In the Old Testament God speaks in personal terms ... and the prophets and psalmists address him in personal terms ... In the New Testament the same conviction as to the personal character of God is embodied in the figure of Fatherhood ..."

3. A third argument appeals to the character of revelation. Thus, W.H. Farmer: "In the thought of revelation there is expressed the sense of God's active approach as personal to man."[5] For orthodox Christian theology, the very concept of revelation is tied up with the possibiliyt of a true knowledge of God, however limited this might be. The personalising content of revelation is taken to incorporate anthropomorphic expressions but to exclude anthropomorphic conceptions.[6] That God is personal must therefore be taken seriously.

4. Then there is a consideration which is not so much an argument but an expression from within a religious tradition. Frederick Copleston is representative here: "If we had reason to believe that God were not personal, we should see the uselessness of worship and prayer; but the statement that God is personal suggests immediately that worship and prayer are in place, even though we have no adequate idea of what the devine personality is in itself."[7]

5. A closely related matter is the argument from religious experience. Christian would argue that they experience God as personal in their

---

[2] J.R. Illingworth, *Personality: Human and Divine*, London: Macmillan, 1894, p.193.

[3] Barth, *CD*, I/1 p.138. Cf. H.H. Farmer, *The World and God*, London: Collins, 1963, p.9.

[4] J. Hick, *The Philosophy of Religion*, N.Y.: Prentice Hall, 1965, pp.9-10.

[5] Farmer, *World*, p.123.

[6] H. Gollwitzer, *The Existence of God*, London: S.C.M., 1965, pp.142-164; A.J. Heschel, *The Prophets*, N.Y.: Harper and Row, vol 2, 1975, chapter 4.

[7] Copleston, *History of Philosophy*, vol 2, p.397. Cf. Gollwitzer, *Existence*, pp.188-196; H.H. Henderson, "Knowing Persons and Knowing God", *Thomist*, 46, 1982, pp.396-397.

lives. This is important, for example, to Webb: "When ... the expression a `personal God' is thus used, without reference to any plurality within the unity of the Divine Nature (i.e. outside a Trinitarian context) what is really in the minds of those who so use it is, I think, always the possibility of personal relations - of worship, truth, love - between **oneself** and God."[8] The content of the claim to experience God as personal takes many forms - the awareness of being "addressed", of meeting another will, of reciprocity, of an unconditional claim on our lives and so on.[9] Arguments from religious experience are notoriously slippery, but the claims must at least be noticed here.

6. Finally, there is the claim that the concept of person refers to that which, in Aquinas' words, is "most perfect in all nature."[10] The personal in God does not yield to a higher order that is not completely personal. God in the communion of his inner life remains the supremely personal reality. There is nothing more ultimate in the divine reality than to be personal, it is the preeminent of all the eminent perfections of God. In Thomist metaphysics this is the working our of the **per viam remotionis et supereminentiae.** But theologians and philosophers of quite different persuasions have been willing to argue that personhood is the most adequate metaphysical category available to us in speaking about God.[11]

A standard reply to this position is to assert that to predicate personhood of God is to detract from his transcendence. The supreme being must be above all categories that can be applied to finite beings. To consider that the deity could be a person is to attribute to him a

---

[8] C.C.J. Webb, *God and Personality*, London: Allen and Unwin, 1919, p.70.

[9] Farmer, *World*, pp.28-35; Gollwitzer, *Existence*, pp.179-187; Henderson, "Knowing", pp.402-417; W.R. Matthews, *God in Christian Thought and Experience*,London: Nisbet, 1930, pp.159-164; Ramsey, "Personal", pp. 61-70; Swinburne, *Coherence*, pp.221ff.

[10] Aquinas, *S.Th.* 1a. 29, 3. On this perspective in Thomist theology see A.J. Kelly, "To Know the Mystery: The Theologian in the Presence of the Revealed God", *The Thomist*, 32, 1968, pp.53-54, "God: How Near a Relation", *The Thomist*, 34, 1970, pp.210-211.

[11] Cf. Macquarrie, *Principles*, p.187; H. Lotze, *Microcosmus*, tr. E. Hamilton and E.E.C. Jones, Edinburgh: T. and T. Clarke, 1984, 9.4, 4.

limiting factor.[12] Those who argue in this way go on to conclude that God's own being must be beyond both personality and impersonality, he is "super-personal" or "transpersonal".[13] Hans Kung summarises his feelings on the matter saying: "It is part of the completely incommensurable nature of God that he is neither personal nor non-personal: since he is both at once and therefore transpersonal."[14]

There is, I believe, an insuperable problem for such views, no content can be given to the claim that God exceeds personality. One way of putting this is to see tht our language only allows us a choice between the personal I-Thou relationship and the impersonal I- It relationship. If we seek to go beyond the personal we find ourselves in the subpersonal.[15] Suppose it is claimed that "supra-personal" means "personal to the nth degree", then we are still in the category of the personal. If however every trace of the alleged anthropomorphism is eliminated how is the allegedly "suprapersonal" distinguished from the merely subpersonal? Cherbonnier explains this in a highly memorable way: "Unless this question can be answered, advocates of the `supra- personal' may fairly be likened to a person crossing the north pole. He believes himself to be going farther and farther north, when in fact he has begun to go south again. Devotees of the 'supra-personal' likewise fancy themselves to have discovered a more exalted term for God. The burden of proof rests with them, however, to show hat they have not unwittingly reverted to the sub personal. Until they do one may conclude that the category of the personal is the north pole of human thought."[16] Such an objection would seem to be

---

[12] Dewart, *Future of Belief*, pp.185-188; Inge, *Plotinus*, vol 1, p.250; G. Legenhausen, "Is God a Person?", *Religious Studies*, 22, 1986, pp.307-323.

[13] F.H. Bradley, *Appearance and Reality*, Oxford: Clarendon, 1969, pp.470-473; K. Jaspers, *Philosophical Faith and Revelation*, tr. E.B. Ashton, London: Collins, 1967, pp.141-145; J. Laird, *Mind and Deity*, London: George Allen and Unwin, 1944, pp.166-168.

[14] H. Kung, *Does God Exist?* London: Collins, 1980, p.634.

[15] Gollwitzer, *Existence*, p.189.

[16] E. La B. Cherbonnier, "The Logic of Biblical Anthropomorphism", *Harvard Theological Review*, 55, 1962, pp.187-190. Cf. Owen, *Concepts*, pp.42-43, H.N. Wieman, "God is More Than We Can Think", *Christendom*, 1, 1936, p.432. It should be noted here that this objection is just as potent when applied to talk of God as he is "in himself" as to considerations of God "towards us".

quite "literally unanswerable": that is, suitable words do not seem to be available to overthrow it.

I have enumerated the above six points in order to demonstrate that for classical theism as a system the concept of a personal God is critic al. In pausing briefly at the last point I have hoped to demonstrate that there is at least one good ph ilosophical reason, in addition to any religiously orientated claims, for believing that the deity must be personal. Altogether this indicates that the subject matter of this chapter is no pseudo-problem but of central importance to the classical theistic model.

B. The Nature of the Personal

Little sense can be made of the claim the at personhood and timelessness are compatible unless a fair independent characterization is first given of what it might mean to be a "person". I am not here interested in the criteria of personal **identity**, but inquiring as to what are those properties we might reasonably expect a person to possess. For purposes of convenience I divide the various models of person-hood into three groups.

(a) Firstly, there are those which emphasise that persons have states of consciousness. In a recent article Daniel Dennett has pointed out that there have been at least six different notions of personhood put forward in the philsosophical tradition, each offered as an individually necessary if not sufficient condition of personhood.[17] "A" is a person only if:

(1) "A" is a rational being.
(2) "A" is a being to which states of consciousness can be attributed.
(3) Others regard or can regard "A" as a being to which states of consciousness can be attributed.
(4) "A" is capable of regarding others as beings to which states of consciousness can be attributed.
(5) "A" is capable of verbal communication.
(6) "A" is capable of regarding his/her/itself as a subject of states of consciousnes.

---

[17] D. Dennett, "Conditions of Personhood", in Rorty, *Identities*, pp.175-196. Dennett gives details as to which philosophers emphasised the particular traits.

It will be evident how strongly the concept of thought or thinking figures for such models. The central definition of "person" adhered to by classical theism, that of Boethius, clearly falls in this category: "Wherefore if person belongs to substances alone, and these rational, and if every substance is a nature, and exists not in universals but in individuals, we have found the definiton of a person. `The individual subsistence of a rational nature.'"[18]

(b) Secondly, there are models which stress personal action or intentionality. This is central to Barth's whole theology, for example: "God is who is in his works ... God exists in his own decision. God lives from and by himself."[19] Or, as Peter Bertocci puts it: "For the personalist ... the word `person' identifies an agent capable of self consciousness and of action in the light of rational and moral-aesthetic-religious ideals."[20] Volition comes strongly to the fore amongst this group of theorists, and there is a very heavy emphasis upon the tie between the concepts of agent-action and personality. Actions are something over and above happenings. They are intersubjective, and they posit both a self and other selves. Austin Farrer finds a tight identity: "If `God's will' means `God's voluntary action' then it is a synonym for `God himself' for what is a person but his voluntary action."[21] Recently, Thomas F. Tracy has built up an argument linking character traits to personal subjects by way of the notion of intentional action.[22] Character trait predicates can only be meaningfully attached to a subject if they are the outcome of some sort of project he is undertaking, that is, the overt behaviour in question must be intentional. This requirement has important implications for any talk about God as personal: as he says : "In using our language of character traits to describe a person's distinctive identity we are

---

[18] Boethius, *Contra Eutychen et Nestorium*, III, in Stewart et al. *Tractates*, p.85. Cf. Aquinas, *S.Th.* 1a. 29, 3.

[19] Barth, *CD*, II/1, pp.260, 272.

[20] Bertocci, *Person*, p.26.

[21] A. Farrer, *Faith and Speculation*, N.Y.: New York University Press, 1967, p.57. For an extended treatment see R.H. King, *The Meaning of God*, London: S.C.M., 1974, Chapter 3. Also worth consulting are H.G. Frankfurt, "Freedom of the Will and the Concept of a Person", *Journal of Philosophy*, 68, 1971, pp.5-20 and A.B. Gibson, "Time and Action", in *Experience, Existence and the Good*, I.C. Lieb (ed), Carbondale: Southern Illinois University Press, 1961, pp.169-177.

[22] T.F. Tracy, *God, Action and Embodiment*, Grand Rapids: Eerdmans, 1984.

calling attention to patterns in the way he conducts his life as an agent of intentional actions. This clearly locates the conceptual hinge on which will turn any talk of God in personal categories ... This language requires that we think of God as an agent of intentional actions."[23] Unless some meaning can be given to timeless will or intention it is difficult to see how God can be a person.

(c) Finally, there are models whose emphasis is upon reciprocity of relationship. For writers along these lines "person" is a concept of relation rather than a concept of substance expressing the nature of something that exists by itself. Personal being means being-in-relaionship. Hegel's position is worth quoting: "It is, in short, the nature of character of what we mean by person or subject to abolish its isolation, its separateness ... In friendship and in love I give up my abstract personality, and in this way win it back as concrete personality. It is just this winning back of personality by the act of absorption, by the being absorbed into the other, which consitutes the true nature of personality."[24] Various philosophers, such as Webb, take the next step and apply this way of thinking to the question of God's personhood: "we should not speak of a personal

God unless we supposed that we could stand in personal relationship with him ... It is upon the possibility of this reciprocal intercourse that the whole question turns."[25] According to this line of thinking unless the divine eernity is compatible with an interrelationship with human persons it will not be appropriate to call God a "person".[26]

C. The Personal and the Eternal

Objections to the concept of an "eternal person" can be broken down into three groupings corrresponding to the three basic models of

---

[23] Tracy, *God, Action and Embodiment*, p.12.

[24] G.W.F. Hegel, *Lectures on the Philosophy of Religion*, tr. E.B. Spiers, London: Routlege and Kegan Paul, 1982, vol 3, pp.23-24. Cf. R. Mehl, *The Condition of the Christian Philosopher*, tr. E. Kushner, London: James Clarke, 1963, pp.86-87; J. Macmurray, *Persons in Relation*, N.Y.: Harper, 1961.

[25] Webb, *Personality*, pp.73, 131.

[26] In this chapter I have deliberately omitted any discussion of the Trinatarian relations. Although the subject has a central place in classical theism it is neither practical nor necessary to consider the matter here.

personhood outlined above. In various ways it has been denied that a timeless person can be conscious, willingly act, and be involved in real interpersonal relationships.

1. Not a few philosophers have made the very strong claim that, logically, any mind must be located in time. So, Galloway: "no mind is conceivable, whether human or divine, which does not imply states of consciousness that change."[27] Also, J.R. Lucas:

> I cannot conceive a mind being conscious of something about whom the question `when?' does not arise ... timeless mind seems inconceivable ... It seems reasonable to say wih Boethius that God is not in space but space is present to, or ... in God. But although we may in this sense say that God is non-spatial, we cannot analogously argue that he is non-temporal, since minds although only contingently located in space are necessarily located in time.[28]

The temporally elongated nature of consciousness, incorporating thought, judgement, reflection, memory and many other activities necessary for personhood has been held to be incompatible with a timeless entity being a "person".[29] If a time less God is incapable of mental activity of any sort he can hardly be personal. Hermann Lotze sums up a srong conviction when he says:

> It is not sufficient to lessen the weight of this objection by the assertion that this educative stimulation is necessary only for finite and changing beings, and not for the nature of God, which as a self-cognisant Idea, eternally unchangeable, always possesses its whole content

---

[27] G. Galloway, *The Philosophy of Religion*, Edinburgh: T. and T. Clarke, 1974, p.479.

[28] J.R. Lucas, *A Treatise on Time and Space*, London: Methuen, 1973, pp.7, 304.

[29] Brightman, *Problem*, p.133; Chung, "Greek and Chinese", p.155; R.C. Coburn, "Professor Malcolm on God", *Australasian Journal of Philosophy*, 40-41, 1963, p.155; Gale, "Omniscience", p.333; Hepburn, "Transcendence", pp.155-156; F.J. McConnell, *Is God Limited?*, London: Williams and Norgate, 1924, pp.252-253; Sorabji, *Time*, p.258.

simultaneously. Though this assertion grazes the truth ... it would make the being of God similar to that of an eternal truth - a truth not merely valid but also conscious of itself. But we have a direct feeling of a wide difference between this personification of a thought and living personality.[30]

I do not consider that the above line of argument has been developed anywhere near enough to be successful. The classical theist may immediately grant that concepts such as reflection, memory and anticipation could not apply to a timeless being (nor to any omniscient being), but this is not to admit that the key concepts of consciousness and knowledge are inapplicable to such a deity. To begin with it is clearly inadequate to move from the premise that the only form of consciousness we are familiar with is temporal to he conclusion that all consciousness must be temporal.[31] Of course, the onus may be laid upon the non-temporalists to give some characterizaion of the concept of non-temporal connections between the simultaneous states of the divine mind. Even our normal language about intellectual activities is of help here, for there does not seem to be any essential temporal element in words like "understanding" or "recognising". These and other terms are "achievement terms" and describe a state of attainment.[32] In finite, limited, temporal beings like ourselves, intellectual activities seem to be invariably connected to successive rational processes, but this is a contingent and not a necessary property of intellection. To "understand", to "be aware", to "know" and so on are not necessarily processive. It is coherent to suppose that an atemporal deity could possess maximal understanding, awareness and knowledge in a single all-embracing vision of himself and the sum of reality. Such knowlege would not be habitual, discursive or compositional,[33] but this is surely a perfection and not a defect.[34] In a

[30] Lotze, *Microcosmus*, p.682.

[31] Cf. R. Purtill, "Foreknowlege and Fatalism", *Religious Studies*, 10, 1974, pp.323-324.

[32] Burrell, *Aquinas*, p.141.

[33] Aquinas, *S.C.G.* 1. 56-58. Cf. Pike, *Timelessness*, pp.124-126. Later I shall consider just how such knowledge might be possible.

[34] "the most perfect being will possess spiritual attributes in a state of pure actuality". Owen, *Christian Knowledge*, p.240. Cf. F.C. Schiller, *Humanism*, London: Macmillan, 1912, pp.217-218.

recent article Jule Gowen has persuasively argued that the states of consciousness of an eternal God could be logically ordered. Such logical ordering could cover not only his purely intra-mental life but also his knowledge and actions vis-a-vis the created order.[35] A logical order is a real order but has no necessary connection to temporality. Whilst temporally ordered events are also logically ordered there is no necessary reason why logically ordered events must be temporally ordered. The temporal succession characterisic of mental states as we know them is replaced in God by an atemporal logical ordering according to priority or entailment. I conclude that although the divine eternal consciousness may be phenomenally very different from our own it is not contradictory to suppose it to be a consciousness none the less.

2. A more congent argument against eternal personhood is directed against the concepts of non-temporal will and intention. Richard Sorabji finds this a major stumbling block:

> there is an objection to the idea of timeless agency, to which I, a last, can see no answer. For it is not clear what it can mean to speak of a **will** which does not exist at any time ... there must be some similarity to human will, if there is to be any point in using the world 'will' at all in application to God. And it is hard to see how something which existed at no times could begin to have the requisite similarity. The consequence, if a timeless God cannot will, is that he cannot act either.[36]

Likewise, Gale thinks an agent must be temporal:

> The necessity for a person to endure in time can also be seen from an analysis of what it is to be a rational agent. An agent performs intentional actions so as to bring about some goal or end. But to have a goal or end, the agent must have desires and values. But only a temporally

---

[35] J. Gowen, "God and Timelessness", *Sophia*, 26, 1987, pp.18-20.

[36] Sorabji, *Time*, p.257. Cf. Hepburn, "Transcendence", p.255; Kogan, *Averroes*, p.230.

incomplete being can have a desire or intention, since one cannot desire or intend what one already has.[37]

J.S. Morreall has developed the argument in fuller detail than others.[38] He breaks down the act of will into four steps:

(1) Entry into a situation with the recognition of doing something.
(2) Deliberation.
(3) A decision to perform an action.
(4) Actually performing the action.

Putting God in relation to the four steps comes out as follows:

(1) A timeless knower cannot **enter** into situations he already knows about.
(2) Timelessness excludes the possibility of deliberation, for there is nothing to be "considered".
(3) A "decision" of God's could not be the end of a deliberation, or the choice of what God desires most. God couldn't decide or will in the sense of "making up one's mind".[39]
(4) God causes by fiat without effort.

Morreall concludes that the differences between divine and human "willing" are too great to be subsumed under the one notion. We can't make any sense of an act of willing which does not occur before or at the same time as an event it is meant to bring about.

I have gone some way towards answering this objection towards the end of the last chapter, where I argued that a timeless being could simultaneously consider an infinity of possibles and will one as actual. Given that God does so will, such an act of will, which is the act of his essence, will express his whole nature, and being subject to no

---

[37] Gale, "Omniscience", p.333. Cf. W.E. Steinkraus, "Time and God", *Philosophical Quarterly* (India), 30, 1958, p.247.

[38] Morreall, *Talking*, pp.43-46.

[39] Cf. Hartshorne, *Divine Relativity*, p.118; Swinburne, *Coherence*, p.214; Ward, *Rational Theology*, p.75.

higher category will be absolutely immutable.[40] This however does not lead to Spinoza's conclusion: "Things could be produced by God in no other manner and in no other order than that in which they have been produced",[41] for this is to confuse absolute with conditional necessity. A real negative sense can be given to God's "decision" to create. In bringing into being **this** world God may be said to have "cut off" various logically possible alternatives. Such a decisive "cutting off", in terms of the action described in the previous chapter, can be conceived as non-temporal. Neither need it be granted that for every case of agent-action a course of "making up one's mind" need be involved. We often use "decide" simply to describe the implementation of an agent's intentions, I "decided" to work on this book today, but I was at no stage conscious of "having to make up my mind to do so".[42] In this sense of realizing-an-act further meaning can be given to non- temporal decision making.

Can positive meaning be given to the concept of intentionality outside of a temporal framework? It would seem so, provided the possibility of purely logically ordered states of mind is accepted. William P. Alston has made a consistent attempt to interpret theological language in terms of functionalism.[43] For his modified form of functionalism: "a functional concept of S (some mental state) is a concept of **law-like connections** in which S stands with other states and with outputs."[44] Such a definition is ideally suited to an analogical interpretation of the states of mind of a timeless being. On such a functionalist account there can never be a gap between the divine intention and the divine action, for a timeless omnipotent being cannot, like us, be impeded from realizing his intentions by his environment. In God, therefore, intention and action can only be logically dstinguished. Mann stresses this: "The concept of an instantaneous intention, whose objective is realized simultaneously

---

[40] Aquinas, *S.Th.* 1a. 19,7; *S.C.G.* 1.76., P.T. Geach, "God's Relation to the World", *Sophia*, 7, 1969, pp.1-9. The unconditional character of God's will is not a deficiency but a mark of sovereign freedom. Farrer, *Faith and Speculation*, p.117.

[41] Spinoza, *Ethics*, Proposition 33. Cf. Schleiermacher, Cf, 54.4.

[42] Cf. B.R. Reichenbach, "Omniscience and Deliberation", *International Journal for Philosophy of Religion*, 16, 1984, pp.231-232.

[43] W.P. Alston, "Functionalism and Theological Language", *American Philosophical Quarterly*, 22, 1985, pp.221-230.

[44] Alston, "Functionalism", p.225.

with its formulation, may tax one's credulity, but therea is no absurdity in the idea of a volition whose object is simultaneously realized."[45]

I believe this way of thinking about the divine mind confirms earlier work undertaken by Geach on the concept of will in Aquinas.[46] For Aquinas, as interpreted by Geach, will essentially consists, not in a peculiar quality of experience, but precisely in the peculiar sort of causality expressed by "knowingly give rise to". A voluntary action is the bringing to a fulfilment of a goal. "Trying" to bring something about is not a necessary condition for volition, as voluntary omissions show. If God knowingly brings about the existence of the world, then, on this account, we may say he "willed" the world's existence. If, by analogy with the above line of reasoning, we suddenly found that we could bring about, or even create, effects in our environment simultaneous with our thinking of these things as desirable states of affairs, we would surely conclude that in some (mysterious) way we were "willing" them into existence. This may only be a faint and inadequate picture of how God realizes his intentions, but enough has been said to illustrate that such talk about the divine mind is not dependent upon its temporality.

3. The final objection to be considered relates to the ability of a timeless being to enter into genuine interpersonal relations with other beings. The key question here is what meaning can be given to timeless reciprocation, can there be a non-successive response from God to the temporal approach of his creatures.

This problem has been felt sharply and expressed strongly by many non-classical theists. Gale comments: "A timeless being cannot interact with other agents, since it cannot be causally affected by what they do. It is no accident that those theists who conceived of God as timeless ... were careful in denying that anything in the world could affect Him."[47] Gollwitzer picks up a matter of religious signficance: "prayer in the real sense ... takes place in the form of `dialogue between two entities'; that is inseparable from it ..."[48] M.J.

---

[45] W.E. Mann, "Simplicity and Immutability in God", *International Philosophical Quarterly*, 23, 1983,p.270.

[46] P.T. Geach and G.E.M. Anscombe, *Three Philosophers*, Oxford: Basil Blackwell, 1961, pp.106- 107.

[47] Gale, "Omniscience", p.333.

[48] Gollwitzer, *Existence*, pp.167-168.

Heinecken goes so far as to say: "Some have said that God is timeless
... But ... eternal ideas cannot lift a finger to help anyone."[49] John
Kleinig is another to see a great problem here: "a timeless being is
static. It cannot change for change is temporal ... it would appear to
be a mark of imperfection were God not able to respond to different
sets of circumstances differently."[50] The list could go on.[51] I do not
intend to debate the point that God cannot respond to finite human
personages. I think that this much must be granted. I do however
wish to spend some time analysing the implications of this fact,
particularly against its metaphysical backgroud. First, however, I
think that it can be established that a timeless being can so act in time
to bring about effects equivalent to those he would bring about if he
were responding.

The argument that a timeless being could not respond, overlooks a
rejoinder as old as Origen: God might changelessley will, say, a
prayer, followed by an outcome "in response". Such a God would
not have to take action **after** the event.[52] Conceivably such a timeless
coordination could cover all the relations between God and finite
persons, and, phenomenologically, would be indistinguishable from
the response in time of a temporal deity.

Paul Helm has filled outpn the details required for such a model.[53]
Helm distinguishes between simple and complex intentions. B is a
complex thing to intend when B is some action the attempt to do which
is consequent upon the action of another. If God has complete
foreknowledge it is impossible that his intention to bring about a state
of affairs only arises **when** another state of affairs takes place. It is

[49] M.J. Heinecken, *Beginning and End of the World*, Philadelphia: Fortress,
1960, p.25.

[50] Kleinig, "Anthropomorphism", *Tyndale Paper*, 17, 1972, p.8.

[51] See, Jantzen, "Timelessness", p.574; Mason, "Worship", p.84; S. Ogden,
The Reality of God, London: S.C.M., 1967, p.105; Steinkraus, "Time", p.248; K.
Surin, "The Self Existence of God: Hartshorne and Classical Theism", *Sophia*, 21,
1982, pp.22-23; E. Stump, "Petitionary Prayer", *American Philosophical
Quarterly*, 16, 1979, pp.81-91; Wright, "Dialogues", p.452.

[52] Sorabji, *Time*, p.257.

[53] P. Helm, "Omnipotence and Change", *Philosophy*, 51, 1976, pp.454-461.
Cf. J.F.X. Knasis, "Aquinas: Prayer to An Immutable God", *New Scholasticism*,
57, 1983, pp.196-221., V. Morris, "Properties, Modalities and God",
Philosophical Review, 3, 1984, pp.46-47; Sturch, "Problem", pp.490-491.

not contradictory to suppose that God wills that B should not occur unless some state of affairs obtain **and** God wills B on account of his foreknowledge that this state of affairs will obtain. This does not introduce contingency into the will of God provided God has ordained the state of affairs sqin question. In this way, for example, God can be said to (timelessly) respond to the prayers of believers, which, if not offered, would receive no answer.[54]

A temporalistic theist may however feel that something is still trlacking, that the "pre-programmed" character of God's dealings with people smacks of a certain "quasi-deism" and does not meet the demand for genuine communion built into what we mean by personhood.[55] As the objection stands it has considerable force, and would indeed be persuasive if the sort of phenomena outlined above were descriptive of an exchange between finite persons. At this point it is necessary to make an excursus into Thomist metaphysics to explain how the relationship between God and creatures can be considered as superlatively personal.

D. The "Real Relation" Debate

In the previous chapter I emphasised that the act of creation presupposed nothing from the side of its effect, viz. the creature. The **sui generis** pure relation of absolute dependence of the creature upon God has important implications for this stage of our discussion.

In the *Summa Theologiae* la.l3.7. Aquinas sets out to answer the query, "whether names which imply relation to creatures are predicated of God temporally". For Aquinas the unique character of "relations" is that they do not signify something inherent in a subject but are in some sense an association between subjects.[56] In question thirteen article seven he distnguishes between three classes of relation.

The first class is called logical relations (**rationis relatio**) or relations according to reason (**secundum rationem**). Both terms in

---

[54] Cf. Gowen, "Timelessness", pp.22-23, who in response to Wolterstorff, "God Everlasting", pp.77-98 builds up a model of God's acting to bring about events subsequent to human decisions where neither the acting nor the plan of God to act occur in time.

[55] Cf. Hasker, "Intelligibility", p.183.

[56] Aquinas, *S.Th.* 1, 28, 1. All subsequent quotations are from *S.Th.* 1a. 13, 7 unless otherwise indicated.

a relation are logically related when the relation: "is in the idea only, as when mutual order or habitude can only be between things in the apprehension of reason." Logical relations are established by the mind and its understanding of the terms and are not due to the terms themselves. That is, the relation is in the apprehending mind. Aquinas gives as one example of this class the relation between genus and species. When two terms are related logically, nothing in the reality of the terms undergoes change since the relation is made in the mind.

The second class are known as "real relations". Aquinas{ says that these "are realities as regard both extremes, as when for instance a habitude exists between two things according to some reality that belongs to both ... (such as) quantity: as great and small ... and the same applies to relations consequent upon action and passion as motive power and the movable thing, father and son and the like." The relation is due to something in the reality of the terms themselves, and what establishes the relation is due to something they have in common, or brings about some change in the terms due to some causality.

A final class is known as "mixed relations". These are real in one term and logical in another. "Again, sometimes a relation in one extreme may be a reality, while in the other extreme it is an idea only: and this happens whenever two extremes are not in the same order." By "order" Aquinas means ontological order. An example of such a relation is that between creature and Creator, he says: "Since therefore God is outside the whole order of creation, and all creatures are ordered to Him, and not conversely, it is manifest that creatures are really related to God Himself: whereas in God there is no real relation to creatures, but a relation only in idea, in as much as creatures are referred to him."

This requires some explication. In the last chapter I have already stressed that to be a creature **is** to exist in a relation of absolute dependence upon God as ontological cause. On the creature side of the Creator-creature relation, creation as passively considered, the relation of creature to Creator is totally real. Since a creature is simply a being-related-to-God, rather than something which stands in relation to God, the real effect of the relation as far as the creature is concerned is the creature. No relation as real as this could occur between two creatures.[57] Creation is actively considered is only a logical relation. The divine power is God himself. When God creates he does nothing else than to be God. The being of creating is not posited in God as though it were God plus something else. This is so because when God creates no **new esse** (being) is produced. Creation, actively taken, is God and only God. It is not an accidental act. It does not add to God's being. Because there is no addition to his being, there is no new reality set up between God and what he makes out of nothing.[58] To put it another way, the act of creation could not possibly condition God, so as to place him in a real relation to the creature, because the creature does not exist prior to or outside of this action. Created being, **qua** created being, can bring nothing to the relationship because it does not exist independently of it. Thus in the Creator-creature relationship we find the deepest possible example of asymmetry and non-reciprocity. That God creates, and conserves, makes an absolute difference to the creature and no difference to God. This is not a mere corollary of the relationship of creation but its very essence.[59] At first glance such a metaphysics of creation may seem to be antithetical to all that is meant by a genuine personal relationship. Not a few theists have so argued. Charles Hartshorne is one of them: "If, then, God is wholly absolute, a term but never a subject of relations, it follows that God does not know, will or love us his creatures. At most we cn say only that we are known, willed and loved by him. Here all analogy fails ... does this strange combination of words mean anything? ... It is awareness that enables relations to make a difference to a thing. Merely being-known or being-loved is nothing to a thing."[60] From a Neo-Thomist perspective Norris Clarke says:

---

[57] Cf. K.L. Schmitz, "Weiss and Creation", *Review of Metaphysics*, 18, 1964, pp.160-169; Aquinas, *S.C.G.* 2, 18, 2; *S.Th.* 1. 45, 3.

[58] Aquinas, *De Potentia Dei* q 3 a 2; *S.Th.* 1.45, 3, *S.C.G.* 4. 11. etc.

[59] Geach, "Causality and Creation", pp.6-7, brings this out clearly. E(x) = there is an x,x = designation for an individual, A = some predicate. "God's creating an individual c would be expressed by a proposition of this sort: There is just one A; and God brought it about that E(x) (x is an A); and for no x did God bring it about that x is an A (i,.e. x is not presuppposed); and c is an A ... The part of this proposition that expresses the creative act (namely the first three conjuncts) does not mention, and explicitly denies that in creating God acted upon any individual."

[60] Hartshorne, *Divine Relativity*, pp.16-17. Cf. Ogden, *Reality*, p.51.

In the past Thomistic metaphysics seem to have been content for the most part to assert and defend the absolute immutability of God and to relegate all change and diversity on the side of the creature. But they have not gone on to explain how He can enter into a truly interpersonal dialogue with creatured persons, how His loving of them and their response to Him in the particular contingent ways which are proper to a free exchange between persons can truly make a difference to Him, how He is not the completely impassive, indifferent metaphysical iceberg, or at least one-way unreceptive Giver, to whom my loving or not loving, my salvation or damnation, make no difference whatsoever, as Hartshorne and other process philosophers have accused him of being. It does seem to me that they have a legitimate grievance against the way Thomists have handled, or failed to handle, this problem.[61]

The next logical step on from the above "observation" is to conclude that **personal** religion depends upon God being temporal. Barth has put this clearly:

As the eternal One He is present personally at every point of our time. As the eternal One it is He who surrounds our time and rules it will all that it contains. How can He be and do all this as the eternal One He does not Himself have His own time ... everything depends upon whether God's temporality is the simple truth which cannot be attached from any quarter because it has its basis in God Himself, which is not then a mere appearance, a bubble constructed by human feeling or thought.[62]

---

[61] W. Norris Clarke, "A New Look at the Immutability of God", in *God Knowable and Unknowable*, R.J. Roth (ed), N.Y.: Fordham University Press, 1973, p.44 cited in B.L. Whitney, "Divine Immutability in Process Philosophy and Contemporary Thomism", *Horizons*, 7, 1980, p.54. Whitney can be consulted for many similar statements.

[62] Barth, *CD*, II/1 pp.613, 620. Cf. E.S. Brightman, "A Temporalist View of God", *Journal of Religion*, 12, 1932, pp.544-555; C. Hartshorne, "The Dipolar

The preceding line of reasoning is, I believe, mistaken. The first thing to note is that the denial of a "real relation" between God and the created order is not to deny a relation **simpliciter.** What is denied is that creation changes God in any way. If no "real relation" simply meant "no relation" then we could not say that God created at all.[63] The difference between the logical relation of God to creatures and all other logical relations, such as between a thing known and a knower, is that a **real** change is effected in the other term of the relation without here having to be any change in the logical term. Such a unique logical relation is only possible because God alone is pure act, but it does mean that there is an "actual relation" to the second term because the second term is really related to the first.[64] David Burrell wants to call the relation of God to creatures an "intentional relation"[65] so as to stress the free action of God in creating the world. This is acceptable providing we keep in mind what was said about the absolutely unconditional freedom of God in the previous chapter and the relationship between intention and action in God in the earlier part of this one. If these previous postulates are coherent, so is the concept of a timeless immutable actual personal relationship of God to creatures.

The critic however may not be persuaded. We are still lacking, he says, that responsiveness needed to generate a true personal relationship. No matter how freely and lovingly God created us, if we cannot affect him the relationship is not genuinely personal. This argument fails because it wants to set the bounds of personhood at what is applicable to human relationships. Shutte, from a different angle, shows how this is inadequate:

> According to Macmurray it is the positive intention of the Other[66] that enables the agent to develop his own power of

---

Conception of Deity", *Review of Metaphysics*, 21, 1967, pp.274-275; Matthews, *God in Christian Thought*, p.257; McGilvary, "Experience", p.144-145; Sutherland, "God, Time and Eternity", p.107.

[63] Cf. T. Weinandy, "Aquinas and the Incarnational Act: `Become' as a Mixed Relation", *Doctor Communis*, 32, n.d., pp.28-29.

[64] Weinandy, "Incarnational Act", pp.86-87.

[65] Burrell, *Aquinas*, p.86.

[66] By "Other" Macmurray means another self we encounter, the capital does not denote divinity. See his *Persons in Relation*, N. Y.: Harper, 1961.

free action. The problem about being given freedom can thus be seen to be related to the question of the acquisition of a positive intention. How does one in fact acquire a positive intention? From another who already has it of course. And from whom does he acquire it? If positive intentions are to exist at all then someone somewhere at some time must have a positive intention that was not acquired but, as it were, self generated. Such a notion is that of a person who does not depend on others for his personhood. A totally independent person is an infinite one.[67]

We have arrived at the concept of perfect self- actualised personhood, an idea fully compatible with the notion of God as **totum simul existens.**

It is possible to go beyond this point and affirm that only as such a being can God be maximally related to his creatures. As invariable **totum simul existens,** he is in relation to the creature all that he could ever be, and it is all that it is by his pure act which communicates to it **esse.** All it has derives from him and all he is is constantly present to it. Only a being who is not in time can be so essentially present in a relationship of undiluted super-generosity. J.F. Anderson stresses this side of things:

> God's causal presence in things ... is He Himself, in Person, immediately ... Filling all things, containing all things creatively. His presence in them is His gift to them of their total being ... In every being that which is innermost is the act whereby it exists ... God is the **esse** of all things (causally), since every being exists by His **esse** alone ... Now it is as the supreme Act of existing that God is omnipresent and operative everywhere by His creative efficacy. Intimately present to the very act of being, from which the actions of each thing flow, God supports all things, animates them from within, moves them to their operations, `applies' them to their acts, so that they are nothing and do nothing except by Him,

---

[67] A. Shutte, "Indwelling, Intersubjectivity and God", *Scottish Journal of Theology*, 32, 1979, p.215.

precisely because their total being entitative as well as operative is given to them, created in them, immediately by Him.[68]

God is more intimately present to things than they are to themselves for **he** sustains them at their ontological root.[69] Thomas Weinandy puts the matter crisply from a comparative angle: "Even Pantheism falls short of such a close relations hip, for in Pantheism God is never fully present as he is in himself, by his essence, but by some lesser emanation or divine spark of his being."[70] I conclude these sections on the nature of the relationship between the eternal and the personal by noting that not only do the two concepts, as discussed, seem compatible, but that, only if God is atemporal fulness of life, can personhood conceivably be given its most eminent meaning. As H.P. Owen says: "the most perfect case of love, and so (if love is the perfection of the will) the most perfect case of willing, would be one in which the lover expressed his whole self toward the object of his love in one necessary and eternal act."[71]

E. Timelessness and Incarnation

The relationship between the timelessness of God and human temporality is raised in its sharpest form by the Christian doctrie of the Incarnation. One must not only grapple with the paradoxical confession that "God truly **is** man, that it is truly **God** who is man, and that it is truly **man** that God is",[72] but try to bring together in a consistent manner the seemingly incompatible predicates of eternity

---

[68] Anderson, "Ubiquity", pp.145, 153, 157, 158. Cf. Rock, "Divine Causality", pp. 35, 39; G. Marcel, "God and Causality", in *Religion and Culture*, W. Leibrech (ed), N.Y.: Harper, 1959, p.211; Redlow, "St. Thomas", pp.16ff.

[69] Cf. Mascall, *Openness*, p.168.

[70] Weinandy, "Incarnational Act", p.27. It is recognised that some of the above comments seem to raise the specture of determinism. A subsequent chapter shall consider this matter in detail.

[71] Owen, *Christian Knowledge*, p.245.

[72] Weinandy, "Incarnational Act", p.16. The exposition below is a self-conscious attempt to remain within the framework of the Chalcedonian Creed. See, J. Stevenson (ed), *Creeds, Councils and Controversies*, London: S.P.C.K., 1966, p.337.

and temporality in one subject. The Incarnation occupies a position of epistemic centrality in classical Christian theism. Brian Hebblethwaite reminds us of this: "Farrer insists that, far from our concept of God ruling out the possibility of incarnation, it is the doctrine of the Incarnation that defines the Christian concept of God. On this reckoning, God **must** be such as to be able, without ceasing to be God, to express himself through a human life."[73] If the time-eternity problem is found to be intractable at the point of the

Incarnation, the whole system of classical Christian theism, on its own terms, is open to dissolution. Given the importance of the question it is therefore rather surprising to find that so little work seems to have been devoted to the matter at hand. In dealing with the subject I will first review a number of unsatisfactory preferred "solutions" before sketching a model whose elements seem to provide us with a reasonable answer.

One response to the problem is to "cut the Gordian knot". This can be done from two sides. On one side is a body of theists who believe that, since the doctrine of the Incarnation is incompatible with the timelessness of God, the latter must b e discarded. The most important voice here is Barth's: "No contradiction or diminution of deity takes place, but the true and fullest power of deity is displayed, in the fact that it has such power over itself and its creature that it can become one with it without detriment to itself. This is just what takes place in Jesus Christ. His name is the refutation of a God who is only timeless."[74] The logical concern here is that it seems contradictory to suppose that one and the same person can be finite and historically conditioned **and** eternal and unconditional. **Ergo,** the constraints of Hellenistic metaphysics must be rejected.[75] The other response is of course not to reject the timelessness of God but to abandon the

---

[73] B. Hebblethwaite, "The Propriety of the Doctrine of the Incarnation as a Way of Interpreting Christ", *Scottish Journal of Theology*, 33, 1980, p.213. Cf. L. Hodgson, "The Incarnation", in A.E.J. Rawlinson, *Essays*, p.401; R.W. Leigh, "Jesus: the one-natured God-man", *Christian Scholar's Review*, 11, 1982, pp.136-137; Pannenberg, "Appropriation", pp.110,114.

[74] Barth, *CD,* II/1. p.616.

[75] R. Niebuhr, *The Nature and Destiny of Man*, London: Nisbet, vol 2, 1943, pp.62-63; A.D. Smith, "God's Death", *Theology*, 80, 1977, p.265. Cf. T. Pierce, "Spatio-Temporal Relations in Divine Inter- actions", *Scottish Journal of Theology*, 35, 1982, p.4.

Incarnation. Tomkinson counsels such a course: "If an analysis of the received concept of God, i.e. as supreme being, leads us to a conclusion which seems at odds with those of revelation, the former may claim the credentials of reason, the analysis being open to inspection by all concerned. If and insofar as the supporting reasoning seems cogent it has a claim upon us logically prior to that of the interpretation of some special experience."[76] It will be argued below that neither of these responses is necessary, for the timelessness of God is not logically icnommensurate with the Incarnation.

A second solution suggested is to leave the matter a mystery or a paradox. Kierkegaard seemed to have handled the matter in that way: "the question is if one will give assent to God's having come into being, by which God's eternal essence is inflicted in the dialectical determinations of becoming."[77] More explicitly, Swinburne, in his 1965 paper, seems to find some virtue in the conundrum: "If our God is a temporal one, his omnipotence is more a mystery than his incarnation; but if God is timeless the converse holds. If we find mysterious what the New Testament authors and the Fathers found mysterious this suggests that their God is the same as our God. The doctrine of the timelessness of God preserves the mystery in the right place."[78] An appeal to enigma however is not convincing for we are not just faced with a riddle but an apparent contradiction.

A third way forward is to see the properties of time and eternity coming together in some way. On the one hand this could mean the "intemporation" of the divine nature.[79] According to this conception, through the Incarnation, time becomes a predicate of God. There is some sort of free assumption of time by God as the mode of his own determination.[80] A corollary of this would seem to be that the whole of the divine life, at least of the Son, becomes temporal. G.D. Yarnold takes such a proposition seriously: "The span of temporality

---

[76] Tomkinson, "Atemporality", p.187.

[77] S. Kierkegaard, *Philosophical Fragments*, tr. D.F.Swenson, Princeton: Princeton University Press, 1936, p.72.

[78] Swinburne, "Timelessness 2", p.486.

[79] E. Brunner, "The Christian Understanding of Time", *Scottish Journal of Theology*, 4, 1951, p.8.

[80] A. Darlap, "Time", in *Sacramentuam Mundi*, K. Rahner (ed), London: Burns and Oates, 1970, vol 6, p.258; K. Rahner, *Theological Investigations*, Baltimore: Helicon, vol 4, 1966, pp.113-114.

between the earthly events of conception and Ascension is eternally purposed, eternally experienced, even eternally remembered; because in the `eternal now' will, and act, and knowledge belong together."[81] I have already argued in an earlier chapter that all attempts to bring together time and eternity in some all embracing synthesis lead to intolerable contradictions.[82] I wish only to restate that position here: If God is timeless he cannot also be temporal. On the other side some have tried not to temporalize the divine nature but to "eternalize" the human nature. Stump and Kretzmann take up this alternative:

> The divine nature of the second person of the Trinity, like the divine nature of either of the other persons of the Trinity cannot become temporal: nor could the second person acquire a human nature he does not eternally have. Instead the second person eternally has two natures; and at some temporal instants, all of which are ET- simultaneous both these natures in their entirety, the human nature of the second person has been temporally actual. At those times and only in that nature the second person participates in temporal events.[83]

This attempt faces many difficulties. It clearly violates the authors' stated desire to remain within the bounds of classical orthodoxy because it introduces into the Trinitarian relations a differentiation other than that of origin. More importantly for our discussion, can we make sense of an "eternal human nature"? Just how is this eternal human nature related to the eternal divine nature of the Son of God, viz. how do we characterize an eternal hypostatic union? How is it that the timeless human nature "has been temporally actual" without undergoing that process of becoming temporal which is explicitly denied of a divine person? If it is **only** in the eternal-and-temporal human nature that the second person participates in temporal events

---

[81] Yarnold, *Moving Image*, p.218.

[82] I do not see how any sense can be made of a statement like the following. "It is really, I suggest, a timeless truth about God that human nature, and the human experience of weakness and sleep and ignorance, are somehow included in His whole divine life." C.S. Lewis, *Mere Christianity*, London: Collins, 1952, p.145.

[83] Stump-Kretzmann, "Eternity", p.453.

have we an act of Incarnation at all? Altogether the picture is very puzzling.

Apparently unknown to Stump and Kretzmann, their model has a number of precursors.[84] The most important of these is the Lutheran doctrine of the communication of attributes (**communicatio idiomatum**).[85] According to this view whatever can be said about one of the natures of Christ can be said of the other. Bonhoeffer represents such a view:

> the particular characteristics of each individual nature can also be predicated of the particular characteristics of the other ... the predicates of the eternal God may and must also be expressed of the human ... The Incarnation remains, even within the Trinity, eternal.[86]

Calvin, and Reformed thought after him, took up a different position. He comments: "the divinity was so conjoined and united with the humanity, that the entire properties of each nature remain entire, and yet the two natures constitute only one Christ."[87] The most important Calvinist argument against the Lutheran **communicatio** was pithily expressed in the phrase **finitum non capax infiniti**, "the finite cannot receive the infinite". The divinization of the humanity implied by the **communicatio** would destroy the integrity of the human nature: a human nature possessing the properties of deity would no longer be human at all. If the human nature of Christ is eternal it becomes impossible to make sense of the "becoming" involved in the Incarnation. The Incarnation becomes a state of being without beginning and not an act of God in time at all. According to the Reformed such a reciprocal relation between the Creator and the creature implied by the **communicatio** not only suggests an unacceptable "fusing" of natures but also places God and his creature,

---

[84] See, H.A. Wolfson, *The Philosophy of the Church Fathers, vol 1: Faith, Trinity, Incarnation*, Cambridge Mass: Harvard University Press, 1970, pp.393, 453 for Patristic examples.

[85] For Luther see Leigh, "God-man", p.126.

[86] D. Bonhoeffer, *Christology*, tr. J. Bowden, London: Collins, 1966, pp.93, 97.

[87] J. Calvin, *Institutes of the Christian Religion*, 2. 14, 1, Macdill: Macdonald, n.d.; p.249.

the unconditional and the conditional, on the same level. For all of these reasons there came into being the doctrine known as the **Extra Calvinisticum**. The eternal Word is not only flesh, but he also is and continues to be what he is in himself. He also exists without (**extra**) the flesh. Nothing peculiar of either of the two natures in Christ is communicated to the other, though the diverse properties may be pred icated of the one Person. There is a real distinction, though not a separation, between the **logos asarkos** ("Word without flesh") and the **logos ensarkos** ("Word in the flesh"). This in no way denies an intimate and constant union of the two natures in Christ.[88] I consider that the above objections to the concept of a ubiquitous human nature are conclusive, and that any way forward will have to follow the broad lines of the Reformed position. Before considering such a positive proposal there is one further model to be considered: the way of kenosis.

The word "kenosis" is from the Greek very **kenoo** meaning "to empty". The verb is used in a description of the Incarnation contained in the seventh verse of the second chapter of St. Paul's letter to the Philippians. Kenotic theories take on var ious forms, but they all share the idea that in becoming a man the second Person of the Trinity laid aside his distinctively divine attributes and lived for a period on earth within the limitations of humanity.[89] The various older forms of kenotic doctrine attempted to hold to the classical doctrine of an immutable God and the received understanding of the Trinitarian relations, **and** tried to make sense of a real relinquishment of the personal properties of divinity. In these forms kenotic theo ries were subject to numerous cogent criticisms. In particular they were incompatible with the model of deity with which they began. Cupitt states the issue clearly: "since the divine attributes belong to God not contingently but analytically it is logically impossible or the deity to

---

[88] On the matters discussed above see Barth, *CD*, I/2, pp.163-170; Berkhof, *Systematic Theology*, pp.323- 326; G.C. Berkouwer, *The Person of Christ*, tr. J. Vriend, Grand Rapids: Eerdmans, 1954, pp.272-283; Hebblethwaite, "Propriety", p.218.

[89] On the history and content of Kenoticism see, J. M. Laporte, "Kenosis: Old and New", *The Ecumenist*, 12, 1974, pp.17-21; G. MacGregor, "The Kenosis", *Anglican Theological Review*, 45, 1963, pp.73-83; J. Macquarrie "Kenoticism Reconsidered", *Theology*, 77, 1974, pp.115- 124; L. Richard, "Kenotic Christology in a New Perspective", *Eglise et Theolgie*, 7, 1976, pp.5-39.

190

doff one like a superfluous piece of clothing."[90] Most specifically, it is a logical contradiction to consider that God could lay aside the attribute of eternity, which is the simultaneous possession of the whole of his life, and take it up again.[91] The most recent kenotic theories realize that these problems are insuperable and seek to circumvent them by reinterpreting the nature of the Godhead in such a way that kenosis is a feature of the eternal movement of God's being. John Macquarrie puts the issue clearly: "For an Absolute who retained the fulness of being within himself might be metaphysically ultimate but could hardly be God in any religious sense. He is God and evokes worship because he comes out from himself and submits himself to the self-limitation that goes along with creative and redemptive love."[92] Self- evidently, what we have here is an abandonment of "perfect being theology" as it has usually been practiced by Christian theologians. A being other than the God of classical theism is considered to have become incarnate in Jesus Christ, on these terms kenoticism is not an option for the working principles of this exercise.[93] A first step towards grasping how the one person can be both temporal and eternal is to understand the character of the union between the divine and human natures in Christ. It is vital to understand that, according to Chalcedonian (orthodox) Christology, whereas there are two natures in Christ there is only one person. This is held to be possible because the human nature of Christ does not possess a self- subsisting personal centre. Leontius of Byzantium[94] was the first to express this doctrine of the **enhypostasia**. Whilst according to the Aristotelian background of thought, a human nature without a personal subsistence (hypostasis) would be a pure abstraction, Leontius argued that a nature can exist

[90] D. Cupitt, "The Christ of Christendom", in *The Myth of God Incarnate*, J. Hick (ed), Philadelphia: Westminster, 1988, p.137.

[91] Cf. D. Baillie, "God Was in Christ", London: Faber, 1961, p.98; T.V. Morris, *The Logic of God Incarnate*, Ithaca: Cornell University Press, 1986, pp.60-61. F. Weston, *The One Christ*, London: Longmans, Green, 1907, pp.119-123.

[92] Macquarrie, "Kenoticism", p.124.

[93] A full reply, which is not practical here, would require a defence of the Anselmian definition of God as "greatest conceivable being".

[94] c.485-543 A.D., Details in H.M. Relton, *A Study in Christology*, London: S.P.C.K., 1917, pp.69-83.

without an independent hypostasis if it possess a hypostasis in virtue of its inherence in a subject. There is a clear logical distinction between the abstraction of a nature without an hypostasis and a nature being an hypostasis. The **enhypostasia** doctrine claims that the hypostasis of the human nature is received from the eternal Word in the act of Incarnation. By itself Jesus' humanity would not only be impersonal in the modern sense of lacking self- conscious personality, but taken by itself Jesus' human being would be non-existent. Hence, it can be conceived by itself only by abstracting from the actual reality of Jesus' existence. In his concrete reality, the man Jesus has the ground of his existence (his hypostasis) not in himself as man but "in" the Logos. The creation of the hypostatised human nature and it's unification with the Logos are one and the same event.[95] Considered passively therefore, from the side of humanity, the personalized human nature becomes absolutely in the act of Incarnation through its union with the Logos. This sort of becoming, as I have argued in a number of places earlier, does not require its creative agent to be in time. That is, this sort of non-sequential becoming (from "non- existent hypostasis" to the enhypostatic state) does not enquire that the assuming power of the Logos, the causal act which brought this to be, be placed in a temporal series. The event is to be subsumed under the atemporal causation discussed in the last chapter.[96] It is true however that the Logos "owns" this particular human nature in a way in which he does no other. The enhypostatic event is not just a becoming in a human nature but the means by which the Logos acquires a new nature by union. Aquinas says:

> Whatever adheres to a person is united to it in person whether it belongs to its nature or not. Hence, if the

---

[95] Cf. W. Pannenberg, *Jesus - God and Man*, tr. L.L. Wilckens and D.A. Priebe, Philadelphia: Westminster, 1968, p.338.

[96] It might perhaps be thought that the sort of origin attributed to the humanity of Jesus is incompatible with what we normally mean by a human being. However, providing that Christ possesses a real human hypostasis, with the properties we usually predicate of an existing human nature, the manner of the coming into being of the humanity is quite irrelevant to its status. See H. McCabe and M. Wiles, "The Incarnation: An Exchange", *New Blackfriars*, 58, 1977, pp.550-553; Morris, *Logic*, Chapter 2, W.L. Walker, *The Spirit and the Incarnation*, Edinburgh: T. and T. Clarke, 1901, p.258.

human nature is not united to God the Word, it is in no ways united to him; and thus belief in the Incarnation is altogether done away with ... Therefore, in as much as the Word has a human nature united to him, which does not belong to his divine nature, it follows that the union takes place in the person of the Word ...[97]

If the Logos is personally united to the human nature then the Logos must have a new form of existing, viz. as a man.[98] The one Person of the Logos exists as both God and man. How though is it possible for the Logos to subsist in a human nature without undergoing the sort of substantial change tht would take place in time? To answer this we must recall what has already been said earlier about the maximal personhood of God as pure act and the ontological status of mixed relations. Weinandy is worth quoting at length:

while a human person is in potency (has potential) to become further relational, divine persons are fully relational, fully actualized relations, fully personal, since they relationally are the immutable and full actualized nature of God as **actus purus** ... Because of this when God in the Trinity of Persons establishes relations outside himself, he is able to do so not by mediating acts which involve change, but by relating the other person to himself as he is. The Persons of the Trinity being fully actualized relations contain no potency which needs to be actualised or overcome through new actions in order to overcome new relations. What needs to be overcome is man's potential to be related ... The Logos being a fully actualized subsistent relation does not have to overcome some potential in order to become man and subsist as man. He does not ... have to change his immutable being or newly express it as incarnational. The Logos being a fully actualized subsistent relation has no relational potency and thus has no need of new mediating actions on his part in order for him to establish an incarnational relation. The

---

[97] Aquinas, *S.C.G.* 3, 2, 2.

[98] This is not equivalent to the Logos acquiring new personal being because the inherence of the human nature is in the Person of the Logos, this is one- sided.

> potency lies in the humanity. It must be related and united to the Logos in such a way that the effect in the humanity is nothing other than the Logos subsisting in it as man ...⁹⁹

This is a thorough-going explanation, in Thomist terms, of how the Logos can become a man without change. As such it no more imputes temporality of the subsistent relation of the Logos to the human nature than does the relation of Creator to creature we saw previously. It is for these reasons that the incarnation can be understood as another example of Aquinas' "mixed relation"; in his own words:

> Now to be man belongs to God by reason of union, which is a relation. And hence to be man is newly predicated of God without any change in him, but by a change in the human nature, which is assumed to a divine person. And hence when it is said 'God was made man' we understand no change on the part of God, but only on the part of the human nature.¹⁰⁰

The real relation of the humanity to the Logos, the created relational effect, is the pattern of the Word in its union with the humanity. The relation of the Logos to the humanity is logical. That is to say, there is an actual relation of the Logos to the human nature but not such that the Logos is changed. The Logos is Incarnate as man not by any substantial change but being the Logos as the Logos in a particular way to a particular (assumed) human nature. Since none of this involves a change in the ontology of the Logos it removes any implication, according to a relational view of time, that the Logos must abandon his eternity in becoming man. It is precisely because he is fully realized being, **totum simul existens**, that he is able to will from all eternty to take to himself a temporal nature at a point in time, and to take up this nature, all without change. As the real term of the relation, the human nature subsists in its temporality in the Person of

---

⁹⁹ T.G. Weinandy, *The Immutability and Impassibility of God with reference to the Doctrine of the Incarnation*, unpublished Ph.D. thesis, University of London, 1976, pp.219ff, ctied in E.L. Mascall, *Whatever Happened to the Human Mind*, London: S.P.C.K., 1980, pp.79-80.

¹⁰⁰ Aquinas, *S.Th.* 3.16, ad 2.

the Logos; but as the logical term of the relation, the Logos remains timeless.

I conclude that the eternity of God is not only compatible with the doctrine of the Incarnation, but, in terms of the discussion above, is both required and entailed by it. Whilst much of what has been said above may seem enigmatic and not to accord with our ordinary way of thinking and speaking this should hardly be a cause for alarm, for the metaphysical properties of an eternal being are unlikely to accord with anything we are familiar with.

F. Summary and Conclusion

The stated intention of this chapter was to demonstrate that there exists no essential incompatibility between the concepts of personal being and timeless eternity as applied to the one individual. This objective was an important one, for excepting it could be realized, the whole structure of classical Christian theism, and not just the notion of the divine eternity as part of it, stood under threat. I believe it has been established that an eternal being may meaningfully be said to be conscious, and conative, even though these terms have to be modified somewhat in their meaning to be truly predicated of the divine mind. Reciprocity, however, was found to be incompatible with timelessness. This was taken not to contradict the claim about eternal personhood but to enhance it, for only a being which possesses all of its life at once could conceivably be a fully actualized person. In analysing in some detail the Creator-creature relationship, extensive use was made of the Thomist doctrine of relations. Whereas an unconditioned deity cannot be changed by its relations to finite persons, this in no way detracts from the meaningfulness of a relation constituted by a change, of an absolute nature, on the side of the creature. In this way it is possible to meaningfully affirm a personal non-temporal relation of God to humanity. These principles were not in any way vitiated by a discussion of the difficult problem of the Incarnation.   Indeed the two-natures doctrine, in its strict Chalcedonian form, would seem to **require** a totally realized being, a **totum simul**, for only such a being could conceivably become man without a change in his Godhead. I conclude that the classical doctrine of the divine eternity has passed one of its most severe tests. Other difficulties remain however, especially those to do with the concept of "foreknowledge". To these we must is Godhead. I conclude that the classical doctrine of the divine eternity has passed one of its most severe tests. Other difficulties remain however, especially those to do with concept of "foreknowledge". To these we must now turn.

CHAPTER SEVEN

THE PROBLEM OF FOREKNOWLEDGE

In the second chapter I categorised the time-eternity relation as a specific example of what has been termed the two-worlds problem", the difficulty of bringing together in some meaningful way two ontologically separate and even antithetical orders of reality. Subsequently I distinguished between two poles of the problem as it confronts my argument, a "vertical" dimension, namely the task of relating the apparent opposites of timelessness and time, and a "horizontal" dimension, the problem of how God can be related to a non-existent past and future. In the last two chapters I have tackled the "vertical" aspect in terms of the concept of a creation **ex nihilo**. In the next two chapters I hope to put these ideas to work with respect to the "horizontal" aspect of the time-eternity relationsip. I have chosen to do this in the context of discussing the question of the divine foreknowledge. This seems appropriate because, from Boethius onwards, one of the strongest motives amongst classical theists for maintaining the doctrine of the divine eternity has been its apparent ability to explain how knowledge of the future is possible.

A. The Problem of the Future

In the third chapter of this book I outlined and defended the theory of absolute becoming according to which only the present is real and both the past and the future are non- existent. Accepting this tensed view of reality immediately makes the concept of foreknowledge, knowledge of the future, highly problematical.

The difficulty has long been recognised. Anselm mentions it: For what is able not to be cannot at all with certainty be inferred to be ... what is able to happen in the future cannot be foreknown, and also what is foreknown is not able note to happen in the future."[1] There would appear to be a genuine ontological barrier to future knowledge, it is simply absurd to suppose that God can know something which is

---

[1] Anselm, *De Casu Diaboli*, 21., in Hopkins and Richardson, *Anselm*, vol 2, p.166.

no. As Geach says: "The truth is that the future is not for **anybody** to see; `seeing the future' is a self-contradictory action."[2] Neither we nor God can experience events before they happen since before they happen they literally are not.[3] This account of course not only presupposes that the 4- dimensional view of reality is false, but that the future is open and undetermined.[4] The next step is to push the objection against the doctrine of divine foreknowledge. The process philosopher Lewis Ford is highly critical: "God knows everything, everything actual as actual and everything possible as possibe. We simply deny that he knows the possible as actual. Classical theism has always recognized that God cannot know contradictions ... To know the future, that which is still indeterminate ... as if it were already fully determinate, excluding all alternatives is to know A as non-A, a contradiction."[5]

An opponent of classical theism may seem to be at an advantage here, for he can appeal to a broad based philosophical framework to support his position on the unknowability of the future. A good deal of work has been done on the logical status of future contingents and propositions about the future.[6] Many contemporary philosophers would want to deny that the law of excluded middle has universal application, that is, a proposition can be "neither true nor false" (or not determinately true or false), and can change its truth value from being neither true nor false to being true, or false. This conviction receives

---

[2] P.T.Geach, "The Future", *New Blackfriars*, 1973, p.209. Cf. *Providence and Evil*, Cambridge: Cambridge University Press, pp.56-58.

[3] See, N.F.S. Ferre, *The Christian Understanding of God*, N.Y.: Harper, 1951, pp.93-94; Hebblethwaite, "Predestination", p.438.

[4] See, Laird, *Theism*, p. 169; J.Ward, *The Realm of Ends*, Cambridge: Cambridge University Press, 1912, p.11., Whitrow, *Natural Philosophy*, p.295.

[5]Ford, "Eternity and Temporality", pp.118-119. Cf. R.H. Ayers, "A Viable Theodicy For Christian Apologetics", *Modern Schoolman*, 52, 1975, p.395; H.M. Relton, *Studies in Christian Doctrine*, London: Macmillan, 1960, pp.24-25; Ward, *Rational Theology*, pp.130-134.

[6] For an interesting review of the medieval discussions see C. Normore, "Future Contingents", in *The Cambridge History of Later Medieval Philosphy*, N. Kretzmann, J. Pinborg, A. Kenny (eds), Cambridge: Cambridge University Press, 1982, pp.358-381.

different expressions, all of which however logically exclude the possibility of a real knowledge of definite future particulars.[7]

Considerations of this kind can be tied to what is known as the "Generality of Predictions Thesis". If the future is open then it is not possible successfully to identify future individuals. There will always be a genuine doubt that there will exist a referent who will correspond to any singular identifying expression for any future indiviual we might like to formulate. To give a name **for** a future individual is not to give the name **of** such an individual. Statements about future individuals are irreducibly general.[8]

It is hardly surprising therefore that theists influenced by the A-theory of time and the matters mentioned above should deny foreknowledge to God in the classical sense. If God can deny foreknowledge to God in the classical sense. If God can know at all this will have to be in a very attenuated sense, rather than speaking of **foreknowledge** it is more accurate to speak about God's usually accurate **predictions** of what will come to pass.[9] Different philosophers have tried to avoid the implications of the above line of thought in a variety of ways. I wish now to look at these alternatives to the classical position in order to demonstrate that if foreknowledge is possible at all it will have to be comprehended in terms of some type of eternal simultaneity.

---

[7] See, for example, G.E.M. Anscombe, "Aristotle and the Sea Battle", *Mind*, 55, 1956, pp.1-15; Baelz, *Providence*, pp.123-124; Broad, *Scientific Thought*, pp.69ff; Gale, *Language*, chapter 8; C. Hartshorne, "The Meaning of 'Is Going to Be'", *Mind*, 74, 1965, 46-58; M.J. Lowe, "Aristotle on the Sea Battle: A Clarification", *Analysis*, 40, 1980, pp.55-59; McCall, "Temporal Flux", pp.273-276; J. Runzo, "Omniscience and Freedom for Evil", *International Journal for Philosophy of Religion*, 12, 1981, pp.131-147; R. Taylor, "The Problem of Future Contingency", *Philosophical Review*, 66, 1957, pp.1-28.

[8] For different forms of this thesis see Broad, *Scientific Thought*, pp. 74ff; Gale, *Language*, chapter 9; W. Godfrey- Smith, "The Generality of Predictions", *American Philosophical Quarterly*, 15, 1978, pp.15-25; G. Ryle, *Dilemmas*, Cambridge: Cambridge University Press, 1954, pp.15-35.

[9] See, Jantzen, *God's World*, pp.65-66; J.R. Lucas, *The Freedom of the Will*, Oxford: Oxford University Press, 1971, chapter 14; A.N. Prior, "The Formalities of Omniscience", *Philosophy*, 59, 1962, pp.124-129, Swinburne, *Coherence*, chapter 10.

1. In outlining some of the logical problems concerning future knowledge Peter Geach has, in a number of articles, suggested that God's control over the future can be secured in dependently of foreknowledge.[10] The idea is a simple one:

> God is almighty: God cannot be thwarted, or taken by surprise, or driven to improvisations, by the perverse misdeeds of his creatures. But this does not mean that creatures have not a real say in the future of the world ... Only God is bound to win, and none the less if he announces some of his moves in advance. If I were playing chess against Bobby Fischer, he might very well in advance announce not only that he would beat me but that he would deliver mate wih a certain pawn; and I am sure he would not need to invent new strategy to do whatever he wills; so here is no doubt that he will win, and he can even tell us how ... On the present view God's knowledge of the future comes solely from, indeed consists in, his perfect control over the future.[11]

Although Geach does not mention it the chess-master strategy ties in with the argument known as foreknowledge by familiarity. God knows our future moves because of his intimate understanding of ourselves as persons, and this cannot endanger our freedom.[12]

The strategy fails for a number of reasons. No matter how well we, or God, know free human persons it is always logically possible for them to act out of character. **Certain** knowledge of the future by means of familiarity is therefore ruled out.[13] In a nuclear age even the

---

[10] Geach, "The Future", p. 215, *Providence and Evil*, p.58. Cf. Hebblethwaite, "Predestination", p.443; R.S. Luhmann, "The Concept of God: Some Philosophical Considerations", *The Evangelical Quarterly*, 54, 1982, p.101. Apparently unknown to Geach the model he suggests is found in W.R. Matthews, *God in Christian Thought and Experience*, London: Nisbet, 1930, p.243.

[11] Geach, "The Future", p.215.

[12] Augustine, *De Libero Arbitrio*, 3. 4, 10-11; Schleiermacher, *CF*, 55.3.

[13] See, H. Bergson, *Time and Free Will*, tr. F.L. Pogson, London: George Allen and Unwin, 1921, pp.183-188; A. Kenny, *The God of the Philosophers*, Oxford: Clarendon, 1979, p.59; Runzo, "Omniscience", pp.135.

wholesale failure of history could conceivably occur because of an unpredicted action. It might be replied that the master hand of destiny would never allow this to occur; but the only manner in which such a positive result could be assured would involve the manipulation of human persons. If we cannot fail even if we want to then we are not truly free.[14] A final factor which makes the chess-master model unsatisfactory is that it places God in a perpetual flux of responsiveness to human action - it is not only human persons whose freedom would be curtailed, but God's also.[15]

2. A second proposed strategy is quite different. Various "gaze" models have been put forward in which God in some way looks into the future.

Nelson Pike[16] took up references in Augustine,[17] Calvin[18] and Boethius[19] referring to a divine "spiritual vision" of the future. He argued that God could perhaps be likened to a crystal ball gazer with the genuine ability to look into the future. Such future vision would be intuitive or immediate, i.e. non inferential, so avoiding any deterministic implications.[20]

"Gaze" solutions like Pike's face an insuperable problem. Unless some grounds can be given for God's knowledge of the future we have no reason to suppose it is knowledge at all, rather than just good guessing, but any suggested grounds would seem to have to posit either an "already existent future", or, be based on causal links with the present, raising again the spectre of determinism. Unless Pike and others can give some sort of explanation as **how** God might be

---

[14] Cf. D. Basinger, "Human Freedom and Divine Providence: Some New Thoughts On An Old Problem", *Religious Studies*, 15, 1979, pp.498-504; Neville, *God the Creator*, p.103.

[15] So, Ford, "Eternity and Temporality", p.120; P. Helm, "Omnipotence and Change", *Philosophy*, 51, 1976, p.460.

[16] Pike, *God and Timelessness*, chapter 4.

[17] Augustine, *City of God*, 11.21.

[18] Calvin, *Institutes*, 3. 21.

[19] Boethius, *Consolation*, 5. 6. Cf. Scotus, *1 Sent.* 29. 5, 35.

[20] Richard Sorabji, *Necessity, Cause and Blame*, Ithaca: Cornell University Press, 1980, p.122 accepts that this model is logically possible. S.T. Davis, "Divine Omniscience and Human Freedom", *Religious Studies*, 15, 1979, pp.314-315 also speaks of a "future vision", but makes no reference to Pike.

supposed to peer into the future the suggested model has no more status than mere stipulation.[21]

One attempt to get around this problem has been to suggest that time is multi-dimensional. A number of such proposals have been put forward in the context of explaining how human precogntion might be possible. Since divine precogntion would seem to be on a logical par with human precognition a brief glance a these representations is justified.

J.W. Dunne tried to explain apparent examples of prescience in dreams by developing a theory of an infinite time series.[22] In certain dream experiences Dunne believed that we have evidence for what we would normally take to be events separated in monodimensional time, i.e. present and future, to be co-present and co-perceptible, that is, existent and perceptible at one and the same **time**. In his scheme time is not eliminated but pushed back, so that we postulate a second dimension of time to account for the co-occurrence referred to above. Dunne argues that the becoming of time always requires a higher order dimension in which to move, thus we start an endless regress which ends at infinity. The immediate problem here of course is that infinity, by definition, has no last term so that the model ends up with no explanatory basis.[23]

Although C.D. Broad rejected the wider aspects of Dunne's model, he thought that part of its structure could be used to explain precognition. He postulated a second dimension of time to make sense of the "co-existence" which is apparently a conditon of veridical foreseeing.[24] Suppose that there are two events, x and y. If a person judges x is simultaneous with y it may be that (a) x is simultaneous with y in both temporal dimensions, or (b) x is simultaneous with y in

---

[21] Cf. Runzo, "Omniscience", pp.136-138. Runzo reminds us that knowledge is **justified** true belief.

[22] J.W. Dunne, *An Experiment with Time*, London: Faber and Faber, 4th ed. 1939. His work is built on C.H. Hinton's *The Fourth Dimension*, 1887. The theory is taken up by J.L. Stocks, *Time, Cause and Eternity*, London: Macmillan, 1938.

[23] So, C.D. Broad, "Mr. Dunne's Theory of Time In `An Experiment With Time'", *Philosophy*, 10, 1935, pp.168-185.

[24] C.D. Broad, "Philosophical Implications of Foreknowledge", *Proceedings of the Aristotelian Society*, 16, 1937, pp.200-204.

the first and before y in the second, or (c) that x is simultaneous with y in the first and after y in the second. Now let us suppose that a person judges that x is before y. It maybe that (a) x is before y in both dimensions (b) x is before y in the first dimension and simultaneous with y in the second, (c) that x is before y in the first dimension and after y in the second. Lastly, let us suppose that a person judges that x is after y. Then it may be that (a) x is after y in both dimensions, or (b) tha x is after y in the first dimension and is simultaneous with y in the second, or (c) * that x is after y in the first dimension and before y in the second. Broad then proposes a causal rule: An event x can be a cause-factor in a causal ancestor of an event y if, and only if, x is before y in **at least one** of the two temporal dimension. This condition is fulfilled in five of the cases above, but in only one of them, *, would an observer in our normal dimension of time judge that x is after y but that x appears to cause y. These events would fall within the class of precognitions.

A hypothesis of another dimension of time might seem a long way to go to try and establish either human or divine precognition. Anyone with an empirical bent would probably require that the evidence for precognition of the human sort, or the veridicality of prophecy, be much stronger than it appears to be to justify such a move. Additionally, there seems to be a fatal object to such a 2-dimensional time schema: It is unable to comprehend the phenomenon of becoming. This is Price's criticism:

> I think we are committed to the event more curious idea of `Partial Becoming'. Suppose that I precognize an event which is to occur next Saturday. In one respect this event has not yet come into being: It is still future and does not yet exist. But in another respect it is past, and so **has** come into being (viz. in the other time dimension). It is so to speak **half-real**; it has **partially become** but not wholly. When next Saturday comes, but not before, it will receive is second instalment of being, and will then be completely real. - Yet will it? For those two halves of its being are so to speak out of step. For when it begins to be in the West-to- East dimension (first time dimension), it

will already be long past in the South to North dimension (second time dimension).[25]

This problem appears intractable. Confirmatory to these philosophical conclusions, mathematical physics suggests that the strucure of the universe needs to be four dimensional if its principal field equations are to be equally valid. Penney concludes his paper on the subject with: "Even if one denies the slightly metaphysical interpretation we have attempted to place on this result, one must grant that the basic mathematical description of the most fundamental physical phenomena shows a remarkable proclivity for four-dimensions."[26]

It seems safe to conclude that as yet no viable model of foreknowlege by "gazing", or by precognition, has been promulgated. 3. I wish now to glance at an idea which has been referred to by certain theists as a possible explanation of divine foreknowledge, that of backward causation. The concept that contingent, rather than logical matter, is not a new one.[27] Stories can be told which are consistent with present actions being done to influence, or cause, past events.[28] If one defines cause and effect in terms of necessary and sufficient conditions then there seems to be no logical objection to effects necessitating causes and so causing their causes whilst temporally posterior to them.[29] Some support for retro-causation has been claimed from the work of the theoretical physicist Kurt Godel, who has put together relativistic models which would apparently enable travel into the past.[30] I have no desire to tackle these complex

---

[25] H.H. Price, "Philosophical Implications of Foreknowledge", *Proceedings of the Aristotelian Society*, 16, 1937, p.225.

[26] R. Penney, "On the dimensionality of the real world", *Journal of Mathematical Physics*, 6, 1965, p.1611.

[27] So, Russell, *Knowledge*, pp.237-238, *Mysticism and Logic*, pp.202-203.

[28] See, M. Dummett, "Bringing About the Past", *The Philosophical Review*, 73, 1964, pp.338-359.

[29] See, Taylor, "Causation", pp.59, 64. Cf. Hinckfuss, *Space and Time*, chapter 6.2 and D. Ehering, "Causal Asymmetry", *Journal of Philosophy*, 79, 1982, pp.761-774.

[30] Godel, "Remark", pp.557-562; H. Stein, "On the Paradoxical Time-Structures of Godel", *Philosophy of Science*, 37, 1970, pp.589-601.

matters in any detail excepting as they have been raised as a way of understanding foreknowledge. Brian Davies argues: "To put it another way, if the notion of backward causation is coherent, then it is coherent to suppose that God can be omniscient, and that P can be free, since it is coherent to suppose tht God's knowledge at t1 that p will act freely a t_2 is caused by P's acting freely at t_2."[31]

For a theist to ride on the back of such a controversial concept as backward causation is most precarious. Very generally, and as even supporters of the logical possibility of the idea admit, it is extremely difficult, if not impossible, to imagine a series of events, or to design an experiment, which would demonstrate that retrocausation, and not forward causation had taken place.[32] Secondly, the idea seems to generate certain absurdities - such as "deliberating" in order to bring about an event in the past which will prevent another (known) event from occuring.[33] Neither is an appeal to Godel helpful, for his model is a mathematical construct enabling backward time travel in the world which it describes, but it is uncertain if it describes **our** universe.[34] Finally, and most significantly, according to the schema Davies is proposing God could only know events in the future if future events somehow "exist" so as to cause his knowlege about them in the past. Since I have already rejected the concept of an already existing future it appears that the idea of retrocausation is unhelpful in explicating how God might be in time and yet possess certain foreknowledge.[35]

4. In recent literature, discussion has been renewed on an old solution to the possibility of foreknowledge without determinism, this is the idea of a **scientia media** or "middle knowledge". Robert Adams explains its meaning:

---

[31] B. Davies, "Kenny on God", *Philosophy*, 57, 1982, p.112.

[32] See, Brier, *Atemporal Causality*, p.12; Mackie, *Cement*, chapter 7; Mellor, *Real Time*, pp.177-183; Swinburne, *Space and Time*, pp.162-167.

[33] So, Gale, *Language*, pp.120ff.

[34] See, Stein, "Godel", p.593.

[35] It is a weakness of Thomas Talbott's paper, "On Divine Foreknowledge and Bringing About the Past", *Philosophy and Phenomenological Research*, 46, 1986, pp.455-469, and of Linda Zagzebski's, "Divine Foreknowledge and Human Free Will", *Religious Studies*, 21, 1985, pp.279-298, that in proposing the foreknowledge problem can be resolved in terms of a "backward dependence relationship" there is no discussion of the ontology of time.

God knows with certainty what every possible free
creature would freely do in every situation in which the
creature could possibly find itself. Such knowledge was
called `middle knowledge' by the Jesuits, because they
thought it to have a middle status between other kinds of
knowledge - between God's knowledge of the merely
possible and His knowledge of the actual; or between His
knowledge of necessary truths, which all follow from the
divine nature, and His knowledge of His own will and
everything that is causally determined by His will.[36]

The theory originated with the sixteenth century Jesuit Theologian
Luis de Molina. Molina's account of God's foreknowledge of human
action appealed to divine knowledge of counterfactual propositions.
God knows what any possible creature would freely do in any
possible circumstance: by knowing this and by knowing which
creatures he will create and which circumstances he will bring about,
he knows what actual creatures will in fact do. Molina explains his
theory of middle knowledge thus:

given his complete comprehension and penetrating insight
concerning all things and causes, he saw what would be
the case if he chose to produce this order or a different
order; how each person left to his own free will, would
make use of his liberty with such-and-such an amount of
divine assistance, given such and such opportunities,
temptations and other circumstances, and what he would
freely do, retaining all the time he ability to do the opposite
in the same opportunities temptations and other
circumstances.[37]

Molina is thus offering a sketch of "possible worlds". God's
knowledge of what will happen in the actual world is based on his
knowledge of which possible world he is going to bring about.

---

[36] R.M. Adams,"Middle Knowledge and the Problem of Evil", *American
Philosophical Quarterly*, 14, 1977,p.109.
[37] Cited in Kenny, *God*, pp.62-63.

Molinism has appeared in a modern form in the work of Alvin Plantinga.[38] Plantinga's account is given in terms of "possible worlds", where these correspond to a complete state-description of a universe. According to Plantinga, God knows all true counterfactuals about the free actions of actual and possible creatures and on this depends which possible worlds he can and which he cannot actualize, God's knowledge of these counter-factuals is equivalent to middle knowledge.[39] Middle knowledge would not suffice for foreknowledge unless God knows which of the possible worlds is actual.[40] If God's decision to create a particular world is to be the basis of his infallible knowledge of free action he must know which possible worlds he can create, and when he is actualizing. Given that, according to Molina and Plantinga, the actual world contains undetermined free human actions, God cannot know which world is actual simply by choosing a coherent world history and erecting it. The content of the actual world depends not only on the decision of God, but on the free decisions of the creatures he makes.[41]

Anthony Kenny believes the "middle knowledge" account to be incoherent. The problem is how can God foreknow the content of the counterfactuals of a world if their truth value is not established independently of the existence of that world as actual. And if he can foreknow which world **will be actual** his middle knowledge (the supposed basis of his foreknowledge) must logically precede his decision to create, but this middle knowledge is supposed to depend for its content on the world **as actual**. Kenny says:

> If it is possible for God to know which world he is actualising, then his middle knowledge must be logically

---

[38] A. Plantinga, *The Nature of Necessity*, Oxford: Clarendon, 1974, chapter 9.

[39] Plantinga, *Nature*, pp.180, 186.

[40] Divine foreknowledge by middle knowledge is therefore not logically equivalent to the case of propositions about the future being reckoned true **now** because they correspond to what **will** take place. **Contra** R. Otte, "A Defense of Middle Knowledge", *International Journal for Philosophy of Religion*, 21, 1987, pp.167-169, what is lacking in the comparison is any explanation of the certitude of the divine knowledge about **which** set of propositions at the present time corresponds to actual future events.

[41] Plantinga, *Nature*, p.184.

prior to his decision to actualize; whereas if middle knowledge is to have an object, the actualization must already have taken place. As long as it is undetermined which action an individual human being will take, it is undetermined which possible world is the actual world- undetermined not just epistemologically but metaphysically. And as long as it is undetermined which world is actual, it is undetermined which counterfactuals about human free behaviour are true.[42]

A reply to Kenny has been offered by Burns:

For God, not for us, whose decisions are infallible, the conception of the actual, prior to all actuality, is sufficient to ground the truth of counterfactuals, and therefore, his knowledge of them ... this knowledge is (loosely) simultaneous with God's conception of what it is to become actual and (logically) prior to the actualization of a world ... therefore God does know which world he is actualizing, and the object of middle knowledge presumes the infallible conceptual of the actual God eternally possesses ... this will be sufficient to permit appropriate individuation (of a world).[43]

If God possesses "an infallible conception of the actual prior to all actuality" then the middle knowledge explanation will succeed. But the problem with this postulate is that it ascribes to God a peculiar property not only beyond anything we possess but contradictory to the way we conceive of reality. To know the actual **before** it is actual presupposes that the actual somehow already exists, but if both God and the world are really in time the actual is something which progressively comes **to be** an can only be known as actual, rather than possible, in its becoming. Although it is not quite clear it seems likely that Burns believes, as David Basinger puts it, that God possesses a "primitive, noninferential ... cognition" which leads him to say: "why

---

[42] Kenny, *God*, p.71.

[43] P. Burns, "Questions and Answers On the Attributes of God", *Heythrop Journal*, 27, 1986, p.175. Cf. Otte, "Defense", p.165.

should we not assume that middle knowledge is, for God, properly basic."[44]   Other philosophers however simply deny that they can make sense of a knowledge of future conditionals which is ungrounded.[45] Although talk of primitives is not subject to the usual canons of rational argumentation the onus is surely on the proponents of "middle knowledge" to do more than assert that God possesses such and such a property. It is fair to ask for some sort of characterisation of how this might be, when, after all, what is being referred to seems so far removed from the usual bounds of our thinking. At this point I can only repeat the comments of others. Normore says: "since the conditional is contingently true the property which grounds it must be contingent. But how can even God know the contingent properties of non-existents?"[46] Duns Scotus is critical also: "There are ideas of non-future possibles just as there are of future ones, since this difference between future and non future possibles is only through the act of the divine will. Thus the Idea of a future possible no more represents that future to exist than does the Idea of a non-future possible ..."[47]

There is one further objection which, whilst only appealing to those influenced by classical theism, nevertheless may be appropriately mentioned in the context of a work of this nature. Middle knowledge, however conceived, introduces an element of passivity into the divine being. Garrigou- Lagrange presents a standard Thomist objection: "Molinism is induced to maintain that God's knowledge is passive with regard to the conditionally free acts of the future, which determine his knowledge instead of being determined by it ... middle knowledge, by positing a possibility in pure Act, could not be a pure perfection ..."[48] The middle knowledge position places God in a

---

[44] D. Basinger, "Middle Knowledge and Classical Christian Thought", *Religious Studies*, 22, 1986, p.421.

[45] Adams, "Middle Knowledge", pp.110, 112.

[46] Normore, "Future Contingents", p.385.

[47] Scotus, *Opus Oxon*, 1.39, in *Philosophy in the Middle Ages*, A. Hyman and J.J. Walsh (eds), Indianapolis: Hackett, 1973, p.591. Cf. B.R. Reichenbach, *Evil and a Good God*, N.Y.: Fordham University Press, 1982, pp.14-15.

[48] Garrigou-Lagrange, *God*, vol 2, p.90. (He has a very extensive discussion from an orthodox Thomist point of view, pp. 465-562.) Cf. Barth, *CD*, II/1,pp. 569-580; Schleiermacher, *CF*, 55.2.

position of receptivity, what he knows is conditioned by the contents of creation. For classical theism this must mean an inversion of the Creator- creature relationship, and as such conflicts with the very concept of creation. Whilst I cannot claim that the theory of middle knowledge has been refuted, I do not believe it has recommended itself sufficiently strongly to be accepted as a reasonable solution to the problem of God's knowledge of the future.

In looking back over the various attempts to hold to the foreknowledge of God within the bounds of a temporalistic theism it seems that no single model can make good the contested claim. I conclude that if God can know the future he must possess the attribute of supratemporality. This brings us back to the major object of this chapter, to make sense of the claim that God can know things which do not yet exist.

B. The Classical Emphasis: The Divine Vision

As a first step in grasping the classical position it is useful to remind ourselves that according to the scholastic position God does not possess "foreknowledge" at all. For example, St. Anselm says: "God's foreknowledge is not properly called foreknowledge. For the one to whom all things are always present does not have foreknowledge of future things; rather He has knowledge of present things."[49] Since God's life is outside of time, since his existence is **totum simul**, because he dwells in the "eternal now" it is not only misleading but false to suggest that he knows things to come, for him nothing is still to come.[50] The most we can say is that foreknowledge is predicated of God after a denominative and analogous manner, to take the matter in any other manner would be to suggest that God belonged to our order of being in space-time, that he had a "location" as we do.[51] If we must speak of the foreknowledge of God at all it is

---

[49] Anselm, *De Casu Diaboli*, 21.

[50] See, Ewing, *Value*, p.285; Maritain, *Existence*, p.114.

[51] Cf. Martin, "Primordiality", p.497; J.F. Ross, "Review of `The God of the Philosophers'", *Journal of Philosophy*, 79, 1982, pp.414-415.

necessary to keep in mind that he has foreknowledge **quoad nos,** according to our standpoint, but not **in se.**[52]

A second, and vital conception for the matter at hand, is that whatever is known is known according to the modality of the knower. The idea is first located in the Neoplatonist Iambilichus, from where it passed to Neoplatonism in general, and via Boethius, into the scholastic understanding of God's knowledge.[53] If God knows things after the mode of his own unconditioned existence, this can only mean that his knowledge lacks all relativity, it determines that which is known for its is their source. More specifically, in Wippel's words: "Given that such and such a thing is future in terms of its own and temporal mode of being, according to the mode of its eternal divine knower it is present, and eternally present to God."[54]

Aquinas' theory of knowledge in God follows the order of principles we have observed elsewhere, God, as fully realized being, cannot receive any of his knowledge from creatures. Since God is pure act and is absolutely simple the act of understanding is one with his essence.[55] If it be inquired how God can know things other than himself the answer can only be that he knows them in himself. The divine knowledge cannot move outside of the divine essence because it contains the likeness of all things, all finite and contingent beings receive their form and being through participation, causally, in his essence. In this sense there is nothing to know outside of himself.[56] The meaning of this theory comes out more clearly when Aquinas tackles the problem of how God can know other things in their particularity. If God's knowledge of creatures is to be true knowledge it is necessary that he know them not as exemplications of a common idea, but as really existing and separate:

---

[52] Cf. Fitzgerald, "Kretzmann and Stump", pp.265-266. Also, J. Zeis, "The Concept of Eternity", *International Journal for Philosophy of Religion*, 16, 1974, pp.68-69.

[53] For relevant references see Sorabji, *Time*, p.259.

[54] J.F. Wippel, *Metaphysical Themes in Thomas Aquinas*, Washington: Catholic University Press, 1984, p.248.

[55] Aquinas, *S.C.G.* 1.45.

[56] Aquinas, *S.Th.* la. 14, 5; *S.C.G.* 1.46.

all that makes for perfection in any creature is to be found first in God, and is contained in him in an eminent degree. But the perfection of creatures is not merely a matter of what they have in common; namely existence, but also of what they have as distinct from one another ... thus all things are found first in God ... the essence of God stands to all the essences of things not as what is common as to what is special in each ... but at the complete actuality stands to incomplete actualities ... since the essence of God contains all that makes for perfection in the essence of every other thing, and more besides, God can know all things in himself with a knowledge of what is proper to each.[57]

Since God is the fulness of perfection, in knowing himself he knows the character of all possible creatures which might participate in him; thus he can know all things in himself with a knowledge of what is proper to each.

At this point we come to a very important notion in Aquinas' theory of God's knowledge of other realities. God's knowledge of things external to himself is not obtained, as with our bodily sight, directly of things outside himself but of things existing within him. This is not to say that he does not know things outside himself as existing outside himself, but that he so knows them because of their presentness in himself as their eminent source. Aquinas explains thus:

But if the adverb `as' is taken to refer to the knower's manner of knowing, it is true that the knower knows the things known only as it is in the knower: because the more perfectly the thing known is in the knower, the more perfect the degree of knowledge. Thus, then we must say that God does not merely know that things are in himself; but, from the fact that he contains things in himself, he knows them in their own proper natures; and all the more perfectly for the more perfect way in which they exist in him.[58]

---

[57] Aquinas, *S.Th.* la. 14, 6; Cf. *S.C.G.* 1. 51-53.
[58] Aquinas, *S.Th.* la. 14, 6.

The clarity of divine knowledge is maximal because God knows things as they are in their origin in him, rather than in the obscurity of created light.[59] If God knew things in any other way than in himself this would be a defect for it would introduce a conditioning source, an accident, into the essence of God so that the infinite intellect would depend on its finite product.[60] There is not in God a finite image derived from finite things, but rather that which is multiplied and divided in creatures is one and simple in him. As Hermann Heppe describes it: "The divine awareness is thus the direct actuosity of the being of God it self and is therefore one, absolutely simple, unconditioned, infinite, simultaneous, eternal, unchangeable and absolutely perfect and certain intuition."[61]

The transition from the understanding above to the express question of whether "God knows the things that are not" is an easy one. Whilst the ultimate inspiration for the Thomist position is Boethius, the answer is given from within Aquinas' own metaphysical position: "Whereas for us there are things knowable which we do not know, for the divine things which do not exist can be known. Whatever can be produced, or thought or said by a creature, and also whatever God himself can produce, that is all that could every possibly come into being is known by God."[62] "Moreover, God knows things by his essence, since his essence is infinitely perfect, by knowing it he knows not only those things which are actual but all things that could ever possibly exist."[63] St. Thomas then makes a distinction between God's knowledge of non-existent things which will never be and his knowledge of things which while not now existing once were or will be. Knowledge of the former is by the **scientia simplicis intelligentiae,** the knowledge of simple understanding, God knows the purely possibles as merely existing in the divine power. On the other hand things which to us are past or present or future are known to God not only as being in His power, but also in their respective

---

[59] Cf. Augustine, *City of God*, 11.7; Dionysius, *De Div. Nom*, chapter 7.

[60] Cf. W.P. Alston, "Does God Have Beliefs", *Religious Studies*, 22, 1986, pp.288-291; Anderson, "Creative Ubiquity", pp.159-160; Garrigou-Lagrange, *God*, vol 2, pp.65-68; Maritain, *Existence*, pp.106-109.

[61] Heppe, *Reformed*, p.71.

[62] Aquinas, *S.C.G.* 1.66, 1; *S.Th.* 1a. 14, 9.

[63] Aquinas, *S.C.G.* 1.66, 3.

causes and in themselves, this is the **scientia visionis**, the knowledge of vision. God sees the existence of things which, in relation to us, do not now exist, because his eternity is by its indivisibility present to all time.[64] I quote him at length:

> There is no succession in God's act of understanding ... it is all at once everlasting ... Wherefore the proportion of eternity to the whole duration of time is as the proportion of the indivisible to the continuous ... of the indivisible that is outside the continuous, and yet synchronizes with each part of the continuous ... since time does not exceed movement, eternity, being utterly outside movement, is altogether outside time. Again, since the being of the eternal never fails, eternity synchronizes with every time or instant of time ... Accordingly whatever exists in any part of time, is coexistent with the eternal as though present thereto, although in relation to another part of time it is present or future. Now a thing cannot be present to, and coexistent within the eternal, except with the whole eternal, since this has no successive duration. Therefore whatever happens throughout the whole course of time is seen as present by the divine intellect in its eternity. And yet that which is done in some part of time was not always in existence. It remains therefore that God has knowledge of those things which are not yet in relation to the course of time.[65]

God's understanding, being his essence, is eternal. Standing outside of time it encompasses all of time, and in such a way as that, because it is simple and eternal, all of it is present to every part of time and every part of time is present to it. This ever-presentness to God is the **nunc stans**, or "standing now", the eternal present to which nothing can be added or taken away. Peter Damien presents the idea powerfully:

---

[64] Aquinas, *S.C.G.* 1.66, 8-9; *S.Th.* 1a. 14, 9.
[65] Aquinas, *S.C.G.* 1.66, 6. Cf. Augustine, *De Libero Arbitrio*, 3.2-4, 4-10, *City of God*, 11.22.

This divine today is the incommutable, indefeasable, inaccessible eternity to which nothing can be added and from which nothing can be taken away. And all things which here below supervene upon and succeed one another by flowing progressively into non-being, and which are diversified according to the vicissitudes of their times, are present before this today and continue to exist motionless before it. In that today, the day when the world began is still immutable. And nevertheless, the day is already present also when it will be judged by the eternal judge.[66]

Prior to examining some objections and difficulties with this concept of foreknowledge I wish to consider an illustration used by Aquinas in order to explain how God can have knowledge of future contingent events:

Things which are brought to the state of actuality in the time series are known by us in time successively, but by God in eternity, which is above time. Hence future contingents cannot be certain to us, because we know them as future contingents; they can be certain only to God, whose act of knowledge is in eternity, above time. In the same way a man going along a road does not see those who come behind him; but the man who sees the whole road from a height sees all together (**simul**) those who are passing along the road.[67]

When Aquinas asserts that God sees all things "simultaneously" he refers to his manner of knowing them in one intuition, not to what is known in that intuition. That God knows all things as present does not mean that God knows all events at our present time, for God's knowledge is not in time. Neither is it meant to exclude a knowledge of what is past or future with respect to other things outside

---

[66] Peter Damian, Opsculum *De Divina Omnipotentiae*, cap 8., cited in Maritain *Existence*, p. 86. Cf. P. Helm, "Timelessness and Foreknowledge", *Mind*, 84, 1975, pp.516-527.

[67] Aquinas, *S.Th.* 1a. 14, 13 *ad* 3. Cf. *De Veritate*, q2.a.12.

himself.[68] God knows things as they are in their successive order without knowing them successively - but in one unchanging comprehensive intuition.

C. The Problem of God's Relation to Non-Actuals

The key question to be resolved in this section is the manner of God's relation to non-actuals, does he simply bear an epistemological relation to them or an ontological one as well. The passages cited above are not unambiguous, on the one hand knowledge of all things God's essence alone places the emphasis on the epistemic, whilst the "knowledge of vision" suggests that in some sense all things possess an ontology. E.J. Khamara[69] thinks that the Boethian view of eternity may be the result of spatializing time. Boethius (and so classical theism) failed to distinguish between the "in" of time and the "in" of space: just as space contains all bodies at one, time contains all events at once. The fallacious assimilation of the temporal sense of "in" to the spatial sense leads to the view of time as a container holding all events "at once", and the suggestion is that it is this view of time that Boethius calls eternity. God sees the whole course of events in their tenseless existence, for they are all there to be seen. Khamara does not stop to discuss the matter, but it is obvious that the suggestion implies that Boethius could have been working with a B-theory or 4-dimensional view of temporality.

That the classical view of eternity in fact presupposes the tenseless theory of time has recently been taken up in detail by Delmas Lewis.[70] He believes that classical theism is deficient at this point because it speaks of all things as being not only "epistemically present" but also "metaphysically present" to God, but, future and past things, as non-existents, do not possess any metaphysical status at all. The relation of epistemic presence does not require that the observer and

---

[68] See, T.J. Kondoleon, "The Immutability of God: Some Recent Challenges", *New Scholasticism*, 58, 1984, pp.299-301; R.W. Mulligan, "Divine Foreknowledge and Freedom: A Note on a Problem of Language", *Thomist*, 36, 1972, pp.293-298.

[69] E.J. Khamara, "Eternity and Omniscience", *Philosophical Quarterly*, 24, 1974, p.208.

[70] Lewis, *God and Time*, pp.11-45. Cf. Shields, "Davies", p.34.

the observed co-exist, e.g. one can have knowledge of a super-nova, an event, which considered as to ontology does not now exist. The relation of metaphysical presence however does require the coexistence of the two terms of the relationship. X is **metaphysically present** to Y if and only if X coexists awith Y in the same "mode of existence". As examples of modes of existence he cites space, time and, if it exists, eternity. According to Lewis, metaphysical presence is a symmetrical and transitive relation, if X is metaphysically present to Y, and Y to Z, X is metaphysically present to Z. He does not seem to want to deny that God may be epistemologically present to all things, for this says nothing about their ontological status, but as a fervent defender of a tensed view of reality he holds it to be contradictory to suppose that God could be metaphysically present to past and future events, for this would require the co-existence of these non-existents with God. On his own terms, and given that I have earlier endorsed a tensed view of reality, Lewis would seem to have a strong case.

The first matter be considered is whether the classical doctrine of eternity goes beyond the epistemic. Much of the evidence would suggest so. Although Boethius' expression "present to itself the infinity of moving time",[71] may seem ambiguous, in that **praesens** can have both a locative (of place) and epistemic sense (registering of awareness) the thrust of the explication of eternity is clearly epistemological. It is God's "knowledge" that is said to "embrace the whole infinite sweep of the past and of the future". Likewise, when Boethius says "this Divine anticipation changes not the natures and properties of things, and so it holds things present before it, just as they will hereafter come to pass in time", we have no suggestion of a tenseless view of reality or of metaphysical co-presence. Similarly: "this ever-present comprehension and survey of all things God has received, not from the issue of future events, but from the simplicity of his own nature ... Hereby also is resolved the objection ... that our doings in the future were spoken of as if supplying the cause of God's knowledge." This last passage seems to reinforce the conclusions reached earlier in our discussion of Boethius, future things are knowable by God because they unfold the fulness of his essense. I

---

[71] Boethius, *Consolatio*, 5.6, and so quotations below, in *The Consolation of Philosophy*, tr. H.R. James, London: George Routledge, n.d., pp.197ff.

conclude that for Boethius eternity does not mean metaphysical co-presence.[72]

The matter is different however with Anselm:

> eternity has its own `simultaneity' wherein exist all things
> ... Just as the present moment encompasses all of space
> without being spatial, the eternal present encompasses all
> of time without being temporal ... just as a spatially
> extended object and its spatially distant points may exist all
> at once in the temporal present, so a temporally extended
> object and the temporally distant points of its history may
> exist all at once in the eternal present.[73]

It can scarcely be denied that Anselm has spatialised time in a manner anticipatory of contemporary tenseless conceptions of reality. In this case he has placed the co-existence of all times in God, rather than in the world, but the metaphysical step is the same. Indeed it generates an intolerable contradiction, that all things exist in the mundane world. How such a bifurcation in existence is possible we are not told, but it clearly represents an unsatisfactory concept of the divine eternity.

It seems too that for Aquinas God eternally knows all things **as existing**:

> All things that have existence in their extramental reality
> with regard to any time whatever, God know eternally
> both by apprehending their extramental reality, and by
> seeing that they exist not only in his cognition but also as
> real existents in the world ... he sees all contingent
> existents in diverse times eternally **as actually present**
> (**praesentialiter**) and not only as having existence in his
> perception. For God does not eternally perceive in things
> that he perceives them, i.e., that they are in his perception.
> Rather, in fact eternally he saw with one glance and will
> see single times and that such and such exists in this time,

---

[72] **Contra** Lewis, *God and Time*, pp.12-14.

[73] Anselm, *The Harmony of the Foreknowledge, the Predestination, and the Grace of God with Free Choice*, chapter 5, in Hopkins and Richardson, *Anselm*, vol 2, pp.189, 190, 191.

and ceases to exist at another time. He not only sees that this thing with respect to preceding things is future, and with respect to future things is past, but he sees that time in which it is present, and that the thing is present in this time.[74]

It is clear from these passages that Aquinas understands the eternity of God in relation to creatures as something more than just a knowledge of what is contained within his own essence (this knowledge by essence is not problematical, for it is timeless), the difficulty seems to come with the further claim that God has a relationship to creatures in their various times. That this relationship is a metaphysical one becomes apparent in further of his comments:

> If ... God was aware only of the intentional existence of a thing or of its existence in the power of a cause, then his cognition would progressively increase through the succession of time. And (for this reason) God is said to know such things by a knowledge of vision ... The divine intelligence observes eternally every contingent thing not only as it is in its cause but as it is in its determinate existence. For **he may behold a thing only while it is really existing**, since otherwise he would know a thing differently after it exists than before it comes to be, and thus from the occurence of things something would be added to his cognition. It follows that God not only saw a thing was future in relation to the power of another thing but observed the very existence of the thing itself.[75]

I believe Lewis has highlighted a genuine contradiction in the Thomist doctrine of the divine eternity, for it is not apparent how God can behold a thing eternally if he can behold a thing only while it is really existing. If Aquinas had stated that God can behold a thing only **as if** really existing this would be compatible with a purely epistemological interpretation, but in stating that he beholds it as it **is**

---

[74] Aquinas, *I Sententiarum* 38.1, 4; 38.1, 5 cited in Lewis, *God and Time*, pp.23-24.
[75] Aquinas, *I Sent.* 38.1, 4, *solutio*; 38.1, 5 cited in Lewis, *God and Time*, p.25 (my emphasis).

in existence we have a conflict with the claim that he knows all things in the (tenseless) present. Aquinas seems to have placed himself upon the horns of a dilemma. If God is conscious of temporal succession **qua** temporal succession then he could not be immutable, for his knowledge would grow as more things came to be, or passed away, but if he beholds all things eternally as existent (cf. **as if** existent) then, whilst immutability is preserved, God sees things as they are not, for not all things are always existent. In order to maintain the divine immutability and the veracity of the divine knowledge Aquinas would seem to be committed to a "block universe" view of reality, for under these conditions God could veridically see all things, temporally, as existing.[76]

The Thomist illustrations of the time-eternity relationship are also problematical. Earlier in the book it was noted that Aquinas compares the simultaneity relation of the centre of a circle with its circumference to the relation between eternity and time.[77] The example is attacked lucidly by Scotus:

> Since time is not a standing circle, but a flowing one, of whose circumference there exists nothing but the actual instant, neither will any of it be present to eternity, which is like the centre, except that instant, which is like the present. If, however, it were supposed **per impossibile** that all of time is all at once standing still (**simul stans**) then all of it may be at once present to eternity just as its centre.[78]

Scotus has acutely grasped the problem. If the classical concept of the divine eternity requires the metaphysical co-presence of God and created things (as we would normally understand these to mean) the whole of time must co-exist.

Several philosophers have attacked the hill top example quoted earlier. Margaret Paton believes it to be a logical impossibility to see

---

[76] Cf. Lewis, *God and Time*, p.25.

[77] Aquinas, *S.C.G.* 1.66, 6.

[78] Aquinas, *I Sent* 39.5, 33 in *Opera Omnia*, v.2 1316. cited in Lewis, *God and Time*, p.38.

the **successive** stages of a hiker along a road **simultaneously.**[79] John Zeis holds that unless the future part of the road is represented by the indefinitely many forking of possible routes Aquinas has given us a deterministic picture.[80] What Zeis apparently has failed to grasp is that God sees the one actual future in its actuality. Others have noticed that the concept of a "timeless observer" seems to be a contradictory one, for perception is a process.[81] Whilst, to be fair to Aquinas, we are only dealing with an illustration, it does seem that no epistemic perspective alone can overcome the basic problem that future things do not exist **at all** for them to be seen.[82]

At this juncture several possibilities open up. We might wish to go all the way with Lewis and to simply accept that the classical doctrine of the divine eternity is radically deficient. Although he does not say it in so many words, it seems that he thinks that God could only be **totum simul existens** if, **per impossibile,** eternity was metaphysically co- existent with all of time. Given that this is not possible on the tensed view of reality, a conclusion that Lewis and many others would come to is that either God's life is successive **or** the **totum simul** in its relation to the world is epistemic only.

An obvious solution to the dilemma would be to take the latter option. All that would be required is to hold on to the affirmation that God knows all that he knows, including created beings, in knowing his own super-eminentessence. Given that his essence is timeless, so would be his knowledge. One likely objection to this tack is that it preserves the eternity of God at the cost of his omniscience; for it is one thing to know something as an idea, but another thing to know that such a thing has existence. Excepting God knows things in their concrete reality he can hardly be supposed to have perfect knowledge.[83] At this point I have no desire to enter into a discussion based on the Kantian objection to the ontological argument "existence is not a predicate": that is to argue that nothing is lost if God does not

---

[79] M. Paton, "Can God Forget?", *Scottish Journal of Theology*, 35, 1982, p.393.

[80] Zeis, "Concept of Eternity", p.67.

[81] See, Khamara, "Eternity", pp.209ff; Mabbott, "Experience", p.165.

[82] So, Lewis, *God and Time*, pp. 41ff.

[83] This is raised as a general objection to a timeless deity by Shields, "Davies", p.33.

know things in their act of existing cf. that they exist and the various relations in which they exist. Thomists would retort that they have always insisted that God knows things in a more perfect way in knowing them in himself as their archetype than in knowing them as they exist in themselves.[84] So nothing would be lost by dropping out the element of metaphysical co-presence which seems present in the classical concept of eternity. The finite cannot contribute to the inifinite so the deletion of this theoretical aspect would in no way impugn the assertion of **totum simul existens**, or of omniscience as the knowledge of all it is logically possible to know.[85] Although I believe it would be feasible to defend such a position, to leave the issue at this point would be to suggest that God is more of a self-enclosed being than Christian theists have thought him to be. I wish instead to go back to some of the sources cited above and take up the matter at the point where the epistemic-metaphysical tension seems to be generated.

In the text from the *Commentary on the First Book of Sentences* (cited above) Aquinas makes three statements which are incompatible with other parts of his philosophy. He says that God sees times "as actually present", that "he may behold a thing only while it is really existing" and that "God ... observed the very existence of the thing itself." It is the notion of a divine "observation" of things in time which is the source of the problem. For by "observation" we usually **mean** observing something which exists at the same time as the act of observation.[86] That is to say, that whilst the epistemic present does not logically entail the metaphysical present, the two are usually conjoined in our thinking. Aquinas, it would seem, moves from the notion of **scientia visionis**, a perceptual analogy, to the conclusion

---

[84] It is to be recalled that for classical Christian theism, finite beings "in themselves", are nothing, and that the passage of time, by the philosophy of time adopted in this book, is not to be interpreted entitatively. That is to say, there is nothing for God to know outside himself other than that which he gives.

[85] It is possible for God to know all things simultaneously in his essence **and** to know temporal events successively, but since to know things in the former manner is greater than the latter the omniscience of the greatest conceivable being must be construed only in terms of the former.

[86] Strictly speaking of course, because of the finite velocity of light, we never obeserve anything at the same time as it occurs, but this point need not detain us here, for we are investigating a line of reasoning in Aquinas.

that God must know all things in their presentness, something which is only possible if in fact they exist, that is, are in their present. But we have seen that all things are not in their present, for some are either "in" the past or "in" the future. The way around this problem is not to argue that an eternal being can know every "now" at once but to drop the metaphor of observation. If we clear away this time-bound concept, the relation between the epistemic and the metaphysical presence of things in God is placed on a new footing. Arguably, the resources are already present in Thomism to clarify the nature of God's relationship to the non-existent "components" of time, viz. the past and the future, and so present a coherent solution to the horizontal dimension of the "two-worlds problem".[87]

Although the majority of Aquinas' interpreters probably adhere to the view that St. Thomas appeals to the eternal mode of the divine being to explain the divine knowledge of future contingents as present,[88] here is another strand in Thomist thought which lays the emphasis upon the eternal and determining decrees of the divine will. It is this aspect of Thomist thought which I wish to take up.[89]

In reply to the question "is God's knowledge the cause of things" Aquinas sets out to determine how, in God, knowledge is productive:

> God's knowledge stands to all created things as the artist's to his products. But the artist's knowledge is the cause of his products, because he works through his intellect; and so the form of his intellect must be the principle of his activity ... But ... an intelligible form does not indicate a principle of activity merely as it is in the knower, unless it is accompanied by any inclination towards producing an effect; this is supplied by the will ... Now it is clear that God causes things through his intellect, since his existence

---

[87] It will be recalled that in chapter four, where various alternatives to the classical model of eternity were critically considered, one of the major conclusions was that all theories with some sort of a perceptual base were fundamentally deficient. That a much more dynamic and practical concept of eternity was necessary seemed to be an implication of that finding. In pushing ahead here with the model based on timeless causation I am filling out that point.

[88] Wippel, *Metaphysical*, pp.263-264.

[89] That God's foreknowledge is a kind of causing was argued by various philosophers in antiquity, for references see Sorabji, *Necessity*, p.122.

is his act of knowing. His knowledge therefore must be
the cause of things when regarded in conjunction wih his
will.[90]

Aquinas, as he often does in talking about the act of creation, takes
up the analogy of a skilled artisan who plans what he is to do and
brings it about through an initiating act of will. In an analogous
manner God's intellect contains exhaustively a knowledge of all
creatures which could possibly participate in his essence, that is,
become actual. When this knowledge is joined to the divine will to
create, some of these possible beings indeed become actual. In this
way what God knows is the source of what exists. The relation
between the knowledge and will of God is to be understood in a
logical and not in a temporal manner, to speak of the joining of the
divine knowledge to the divine will in order to bring about the act of
creation is to speak of sequence in the intelligible order. In God we
must suppose these things to be indivisible.[91] Also, according to this
conception, the power of God is his knowledge in action.[92]

The next step is to relate God's "knowing things into being" to his
knowledge of them in being. Aquinas says:

> God ... knows himself perfectly: otherwise his being
> would not be perfect ... But if something is known
> perfectly, its power must be known perfectly. Now the
> power of a thing cannot be known perfectly unless the
> objects to which the power extends are known. Hence,
> since the divine power extends to other things by being the
> first cause which produces all beings ... God must know
> things other than himself ... Hence whatever effects
> pre-exist in God as in the first cause must be in his act of
> knowledge[93] ... The knowledge of God, furthermore,
> would not be true and perfect if things did not happen in

---

[90] Aquinas, *S.Th.* 1a. 14, 8.

[91] Cf. Wright, "Dialogues",pp.454-455.

[92] Cf. Schleiermacher, *CF*, 55.1; Leibniz, *Second Letter to Clarke*, 5, *Third Paper to Clarke*, II, *Fourth Letter to Clarke*, 30, *Fifth Letter to Clarke*, 87, in Loemker, *Leibniz*, pp.677-679, 689, 711.

[93] Aquinas, *S.Th.* 1a. 14, 5.

the way in which God knows them to happen. Now since God knows all being, and its source, He knows every effect not only in itself, but also in its order to each of its causes.[94]

In point of fact we have arrived back at the logic of creation. It seems that if the world is produced **ex nihilo** and sustained by the same act, then God must have an exhaustive knowledge of all that has, does, or will exist. As the absolute ground of all things divinity is no mere onlooker at the course of the world but takes in the whole of reality because it wills it as its source.[95]

We must here recall that the Creator-creature relationship is an example of what Aquinas called "mixed-relations". The creature, as pure relation and effect of the divine action, exists in a real relation to God, but God, as unconditioned pure act and cause of the creature, undergoes no change because of the existence of the creature. In terms of the metaphysical relationship of God to the creature this means that whilst all creatures are present in God **totum simul** as in their timeless cause they can never be there in their particularity as successive intemporated beings. That is to say, the one sided nature of the Creator-creature relationship, which ensures God's timelessness excludes the possibility ofmetaphysical co-presence. If God is the creator and sustainer of the universe in a manner outlined earlier, and orthodox Christian theism can hardly be expected to abandon such a position (with close to confessional status) then God cannot be present to particular entities in their own times and so cannot know them in their times. God is present to all times timelessly by the relation of causal creation but no times are present to God in their status of becoming. God must experience every aspect of his creation **totum simul** because what he really experiences is not his creation but himself as Creator, and as Creator his creative and sustaining act is **totum simul**.

Unless an alternative form of the doctrine of **creatio ex nihilo** supplant the one accepted earlier I see no way of escaping from the web of ideas expressed above. Many might say than an alternative

---

[94] Aquinas, *S.C.G.* 1. 67. 7.

[95] Cf. K. Rahner and H. Rondet, "Predestination", in *Sacramentum Mundi*, vol 5, p.90.

doctrine of creation is indeed justified to secure a meaningful relation between God and the creature. The problem with this suggestion is however that it is not immediately apparent what doctrine of God, other than the classical one, could be consistent with **creatio ex nihilo**. This is because at root the notion of fiat creation seems explicable only if God is a subsistent **esse** whose proper effect is **esse**, i.e. the being of creatures.[96] It is the view of God as a subsistent being, as an **actus purus**, which is the beginning of the chain of ideas which has led us to this point. The decision seems to be either an amended concept of eternity or an abandonment of classical theism altogether. It is now appropriate to consider the implications of the findings above to see whether classical theism is seriously under threat.

D. The Divine Eternity and the Limits of Knowledge

If a timeless God cannot apprehend things in their mode of becoming but only knows the world in his immutable eternity does this mean that either God is deceived or that time is unreal? Peter Geach thinks so:

> To say that God sees future events as they are in themselves, in their presentness, and not **as** future, is to ascribe to God either misperception or a patently self-contradictory feat. Misperception ... if God is supposed to see what is really future not **as** future but as present; flat self contradiction, if what God sees is **both** future **and** simultaneously (since in itself it is just as God sees it) also present ... if one says `Time is real from our point of view, but not from God's' the question has to be pressed: is the world temporal and changing or is it not?[97]

---

[96] On this subject see T.C. O'Brien, "Appendix 1: *Esse*, The Proper Effect of God Alone", *S.Th.* vol 14, pp.169-175.

[97] Geach, *Providence and Evil*, pp.57, 43.

Charles Hartshorne has produced a similar argument.[98] If the awareness of time is of an immutable whole then time must be an immutable whole. But classical theism accepts the reality of becoming, therefore it can give no consistent explanation of the reality of time.

The above objection seems to be based on a number of misconceptions. The first of these involves a confusion between the epistemic and the ontological. From the fact that X perceives Y as a Z we cannot conclude that X is a Z. How a thing is known does not determine what is known. The timelessness of God's apprehension of temporal events does not entail that these events must be timeless.[99] It may seem that we have impaled ourselves on the second horn of the dilemma - God, by perceiving timelessly misperceives reality. Several points need to be made here. Firstly, the criticism seems to suppose that the only knowledge of change can come from changing, but, as Bowne puts it: "The concept of sequence ... does not involve a sequence of conceptions".[100] It is reasonable to assume that God has a conceptual grasp of many phenomena which, as infinite spirit, he could never experience, e.g. physical pain, boredom. There is no reason to suppose that a timeless God could not have a concept of time even if he could never experience it. God could only be said to **misperceive** if he took his perception to be in correspondence to things as-they-are. Yet if God is cognitively aware of the nature of time, viz. of the reality of becoming, he does not believe that the world is all- together and so he is not deceived. Finally, it seems to be confusing, if not erroneous, to say in anything but the most metaphorical sense that God "perceives", perception involves the sort of passivity which I have tried consistently to deny of God. Things are what they are because of the way God wills them to be. It seems logically coherent to suppose that the divine intellect could eternally envisage created temporal determinations and through being joined to

---

[98] Hartshorne and Reese, *Philosophers*, p.93. Cf. Galloway, *Philosophy*, p.479; Lewis, *God and Time*, pp.34, 91; L. Reitmeister, *A Philosophy of Time*, N.Y.: Citadel, 1962, p.19; Stout, *God and Nature*, p.228; W. Temple, *Christus Veritas*, London: Macmillan, 1954, p.94.

[99] Similarly, no one supposes that God's spaceless perception of things means that space is unreal. Cf. Hasker, "Intelligibility", pp.191-192.

[100] Bowne, *Metaphysics*, p.233.

the divine will timelessly cause such temporal determinations.[101] Only if it is somehow contradictory to suppose that an eternal being could create, a matter denied earlier in this work, could the timeless bringing to be of real temporal determinations be rejected. God as its creator, can very well know that time is, without knowing, i.e. experiencing, time.

Of greater concern is the alleged incompatibility between the properties of timelessness and immutablity. Arthur Prior began the debate with an argument designed to show that the timeless knowledge of a timeless God would be restricted to truths which are themselves timeless. For example, he says:

> God would not, on this view I am considering, know that the 1960 final examinations at Manchester are now over. For this isn't something that he or anyone else could know timelessly, because it just isn't true timelessly. It's true now but it wasn't a year ago (I write this on 29th August, 1960) and so far as I can see all that can be said on this subject timelessly is that the finishing date of the 1960 final examinations is an earlier one than the 29th August, and this is not the thing we know when we know that these examinations are over. I cannot think of any better way of showing this than the one I've used before, namely the argument that what we know when we know that the 1960 final examinations are over can't be just a timeless relation between dates, because this isn't the thing we're pleased about when we're pleased the examinations are over.[102]

The form of the argument should be familiar from our earlier review of the A and B-theories of time, in particular as to whether tensed sentences can be translated into untensed sentences without loss of meaning.[103] What in fact Prior is claiming, and in this he is

---

[101] Cf. Neville, *Creator*, pp.115-116.

[102] A.N. Prior, "Formalities of Omniscience", *Philosophy*, 59, 1962, p.116.

[103] The paper referred to by Prior is his "Thank Goodness That's Over", *Philosophy*, 34, 1956, p.17.

followed by a considerable body of other philoophers,[104] is that A, or indexical propositions, depend for their truth value upon the time of their utterance. If God, as timeless, cannot know the time of utterance of this class of propositions then he is unable to judge their truth value, therefore a timeless being cannot be omniscient. A body of philosophy on the other side claims that what has been idenified is not a range of facts that a timeless being could now know, but only a certain form of words that such an individual could not use when formulating or reporting this knowledge.[105] For these philosophers there is no logical incompatibility between timelessness and omniscience.

Given that I have already endorsed the A theory of time in chapter three, and have advanced metaphysical reasons for the conclusion that God cannot be said to know events as they are happening, I must agree with Prior and others that God cannot know the truth of tensed sentences. This is not to say however that God is not omniscient. This becomes clearer when we consider what it is that a timeless God cannot know. Presumably God can still exhaustively comprehend all true B- expressions, those which make no use of tense, as the Creator he knows all about the nature of beings and their interrelationships with the exception of knowing **when** in time these things are located. How much of a loss is this to God or to us?

It seems that it entails no loss to God, for his being **in se**, his being Creator, Preserver, Redeemer and whatever other functions we might like to attribute to him, does not depend upon a knowledge of when it is now now. He does not come to know "our hour of need is now" by observing when our hour of need is, but by timelessly bringing

---

[104] See, Gale, "Omniscience", pp.319-322, P. Helm "Time and Place for God", *Sophia*, 24, 1985, pp.53-55; Kenny, *God*, chapter 4; N. Kretzmann, "Omniscience and Immutability", *Journal of Philosophy*, 63, 1966, pp.409-421; Lewis, "Eternity Again", pp.78-79; Sorabji, *Necessity*, p.126; Time, pp.258-259; Vaughan, *Eternality*, pp.72-78; Wolterstorff, "Everlasting", pp.93-95.

[105] See, H.N. Castaneda, "Omniscience and Indexical Reference", *Journal of Philosophy*, 64, 1967, pp.203-210; Davies, "Kenny", pp.108-110; Geach, *Providence and Evil*, p.40; Hasker, "Intelligibility", pp.186-188; M. Macbeath, "God's Spacelessness and Timelessness", *Sophia*, 22, 1983, pp.23-32; R.H. Nash, *The Concept of God*, Grand Rapids: Zondervan, 1983, pp.66ff; Pike, *Timelessness*, chapter 5; Stump and Kretzmann, "Eternity", pp.453-457; Swinburne, *Coherence*, p.166.

into being all things, including those conditions which constitute "our hour of need". In terms of classical theistic thought, God, as **actus purus**, can never respond to any contingent situation but as utterly dynamic must condition all situations. This does not mean that we will not receive help in "our hour of need", but it does exclude a **response** to temporally located events.[106] To put the same point another way, God does not need to know what time it is to be God, he does not need the action - and emotion-guiding force of tensed propositions like we do, for he is already fully active and involved with his world, timelessly. Richard Gale[107] wants to pursue the matter further, he anticipates a reply to the A-theory arguments by classical theism, and tries to show that there is no way of escape. A theist might argue, he says, that timelessness is essential to perfection, hence, necessarily, God is timeless. Yet, if God is timeless, and it is logically impossible for a timeless being to know A-propositions, it is logically impossible for God to know A-propositions. Since it cannot be asked of God to do the logically impossible, it is no stain on the sort of omniscience that God has not to know the truth of tensed expressions. Gale believes this line of argument faces "two insuperable difficulties". One, which he does not pause to examine, is that an omnitemporal being might be perfect.[108] The other states:

> by relativizing God's omniscience to what a perfect being can know ... it creates a paradox of perfection - that an absolutely perfect being possesses a lesser degree of omniscience than is possessed by some possible non-perfect omniscient being, assuming, as seems reasonable, that a being could possess one of God's omni-properties without possessing every other one. This non-perfect omniscient being, provided it is in time, would know more than an absolutely perfect being does, since it would know every proposition known by the latter plus

---

[106] Cf. Sorabji, *Time*, pp.259-260.

[107] Gale, "Omniscience", pp.331-332.

[108] I take up the relationship between timelessness and perfection in some detail in chapter nine.

A-propositions. Thus God winds up with a second-class type of omniscience.[109]

My reply to this is two fold. The first section of this chapter was devoted to the question of whether a temporal God could conceivably be omniscient, there it was concluded that this was not possible. If the A-theory of time is true, and it is reasonable to request grounds as to how a temporal being might know the future, I do not see how any temporally bound God could know that which is not yet actual. On this basis alone I believe Gale's objection fails. Additionally, Gale seems to have failed to take into account the problems created for temporalistic theism by the relativity of simultaneity. In our earlier discussion on the process view of eternity it was observed that no single consciousness in time could apparently comprehend the diversity of "nows" associated with the infinitely many reference frames of the cosmos. I cannot see how any temporal observer, God or otherwise, could have the sort of knowledge of this plethora of "nows" which an argument such as Gale's persupposes.[110] James Ross makes a similar point in response to a like argument by Kenny:

> Kenny never asks whether the problem is, in the context of the whole universe, even coherent. What time is it **where**? ... Suppose `What time is it now?' changes instant by instant, then no one knows what time it is; all clocks that run are wrong every time because they can't move instantly. **Where** is God to know the time? With the earth rotating at 1000 m.p.h., in solar orbit at 65,000 m.p.h., with the sun moving at hundreds of thousands of miles per hour in the reaches of the Milky Way ... Where is it that God must know `the' time. The whole project is cosmologically incoherent.[111]

---

[109] Gale, "Omniscience", p.332.

[110] The relativity of simultaneity does not of course in any way effect the character of the **timeless** relationship between God and the world. God cannot be located in accord with any physical theory of time. Cf. Martin, "Primordiality", p.567.

[111] Ross, "Review", p.413. Cf. "Creation 2", pp. 136-137; Sorabji, *Time*, p.254. George N. Schlesinger, "Divine Perfection", *Religious Studies*, 21, 1985, p.148, misses this point when he supposes that a temporal omnipotent deity could

I do not see how any time bound God could know all the truth that an eternal God could know let alone the truth of all (relativized) A-expressions. If, therefore, no such a being could conceivably exist the timeless God is that being which has the greatest conceivable knowledge, and this is sufficient for classical theism's understanding of omniscience.[112]

E. Summary and Conclusion

The intention of this chapter was to bring about a meaningful resolution of the "horizontal" dimension of the "two-worlds problem", to comprehend how a timeless God could be related to the non-existent past and future. After setting forth this problem as a genuine ontological one, various posited solutions to he problem of foreknowledge from within temporalistic theism were examined. None of these seemed to be able to provide the requisite grounds that a temporal deity could genuinely know future events in their futurity. The classical understanding begins on quite a different footing, for its primary emphasis is that God's knowledge of contingent beings is through his own essence. This does not entail **foreknowledge**, or, strictly speaking, anything beyond God's own self-understanding. In

---

"survey instantaneously the whole of the universe". What he is proposing presupposes a "universal now", in pre- relativistic terms, to be known immediately.

[112] In addition to the matters above there would seem to be another major obstacle against a temporal God possessing foreknowledge. It is difficult to see how foreknowledge of one's own future actions and state of mind can be reconciled with the attributes of intentionality and decision making. That is, divine foreknowledge would seem to rule out divine free choice. For those who believe this is a real problem see: T. Kapitan, "Can God Make Up His Mind?", *International Journal for Philosophy of Religion*, 15, 1984, pp.37-47; R. La Croix, "Omniscience and Divine Determinism", *Religious Studies*, 12, 1976, pp.365-381; Runzo, "Omniscience", p.141; Swinburne, *Coherence*, p.177. For a denial see: D. Basinger, "Omniscience and Deliberation: A Response to Reichenbach", *International Journal for Philosophy of Religion*, 20, 1986, pp.169-172; P.L. Quinn, "Divine Foreknowledge and Divine Freedom", *International Journal for Philosophy of Religion*, 9, 1978, pp.225-236. It is worth noting this subject here because it is often supposed that the concept of the omniscience of a temporal deity is less problematical than that of an eternal one.

commenting upon the work of Delmas Lewis it became apparent however that several of the major classical figures wished to claim a knowledge for God of things in their temporal particularity. This however generates a contradiction for it supposes that it is coherent to know non-existents as existing. The root of the problem seems to lie in the inconsistency of supposing that a fully actualized being could observe the flux of mundane processes. Once this possibility is denied, and recourse is made to the **scientia visionis intelligentiae** and the nature of God's relation to the world in terms of timeless causation, it becomes evident that God's knowledge of things is a knowledge of effects as they are contained in his own creative power. If God knows things in this way, viz. in a "mixed relation", he does not know created things in their own times but only in his own absolute simultaneity. In brief, God can never know what time it is.

The implications of this fact are however nowhere near as severe as may first appear. The epistemological reality that God does not know what time it is has no implications for the metaphysical status, of time, for the two subjects bear no relation. God as Creator can quite clearly know that there is such a "thing" as time and know the order in which events occur throughout time, as such he cannot be said to be deceived. It seems undeniable that a timeless being cannot know the truth of A-propositions, but no-one has been able to show that this involves any real religious or theological loss. That is, it does not interfere with the status and function of God as Creator-Preserver, neither does it negate his omniscience. Although the sort of knowledge which a timeless God can have of temporal events (being unable to distinguish between past, present and future in the temporal series) may surprise us, and be incomprehensible, it is nevertheless not contradictory and is fully consistent with the findings of the earlier parts of this book. Analysis of the results of this chapter reveal that the "horizontal" dimension of the "two-worlds" problem has not so much admitted a solution but proved itself to be a pseudo-problem. An eternal being has no "real relation" to the temporal series. As indicated above however, this has no material conseqences.[113]

---

[113] It is interesting to see how Aquinas almost apologises for the conclusion that God has practical as well as speculative knowledge of things other than himself. He takes this to be acceptable because the practical knowledge does not diminish the excellence of the speculative, (*S.Th.* 1a. 14, 16 *ad* 2). If these

Throughout the last three chapters of the book considerable use has been made of the concept of timeless causation, and more particularly of the nature of this causal power in creating the world **ex nihilo** and preserving it in being. Even if the course of the argument has been acceptable so far there yet remains one area of tension which has repeatedly surfaced even within the context of classic Christian theism. This is the problem of how to reconcile God's universal causality with finite freedom. It is this subject which forms the centre of concern of our next chapter.

---

intuitions had been worked through more thoroughly they could easily have led to the sort of conclusion found in this chapter.

CHAPTER EIGHT

THE DIVINE ETERNITY AND HUMAN FREEDOM

The subject matter of this chapter is the apparent need to reconcile the concept of the divine eternity with genuine human freedom. The problem has a number of aspects; in the first place a number of philosophers have wanted to argue that omniscience and indeterminism are incompatible. Only if the future is fixed can it be knowable, hence either God is not strongly omniscient or there is no free will. Another dimension of the problem concerns causation, the difficulty here is not restricted to those forms of theism which believe that God is timeless, but to all which would adhere to a concept of universal divine causation. How is it possible for God to cause human actions and for such actions to remain free? This book is committed to finding some sort of a resolution to this problem on a number of counts. In the first place I have interpreted the divine eternity in its relation to the world in terms of an all embracing timeless causation. If free human acts were omitted from this scheme it would preclude God from being **totum simul existens**, that is, there would be a realm of existents which did not participate in the divine essence. In some way it would have to be supposed that these entities were self-caused, and once this was admitted, the entire framework of the classical system would collapse, for God would no longer be necessary in the explanatory scheme of things. Even if this implication could in some way be avoided, at the very least the existence of a realm of events not divinely caused would create a lacuna in the divine causal knowledge. Amongst many other things, the classical doctrine of omnipotence and providence would be threatened. Much more could be said here of the implications for classical theism of accepting that finite free wills could be essentially independent of God, but enough has been indicated to show that a serious problem confronts any view which presents a doctrine of eternity in terms of causation.

A. Foreknowledge and Freedom

One of the ongoing debates in contemporary philosophy of religion is over the compatibility of God's omniscience and human freedom. If God is everlasting and omniscient, then it might seem that my freedom now to do other than what I am doing must be the freedom so to act that a fact about the past, viz. God's prior belief about my present activity, would not be a fact about the past. But since the past is "fixed", it seems that if God exists, then I am not now free to do other than what I am doing. Although this problem is of negative interest, in as much as if foreknowledge and free will are found to be incompatible a theist might have more reason to consider that God is timeless, it is not a matter of positive concern here because a timeless God does not have **foreknowledge** at all.[1]

A number of philosophers however, have wanted to argue that even the sort of "foreknowledge" attributed to a **timeless** God is incompatible with human freehold. Paul Helm says: "The notion of foreknowledge expresses a temporal knower's belief or recognition that certain events were known timelessly **before this time**",[2] and goes on to repeat the usual argument for the incompatibility of foreknowledge and freedom. At the end of his paper he comments: "Hence there cannot be free will, even if God's knowledge of human actions is timeless".[3] Helm has made a bad mistake here, as a timeless God's knowledge is not timeless **before** any time, simply because timelessness has no temporal relation to time at all. Without this relation of antecedence, the imputed deterministic implication cannot get off the ground.

Of greater interest is Ayers argument:

> If God knows with absolute certainty the totality of one's existence from eternity, then his life is complete before he himself has actualised it in time. Strictly speaking, then

---

[1] For articles which review the discussion and indicate current issues see: J.M. Fischer, "Pike's Ockhamism", *Analysis*, 46, 1986, pp.57-63; W. Hasker, "Foreknowledge and Necessity", *Faith and Philosophy*, 2, 1975, pp.121-157; O.G. Ramberan, "Omniscience, Foreknowledge and Human Freedom", *Canadian Journal of Philosophy*, 15, 1985, pp.483-488.

[2] Helm, "Divine Foreknowledge", p.526 (my emphasis).

[3] Helm, "Divine Foreknowledge", p.527.

men's live cannot be otherwise than God knows them to be. Tomorrow's choices are already set for man because their lives are constituted for God before they are constituted for them. However men may think they are free to make choices such freedom is an illusion. To say that while God **knows** that all events are actual, He does not **predetermine** all events is but an empty and meaningless locution. If God knows all choices future as well a past and present, as actual, then however much one may think he is free with respect to future choices the particular choice he will make is already actual in God's absolute knowledge and he will be unable to choose anything other than what he does in fact choose.[4]

Ayers has failed to come to grips with the notion of timelessness at a number of points. This comes out in his use of "before" and "already" in specifying relation between God's eternal knowledge and a man's choices. Both of these words are temporal locators and so inapplicable to timeless knowledge, once this is recognised it is plain that God's full knowledge of all choices in time does not precede any of these choices. Therefore any deterministic implications, by way of sequence, are removed. To attend to Ayers second point, it is not an empty locution to suppose that God can know all events as actual without predetermining them. **Predetermination** is immediately ruled out by the concept of timelessness, and is replaced by the concept of a timeless causal effecting of human choices, whether this idea is compatible with freedom of choice remains to be seen, but it is not an empty concept, and if incompatible with freedom will be so on different grounds then those suggested by Ayers whose logic unwittingly remains restricted to temporal determinations.

D.P. Lackey recognizes that the "timeless solution" to the problem of omniscience and free will is more subtle than some seem to allow, but puts the objection in a slightly different form which he believes is successful:

The proposition that causes problems for those who believe in free will is not `God knows now what I will do tomorrow', but rather, `it is true now that God knows

---

4 Ayers, "Theodicy", p.395.

what I will do tomorrow'. This second statement does not say that God knows **now**, but only that, for us, it is now true that he knows. The contradiction between foreknowledge and free will cannot be resolved by placing that knowledge in a non-temporal being.[5]

The line of Lackey's objection becomes clearer if it is put a little differently. If God knows what I will do tomorrow he could communicate to someone else today the infallible information about my actions tomorrow, but such infallible knowledge of subsequent events presupposes that it is logically impossible that any alternative will take place, therefore my future actions must be determined. Where this objection fails is that it does not come to terms with the ontology of God's knowledge of the future. Classical theists have always insisted that what God knows is events in-their- occurring, that is to say that what is future to us is known by God in its actuality.[6] Since the transmission of knowledge **per se** could not have deterministic implications, Lackey's argument will only succeed if it can be established that there is something in God's knowing events in-their- occurring (from outside the temporal sequence) that entails determinism. It is difficult however to see how a knowledge act could determine that which is known?[7]

It is not unlikely that what Lackey and others take to be the source of the deterministic implications of omniscience is the conviction that no concept of necessity is compatible with freedom of choice. If God's information about what I will do tomorrow is infallibly true now then tomorrow's actions will be necessary **simpliciter.** This line of reasoning however fails to distinguish between conditional and

---

[5] D.P. Lackey, "A New Disproof of the Compatibility of Foreknowledge and Free Choice", *Religious Studies*, 10, 1974, p.317. Cf. S. Haack, "On a Theological Argument for Fatalism", *Philosophical Quarterly*, 24, 1974, pp.156-159; R.P. McArthur, "Timelessness and Theological Fatalism", *Logique et Analyse*, 20, 1977,
pp.475-490.

[6] See, for example, Anselm, *Harmony*, 1.5; Aquinas, *S.C.G.* 1.68; W.J. Hill, "Does God Know the Future? Aquinas and Some Moderns", *Theological Studies*, 36, 1975, pp.3-18.

[7] Lackey is not concerned with the concept of causal knowledge, this is a problem I will take up shortly.

absolute necessity. In the earlier discussion on God's freedom in creating I made the point that only God's own being is absolutely necessary, he could not not-be. All other things that do exist have conditional necessity; they could (logically) have not been, but given that God has created this actual world they have a necessity as-existing. That is, in existing they necessarily exist. Since God knows things as-existing the knowledge he has of creatures is one of conditional necessity, and conditional necessity is not logically incompatible with free choice. There are many ways of putting this. I quote Anselm for clarity:

> What will be, of necessity will be ... For this necessity signifies nothing other than what will occur will not be able not to occur at the same time ... if it were not necessary that everything which is going to happen were going to happen, then something which is going to happen could not be going to happen - a contradiction ... we are saying that an event which is going to occur is, necessarily, going to occur ... God ... sees all things as they are - whether they be free or necessary; as He sees them so they are.[8]

C.D. Broad sheds light on this problem from another angle. He makes a useful distinction between the terms "predeterminate" and "predetermined". Predeterminism involves an inflexible relation, or logically necessary entailment, between a certain event at one point in time and some later event, it is therefore incompatible with human freedom. He explains predetermination in the following way.

> Let c be any characteristic that can be manifested in time. Suppose that a judgment is made at any moment t to the effect that an event manifesting the characteristic **will** happen in a certain place or in a certain mind at a certain

---

[8] Anselm, *Harmony* 1.3. Cf. Augustine, *City of God*, 5.9; Burns, "Kenny", 175; E. Langerak, "On Foreknowledge and Necessity", *Mid West Studies in Philosophy*, 1, 1976, pp.12-16; R.H. Teske, "Omniscience, Omnipotence and Divine Transcendence", *New Scholasticism*, 53; 1979, pp.277-294. I would prefer to say that God sees all things as they are in himself as causing them atemporally, but the basic point remains unchanged.

future moment t_2. Then this judgment is **already** true or **already** false, as the case may be, at the time t when it is made. The actual course of future history will **show** that it **was** false, as the case may be; but the judgment will not **become** true or **become** false, from being neither one nor the other, when the moment t_2 is reached. I do not know whether this proposition is important or is a mere triviality; but, whichever it may be, it is all that is meant by saying that `the future is already predeterminate'.[9]

Whilst Broad's definition may seem no more than the rehearsal of a debatable theory of timeless truth, there lies behind it a conviction about the nature of reality. However many possible futures there may be there can only be a single actual future, there must therefore be a one to one correspondence between a certain set of propositions able to be (logically) formulated now and this determinate future. What God may be said to know (timelessly) is that assemblage of propositions corresponding to the future (for us) as it will be. This in no way implies determinism. Martin Luther felt that foreknowledge and freedom were contradictory, his argument seems to be one from the immutability of God to the fixity of human decisions.

If his knowledge is an attribute of his will, then his will is eternal and unchanging, because that is his nature, if his will is an attribute of his foreknowledge, then his foreknowledge is eternal and unchanging, because that is his nature. From this it follows irrefutably that everything we do, everything that happens, even if it seems to us to happen mutably and contingently, happens in fact nonetheless necessarily and immutably, if you have regard to the will of God.[10]

Luther's thought moves from: God's will and knowledge cannot be changed, to: what God wills and knows could not be other than what it is. The logical fallacy is a well known one, it comes out when we

---

[9] Broad, "Philosophical Implications", p.206.

[10] M. Luther, *On the Bondage of the Will*, tr. P.S. Watson, London: S.C.M., 1969, p.119.

compare the following. "Whatever God knows he necessarily knows", "whatever God knows necessarily is". The necessity and immutability of the divine knowledge cannot be transferred to what is known. Or to put it another way: "Whatever is willed/known by God must necessarily be" is true when taken indivisibly, for God's will and knowledge is perfect, but false when taken in a divided manner, the **things** known are contingent even if necessarily **known** by God.[11]

Luther, I suggest, may have fallen into this logical error because he was thinking of God's will and knowledge as preceding that which was willed or known. But this is impossible if God is a timeless being. We must think rather of a timeless coincident relation between the causal power of God and finite effects. God immediately co-operates with the operations of his creatures.[12] There seems to be no logical reason why a coincident relation of causal **co-operation** should impute necessity to the finite effect, even if, as per necessary, the causal willing and knowledge of God involved in the relation is immutable. That is to say, Luther has justly recognized the inflexible, because timeless, nature of the divine operation, but in failing to acknowledge that the relation between time and eternity is irreflexive has unnecessarily attributed fixity to the finite effect.[13]

I conclude this introductory section of the chapter with the observation that there appears to be no logical reason why exhaustive timeless knowledge of finite entities, viz. omniscience, should be considered incompatible with human free will. The major challenge to the compatibility of a timeless deity and human freedom is not however epistemological but ontological. Does the nature of timeless causation leave room for real contingent finite willing?[14]

---

[11] Cf. Aquinas, *S.Th.* 1a.14, 13, 3; M.R. Baumer, "The Role of 'Inevitability at Time T' in Aquinas' Solution to the Problem of Future Contingents", *New Scholasticism*, 53, 1979, pp.147-167; Kenny, *Aquinas*, pp.258ff; Sorabji, *Necessity*, pp.122-123.

[12] Cf. Gilson, *Christian Philosophy*, pp.198-199.

[13] For discussions of time-eternity coordination see C.S. Lewis, *The Screwtape Letters*, London: Geoffrey Bles, 1942, pp.138-139; Owen, *Concepts of Deity*, pp.82-87.

[14] Also worth consulting on the relationship between foreknowledge and freedom are P. Fitzgerald, "Review of Fate, Logic, and Time", *Philosophy of Science*, 38, 1971, pp.121- 126; J.L. Walls, "A Fable of Foreknowledge and Freedom", *Philosophy*, 62, 1987, pp.67-75.

B. Timeless Causality and Human Freedom

Before moving on to consider the relationship between the causality of God and human free will it is necessary to recall that there is, philosophically, more than one way of understanding freedom. "Soft determinists" believe that it is possible to meaningfully hold together a belief in determinism and human freedom, where freedom is defined in terms of the absence of external restraint, or non-coercion. Bertrand Russell expresses such a view: "Freedom in any valuable sense, demands only that our volitions shall be, as they are, the result of our own desires, not of any outside force compelling us to will what we would rather not will."[15] This position is frequently termed "compatibilism" for it wants to affirm determinism and freedom-with-responsibility, or it's view of free will is termed "liberty of spontaneity", emphasising that an agent can truly will what he wills.[16]

Views similar to these have proved attractive to many theists. It is likely that it was the final position of Augustine: "To will or not to will is in the power of the one who wills or does not will in such a way as not to impede the divine will and not to overcome its power...He (God) has the wills of men more under control than they themselves have."[17] Augustine is satisfied that a man is free if he can will what is in his mind to bring about, but he does this in the framework of the sovereign conditioning will of God. Luther, especially in his controversy with Erasmus, denied free will, in any other than a compatibilist sense, most vehemently:

> free choice is an empty name and all that we do comes about by sheer necessity ... we will discuss the proposition that necessity has neither merit nor reward. This is true if we are speaking of a necessity of compulsion, but if we are speaking of the necessity of immutability it is false ... man apart from the grace of God

---

[15] Russell, *Knowledge*, p.237.

[16] For a recent compatibilist treatment see D.C. Dennett, *Elbow Room: The Varieties of Free Will Worth Wanting*, London: M.I.T. Press, 1984.

[17] Augustine, *De Corruptione et gratium ad Valentinum*, 14.43,45, cited in R. Portalie, *A Guide to the Thought of St. Augustine*, tr. R.J. Bastian, Westport: Greenwood, 1975, p.197.

242

remains nonetheless under the general omnipotence of God, who moves, and carries along all things in a necessary and infallible course ...[18]

Luther denies that men are under compulsion, but accepts that they cannot do other than they do (this is the necessity of immutability). Everything lies within the divine determination, but this does not remove responsibility. Calvin adopts a similar position:

> If God merely foresaw human events, and did not also arrange and dispose of them at his pleasure, there might be room for agitating the question, how far his foreknowledge amounts to necessity; but since he foresees the things which are to happen, simply because he has decreed that they are so to happen, it is vain to debate about prescience, while it is clear that all events take place by his divine appointment.[19]

Many other examples could be given, but enough has been said to show that the present book could, without abandoning its claim to working within the tradition of classical Christian theism, take up and defend a compatibilist position.[20] In many ways this would make the task of this chapter very much easier, for what is here being defended is that a particular type of causality, divine and timeless, is compatible with human free choices. Given that a compatibilist already accepts that acts of free will fit, somehow, into the universal web of causation the position taken up could merely be a variant of popular compatibilist views. That is, divine determinism would substitute for material determinism, the basic logic of the problem remaining unchanged.

The most telling objection to the compatibilist position is that freedom as spontaneity does not seem to entail, logically, moral

---

[18] Luther, *Bondage*, pp.190, 211, 287.

[19] Calvin, *Institutes*, 3.23,6.

[20] For a contemporary acceptance of divine determinism see Davies, "Kenny", pp.144-177, and his *Introduction to the Philosophy of Religion*, Oxford: Oxford University Press, 1982, pp.88-89. Also worth consulting are Kenny, *God*, chapter 6, and A. Flew, "Divine Omnipotence and Human Freedom", in *New Essays in Philosophical Theology*, A. Flew and A. MacIntyre (eds), N.Y.: Macmillan, 1955, pp.144-169.

responsibility. Even if a choice is my own, if I could not have done differently in the circumstances, how can my action be interpreted as one deserving of moral praise or blame.[21] Or, more seriously, if God is the ultimate cause of all of my actions, in that he moves me freely to will them, will not God be responsible for evil deeds as well as good ones.[22] If this implication cannot be avoided it seems to be too high a price to pay for preserving an interpretation of divine eternity in terms of timeless causation. I have no desire at this point to become embroiled in the debate over whether a compatibilist thesis can be defended by a theist, although I am inclined to think it can be, I do not think that it need be. So far I have argued a position asuming that determinism is not true, I shall continue in this way for the rest of the time noting only that the particular view of timelessness here argued does not depend on the truth of indeterminism.

That view which is opposed to soft determinism emphasises the ability of the human person to act other than he did in fact act in a situation even if all known circumstances were unchanged. Such a theory understands free will as "liberty of indifference". It involves not only the ability to act otherwise than one did in fact act but also to choose other than one did in fact choose.[23] Jacques Maritain is worth quoting at this point:

> Freedom of spontaneity is not, as free will, a power of choice that transcends all necessity, even interior necessity, and all determinism. It does not imply the absence of necessity, but merely the absence of constraint. It is the power of acting by virtue of its own internal inclination, and without undergoing the coaction imposed by an exterior agent (e.g., an electron spinning freely). When freedom of spontaneity passes the threshold of the spirit, and is spontaneity of a spiritual nature, it becomes properly freedom of independence. To this extent it does not consist merely in following the inclination of nature, but in being or making oneself actively the sufficient

---

[21] See, for example, N. Smart, *Philosophers and Religious Truth*, London: S.C.M., 1969, pp.55ff.

[22] So, Kenny, *God*, pp.86-87.

[23] For a recent exposition see P. van Inwagen, *An Essay on Free Will*, Oxford: Clarendon, 1984.

principle of one's own operation. This, then, is why freedom of independence exists only in beings which also have free will; and presupposes the exercise of free will in order to arrive at its end.[24]

Theistic indeterminists or incompatibilists insist that a person can only be free with respect to an action if God does not causally determine that the person do the action.[25] It should be noted that a theistic indeterminist can maintain that God **causes** the person to do the action without causally **determining** the action; this is the view which shall be defended in this chapter.[26]

1. Prior to proceeding to a positive exposition of the relationship between divine and contingent causality it is necessary to specify in more detail where the alleged difficulties are believed to be. I shall then reply to these difficulties **seriatim**. Rudolph Gerber summarises a widespread conviction when he says: "At bottom, the contemporary problem for the theist is the reconciliation of two absolutes, the all-creating God and the self-creating man."[27] The felt tension is between the doctrine of **creatio ex nihilo** and human creativity. Can the concept of a God who brings all things into being and sustains them in being, and apart from whose power nothing can happen, be coherently combined with the notion of persons as self produced entities? More specifically, does the doctrine of creation as understood by classical theists leave room for the sort of secondary causality that

---

[24] J. Maritain, *Freedom - Its Meaning*, p.636 cited in Redlon, *Creative Act*, p.8. Cf. R. Guardini, *Freedom, Grace and Destiny*, tr. J. Murray, Westport: Greenwood, 1975, pp.90- 97; Scotus, *Oxford Comm*, 1.39, in Hyman, *Philosophy*, pp.593- 595.

[25] Cf. Plantinga, *Necessity*, pp.169-184; Kenny, *God*, Chapter 5.

[26] The main theistic objection to the "liberty of indifference" view is that it seems to contradict the sort of freedom it is supposed that God has, and that glorified human persons enjoy in the beatific state. In both cases, it is argued, maximal freedom is enjoyed whilst there is no possibility of doing other than the highest good. See, Copleston, *History*, vol 2, p.532; Pontifex, *Providence*, pp.84-85; T. Sutton, *S.Th.* vol ll, p.219.

[27] R.G. Gerber, "Causality and Atheism", in *Philosophy and Christian Theology*, G.F. Maclean and J.P. Dougherty (eds), Washington: Catholic Universiy of America, 1970, p.240.

seems essential to the world as we know it and the persons we seem to be. Keith Ward attacks Aquinas on this point:

> Although Thomas speaks of contingency in the world, it is clear that what he means is that proximate causes are contingent - considered in themselves they do not entail their effects. Still, all that happens is determined solely by God himself ... For the divine act of creation is timeless and changeless, and thus unaffected by what it creates. There is accordingly no place for a real efficient causality other than God's which may modify his knowledge or responsive action.[28]

Lewis Ford has been just as carping.[29] He questions whether the notion of created freedom makes sense, and decides that it does not because the whole idea of freedom precludes the concept of a completed essence produced by a creative act external to ourselves. Another objection tries to impale the classical theist on the horns of a dilemma. If God wills all states of affairs that exist, he is either responsible for them, and so culpable in the case of evil acts, or responsive to their initiating finite causes in bringing them about, and so is conditioned by finite events. Neither of these alternatives can be embraced by classical theism, therefore its concept of God's causal relation to the world must be faulty. Ford poses the problem:

> Does God (consequently) will what happens because I will it, or do I will it because God wills it? If the later, then God is ultimately responsible for whatever evil I commit; if the former, then God's willing that it should happen according to my will means that the concrete determination of God's willing in this particular case is contingent upon my willing.[30]

---

[28] Ward, *Rational Theology*, p.79. Cf. Langford, *Providence*, pp.99, 162-163; W.G. Pollard, *Chance and Providence*, London: Faber and Faber, 1958, p.149;T.F. Torrance, *The Ground and Grammar of Theology*, Charlottesville: University of Virginia Press, 1980, p.69.

[29] L.S. Ford, "Can Freedom be Created?", *Horizons*, 4, 1977, p.186.

[30] Ford, "Eternity", p.118. Many other authors feel that a universal divine causality would entail determinism. See, Farmer, *God and World*, p.230,

2. I wish briefly to respond to these criticisms before turning to a positive exposition. I do so here, because, as will become evident through the exposition, they reflect certain basic misunderstandings.

It is patently inaccurate to maintain, in Ward's words, that according to Aquinas: "all that happens is determined solely by God himself". The key word here is "solely", no Thomist would deny that finite events are caused **wholly** by God, but this in no way excludes the real efficacy of finite causes in their own order of being (which is other than that of God's action). The objection cannot be sustained unless the metaphysical pluralism essential to the doctrine of **creatio ex nihilo** can be demonstrated to be incoherent. Likewise, to move from the existence of a timeless and immutable cause which governs all reality to the conclusion that this is the only cause is to presuppose that there can only be one (ontologically) type of causation. This is exactly what classical theists wish to deny.

Ford's first objection, that persons must make themselves, and so cannot be created, is confused as to the meaning of creation. He seems to be attacking the strong **creatio continua** position examined, which interprets reality in terms of infinitely many repeated acts of creation **ex nihilo**. If there were no duration, as this view suppposes, then indeed there would be no room for the genuine becoming of persons, and his objection would be sustained, but this doctrine is not the classical position. According to the classical position finite entities are maintained in continuous being by the creative power of God and so can develop their potentialities through time. One such potential is that of becoming a person, on this understanding what God wills timelessly comes into being immediately, and as such the suggested deterministic implications are avoided. Ford's second objection poses a false dilemma because it fails to take seriously the idea of timeless causation. Temporally speaking, the will of God is neither consequent to that of the creature nor vice versa, since God's will has no temporal relation to the creature at all. Hence the alleged difficulty simply evaporates. On the other hand the will of God has a logical and ontological priority over the creature's will for excepting God wills the creature (with its will) there would be no creature to will. But this sort of priority neither entails determinism nor makes God responsible for my evil actions,

---

Hartshorne, *Divine Relativity*, pp.30, 135; R.T. Wallis, "Divine Omniscience in Plotinus, Proclus and Aquinas", in Blumenthal and Markus, *Neoplatonism*, p.231.

such would only follow if it can be established that I do not freely, although in dependence upon God, will my own actions. Even in the case of human generation we do not suppose that the (temporally situated) ontological priority of the parent affects in any way the moral responsibility of the child. What Ford and others have crucially failed to show is that our ontological dependence upon God as Creator obviates our personal responsibility for our own actions. It is this question which will bulk large in our subsequent discussion.

3. As a next step towards a positive position it is worth noting how seriously classical theism takes the order of contingent things and its reasons for doing so.

The doctrine of creation, far from in some way diminishing the reality of creatures, can be taken as the source and establishment of their real being and efficacy. In previous chapters it has been argued that creation is a relation of pure dependence on God; as a mixed relation, creation, at one and the same time, places the creature in absolute dependence upon the Creator, whose proper effect is **esse**, and is utterly incompatible with any form of pantheism - for God has no real relation with the creature. This type of relation means that real beings are produced, what comes into existence is not an aspect of God but something which perdures. There are several ways of making this point. Neville puts it thus:

> The dependence of B (a creature) ... on A (God) is not a feature of B's specific determinate character ... Hence, the dependence of B on A cannot in any sense interfere with B's integrity, although the dependence is the source of the integrity. The dependence of B is its own nature or being. The integrity of the created realm is precisely the mundane character that it has. Whatever is has its integrity because of the creative act of God giving being to what is, this is the integrity of its own nature. The only way in which non divine beings can have their integrity is in depending for their whole being on God's creative power.[31]

What is here being appealed to is the radical nature of **creatio ex nihilo**, the dependence of the creature on the Creator is not something which could possibly interfere with the creatures own separate identity

---

[31] Neville, *God the Creator*, pp.102, 103.

because it is the source of this very identity. To be a creature is to be a real determinate dependent being. This gives to the creature **qua** creature an identity and status wholly other than that of the Creator. This unbridgeable ontological divide is the meaning of creation. That God could somehow "interfere with" the creature's creaturehood is to suppose an internal contradiction, for this is precisely what he gives it. Frederick Wilhelmsen is getting at this point when he says: "even if `being-a-creature' is principally the creature, the `towards God' constituting creaturehood exists in the subsisting thing. A denial of this proposition ... converts things into being nothing more than creatures, into being nothing but **pure and sheer dependence.** This last subverts the propositon that God makes horses and dogs and cows."[32] The genuine ontological status and proper functioning of contingent realities, finds its source, and not its threat, in the doctrine of creation **ex nihilo.**[33]

In the context of classical, especially Thomist, metaphysics, the next step is to realise that part of the meaning of being an actual existent is to be involved in the production of other things: "To be is to act". Since created things are real they have real causal power. This is the scheme of the "great chain of being". Every being acts in as much as it is act, that is, in as much as it **is.** In acting (in being itself), it produces an effect similar to itself, God as pure act or self-subsistent being thus produced beings. These in turn are finite acts able to produce (but not absolutely) other beings. For Thomism all effects are themselves efficient causes.[34] It is a view of causation like this one which was taken up in the earlier discussion about the logical possibility of timeless causation. There it was emphasised that within such a context efficient causation is not to be thought of as something over and above the agent- in-act but is this very phenomenon. In other words to cause is something natural or intrinsic to every created thing as part of the order of creation.

In a passage worth quoting at length Bernard Lonergan takes the model a step further by specifying the relation betwen such a view of finite causation and the activity of God.

---

[32]Wilhelmsen, "Relation", p.119.

[33] Cf. Langford, *Providence*, p.48 on Aquinas' conflict with the deterministic views of Arabic philosophy.

[34] See Gilson, *Christian Philosophy*, p.206; O'Brien, *"Esse"*, p.173.

Finite causes are instruments, naturally proportionate to producing effects as actual occurrences ... finite causes are all conditioned. Since no finite cause can create it must presuppose the patient on which it acts, suitable relations between itself and the patient, and the non-interference of other causes. Over these conditions the finite cause has no control, for the conditions must be fulfilled before the finite cause can do anything. Next, though the condtions are finite entities and negations of interference, though the conditions of the efficacy of one finite cause may be fulfilled by suitable operations and absentions on the part of other finite causes, still it remains that all the other finite causes equally are conditioned. Hence, appeal to other finite causes can do no more than move the problem one stage further back; it can do that as often as one pleases; but never can it solve the problem. The only solution is to postulate a master-plan that envisages all finite causes at all instants throughout all time, that so orders all that each in due course has the conditions of its operation fulfilled and so fulfils conditions of the operation of others. But since the only subject of such a master-plan is the divine mind, the principal agent of its execution has to be God. Demonstrably, then, God not only gives being to, and conserves in being, every created course, but also He uses the universe of causes as His instruments in applying each cause to its operation and so is the principal cause of each and every event as event.[35]

Two things attract our attention here. The first is that the required master plan encompassing all of time and the order of finite effects fits neatly with the notion of universal timeless causation developed earlier. The second is that Lonergan's scheme affirms the

---

[35] B. Lonergan, "Review of **De Deo In Operatione Naturae Vel Voluntatis Operante**", *Theological Studies*, 7, 1946, pp.605- 606. I must stress here that I am not trying to **prove** that this is the way things are with respect to the ordering of finite causes and God's relation to them, I doubt if such matters can ever be irrevocably established. Rather, here, as else where in this chapter, I am arguing for the compatibility of God's universal timeless causation and the freedom of human persons **within** a designated metaphysicl system.

reality of secondary causes at the same time as emphasising the priority of divine causation. In this context the creature is nothing other than a created causing cause.[36]

It may be questioned at this point whether we have in fact escaped the net of determinism, even if it is granted that God causes the creature to cause this may mean nothing else but he determines it to determine. The contemporary Thomist reply to such an objection, "the theorem of divine transcendence",[37] seeks to reconcile the infallibility of the divine causation with the contingency of finite effects. Aquinas' views can be conveniently traced through a series of major texts.[38]

In his *Commentarium in Sententias Peter Lombardi* d. 38, q.l, a.5, Aquinas takes up the question as to whether the divine knowledge is compatible with contingency in things. He replies that it is, because neither the fact that God is the necessary cause of all things, nor the fact that knowledge presupposes a determination in the thing known precludes the existence of contingent things through God's knowledge of them. The first does not because the necessity or contingency of the effect follows the proximate cause and not the first cause. This does not imply that the secondary cause can impede the first cause because, as we have discussed earlier, the divine knowledge, as atemporal, relates to things as they are in their conditional necessity. An advance on this position occurs in later works, such as in the *Summa Theologiae*, la. 19, 8, where Aquinas gives an explanation not in terms of the divine knowledge but in terms of causation:

> From a fully effective cause in operation an effect issues not only to the fact that arrives but also to the mode of its coming and being ... Since God's will is of all causes the most effective, the consequence is that not only those things come about which God wills, but also that they come about in the manner that God wills them to ... the ultimate reason why some things happen contingently is not because their proximate causes are contingent, but

---

36 Cf. Rock, "Divine Causality", p.39.

37 B.J.F. Lonergan, *Grace and Freedom*, J. Patout Burns(ed), London: D.L.T., 1971, p.79.

38 I follow here B. McGinn, "The Development of the Thought of Thomas Aquinas on the Reconciliation of Divine Providence and Contingent Action", *Thomist*, 39, 1975, pp.741-752.

because God has willed them to happen contingently, and therefore has prepared contingent causes for them.

St. Thomas fills out this matter somewhat in the *De Veritate*, q.23, a.5, *ad* 1 where the divine will is held to have the power to bring about the mode of its effects because it is a voluntary cause. If God's causal power were merely natural it would produce only necessary effects, but as voluntary it can specify (in its omnipotence) that some of its effects will be contingent. Such a will stands outside of the line of finite causes, viz. it is transcendent, and simultaneously wills things to be either contingent or necessary disposing the order of causes to produce the thing in its proper mode. The theorem is present in all its particulars in *Contra Gentiles* 3. 94:

> But God, who is the governor of the universe, intends that some of his effects be produced here with the modality of necessity, there with that of contingency. And to do this he adapts causes differently, for some effects, using necessary causes, for others contingent causes ... for divine providence is the **per se** cause that this effect come about contingently. And this cannot be impeded.

By building upon the notion of the divine causation, Aquinas, and classical theology which follows him, believe that a position has been reached where both the primary causality of God in all its necessity and the real contingency of finite effects is affirmed. The key idea is that of a voluntary cause which transcends finite causes (and as such it must be outside of time) is able to, as a **per se** or necessary cause, bring about even contingent effects. Before going on to examine certain criticisms of a position such as this one I wish to delve a little more deeply into the metaphysical nexus which is the basis of its conceptualization.

4. A key idea in the whole classical insistence of the ultimate compatibility of divine and contingent causation is that of different levels of causation. This is a logical outworking of the concept of an order of being or hierarchy of perfection - God as supreme being and first cause can only be compared analogically to his effects, created beings, and their causal activity. Aquinas makes direct use of these ideas in attempting to demonstrate how the same effect can be from God and a natural agent:

In every agent, in fact, there are two things to consider, namely the thing itself that acts, and the power by which it acts ... But the power of the lower agent depends on the power of the superior agent, according as this superior agent gives this power to the lower agent whereby it may act; or preserves it ... So, it is necessary for the action of a lower agent to result not only from the agent by its own power, but also from the power of all higher agents; it acts then, through the power of all. And just as the lowest agent is found immediately active, so also is the power of the primary agent found immediate in the production of the effect. For the power of the lower agent is not adequate to produce this effect of itself, but from the power of the next higher agent; and the power of the next one gets this ability from the power of the next higher one; and thus the power of the highest agent is discovered to be of itself productive of the effect, as an immediate cause ... So, just as it is not unfitting for one action to be produced by an agent and its power, so it is not inappropriate for the same effect to be produced by a lower agent and God: by both immediately though in different ways ... the natural effect does not produce it except by divine power ... It is also apparent that the same effect is not attributed to a natural cause and to divine power in such a way that it is partly done by God, partly by the natural agent; rather it is wholly done by both, according to a different way, just as the same effect is wholly attributed to the instrument and also wholly to the principal agent.[39]

It will be observed how this line of thinking resembles that of the cosmological argument. In both cases we have an ascent through a hierarchical series of causes until we arrive at an unconditioned cause, viz. God.[40] The prime cause however is not to be thought of as the head of the series, his power is not qualitatively related to that of the members of the series but creatively establishes the whole series and all of its members' dependence upon himself. It is this which sets the

---

[39] Aquinas, *S.C.G.* 3.70, 5 & 8. Cf. *S.Th.* 1a.105, 6.
[40] Cf. Mascall, *Existence*, p.86.

divine causality apart from all finite causality, (as the giver of being to the giver of becoming)[41] and gives to it an intimacy, an immediacy and a profundity outside of the category of creaturely causation. As beyond the created orders of necessity and contingency the transcendent divine causal power cannot "impose" itself on the creatures it constitutes.[42] It is the difference between ontological and cosmological causation which ensures that the freedom of the creature is not violated but established. As Journet says: "But human action (created) and divine action (uncreated) are not in the same place. Divine action (in relation to human action) is one of envelopement: it gives rise to it, gives it being and continuance ..."[43] In all this matter it must be constantly borne in mind that we are dealing with a **sui generis** relation: the divine causation has nothing in common with the way we think of mechanical causation in terms of push and pull,[44] for it always works from "within", neither is it in any way comparable to "Humean causation".[45]

Many different analogies have been appealed to in order to throw some light on the nature of the divine causal power and its relationship with the world. Favourites include the analogy with basic human actions,[46] the relationship between our thoughts and our movements,[47] the dependence of a dream on a dreamer or a song on a singer,[48]

[41] Cf. Anderson, "Ubiquity", p.149.

[42] Cf. T. Gilby, "The Single Causal Origin: Appendix 11", *S.Th.* vol 2, pp.209-212; B. Lonergan, "St.Thomas' Theory of Operation", *Theological Studies*, 3, 1942, p.390.

[43] C. Journet, *The Meaning of Grace*, London: Geoffrey Chapman, 1962, p.20. Cf. Maritain, *Existence*, pp.41, 88. For many theists it is difficult to conceptualize how freedom could exist if it were not created, that is, dependent upon God's causal power, for the alternative would seem to be either an uncaused act or the determinism of particular causes. See, T. Gilby, "Translators note to *S.Th.* 1a.22,4" vol 5, pp.104-105.

[44] Cf. R.C. Richardson, "The `Scandal' of Cartesian Interactionism", *Mind*, 91, 1982, pp.24-26.

[45] Ross, "Review", p.416.

[46] A. Farrer, *Faith and Speculation*, N.Y.: New York University Press, 1967, p.62.

[47] B.L. Hebblethwaite, "Providence and Divine Action", *Religious Studies*, 14, 1978, pp.239-232; Langford, *Providence*, p.70.

[48] Ross, "Creation 2", pp.126-127.

and the timeless creative influence an author has over the free
interactions of the subjects of his plots.[49] So far I have tried to resist
appealing to analogy because, if creation is the establishing of all
things "from nothing" all intra-cosmic analogies must be deficient.[50]
Language and thought must fail us in this matter, for even to speak of
a "first cause" is to imply that we are dealing with something which is
merely higher and superior to other causes, and not with a completely
different order.[51] J. Lachs, who seems to be no friend of theism, puts
the matter very perceptively:

> The trouble, of course, is with his (John Cobb's) thought
> that if God be not the cause of events he might just as well
> not be. The very opposite of this seems to me true: unless
> we transcend the idea of God as cause, we might just as
> well do, we will in fact have to do, without it. The reason
> for this is that a being responsible for actual events is, in
> truth, not God.[52]

If the Thomist solution to the reconcilability of finite free action and
divine causal power is to work, then both for the sake of creaturely
contingency **and** the maintenance of the divine status, God cannot be
inserted into the world's causal chains, the divine causal influence, as
ex nihilo, cannot and must not be thought of as univocal with other
causes. As in all other things, God is not to be conceived of as a
"cause" in the categorical sense; he does not belong to any categories
precisely because he is the "cause" of them all.[53]

---

[49] See, D.M. Mackay, "The Sovereignty of God in the Natural World", *Scottish Journal of Theology*, 21, 1968, pp.15-16; D.L. Sayers, *The Mind of the Maker*, London: Methuen, 1941, *passim*.

[50] Cf. D. Emmett, *The Nature of Metaphysical Thinking*, London: Macmillan, 1953, p.185.

[51] Barth is particularly strong, and useful, on this point. *CD* II/1, pp.581-582, III/3, pp.98-99, 103, 106, 135-136, 140. Cf. Berkhof, *Systematic Theology*, p.173; G.C. Berkouwer, *The Providence of God*, tr. L. Smedes, Grand Rapids: Eerdmans, 1952, p.166.

[52] J. Lachs, "God's Actions and Nature's Ways", *Idealistic Studies*, 3, 1973, pp.223-228. He is responding to John Cobb, "Natural Causality".

[53] See, P. Schoonenberg, *God's World in the Making*, Pittsburgh: Duquesne University Press, 1964, pp.30-31, 48. Cf. R.W. Hepburn, *Christianity and*

THE TIMELESSNESS OF GOD

By these last comments it may seem that I have almost qualified out of existence what was initially offered as a positive contribution to the problem of the relationship between God as Creator and the freedom of creatures. Qualification is however not negation, and the dialectical approach above arguably reflects the only way of consistently speaking about a being who is believed to be not like us. In concluding this section I would wish to hold together the two emphases in the respective quotations below. First from Chifflot, then from Garrigou-Lagrange:

> We are brought back, therefore, to the mystery of creation by the study of the cooperation of God and second causes. The `solution' of this second problem is also in the order of `mystery'. To conclude, as we have done, that the second cause finds its efficiency only in the creative causality of God, is not to `explain' the second cause, but, on the contrary, rather to shine upon it the mystery of Divine action. It is not to give a solution to the pro blem of its cooperation with the first cause; it is at most to indicate the **place** - in an inaccessible light - where the problem is solved in the infinite intelligibility of the Divine Mystery.[54] Then: But who could demonstrate that there is any **contradiction** in maintaining that the **creator of free will**, who is **more intimately associated** with the **will than freedom itself is**, can infallibly move the will to determine itself freely to act? Infallibility is not necessity.[55]

5. There are however a number of objections to the line of thought developed above by philosophers who are convinced that the notion of God entertained by classical th eists, and the concept of creaturely freedom, are contradictory. One difficulty arises over the logical status of the sort of causation associated with the divine production of human free acts. If the classical theist wishes to claim that what God wills infallibly comes about then it seems that the divine causation

---

Paradox, London: Watts, 1958, p.175. It will be recalled that in chapter 5 I gave reasons for talking about timeless "causation", that is, the term is not equivocal.

[54] Th. - G. Chifflot, cited in Rock, "Divine Causality", p.41.

[55] Garrigou-Lagrange, *God*, vol 2, p.76.

must be identified with logical necessity. Gary Gutting finds a
problem here: "it would seem to be of the essence of a causal relation
that the connection between cause and effect not be logical. Whatever
the necessity of the connection, there is, as Hume urged, no
contradiction in asserting the existence of the cause and denying the
existence of the effect."[56] It might seem that the only way in which
the two concepts in question can be brought together so that the causal
relation has logical necessity is if some form of pantheism is
endorsed.[57]

Whilst I would wish to endorse the point for cosmological
causation, the matter at hand does not negate the reality of God's
ontological causation but reinforces what has been said so far about its
nature and status. Milton Capek, in discussing the character of
causation in a context quite unrelated to the thrust of our present
discussion, points us in the right direction when he argues that
ordinary every day causation cannot be deterministic because it is
temporal, for only non-temporal relations can logically implicate. That
is to say, the truths of mathematics and of logic are timeless, but cause
and effect in the world partakes of temporal flow, and as such must be
indeterministic.[58] If causation were timeless, then there would be no
temporal phase between the cause and its effect, nothing could
intervene between the two; provided a cause is sufficient for a
particular effect the effect will ineluctably follow. In the case of God's
timeless causal power the last condition is always met, that is, the
infinite power of God is always sufficient to bring about any finite
effect, therefore divine causal action will in e very case logically entail
the end to which it is directed. Not only however will the divine cause
be logically sufficient to bring about its effect, but if it is a **creative**
cause it will also be logically necessary, for this type of cause brings
its effect into being. It might perhaps be supposed that a logically

[56] G. Gutting, "Is Ross's God the God of Religion?", *Journal of Philosophy*,
77, 1980, p.630. Cf. Taylor, "Causation", p.62.

[57] So Bergson, *Time*, pp.208-209; R. Oakes, "Theism and Pantheism Again",
Sophia, 24, 1985, pp.30-37; D.R. Griffin, "Divine Causality, Evil, and
Philosophical Theology: A Critique of James Ross", *International Journal for
Philosophy of Religion*, 4, 1973, p.183.

[58] M. Capek, "Toward a Widening of the Notion of Causality", in *Process
Philosophy*, J.R. Sibley and P.A.Y. Gunter (eds), Washington: University Press of
America, 1978, pp.87-93.

necessary and sufficient divine causality leaves no room for genuine creaturely causality, and leads inevitably to a deterministic position. The first consequence would follow if the cause and its effect were on the same ontological level, but I have tried to establish at some length above that this is exactly what is denied in the case of the relation between God's causal power and that of finite beings. If such a metaphysical pluralism is coherent then the alleged difficulty disappears for the finite cause is left room to operate on its own level. The second alleged difficulty, the problem of determinism, is avoided once it is realized that the divine causation invariably produces its effect because it is absolutely coincident with its effect. It cannot be said that God's causal power **predetermines** its effect, because it does not exist before its effect, neither, on the other hand, is any entity preceding, or waiting to receive the effect. We are back once more to the unique relation which is meant by creation. Any objector must establish that to be created is to be determined, i.e. created freedom is a contradiction.

This objection has in fact been taken up, especially by process theists. Charles Hartshorne says: "it is impossible that our act should be both free and yet a logical consequence of a divine action which 'infallibly' produces its effect. Power to cause someone to perform his own choice or act precisely defined by the cause is meaningless."[59] Griffin wants to argue that the idea of causing someone else to act is simply a contradiction. He wants to insist that free action is incompatible with metaphysical dependence on another: "For, entailed in the idea of 'real (i.e. actual) being' is the element of power. And if the beings of the world are metaphysically dependent ... upon God, then they have no power of their own. If they have no power, they have no actuality."[60] To act is, by definition, not to be determined totally by something else. If on the other hand we have real causal power the notion of God's efficient causal influence is empty. The classical theist, he wants to insist, cannot have it both ways.

To these objections one can only repeat what has been said so far: creation constitutes the creature causing, it gives it reality and integrity at its own level. Not to take this concept seriously is implicitly to refuse to entertain the notion of a metaphysical pluralism, it is, in the

---

[59] Hartshorne, *Divine Relativity*, p.135.
[60] Griffin, "Divine Causality", p.177.

language I have used throughout, effectively to deny that there is, or can be, a "two-worlds problem". We are back again at the difficulties confronting rival **Weltanschauungen**. Again, I would judge that what is being denied is the logical possibility of being a free-creature. From a classical viewpoint what the objectors are asking for is impossible, viz. that free human persons as such possess some non-dependent ontologic al status. The classical Christian philosopher cannot move from his conviction that creation **ex nihilo** is a basic datum, and it is difficult for him to see, from within the context of his own metaphysical pluralism, that a genuine contradiction has been highlighted.[61]

C. The Doctrine of Concursus

The doctrine of **concursus** is concerned with what is sometimes termed the "paradox of double agency",[62] the problem of how the divine and the human co-determine man's free actions.[63] The problem is a complex one, with a long history and a large literature,[64] and, from the side of classical theism, seeks to give specific application to the principles enunciated and defended in the section immediately completed above. Enough has been said there, I believe, to show that the notion of **creatio ex nihilo**, or universal timeless creative

---

[61] Morreall, *Analogy*, pp.41, 50, 52, wants to deny sense to talking about God's action in the world because science can seemingly explain all natural phenomena. The objection misses the point, no classical theist supposes God's will to work intra-phenomenally, simply because it causes all phenomena to **be**.

[62] B. Hebblethwaite, "Austin Farrer's Concept of Divine Providence", *Theology*, 73, 1970.

[63] Cf. E. Niermann, "Providence", in *Sacramentum Mundi*, vol 5, p1132; J. Zeis and J. Jacobs, "Omnipotence and Concurrence", *International Journal for Philosophy of Religion*, 14, 1983, pp.23-24.

[64] Major sources include: Aquinas, *S.C.G.* 2.68.8, 3.72-74, *S.Th.* 1a. 1q.8; 23,5; 83,1; 105; 3; Barth *CD* III/3, p.49; A. Farrer, *Freedom of the Will*, N.Y.: Scribner's, 1958, pp.309-315; Gilson, *Medieval Philosophy*, chapter 15; P. Helm, "Grace and Causation", *Scottish Journal of Theology*, 32, 1979, pp.101-112; Journet, *Grace*, pp.20ff; Knasas, "Immutable God", pp.203-214; Lonergan, *Grace*, pp.97-116; K. Rahner, "Grace and Freedom", in *Sacramentum Mundi*, vol 2, pp.424-427; Ross, "Creation 2", pp.128-134; Wright, "Dialogues", pp.466-477; L.H. Yearley, "St. Thomas Aquinas on Providence and Predestination", *Anglican Theological Review*, 49, 1967, pp.409-423.

causation, is not incompatible with genuine finite freedom. It is neither necessary therefore, nor is it within the scope of this book, to give a full exposition of the theory of concurrence. More for the sake of completeness than for anything else I wish only to sketch the outlines of a satisfactory model detailing the working together of the will of God and the will of man.

As preliminaries the following should be kept in mind. Firstly, that in a created universe, any genuine difference between the creature and God has been posited precisely by God's own causal action. Any "coming" of God to the creature is to a being prepared for such a concurrence. Secondly, and in the light of what creation means, the working out of God's will in the world through the creature must be understood in terms of enabling the creature, rather than subordinating it. Robert King says it well: "Rather than supposing that he can accomplish his intention only by overpowering the creature, we ought to suppose that he does so by empowering him ... communicating to the creature a capacity for action of his own."[65] Thirdly, it is a thoroughly misleading picture to conceive a God "acting upon" the creature's will, as if it stood over against him as one human being stands over against another in a situation of mutual influence. If God is the creatures' **esse**, causally, then we have a **sui generis** relation between the divine causing and the creature's willing of the most intimate and interior nature. So, Smulders: "the creative act of God is not to be considered as an extrinsic condition of or supplement to the intrinsic activity of the creature, but as its inmost cause."[66] We have not the case of one cause influencing another, as might make sense for finite causation, but which in the present circumstance would entail determinism, but that of an agent which can cause the motion of the will of another without doing violence to it because, and only because, it is the intrinsic principle of this same motion, it is, in the order of being, the very power of the will itself, the cause without which the will could not be itself. To put to gether these matters in a different way: God creates beings-in- their-doing. As Ross puts it: "God does not make the person act; he makes the so acting person **be**."[67] What God instantiates are human beings free to do or not do what they do do, it is the whole being, doing as it does, that is wholly produced and

[65] King, *Meaning*, p.93.

[66] P. Smulders, "Creation", in *Sacramentum Mundi*, vol 2, p.28.

[67] Ross, "Creation 2", p.130.

sustained by God. God makes all the free things that do as they do, for they, and not God, are the agents of their own actions.

The above however are only boundaries of thought and limits upon our thinking, intended to guide it in the right direction. It is not to be supposed that the problem of concurrence really admits of an "explanation". One can only make preliminary sketches, for the question is tied to the inscrutability of God's mode of knowing and relating to the world. Rahner perceptively remarks that in this matter we are dealing with what are for us fundamental ontological data, our existence as persons on the one hand and our derivation from God on the the other. Since these relate to using a way logically prior to all our questions about them, they must be taken as primordial and cannot be rendered intelligible by any external or "higher" concepts under which they might mistakenly be subsumed.[68]

An analysis of the relationship between the free finite act and the causal power of God would have to include the following, and if adequate, develop each stage in detail.[69] The following order of elements are to be found simultaneously in the one existential event of created free choice:

(a) God conserves the free agent and his will in being. This includes giving the creature the power to act.

(b) The divine will moves the created agent to act, to choose freely among the various actions that are open to him. The divine influence does not **determine** what the choice will be, but only that there will be a choice. The choice is the creatures', but it is really available to the creature in its dependence upon God because he in his infinity is able to actualise any act of will that it might make.

(c) The creature freely orders his active power to one effect. It directs its active indifference to the realization of one definite course of action.

(d) The divine will is united to the divine mind, that is,God knows and causes (atemporally) the free created action.

(e) The existence of the free action is received in time.

---

[68] Rahner, "Grace", p.426.

[69] Cf. Knasas, "Immutable God", pp.210-214; Wippel, *Metaphysical Themes*, pp.259-260; Wright, "Dialogues", pp.469- 472.

261

I take it that the above outline on the matter of the problem of **concursus** is compatible with indeterminism, and that nothing is required of it in its metaphysical context which is incompatible with the timeless ordering of the will of God.

It may be suspected however that even if the metaphysics of the previous discussion falls into place the doctrine of divine causation outlined above has moral implications unacceptable to any form of theism. If God as primary cause is the co-determiner of every creaturely action then either God is responsible for moral evil, or, alternatively, since all acts are equally willed by God, there can be no such thing as sin.

The solution to this problem arises out of what we have already considered, the creature freely orders its own active power to one effect. It is not to be denied that in doing so it depends upon the power of God, but this does not mean that all that is intended by the creature in willing an evil act is intended by God in permitting this act to be. That is, for God to cause the creature's action does not logically entail God intending the creature's action in its moral element.[70] The moral is not coterminous with the metaphysical, all that there is of the mental and physical component of the sinful action derives from God, but all that there is of moral deviation comes from the creature.[71] It is at this point that the traditional emphasis of classical theology upon evil as a **privatio boni,** a falling away from the good, comes into its own.[72] It is a mistake to take this doctrine as teaching that evil, as it were, were some sort of "negative substance", but rather the emphasis on evil as something deficient relates to the form of the sinful act. The evil act is construed as evil because it departs from the moral order of God, which is the order of highest good. Considered materially all acts are equally good, for they are no more than that, created acts. But considered formally the evil act carries an ethical quality that derives

---

[70] This is Bruce Reichenbach's point in "Omniscience", p.225: "This is the case where the bringing about of certain evils ... is the result of the performance of a good action. Though God intends and acts to bring about the good, the action is such that evil also results ... though his creation of persons was intentional, his creation of persons who do evil was non-intentional." This is not to say of course that God's action in creating was inadvertant or accidental.

[71] So, Journet, *Grace*, p.25.

[72] For example, Anselm, *Harmony*, 1.7; Aquinas, *S.Th.* 1a. 2ae. 79,1; Augustine, *City of God*, 11.22; 12.7.

from the creature and not from God, in this sphere of willing to be outside of the divinely decreed **moral** order the creature may be considered to have sovereign initiative. The priority here of course is not to be construed temporally, for God eternally actualizes the creature's choice, neither is it ontological, for the creature's act is absolutely dependent upon the enabling of God, but it is a priority in a negative sense only, of not choosing the best.[73] In this way the full moral responsibility for that deficiency which is sin is laid at the creature's door, whereas God, from whose causal sway nothing is omitted, remains blameless.[74] The creature is truly culpable, because it is free, and yet God is not the author of sin because it cannot be required of him (coherently) to cause something, viz. evil, which is essentially negative. In this way the universal causal power of God which is the central component of this book remains affirmed without unacceptable moral implications.

D. Timelessness and the Significance of History

A matter that can in a general way be subsumed under the question of the relationship between divine causality and human freedom is the charge that if God is timeless history cannot be meaningful.

There are a number of related objections here, but they do not seem to have been brought together in a systematic manner in any one author. One suggestion is that if we are to affirm the importance of time we cannot consider the timeless as somehow ultimate, because for the medievals, the great protagonists of the divine eternity, history did not matter.[75] This however is not a logical argument, but one based on correlation, and so it need not concern us here. More seriously there is the charge that if the world and all its events are the product of one simultaneous act of the divine will then the personal history of the individual is lost sight of.[76] Other philosophers consider that history must first be important for God before it can be important for us. What seems to be meant here, is not only that God

---

[73] Cf. Pontifex, *Providence*, pp.77-79.

[74] The above is not meant to be an adequate theodicy, it would be improper here, for example, to suggest why God does not prevent evil actions.

[75] So, Gunn, *Problem*, p.43.

[76] See, W.L. Moore, "Schleiermacher as a Calvinist", *Scottish Journal of Theology*, 24, 1971, p.182; Pinnock, "Neoclassical", p.40.

acknowledges the reality of contingent events, but that history is taken up into God's own being. Leslie Dewart says: "To think of him as existing in a simultaneous duration above time is to force the Christian faith into a hellenic mold which is not large enough to contain it. The Christian God's substance is not above history; it is the substance - that is, the signification, the meaning of history itself ... we must conceive God as historical **or not at all.**"[77]

Closely related to the last perspective is the orientation which gives a certain place of ultimacy to the evolving and dynamic aspects of reality. This view point is especially prominent in the works of Nicolas Berdyaev. For example, in a famous passage he says:

> A true and non-disintegrated time, one that knows no cleavage between the past and future, a numeral and not a phenomenal time, is also operative in history which is assailed by a false, devouring and annihilating time ... A false time brings about a cleavage between the metaphysical and the historical, while the metaphysical origins of history ought, on the contrary, to establish a tie between them. The cleavage between the eternal and the temporal is both the greatest delusion of consciousness and an obstacle to the foundation of a true philosophy of history.[78]

For philosophers like this, to refer to a timeless principle as the ultimate factor in explanation is to, at the very least, detract from the importance of the historical.[79]

If the eternity of God genuinely diminishes the significance of history, as the above authors suppose, it is, **prima facie**, strange that no classical Christian theist has denied the real status and value of historical events. If anyone can claim to be the father of the Christian view of history it is Augustine, whose exposition of the reality and

---

[77] Dewart, *Future*, pp.197, 199. Cf. R. Hazelton, "Time, Eternity and History", *Journal of Religion*, 30, 1950, pp.10- 11, *Providence*, London: S.C.M., 1958, Chapter 5; McConnell, *God Limited*, p.55; Pringle-Pattison, *Idea*, p.363.

[78] N. Berdyaev, *The Meaning of History*, London: Geoffrey Bles, 1936, pp.74-75.

[79] See Baltazar, "Evolutionary Perspectives", p.148; Brightman, "Temporalist", p.546; Capek, "Causality", p.86; Ferre, *Understanding*, p.72.

centrality of salvation history grew up **alongside of** his understanding of the nature of the divine eternity.[80] If, as I have argued, the doctrine of fiat creation is central to an understanding of God's timeless relation to the world, and if "time" is thus to be understood as a created entity, the reality of time is given the most sure basis and so history cannot be threatened. Ronald Hepburn strikes this point: "Time is as much a God-created (therefore real and good) feature of the world as are the substances the world contains. And however we interpret the words `In the beginning God', they clearly announce a linear, not a cyclical view of time. Thus room is left for real progress, real regress, real novelty."[81] The critical issue, and that which none of the above opponents of the divine eternity address in detail, is whether the notion of timeless creative causation diminishes the ontological status of the entities and events in time which comprise the process of history. I have argued at length throughout this work that the very reverse is the case: the divine causal power establishes creatures in an undiminished dignity. If the argument is consistent then the objection in question proves itself to be a pseudo-problem.

More positively, the concept of God as **totum simul existens** in relation to the created order adds a teleological dimension to history unavailable to temporalistic theism. There is no part of space-time which does not fall within the single all-encompassing embrace of the purposeful divine will. Such a standing teleological order, **sub specie aeternitatis**, gives meaning not only to each individual instant but to every existing thing in relation to **every other** existing thing, and this, infallibly. S.G.F. Brandon puts this well:

The whole world-order, the whole course of human history, and the life of each individual being, were integrated into the transcendent purpose of God. Time ... was meaningful, for it was the progressive manifestation of the Divine Will. Hence the Christian believed that he had a part in a mighty process that was moving slowly and

---

[80] Augustine, *City of God*, Books 11 and 12. Cf. Gundersdorf von Jess, "Augustine", pp.91-92; M.E. Ravicz, "St. Augustine: Time and Eternity", *Thomist*, 22, 1959, p.544.

[81] Hepburn, "Creation", p.252.

majestically to its ultimate conclusion, which would be the complete achievement of God's providence.[82]

E. Summary and Conclusion

The aim of this chapter was to come to terms with a possible major objection to the thesis of divine eternity understood as timeless creative causality, namely, that such a concept is incompatible with genuine human freedom.

A small group of philosophers desire to put the objection in the form of a contradiction between omniscience and freedom. In the case of several of these authors there is a failure to come to grips with what is meant by timeless knowledge, so that once this is appreciated the purported problem disappears. Other, more tightly logical protests are raised, but these fall to the ground when the unique nature of timeless knowledge, as grasping things in-their-occurring is recognised. There seems to be no grounds upon which it could be supposed that knowledge **per se**, simply knowing that such and such occurs, even if the object does not as yet have concrete existence, can entail determinism.

Moving on to consider the relationship between divine **causality** and human freedom more closely it was observed that many prominent theists who would affirm the classical concept of God yet deny human "liberty of indifference". That such philosophers and theologians are "soft (theological) determinists" is significant, for even if the stated intention of this chapter is not achieved the doctrine of the divine eternity is not rendered intrinsically untenable. However, I subsequently argued that universal divine causation is consistent with a strong incompatibilist position. Before embarking upon a more positive exposition of a theistic incompatibilism certainly preliminary objects were dealt with; the principal of these claimed that no room was left for real creaturely causation if God's causal power is universal. This has always been denied by classical theism, and the bulk of the rest of the chapter aimed at demonstrating why.

In the context of a classical, and especially Thomist metaphysics, it is inconceivable that the contingent members of the created order, deriving from God as pure act, should not act, and that their action

---

[82] Brandon, *History*, p.208. Cf. Royce, *World*, pp.149-150; Yarnold, *Moving Image*, pp.162-163, 196.

partake of the character of their mode of being, that is, contingency. If God really causes creatively, if he is an omnipotent being who acts from outside the world's causal chains, it seems difficult to deny that he can bestow on his creatures the genuine power to bring about finite effects, all the while in dependence upon himself. An indispensible concept here, and one which has been presupposed in the earlier chapters, particularly as part of the metaphysical background of **creatio ex nihilo,** is that of ontologically different levels of causation. It is this idea which makes sense of the notion of the divine cause sustaining all other causes in being without competing with them.

Upon examination it is apparent that the sort of divine causation being considered must have the status of logical sufficiency and necessity for its effects, this does not however imply determinism, for the cause in question, as timeless, does not predate its effect but is the coincident source of its integrity. These principles find their ultimate application in the doctrine of **concursus,** the explanation of the harmony of the joint causal power of the finite and the infinite cause in bringing about contingent effects. A possible objection, that such a scheme makes God the author of evil, is seen to be misplaced if it is accepted that sin is not a thing, but rather a defect or deformation, and so is not something which God could, logically, cause.

A final matter for consideration concerned the importance of history in the light of the timelessness of God. The answer to this question depends upon the ontological status of entities and events in the temporal sphere, and since these phenomena have not been denied but positively affirmed by the doctrine of **creatio ex nihilo** it makes no sense for a classical theist to devalue history. Indeed, it is argued that classical theism, via the notion of **totum simul existens,** emphasises the teleological aspect of history in a manner unavailable to temporalistic theism.

In summing up the discussion of this chapter I am conscious of its heavy dependence on Thomist metaphysics, such as emphasis will likely disqualify its contents in the eyes of many philosophical theologians. Nevertheless, I do not believe that any of the major objections considered have patently demonstrated that God's causal power, construed in terms of **ex nihilo** and as the source of creaturely being, is incompatible with human freedom. More than this it is difficult, at last for a theist of generally orthodox Christian persuasion, to think of a more secure base for a belief in free will than the doctrine of creation.[83] If this much is granted then it might be plausible to suppose that, via the notion of **creatio ex nihilo,** only if God is timeless can man be free. At the very least I do not think that the obverse of this has been established.

---

[83] It is my conviction that it is very difficult to demonstrate, with any degree of certitude, in terms of general philosophical argumentation, that the concept of human freedom is meaningful and consistent.

CHAPTER NINE

PROVIDENCE AND PERFECTION

The thrust of the book so far has been primarily explanatory and defensive. I have sought to give content to the idea of God's timelessness, especially in terms of the concept of creative timeless causation, and to defend and expand this notion in response to a variety of objections. Now I wish to discuss two major areas of theism which have traditionally been correlated with the concept of the divine eternity: the notions of providence and the divine perfection. I am returning here to a position briefly adumbrated in my introductory chapter but which has only been implicit in the argument thus far, that God is the "greatest conceivable being". "Perfect being theology", as referred to in the introduction, stresses the superior and transcendent nature of the divine being over the world, but it does so in many contending forms. It is the intention of this chapter to demonstrate that the proper sovereign control of God over the world's history can only be achieved if he is timeless, and that the greatest conceivable being must of necessity possess all of its life simultaneously. If these two points can be reasonably established there would seem to be, not only the logical possibility that God might be timeless, but some positive ground for believing that **God** must be **totum simul existens**.

A. The Notion of Providence[1]

In introducing the question of providence it will be recalled that Boethius (**Consolation** 4.6) understood the eternity-time relationship as analogous to that between providence and fate. Providence, in God, is a single undifferentiated plan for the world, fate, its temporally extended multiform outworking.[2] Later in the **Consolation** the specific question of eternity is taken up in a providential context, the problem of reconciling of foreknowledge and

---

[1] For a useful bibliography see L. Jacobs, "Current Theological Literature: Providence", *Judaism*, 17, 1968, pp.197-202.

[2] These ideas preceded Boethius, being found in the Neoplatonists, Proclus and Ammonius. For details see Sorabji, *Time*, p.255.

human freedom. Although the link between providence and God's eternity is not as overt in other classical theologians as it is in Boethius, nevertheless, for many such theologians, the divine eternity functions as a necessary metaphysical background to questions of providence.[3]

The English "providence" is from the Latin **providentia** whose primary meaning is foresight or prescience, but with time other meanings have been acquired. A useful definition is given by H.P. Owen: "The idea of providence has four main aspects. It indicates firstly that God foresees future events, secondly that he controls them, thirdly that he cares for his creatures, and fourthly that he is working out a purpose for them."[4]   Strictly speaking, for the sort of metaphysics espoused in this book, the distinction between conservation and providence is only denominative,[5] but the distinction may be allowed to stand, for not only has it a certain religious significance,[6] but it also brings to the fore the other side of the problem discussed in the last chapter - how can God control the world if man is free.

For classical theology God is unreservedly conceived of as the sovereign ruler of the created order.[7] D.M. Baillie sums this up: "Christian Faith assures us that everything that happens in the universe happens by the will of an infinitely wise and powerful and loving God ... nothing can happen ... which is not appointed by his unfailing providence ... even the wrong acts of sinful men may be `permitted' if not `ordained' as part of God's plan for the world - a purpose which

---

[3] Aquinas' treatment of providence in *S.Th.* 1a. 19-25, 103- 105 includes the important concepts of primary causation and **creatio continua** which have been a major part of this book.

[4] H.P. Owen, "Providence and Science", in *Providence*, M. Wiles (ed), London: S.P.C.K., 1969, p.77.

[5] See, Macquarrie, *Principles*, pp.219, 223; Neville, *Creator*, p.260.

[6] See, Stocks, *Eternity*, p.2.

[7] On the biblical material to this end, see, Berkhof, *Systematic Theology*, pp.168-170; Garrigou-Lagrange, *Providence*, chapters 15-17; C.K. Robinson, "Biblical Theism and Modern Science", *Journal of Religion*, 43, 1963, pp.118-138; M. Ward, "The Biblical Doctrine of Providence", in Wiles, *Providence*, pp.15-34.

cannot in any degree be thwarted or suffer or fail."[8] Viewed more
metaphysically the certitude and sufficiency of providence depends
upon two things, one is God's universal causation and the other is the
divine eternity. The former means that God has power over all things,
whether necessary or contingent, determined or free, the latter is
equally important because it ensures that the whole world order and
history can be ordered as one event to one end. **Sub specie
aeternitatis**, the universe of space and time is embraced and directed
as a unity, outside of which nothing falls. In effect these matters have
been discussed at length, from a different angle, in he last four
chapters of this book.[9]

On the other hand many contemporary philosophers and
theologians think that the traditional doctrine of providence is so
wedded to the unacceptable classical metphysics that at least it must be
modified, if not abandoned. Prominent here are the existentialists and
process philosophers.[10] A recurrent motif is that God "does his best"
with what he has at hand. Peter Baelz, for example, says: "his love is
doing and will do everything that it can, but ... it is in real sense
limited by the conditions of the world and human freedom."[11]
Langford finds he following analogies helpful: "the description of the
helmsman steering his craft within the confines of the river, and the
picture of the artist working within the limitations of his medium."[12]
The majority of these thinkers would probbaly be happy with the
distinction that John Wright makes between "general" and "specific"
providence. The general, or antecedent, plan of God relates to the

---

[8] D.M. Baillie, *Faith in God*, London: Faber and Faber, 1964, p.266.

[9] For useful references to the classical approach see I.G. Barbour, *Issues in
Science and Religion*, N.J.: Prentice Hall, 1966, pp.425-428; J. Collins, "God's
Eternal Law", *Thomist*, 23, 1960, pp.497-532; R. Garrigou-Lagrange, *Providence*,
St. Louis: Herder, 1937; Pontifex, *Providence, passim*; Ysaac, "Certitude", *passim*.
For a non-classical theist who takes up a position theologically akin to the above
see Barth, *CD*, III/3, pp.14-57.

[10] For references see Barbour, *Issues*, pp.431ff; Langford, *Providence*, pp.79-87.

[11] P. Baelz, *Prayer and Providence*, London: S.C.M., 1968, p.121.

[12] Langford, *Providence*, p.91. Cf. Hartshorne, *Divine Relativity*, pp.23-24,
137-138; Keith Ward, *Holding Fast to God*, London: S.P.C.K., 1982, p.96. Cf.
More radical approaches, G. Kaufman, *God the Problem*, Cambridge, Mass:
Harvard University Press, 1972, chapter 6; M. Wiles, *Working Papers on Doctrine*,
London: S.C.M., 1976, chapter 11.

good he desires for the entire created order, the consequent, or specific, providential working is restricted to that which is actually accomplished of his general plan. God wills the general but accomplishes only the specific, and this because of the barrier of finite human freedom. Nevertheless, there is a measure of certitude about divine providence in that some creatures will definitely respond to the divine overtures.[13]

B. The Religious Request and the Temporalist Reply

H.H. Farmer finds the doctrine of providence to be of great significance: "It has been said that faith in providence is religion itself, and again, that denial of providence is the denial of all religion."[14] Can **any** sense be made of the doctrine of providence by temporalistic theists of the sort named above? There have been many philosophers and theologians who have insisted that religion demands full sovereignty from the deity and that logic specifies that only an atemporal God can meet this demand. If God cannot know future free actions how can he possibly answer prayers which bear on future free behaviour[15] and what assurance is there that the believers hope in God will not be frustrated?[16] More specifically, for biblically based religions, if trust is based on putative prophecies, and God is not fully provident, the prospect of deception (misplaced trust) cannot be eliminated.[17] To put the matter another way, in Walls' language: "if he did not know everything that could and would flow from his creation of this universe, then something might develop which he did not anticipate and which he could not control. Thus, if he were limited in what he could know, he would not be omnipotent."[18] Schleiermacher went so far as to say that if God's knowledge of

---

[13] J.H. Wright, "The Eternal Plan of Divine Providence", *Thomist*, 27, 1966, pp.27-57.

[14] H.H. Farmer, *The World and God*, London: Collins, 1963, p.89.

[15] So, Charnocke, *Attributes*, p.1610.

[16] See, Langerak, "Foreknowledge", p.13; Luther, *Bondage*, p.122; Yearley, "Aquinas", p.410.

[17] See, P. Helm, "God and Whatever Comes to Pass", *Religious Studies*, 14, 1978, p.323; Normore, "Contingents", p.373; Zeis, "Eternity", p.69.

[18] J.L. Walls, "Can God Save Anyone He Will?", *Scottish Journal of Theology*, 38, 1985, p.161. Cf. Hebblethwaite, "Farrer", p.543.

history is not exhaustive, "the idea of providence must be wholly given up."[19]

Most Western theists would probably be unhappy about this conclusion for a number of reasons. It is not surprising to find the doctrine of timelessness attached as a misrepresentation of the real issus at this point. Nash thinks this is so: "The timelessness of God and the sovereignty of God are clearly independent notions ... God's sovereignty is not compromised in any way by the Scriptures' assertion that God acts in time and is thus an everlasting being."[20] For such theists the real issue is not God's eternity but his Lordship over time, and this can stand without any appeal to timelessness.[21]

C. The Classical Reply

In taking up the temporalistic challenge I can only reiterate the treatment in the early part of the seventh chapter of this book: **how** can a temporal deity possess the foreknowledge upon which **any** sure exercise of sovereignty would seem to be dependent? In that chapter I reviewed the chess-master strategy of Peter Geach, various "gaze" solutions of divine prescience or precognition, and the concept of middle knowledge. It was decided at that point that the proposals were either inadequate to ensure future knowledge or else were vacuous assertions that God could "just know" what would come about. I do not believe anyone has as yet shown how foreknowledge could be logically possible without recourse to doctrine of atemporality.[22]

To put the point I am making here a little more clearly:

---

[19] Schleiermacher, *CF*, 55.3, in Mackintosh translation, p.227.

[20] R.H. Nash, *The Concept of God*, Grand Rapids: Academie, 1983, p.82. Cf. Wolterstorff, "God Everlasting", p.303.

[21] See, Brunner, *Dogmatics*, vol 1, pp.266-270; Galloway, *Philosophy*, p.480; Jantzen, *God's World*, pp.59ff; Matthews, *God*, Chapter 12.

[22] V. White, *The Fall of a Sparrow: a concept of special divine action*, Exeter: Paternoster 1985, p.147 comes to conclude in his specialized study of the question of providence that only an extra-temporal deity could act providentially. I concur with his negative conclusion, he however goes on to envisage this extra-temporality in terms of an extended "specious present", a position examined and rejected in the fourth chapter of this book.

1. Providence requires foreknowledge.
2. Foreknowledge requires atemporality.
3. Providence requires atemporality.

If the earlier argument of chapter seven was valid, the objector might turn on the first premise and seek to establish that providence, in whatever sense he might like to give it, does not require foreknowledge. Yet it is extremely difficult to see how anything but verbal assent could be given to the doctrine of providence without a prescient deity. If God's knowledge is temporally bound like ours, and the world is not absolutely deterministic, he must wait to see, and so, just accept, the free actions of his creatures. The consequences of such a view are enormous. David Basinger has highlighted the issues:

> Consider, for example, God's initial creation ... what kind
> of creative options did God have 'before' creation if he
> had only present knowledge. He could have conceived of
> many possibilities. But assuming that he desired to create
> a universe containing significantly free individuals, he did
> not know 'before' creation exactly what would happen.
> He knew he would veto anything he did not want. But he
> did not know with certainty which type of free will
> universe ... would develop ... He did not even have the
> assurance that he would not need to remove freedom
> totally to 'save' his creation from destruction. In short,
> for a God with present knowledge, the creative act was a
> significant gamble.[23]

I cannot see how a time-bound God can be anything but one step behind his creatures, so that the logical possibility of frustrating his plan at any, and so every, point cannot be denied. In such a scheme not even "specific providence" is certain.[24] Some theists might reply that God knows all that was, is and could have been, and religious people must be satisfied with things as they are. It is just not logically realistic to expect any more from God.[25] Yet could this sort of a being really qualify as God, not just the God of religion, but as the ultimate

---

[23] Basinger, "Middle Knowledge", pp.410-411.

[24] Cf. Kondoleon, "Immutability", pp.304-306; White, *Sparrow*, pp.82-86.

[25] So, R.L. Factor, "Newcomb's Paradox and Omniscience", *International Journal for Phiosophy of Religion*, 9, 1978, pp.39-40.

being of any thoroughgoing philosophy? In the first place the attribute of omniscience would have to be severely qualified, limited to the immediately observable and the surely predictable. Secondly, the attribute of omnipotence must be seriously attenuated, a temporal deity is logically incapable of executing a universal plan. A God in time would be a God in flux and a God without foreknowledge could know neither his own future free actions nor human responses to them.[26] Such a being could, conceivably, in Tillich's words: "be subject to the anxiety of the unknown."[27] For all of these reasons I believe that the doctrine of providence, through its religious and philosophical implications, can only be satisfied in any meaningful way if God is timeless. Or, to put it in Bernard Lonergan's rather tortuous words: "It is only in the logico- metaphysical simultaneity of the atemporal present that God's knowledge is infallible, His will irresistible, His action efficacious."[28]

D. Timelessness and Necessary Being

In the present section I wish to briefly examine the relationship between the idea of God as a necessary being and that of the attribute of timelessness. In classical thought there is a long history of the insistence that God is the sort of being who must exist. Perhaps the best known example of this is Aquinas' exposition: "I maintain then that the proposition 'God exists' is self evident in itself, for, as we shall see later, its subject and predicate are identical, God in his own existence ... Therefore, since in God there is no potentiality ... it follows that in him essence does not differ from existence. Therefore

---

[26] See, Ferre, *Understanding*, p.94; Leibniz, "Second Letter to Clarke", 9; Swinburne, *Coherence*, p.177.

[27] Tillich, *Systematic Theology*, vol 1, p.276.

[28] Lonergan, *Grace and Freedom*, p.116. Cf. Neville, *Creation*, p.261. It is realised that strictly speaking the classical view of God as atemporal does not of itself **entail** the doctrine of providence. (An apathetic atemporal Creator might, for example, not be providential.) Rather, what I have argued is that if there are good grounds for wanting to assert a doctrine of providence, as there would seem to be within the context of a "perfect being theology", then providence requires God's timelessness. Cf. Westphal, "Dipolar", p.556.

His essence is his existence."[29]   To put it roughly, to be God is to exist. Thomas Gilby remarks: "God is not **an** essence nor **an** existence. He is the godhead, and the godhead is **esse**."[30]

There has been a considerable amount of discussion in recent philosophical literature about the possibility of a necessary being. Much of this has been generated by J.N. Findlay's now famous "ontological disproof" concerning the existence of God. Findlay contended that God as a fit object of worship must be thought of as necessarily existing. But existentially necessary propositions cannot be true, for necessity is a logical characteristic of propositions, not of reality. Therefore, God cannot exist.[31] Replies to Findlay have been many and varied, and here is not the place to rehearse them. It is sufficient for the purposes of this book to work with the idea of God as a "factually necessary being", that is, a being whose necessity relates to its existential or ontological properties.[32] This is usually interpreted in terms of non-contingence, that God is a being who is caused to exist by no other being. Robert Taylor does so: "a being that is non contingent, and hence not perishable ... If it makes sense to talk about an impossible being, or something that by its very nature does not exist, then it is hard to see why the idea of necessary being ... should not be just as comprehensible."[33]

Views such as these however do not satisfy anti-theists as hard-bitten as J.L. Mackie:

> Since it is always a further question whether a concept is instantiated or not, no matter how much it contains, the existence even of a being whose essence included

---

[29] Aquinas, *S.Th.* 1a. 2,1; 3,4. Cf. Philo, citations in Hartshorne and Reese, *Philosophers*, pp.43-44; Maimonides, *The Guide for the Perplexed*, 1. 57. etc.

[30] T. Gilby, "Simplicity and Unity: Appendix 12", *S.Th.* vol 2, p.216 (my emphasis).

[31] J.N. Findlay, "Can God's Existence Be Disproved?", in Flew and MacIntyre, *New Essays*, pp.47-56; Cf. Ewing, "Proofs", pp.33-34.

[32] Cf. J. Hick, "God as Necessary Being", *Journal of Philosophy*, 57, 1960, pp.725-734.

[33] Taylor, *Metaphysics*, p.111; cf. R. Franklin, "Necessary Being", *Australasian Journal of Philosophy*, 35, 1957, p.100; Geach, *Three Philosophers*, pp.114-115; T.V. Morris and C. Menzel, "Absolute Creation", *American Philosophical Quarterly*, 24, 1986, p.360.

existence would not be self-explanatory; there might have failed to be any such thing ... if it is alleged tht this being nonetheless exists by a metaphysical necessity, we are still waiting for an explanation of this kind of necessity.[34]

Mackie's challenge, which reminds us of Kant on the ontological proof, seems to be that even if the concept of a self-explanatory being makes sense, so that if such a being exists it makes no sense to ask why it exists, one can still ask if such a being is in fact actual. Mackie has in fact pointed us in the direction of sharpening up our concept of God's necessary existence. Any being whose essence was such hat it could not but exist in every possible world would have to be a very special sort, not only non-contingent, or the source of all continge nce, but with properties whose non- instantiation is not strongly conceivable.[35]   Arguably, one such property is the divine simultaneity. Charles Hartshorne points this out:

> The very meaning of eternal is dubious apart from necessity. Without necessity, nothing could establish the least probability of eternity; one would have to wait, so to speak, forever to see if the thing did always go on existing. Nay more, since the future is potential rather than actual, even God Himself could not know that He would never cease to exist, except by knowing this to be impossible; and how could he at the same time know that this non-existence was (is?) eternally conceivable is utterly beyond even the vaguest imagining.[36]

By "eternal" Hartshorne means everlasting and not timeless. His point is an important one. It is difficult to find a reason, apart from necessity, why any temporal being should be everlasting. But Hartshorne does not posit for us a reason why a sempiternal God should be necessary. Richard Swinburne seems to be closer to the mark when he posits two ways in which God's existence as an inexplicable brute fact can be spelled out. One is to say that God is a

[34] J.L. Mackie, *The Miracle of Theism*, Oxford: Clarendon, 1982, p.84.

[35] For a full reply to Mackie see L. Garcia, "Can There Be a Self-Explanatory Being?", *Southern Journal of Philosophy*, 24, 1986, pp.479-488.

[36] C. Hartshorne, *Anselm's Discovery*, La Salle: Open Court, 1965, p.129.

being of such a kind that if he exists at any time he exists at all times. The other is to suppose that God's existence from time to time is itself an inexplicable brute fact. As Swinburne confesses, neither of these explanations makes God's being other than logically contingent.[37]

Whilst I do not wish to push the point about **logical** contingency, I believe there is something amiss with these temporalistic positions. Norman Malcolm wants to argue that the duration of any entity is contingent **fact**. Even if something were to have endless duration its existence would be just as contingent as that of finite things for duration is univocal. If something has endless duration it will **make sense** (although it will be false) to say that it will cease to exist, or to say that something will cause it to cease to exist.[38]   Malcolm's argument seems to be a combination of linguistic and metaphysical stipulations.   The former need not detain us here, though it seems correct that we can always meaningfully ask whether a temporal deity will go on existing. A temporalistic theist is likely to fend off such a problem lightly by saying that God possesses properties over and above his temporality which make his everlasting instantiation certain. Appeal might be made to God's omnipotence at this point, but omnipotence is not usually conceived in terms of the power to preserve one's own being. Probably, the defense would come to rest with God's "incorruptibility".   The problem with this position however is that is seems logically dependent on other elements of an attribute cluster usually identified with classical theism, in particular simplicity, immutability and eternity. It would seem extremely difficult to attribute the first two properties to a temporal God, at least a temporal deity who did anything. It is not unlikely therefore that the temporalist will just have assert the continued existence of God to be a brute fact.

The classical theist is in a much stronger position. It does not seem to be meaningful to ask questions about the possibility of an atemporal deity who is **totum simul existens** going out of existence. Such a question would quite simply be misplaced. If such a being exists it is self-evident that it exists necessarily. Aquinas puts the matter in the

---

[37] R. Swinburne, *The Existence of God*, Oxford: Clarendon: 1979, p.93; Cf. Coburn, "Malcolm", pp.150, 152.

[38] N. Malcolm, "Anselm's Ontological Arguments", *Philosophical Review*, 69, 1960, p.48. Cf. Leibniz, *Fifth Letter to Clarke*, 50; Tillich, *Systematic Theology*, vol 1, p.275.

following interesting form: "Now every necessary thing either has a cause of its necessity from without, or has no such cause, but is necessary of itself. But we cannot go to infinity in necessary things that have causes of their necessity from without. Therefore we must suppose some first necessary thing which is necessary of itself: and this is God ... Therefore God is eternal because whatever is necessary of itself is eternal."[39] This is hardly a proof that God's necessity is his eternity, but it is in a way a **reductio**. If God were temporal we could always ask "What causes him to exist now?" In answering this we would have to proceed **ad infinitum** is a description of his preceding state, but at no point would the regress come to a final solution.[40] Such a deity would seem to possess the same existential status, as say, the everlastingness of matter in Hellenistic thought. We are surely a long way from the "greatest conceivable being".

At this point one begins to appreciate the positive character of the classical concept of eternity; eternity is not just the negation of motion, change, temporality and beginning and end, but it expresses the necessity which God's existence has by virtue of his own essence.[41] Eternity is, as it were, the way in which God's absolute illimitability is to be expressed and understood. Whilst it is not possible to logically demonstrate that a sempiternal being could not be a necessary being the notion of atemporal simultaneity, if coherent, adds a dimension of explanatory power to the concept of God as necessarily-existent that moves us beyond the realm of a bare assertion. Whilst these sort of matters are not easy to weigh up, it does seem to me, as classical theists have always insisted, that the attributes of eternity contributes to the intelligibility of the concept of an ultimate being. In this way I believe that we have a positive reason for affirming the notion of the timeless life of God.[42]

E. Eternity and the Greatest Existent

Throughout this book I have used the terms "eternity" and "timelessness" as though they were interchangeable, strictly speaking

---

[39] Aquinas, *S.C.G.* 1.15,4.

[40] See, Owen, *Concepts*, p.20.

[41] Cf. Wolfson, *Spinoza*, vol 1, pp.363-366 for references to medieval sources.

[42] These last comments of course presuppose that the notion of an ultimate being is in some way meaningful.

THE TIMELESSNESS OF GOD

this is not so, for whilst eternity embraces the idea of atemporality it is not exhausted by it, for the divine eternity, unlike timelessness, includes the notion of fulness of life. Unfortunately, the privative emphasis on eternity as the negation of time has come to the fore in the writings of a number of theists in such a way as to perhaps mislead readers into thinking that this is the primary element in the classical concept of the divine eternity.[43] The emphasis in many classical authors that God lives in an "eternal **now**" indicates that his being has little in common with the static unchanging atemporality of numbers and logical principles. It is enough to remind ourselves that the Boethian definition ("the complete possession all at once of illimitable life") is about a **life** to indicate that eternity is essentially a positive concept.[44] It is one thing however to read this as part of a definition and another to discourse about this concept in a way which truly reflects the positive intention of its formulators.

Thomas Gilby makes an important point when he suggests that the eternal is: "a notion which negatively represents the non-negative in our mind."[45] As indicated in the introduction, it is impossible to hold together **at the same time** in our minds the many attributes which are believed to make up the divine life in its simultaneity. The best we can do as essentially successive beings in order to intuit what is meant by **totum simul existens** is to strip away from our thinking about God concepts which are antithetical to the divine eternity, such as motion, change and time. The negation of these properties is of course not meant to imply that God is these negations, even if we cannot but think of him in this way. That is to say, it would be a mistake to think that in knowing what God is not we have adequately grasped what he is. H.A. Wolfson has made the helpful note that there is a distinction between two types of negation, "privation", and what the Neoplatonists termed "remotion". In the case of the negation by remotion the opposite of the negated proposition cannot be asserted, whereas for privation it may be. This is because negation by remotion serves to exclude a subject from the universe of discourse of the logical type to which both the original predicate and its simple negation

---

[43] See, for example, Galloway, *Philosophy*, p.478; Hegel, *Philosophy of Nature*, p.258; Kneale, "Eternity", pp.227-228; McTaggart, "Relation", p.344; Pringle-Pattison, *Modern Philosophers*, pp.344-345; *Image*, pp.22, 146.

[44] Cf. E. Frank, "Time and Eternity", *Review of Metaphysics*, 2, 1948, p.40.

[45] T. Gilby, "Eternity: Appendix 16", *S.Th.* vol 2, pp.227-228.

are appropriate.[46] To negate temporality of God is not therefore to imply that he is the literal opposite of the temporal, but that his atemporality refers to a mode of existence outside the logical containment of temporal or non-temporal qualifiers.[47] It is to suppose that God has a certain special mode of existence appropriate to himself. In one way the goal of this book has been to say what can be said about this existence, given the necessary inadequacies of thought and language. Classical theists have tried to sum up the character of the divine existence by reference to the idea of "perfection".

This idea is not an easy one to tease out , but it would seem that it must reasonably include the following elements. A perfect being must be essentially and necessarily unsurpassable in positive value by anything that could ever be conceived as actual.[48] As such it must possess the sum total of all logically compossible attributes which could be reasonably conceived as bestowing value on their bearer.[49] Finally, it must possess all of its positive, or great making attributes in an infinite manner, that is inexhaustibly and free of all limi tations.[50] This does not get us very far, except perhaps to reiterate briefly what is meant by Anselm's "greatest conceivable being", or to say that deity must be compatible with "the highest we know".[51] Yet it is unlikely that many theists in the Judeao-Christian tradition would wish to deny these few principles, even though they might be given enormously varied specific content. This is just to say that in a very general sense most Western theists would accept that God cannot be properly thought of as other than perfect.[52]

It is but a little step from what has been said in this section so far to understand why so many theists have felt that a perfect being **must**

---

[46] H.A. Wolfson, "Negative Attributes in the Church Fathers and the Gnostic Basilides", *Harvard Theological Review*, 50, 1967, pp.145-156.

[47] See, Tomkinson, "Atemporality", pp.183-184.

[48] See, D.A. Pailin, "The Theologian and the Nature of God", *Religious Studies*, 12, 1976, pp.141-142.

[49] See, Kretzmann, "Omniscience", pp.419-420; D. Blumenfeld, "On the Compossibility of the Divine Attributes", *Philosophical Studies*, 34, 1978, pp.91-103.

[50] So, Owen, *Concepts*, pp.28-29.

[51] C.A. Campbell, *On Selfhood and Godhood*, London: George Allen and Unwin, 1957, p.307.

[52] See, Morris, "Perfect Being", p.20.

eternal. The Protestant scholastic Stephen Charnocke wants to stress this:

> As immortality is the great perfection of a rational creature, so eternity is the choice perfection of God, yea, the gloss and lustre of all others. Every perfection would be imperfect if it were not always a perfection ... But since God is the most sovereign perfection, than which nothing can be imagined greater by the most capacious understanding, he is certainly eternal; being infinite, nothing can be added to him, nothing detracted from him.[53]

When Charnocke says the infinity of God excludes all addition from his being he means that as eternal there is "no room" for development in God, the temporal is wholly inapplicable to a being who cannot change because he "already" contains within himself all that is worthy of possessing.[54] It is at this point that I must protest at the false representation of the classical doctrine of immutability as a type of static immobile necessity. The very reverse is meant by this doctrine, and by the divine eternity. Development, change and enrichment are inapplicable to an **actus purus** not because it is limited but because it is beyond all limits.[55] God is unchangeable because he is absolutely active, this is what it means to possess a life all at once.

This comes out more concretely when attention is focussed on God's life. Whatever is meant by "life" we surely intend a particular type of category of existence which is positive or valuable. Intuitively we consider that there is some sort of a scale of existence from the inanimate through the lower to the highest forms of animate life known to us, viz. ourselves. There seems nothing problematic in conceiving high forms of life than man, angels might be a good

---

[53] Charnocke, *Attributes*, pp.356-358.

[54] Cf. Brabant, *Eternity*, pp.168, 173; Gundersdorf von Jess, "Augustine", p.77, note 10; p.95.

[55] See, J.F. Anderson, "Must Scholasticism Go?", in *The Future of Belief Debate*, G. Baum (ed), N.Y.: Herder and Herder, 1967, p.44-45; J. Richmond, "God, Time and Process Philosophy", *Theology*, May, 1965, pp.234-241; Schiller, *Humanism*, pp.210-211; Ward, *Ends*, p.471; Weinandy, "Aquinas", pp.15-16.

candidate, or a temporal omnipresent being. The point is that unreflectively we already rank existents in terms of their possession of life. By "God" classical theism means a being who "goes off the scale" we have been referring to in that he possesses all his life in a maximally conceivable fashion, that is, he is eternal.

Von Hugel's words are memorable: Eternal life, in the fullest thinkable sense, involves three things - the plentitude of all goods and of all energizings that abide; the entire self-consciousness of the Being which constitutes, and which is expressed by all these goods and energizings; and the pure activity, the non successiveness of simultaneity, of this Being in all that It has, all that It is ... Eternal Life excludes space and clock-time because of the very intensity of its life. The simultaneity is here the fullest expression of the supreme richness, the unspeakable concreteness, the overwhelming aliveness of God; and is at the opposite pole from all empty unity, all more becoming - any or all abstractions whatsoever.[56]

It is difficult to go beyond von Hugel's spirited language. He is trying to describe the uncircumscribable, the absolute fulness or "pleromic" quality of a life that is unsurpassably all-in-all, that is, supreme.[57]

Another way of reflecting on this matter is to note the essential partiality and fragmentariness of temporal existence. To exist in time is to exist in a divided state, for there is not time apart from a succession of instants: without a past that is no longer, a present that is vanishing and a future which is not here.[58] Many authors have pointed out that there seems to exist in man a longing to know things whole and entire, to grasp reality as it were all-together.[59] If time is real for God as it is for us then he too must have a scattered existence. Even a sempiternal being must be limited, for temporality by its very

[56] von Hugel, *Eternal Life*, p.383.
[57] Cf. Bowne, *Metaphysics*, p.240; Garrigou-Lagrange, *Providence*, pp.112-113.
[58] Pontifex, *Providence*, p.25. Cf. Hatano, *Eternity*, pp.85-88.
[59] See, Bosanquet, *Value*, pp.300, 304-305; Gilby,"Eternity", p.229; Taylor, *Elements*, pp.262-263.

nature is limiting. As to the past, even a perfect memory cannot be taken as equivalent to knowing something in its actuality, nor would perfect foresight, even if possible, give to a temporal God a group of real future beings. However God might enjoy the present, a temporal deity would be unable to experience more than the present and so his life could not be conceived as illimitable.[60] C.S. Lewis puts the matter succinctly:

> God has no history, He is too completely and utterly real to have one. For, of course, to have a history means losing part of your reality (because it has already slipped into the past) and not yet having another part: (because it is still in the future): in fact having nothing but the tiny little present, which has gone before you can speak about it. God forbid we should think God was like that.[61]

The discussion so far in this chapter has been about a very fundamental point: how great is the greatest being or the ultimate existent. I have argued that a temporal deity could only possess omniscience and omnipotence in a very attenuated sense, and so could not assuredly be considered providential. If such a being did exist its very existence would have about it an air of mystery, for unlike all other temporal entities we know of, which are, apparently, radically contingent, this being must, somehow, by very definition, be necessary. Finally, the perfection of this purported deity is limited to the range of its temporally bound existence and cannot be construed as illimitable. Whilst none of these considerations logically compel us to think that such a being does not exist, nor demonstrate that the

---

[60] See Tomkinson, "Atemporality", pp.178-188; Trethowan *Mysticism*, pp.35-36, 157. The divine eternity in the way I have represented it is such that God, strictly speaking, experiences neither past, present nor future, that is, he does not know existents in mutual relation to himself at all. That this does not rob God of any quality of experience is due to the fact that he is construed as possessing in his own essence, without creatures, fullness of life. An adoption of this notion by temporalistic theism to overcome the immediately mentioned problem is not possible, simply because the given specification is inherent in the very notion of timelessness itself. To think of a temporal deity as "quasi- **ipsum esse**" or "semi-**actus purus**" and so able to stretch his life backwards and forwards in time is simply contradictory.

[61] Lewis, *Mere Christianity*, p.145.

supreme existing being is eternal, nevertheless, one is left with the feeling that the very logic of "God" has been altered beyond recognition. There are not lacking however many theists who would argue that this is just as it should be.

Robert Coburn, in moving along this track, claims that it is difficult to see why necessary existence should make a thing more perfect, and cites the example of the logically necessary existence of the prime number between 21 and 24. Alternatively, he says, why shouldn't something be eternal (non-temporal), and also be logically capable of non- existence?[62] These objections do not touch the classical understanding of the divine eternity. The necessary perfection of God is not like that of a number, but is construed to be that of a living being, God's necessity is an expression of his perfect **life**. To be alive and contingent is less perfect than to be alive and necessary for the former raises the spectre of not being alive at all. Similarly, when the meaning of **totum simul existens** is grasped, the notion of God failing to exist (if he does exist) is seen to be impossible. No specification can be given as to how a being who **is** infinite life could go out of existence.

Of greater significance is the assertion that perfection could or must include change. One appeal here is to the portrayal of the active loving nature of God in the Bible, that is, to a non-Hellenistic concept of perfection.[63] Aside from the fact that it is a fundamental mistake to treat the Bible as a metaphysical treatise, I have argued consistently in this book that the notion of eternity is not incompatible with a God who acts and provides for his creation. More usually however, the appeal is not to the authority of revelation but to the demands of reason. Why might there not be progress **in** perfection?[64] Steinkraus puts up the challenge: "Cannot the meaning of perfection be **expanded** to include development?"[65] Or, in the case of process theism, there is the repeated charge that to interpret perfection in terms of timelessness is to exclude all novelty and so enrichment from the

---

[62] Coburn, "Malcolm", pp.146, 151.

[63] So, J. Barr, *Fundamentalism*, London: S.C.M., 1980, p.277; A Heschel, *Man Is Not Alone*, N.Y.: Octagon, 1951, p.101; Mason, "Worship", p.88.

[64] See, Gunn, *Problem*, p.339.

[65] Steinkraus, "Time", p.247 (my emphasis).

divine life.[66] If life as we observe and experience it is always associated with change must not changelessness mean death and perfect life entail unbridled dynamism.[67] Charles Hartshorne has thrown the subject into clear perspective by his process reinterpretation of the meaning of the Anselmian dictum "greatest conceivable being". "To be worthy of worship a being must not be (conceivably) surpassed by another, but it need not, in all respects, be unsurpassable absolutely for it may, indeed it must, in some respects be self-surpassable."[68] God is a perfect being, but only in the sense that he cannot be surpassed by any other being. This allows the possibility that God can surpass himself. Creaturely beings are in no sense necessary to God's existence, to this extent God is self sufficient, but, according to process philosophy, God depends on his creatures in order to surpass himself. On this view God possesses a relative perfection, God is perfect in relation to others, but not in relation to himself. God freely chooses to surpass himself because his perfect being entails that he be receptive to change, and not static, that he be creative, and hence possess potential. A perfect being cannot be static, since its ability to respond to changing events requires it to be dynamic: the God who knows, loves, wills and creates cannot be a being who stands in no need of anything else.[69] Hartshorne again: "Not finitude but fragmentariness is the mark of the non-divine. Hundreds of thousands of scholars have managed to miss this distinction."[70]

I suspect that these alternatives to the classical understanding of perfection simply beg the question against it in that they presuppose

---

[66] See, Ford, "Boethius", p.50; "Non-Temporality", p.362- 363; C. Hartshorne, "The Idea of a Worshipful Being", *Southern Journal of Philosophy*, 2, 1964, p.165.

[67] See, Brightman, "Temporalist", pp.547-548; Leighton, *Man*, p.515; Weiss, *Modes*, p.34.

[68] Hartshorne, "Worshipful", p.165.

[69] See Hartshorne and Reese, *Philosophers*, p.509; Hartshorne, *Anselm's Discovery*, pp.28-32, "Dipolar Conception", pp.274-275, *Creative Synthesis and Philosophic Method*, London: S.C.M., 1970, p.235; J. Felt, "Invitation to a Philosophic Revolution", *New Scholasticism*, 45, 1971, pp.104-105; Ogden, *Reality*, pp.59ff; S. Sia, "On God, Time and Change", *Clergy Review*, 63, 1978, pp.380-381; Surin, "Self-Existence", pp.30-31.

[70] Hartshorne, "Worshipful", p.165.

that there cannot be a fully actualized being. If such a being is logically possible then to talk about progress in perfection at an expansion of the idea of perfection is contradictory, the absolute as absolute cannot be extended. If God exists as **totum simul,** in the manner that has been argued throughout, then to suppose that he could be enriched is to suppose that the Creator of all could receive back from his creation something which he himself did not give it. But this is impossible. There is a web of concepts here: **actus purus, creatio ex nihilo,** aseity, and there is nothing in the alternative suggestions about perfection to indicate that the web must break down. Perhaps one just grasps the concept of a being whose mode of existence does not admit of increase, because perfect, or one does not. Many have claimed that the notion of such a being is conceivable, even if not imaginable. I just do not feel any force in the non-classical assertions at this point.

If the concept of absolute simultaneity in the divine life, or pure act, is not coherent, then Hartshorne's understanding of perfection is probably correct in its basic outlines. The greatest that a temporal being could hope to be would be to possess the maximal realization of values at any particular time, so that an increase of value would always be logically possible. On the basis of such a conception, God's existence might be independent of the world but **what** God is like must be intrinsically dependent upon the world. Such a God is not only a being "on his way", like all other beings,[71] but a being who can never reach completeness as long as the universe is never complete, which, on a process philosophy in terpretation, is never. If the universe really is a contingent entity, that it might never have been, or might never be, is a logically possible state of affairs, in which case there might never have been growth in God, or, growth in God might cease. A process philosophy would seem only to have recourse to two alternatives at this point. It can argue that the universe is not contingent considered **in se;** but this would give it the same logical status as God's existence. Or it can fall back upon the primordial nature of God as an ultimate principle of explanation for growth in God-and-the-world; but this would be to fall into the arms of classical theism. That is, the consequent or concrete nature of God with its "relative perfection" would become dependent upon the primordial or

---

71 Cf. J. Macquarrie, *Twentieth-Century Religious Thought,* N.Y.: Harper and Row, 1963, p.277.

abstract nature of God, which is a reversal of what process theism wishes to maintain, viz. that the abstract is fulfilled in the concrete. Doubtless a process theist might maintain that God, in freely deciding to create the universe, willingly choose to be incomplete and the bearer of a "relative perfection".[72] Broken down in terms of the analysis above this can only mean that for God to choose to be dependent (on the world) was a higher act than to choose to remain independent; it was better for God to need the world than not to need the world. To be wholly dependent upon the existence of other entities for one's (relative) perfection becomes an element in perfection itself (or perfectibility). For classical thought this is simply to reduce the Creator to the status of a creature. Leaving aside all the problems faced by process metaphysics outline in chapter four, one suspects that the whole meaning of "perfect" has been altered. I think we have reached again a terminus in thought where one must decide in favour of a certain type of metaphysical ultimate principle: dependence, as per process thought, and perhaps for all 'temporalistic theism, or independence. To choose for the latter is to endorse God as **totum simul existens**.[73]

Allied to the above attack on the classical concept of timeless perfection is the insistence that a timeless being could not be appropriately worshipped. The relevance of this consideration arises out of Hartshorne's interpretation of "greatness" is the Anselmian definition of God in terms of a being worthy of worship.[74] This may be allowed at this point.[75] An absolute God in the classical sense, Hartshorne argues, must possess an existence exclusive of that of finite entities, as such he can only be conceived of as an abstraction

---

[72] If God had not chosen to create he could not be "relatively perfect", for there would be nothing other than himself against which he could measure his perfection or out of interaction with which he could grow to surpass himself. That is, considered empirically, he would have had to be perfect **simpliciter.**

[73] A consideration of what creatures might get out of creation is not relevant at this point for they exist only subsequent (logically) to the act of creation. (It is appreciated here that we are not dealing with the traditional doctrine of **creatio ex nihilo** but with the logical question of dependence.)

[74] Hartshorne, *Anselm's Discovery*, pp.25-26.

[75] For alternative interpretations see Pike, *Timelessness*, pp.130-149.

and so not fitting of worship.[76] We are to worship God, and not certain philosophical abstractions inherited from the Greeks: "I take `true religion' to mean serving God ... contributing value to God which he would otherwise lack. Even in this religious case to `serve' is to confer benefit, in precisely the sense that the served will to some extent depend upon the server ... God ... lacking dependence is not the God we can serve or, in what I think is the proper meaning, worship."[77] Many other philosophers have taken up this point: a timeless deity would have to be a complete spectator concerning worldly events, and so could not be reverenced,[78] We worship God, Wolterstoff says: "not because he is outside of time ... (but) because of what he can and does bring about within time ...",[79] the **Deus philosophorum** of classical thought is entirely detached from religious experience,[80] and so on.

One hardly need pause to reply to many of these statements. Some of them seem patently eudaimonistic - we should only worship God if he can help us, a timeless God can't help us, so he shouldn't be worshipped. Surely however the question about God's worshipfulness is one about his worth or intrinsic value, and not about his value for - us. Other comments have the tone of religious preference - God must need us or else he couldn't be God. Yet this line of thought presupposes the position that dependence is a perfection, something I have rejected above. It is correct to note that atemporality of itself does not and should not evoke worship, but no classical theist has ever claimed that the divine eternity is merely the negation of time. Rather, as I have stressed in this chapter, it is the **pleroma** of the divine life, it is the absolute standing fulness of the divine existence - it is God in all that he is, all-together, simultaneously. It is this positive conception of eternity which is compatible with worship. More than this, I have struggled in this book to demonstrate that God can be actually related to contingent beings in the most intimate fashion, not despite, but because of his

---

[76] C. Hartshorne, "Absolute Objects and Relative Subjects", *Review of Metaphysics*, 15, 1961, p.169.

[77] Hartshorne, "Dipolar Conception", p.274.

[78] See, Alexander, *Space*, vol 2, p.399; Galloway, *Philosophy*, p.479.

[79] Wolterstorff "Everlasting", p.98. Cf. Pike, *Timelessness*, p.161.

[80] Matthews, *God*, pp.101-110.

timelessness. I return here to the centrality of the doctrine of **creatio ex nihilo**.

For most theists, at least in the Judeao-Christian tradition, worship would seem to be a response to a perceived otherness in God, to an apprehension of unlimited superiority.[81] I believe Neville is correct in pointing to the concept of creation as the most thorough and arresting expression of the supremacy of a God who acts, for it requires neither objects upon which to exert power nor a medium through which to exert it. It is because God in relation to us is absolutely independent of us that he is to be worshipped.[82] Ronald Puccetti puts the matter well:

> The least one requires of an adequate object of religious attitudes is of course its superiority to oneself and to others around one. But for the reflective theist this is not enough. To him religious attitudes are really only appropriate to an object which towers **infinitely** over all actual and possible objects of such attitudes. Thus one is driven to a conception of a being possessed of unlimited superiority, both in thought and in reality to anything else we can conceive.[83]

If this perspective on religious thought is correct, as I believe it is, then not only is the classical concept of divine eternity compatible with worship, but it is properly required by it.[84]

In concluding this brief discussion of the relationship between the divine perfection and the divine eternity it would seem evident that one of the motivating forces behind the development of the latter concept is the desire to maximize conceptually what is contained in the idea of God. Rather than there being any incompatibility between eternity and perfection, if the former is appreciated in its truly positive emphasis, the two umbrella concepts would seem to be entailing. This is more

---

[81] Rudolph Otto's famous thesis is relevant here. *The Idea of the Holy*, tr. J.W. Harvey, London: Oxford University Press, 1931. See also W.D. Hudson, "Divine Transcendence", *Religious Studies*, 15, 1969, pp.197-210.

[82] See, Neville, *Creator*, pp.190, 195-196, 265.

[83] R. Puccetti, "The Concept of God", *Philosophical Quarterly*, 14, 1964, pp.237-238.

[84] Assuming, that is, that a fitting object for acts of worship **exists**.

evident when we remember that eternity is not an attribute specifying the logical status of a divine operation as, for example, omnipotence is, nor is it primarily negative, as, for example, immutability is, but it is a way of describing the mode of being of **all** that God is. In this way it is a sort of super-attribute,[85] specifying the absolutely intensive manner in which all of the attributes of God exist together in the divine nature. We are at the limits of thought here, and certainly beyond that of imagination, but if a perfect being exists an aspect of its ineffably exalted nature would seem to be that it must exist **totum simul**.

F. Summary and Conclusion.

The stated purpose of this chapter was to offer some positive reasons for believing that God, broadly understood in the tradition of Western theism, must be eternal. The first part of the chapter was essentially an outworking of the material in chapter seven concerning the limited knowledge of a temporal deity. If foreknowledge of future free acts is logically denied any being then the inevitable conclusion seems to be that not even the most general divine plan for the good of creatures is capable of certain resolution. It might be argued that religion just has to be satisfied with a God who only in a very attenuated sense is able to know and operate in the world. The whole thrust of this work however has been to try and demonstrate, in terms of the divine eternity and its corollaries, that such a diminution of the concept of God is not logically demanded. If the concept of the divine eternity is coherent, and if God possesses certain other attributes, such as goodness, then a very strong doctrine of providence would seem to be entailed. To deny eternity at this point would to make the relationship between the Creator and the creature in many ways nominal, and this because of what can only be conceived of as a limitation in the former.

The deficiencies of temporalistic theism as a rationally balanced system come out more clearly when it is considered what sense can be given to the idea of God as necessary being. Since everything we know **sub specie temporalis** exists with radical contingency it seems extremely difficult, if not impossible, for temporalistic theists to fend off the claim that God must be a contingent being also. To accept

---

[85] That is in the **ordo cognoscendi** (order of knowing), rather than in the **ordo essendi** (order of being).

this however would be to deny the concept of deity the explanatory position it has generally been accorded in Western theism. Once this step was taken the case for atheism would be greatly strengthened. The non-classical theist seems forced into a position where he must claim that "God, though temporal, is nevertheless necessary", is just a brute fact. Classical theism however avoids altogether the apparent conflict of claiming that some temporal being must exist by defining the mode of God's existence in such a way that if he does exist he must exist necessarily. Any being who is atemporal and has it's life **totum simul** cannot but exist in a, factually, necessary manner. Although this whole discussion takes place within an accepted theistic framework, it would hardly seem deniable that, as a matter of logic, classical theism has the greatest explanatory power at this point.

Whilst from the time of its formulation the Anselmian motto "greatest conceivable being" has been subject to controversy it nevertheless possesses plausibe appeal in emphasising that the deity must possess maximally consistent perfection. Even if the very notion of "perfection" is not self-evident, the point of contact between the major rival forms of Western theism enables genuine dialogue on this matter. I have argued in this chapter that when the divine eternity is appreciated in its positive aspect it presents a higher view of perfection than alternative positions, because it alone asserts that God possesses all of the good that can ever be possessed in simultaneity. There seems no way of escaping the conclusion that **any** temporal being must exist in a dispersed fashion, and so lacks at any given time some of the goods that could logically be possessed "always" by an eternal being. If this perspective is correct there would seem to be strong grounds for supposing that eternity and perfection are mutually entailing.

To sum up, as I have stressed at several points throughout the book, to consider adequately the attribute of the divine eternity is not to look at a mere facet of the divine existence but to make a decision about what sort of a being God is. If God is timelessly eternal, as Davies puts it: "He is immeasurably superior to anything we can imagine."[86] The whole metaphysical structure of a variety of contemporary theistic systems, of which process philosophy is the most influential, seems to be oriented towards avoiding a conclusion such as this. If however the arguments of this chapter, and the related

---

[86] B. Davies, "God, Time and Change", *Clergy Review*, 63, 1978, p.60.

material preceding it, are valid, we are confronted with a choice between the unbounded deity of classical theism, entirely independent of the world, and what may be called a "superman idea of God",[87] of a deity much greater than us but in some measure dependent upon us. I submit that only the former concept is true to the very logic of "God".

---

[87] Swinburne, "Timelessness 1", p.334.

CHAPTER TEN

CONCLUSION

The stated intention of this book in its introduction was to defend and develop the classical doctrine of the divine eternity in the face of a contemporary onslaught of philosophical objections. This was felt to be a topic worthy of investigation because of its implications as to what sort of a being God might be. This indeed became evident through the historical discussion of chapter two, where it was observed that a line of intellectual descent from Plato and Aristotle divided the classical tradition into two camps over the mode of God's timeless relation with the world. It was decided at this early stage to follow through the latter model with its emphasis upon causation rather than to attempt a reconstruction of the Platonic doctrine of emanation. This means that even if the present work is judged to have failed to meet its own self-stated criteria of consistency and coherence it may nevertheless be the case that an alternative model of God's timelessness can be rationally defended. This in itself is a significant observation, for all too often the critics of the classical concept of God's eternity assume that to have demonstrated a difficulty in the doctrine as it is presented in one classical theist, say Aquinas, is to have demonstrated its radical inadequacy for all classical theism. One major conclusion of this book is that if the opponents of the classical doctrine of the divine eternity wish to show unequivocally that this notion fails altogether, when measured according to the canons of reason, then they will have to investigate much more thoroughly the nuances of the individual expressions of the idea as it appears in individual philosophical theologians.

Another important observation made in the early part of this work, which, though almost self-evident, is virtually ignored in the relevant literature, is that the cogency of the classical doctrine can only be assessed in the light of a viable philosophy of time. It is not adequate to assume, as many publications seem to do, that we know what time is, for the question of the ontological status of time is one of considerable complexity. Perhaps one of the major stumbling blocks in discussions of time and eternity is the hidden presupposition, or at least a certain use of language, which treats time as an entity, rather than a relation. This approach has falsely exacerbated the tensions between the temporal and the eternal. It is simply not good philosophy to think of time as an ultimate posit, a "thing", with which any doctrine of God must come to terms. In this sense time does not exist. Nevertheless, this is not to deny the existence of time **simpliciter**, for temporal relations are real. Here again it was necessary to consider a matter to which philosophers of religion have paid for too little attention, the reality of tense. An enormous difference is made to the parameters of the time-eternity question if it is judged, along with a prominent theory of the nature of time unfamiliar to classical scholars, that all reality exists **totum simul**. Although this essay chose against the tenseless view of time, there remains here a large area of research for the philosophy of religion, for to my knowledge no major attempt has been made to re-interpret the classical understanding of God's relationship with the world in terms of such a position.

In aligning myself with a relational view of time which accepts the reality of becoming and the unique ontological status of the present, I self-consciously adopted a stand, which according to the majority of recent scholarship is incompatible with the classical understanding of God as **totum simul existens**. I chose to define the difficulty here in terms of the so-called "two-worlds problem", the problem of bringing together two proposed components of reality which seem to have nothing intrinsically in common. There seems to be two aspects to this problem in the case of the time- eternity relation, the antithesis of succession and simultaneity, what I termed the "vertical" dimension of the problem, and the difficulty of relating God's being to a non-existent past and future, the so called "horizontal" problem. These two aspects of the time-eternity problem are not always clearly distinguished in the literature, with the result that some confusion exists as to what a coherent doctrine of eternity must thoroughly establish.

This matter became apparent when I surveyed the various major twentieth century attempts to solve the time-eternity problem. Concerning most of these models, many of which self-consciously seek to re-define what is meant by "eternity", one can only express disappointment, insomuch as they do not exhibit the degree of attention and philosophical rigour which is usually found in philosophical theology. Apart from process thought, there appears to be no thorough attempt in Western theism[1] to give an alternative metaphysical grounding to an alternative to classical thought which will do more than place God in the time stream in the same way as finite and contingent beings. This observation may however be improper, for it may just be that temporality and atemporality are the only two real and consistent alte rnatives open to ratiocination in this area.[2] Turning to process thought, it was closely argued that the central notions of dipolarity and process in the deity lead to a number of serious difficulties when the relativistic nature of the universe is treated seriously. Although this matter was picked up in detail only for process philosophy the bizarre character of our world suggested by the relativity of simultaneity is a major problem which has not been adequately dealt with by those forms of theism which place God in (which?) time. One suspects that many pre-Einsteinian concepts are still at work here. I concluded the survey of contending contemporary views with the observation that what seemed to be needed if the "two-worlds problem" in its relevant form was to be solved was a dynamic model of God's relationship to the world. This dynamic, I have argued, is supplied by the idea of a timeless creative causal power.

The concept of timeless causality is controversial, and one which does not readily appeal to the empirical and analytical temper of most modern philosophy. Nevertheless, I have argued that there is a philosophicl tradition, whose emphasis I term "productionist", which provides a context in which this idea can begin to take shape. If it is legitimate to think of causes as "bringing things about", and if the concept of action does not analytically require the notion of passage, then the idea of a timeless causal agent would seem to be free from logical objections. It is at this point that the bulk of the book will be considered to stand or fall, for if the idea of a timeless cause is not accepted I can see no way of meaningfully relating an atemporal God to a temporal world. Given the feasibility of the concept however, it becomes relatively straightforward to interpret the "vertical" and horizontal" dimensions of the "two worlds" problem in terms of the classical, and especially Thomist, doctrine of **creatio ex nihilo**.

---

[1] I am excluding here pantheistic systems, like that of Spinoza.

[2] The best hope for an alernative here would seem to lie in a model which could coherently construe time as multi- dimensional with God in one or more dimensions other than our own.

However strange the doctrine of creation may initially appear, it possesses just those features which are required to ensure a compatibility between a God who is never changing and a world which is always changing. Arguably, if, on their own terms, creation and preservation as explicated by traditional Christian theism are the sort of acts which do not require temporality, then God can be related to the whole finite order throughout space and time in the most intimate manner, yet timelessly.

When viewed **sub specie aeternitatis**, or in terms of the **creatio ex nihilo**, the problem of God's relation to the non-existent past and future is seen to have no different logical status to that of his relation to the "present". This is because the relation of creation is one sided only, being the creature's absolute dependence for its existence upon the Creator. Since the presently existing creature no more pre-exists the action of God than do the past or the future, for considered apart from the creative act past, present and future are all "equally non-existent", God cannot be understood as passively re lating to things in-themselves, for nothing exists in itself. Or, put more positively, God does not relate to things other than as they exist in himself as their total causal origin. There is no possible point of contact between a Creator and his creatures in that, by virtue of the very relation of creation, they receive their entire being from the Creator. All that God knows and all that he does concerning his creatures he knows and does in the simple undivided act of his own existing. Temporality cannot touch such a Creator's life for it too is the result of creation.

This means of course, and in accord with various criticisms of the classical concept of the divine eternity, that God can not only not experience succession but he can never know "what time it is". Some have felt this to be a major loss, and indeed it would be if God needed to relate to the world in any temporal sense. Yet if God is the creator and preserver of the whole space-time history of the cosmos, and this atemporally, then there is not the slightest flicker of existence, past, present or future, for which he is not causally responsible. God as **totum simul existens** may be ignorant of the fact that I am "now" writing this, in the full tensed sense of "now", but it seems impossible to specify how this ignorance has any serious philosophical or religious implications. The continuing debate in the philosophical literature concerning the compatibility of omniscience and immutability (or timelessness) is, on these terms, misplaced, a timeless being, as a timeless being, cannot be in possession of the sort of knowledge conveyed by token-reflexive sentences. This however is not a loss, for, according to my argument, the same fact which makes this sort of temporal knowledge impossible for God, his being creator-preserver of all things **ex nihilo**, gives him a scope of knowledge (of a non-tensed sort) and familiarity with the finite order immeasurably superior to that which can conceivably be possessed by any temporal deity. The objections raised in this area, as in others, against the classical concept of eternity, just do not seem to come to grips with the radical ontological disparity between the Creator and the creature, which, far from making the time-eternity problem insuperable, when properly grasped, show that no real problem exists. I am again here supposing that ideas like **actus purus, ipsum esse** and creation **ex nihilo** are logically tenable, they very well may not be, but what the crtics of the concept of the divine eternity have failed to address is the question of whether this idea is explicable in the light of these larger metaphysical ideas. There is a challenge here for temporalistic theists to properly engage the classical concept in its broader context.[3]

Perhaps one of the most surprising conclusions of the book comes from an area of investigation where there can be little doubt that classical theism is at its weakest. This concerns the nature and necessity of a personal God. It involves those attached to classical Christian theology to pay more attention to this area, not only because some of its major working ideas, like "being" and "act" are not self-evidently personal. This concern aside, providing we do not excessively anthropomorphise our understanding of personhood so as to exclude God from this category at the beginning, there seem to be no serious logical obstacles preventing us from making sense of timeless personhood. The properties of consciousness and volition are readily associated with atemporality once it is grasped that thought and will can be understood in terms of invariable logical, rather than temporal, ordering. It seems impossible however to give any meaning to a reciprocal relationship between a timeless God and the temporal world, at least if the relation of creation is accepted. Close investigation however indicates that this is not a weakness but a strength in the classical system, for it enables God to be viewed as the

---

[3] To be fair, Nelson Pike's *God and Timelessness* did attempt to do this, but there has been no comparable effort since and opponents of the classical position have often been heavily dependent upon Pike.

supremely eminent person, the one who is able to give all without receiving anything in return, and being outside the finite order of personhood (with its utter dependence on reciprocity), he can be understood as the ultimate explanatory principle of the reality of the personal. This is a point which seems to have been missed by the many critics of the idea of a "timeless person", and until the question is taken up by them the notion of God as personal must be taken as a plus and not a problem for classical theism.

Again, much more work needs to be done by all sides on the relationship between God's eternity and the Christian doctrine of the Incarnation. Reviewing the literature opposed to the traditional concept of the **totum simul** it would be fair to say that the surface has only been barely scratched, where attempts have been made at all, in uncovering the real difficulties in this area. Any attempt in this book can hardly rank as more than a beginning in what is a most complicated question. Yet, because it is a beginning which has gone as far as spelling out some of the principle of Incarnational theology, I believe it has gone much further than any of the critics have gone at this point.[4] There is at least contained herein an argument attempting to show how the idea of God's eternity and the Incarnation can be brought together, and not just an assertion that this is so. I cannot but conclude therefore that the Incarnation and the divine eternity are compatible.

A problem of lesser significance was raised by the question of the compatibility of God's eternity and human freedom. I chose to deal with it in context because it is raised frequently in the literature, despite the fact that many prominent theists, and myself, would not want to insist that man is free in the incompatibilist sense. Nevertheless, it is quite clear that timeless knowledge poses no threat to freedom, however defined. The situation with respect to the relation between timeless causality and human decision making is far more complex. At this point I found it necessary to do little more than repeat the standard Thomist procedure in reconciling the real joint efficacy of primary and secondary causes. The position is however a very subtle one and eminently compatible with what I have argued in the central chapters of the book. It is a model which I consider to be defensible,

---

[4] My comments here refer to the very specific question of the Incarnation and timelessness, and not to discussions
concerning the logical tenability of the concept of the Incarnation in general.

even if not compelling. Perhaps the relevant chapter makes its greatest contribution by specifying in further detail the sort of causation that has been spoken about throughout the essay.

In the last chapter I turned to consider some positive reasons for adhering to the doctrine of the divine eternity. In a way this was an attempt to do further justice to the very positive emphasis in the classical concept that God possesses "unsurpassable life". Although this is implicit in the very idea of creation and preservation, as well as what I have said about maximal personhood, it comes out more clearly when these matters are subsumed under the concepts of providence and perfection. I have argued, via the question of foreknowledge, that only an atemporal deity of the sort outlined throughout can enact, with certainty of success, even a very general plan for the good of his creatures. This is not just an argument based on what certain people might desire religiously, but is correlated with the important philosophical ideas of omniscience and omnipotence. Similarly the concept of necessary existence, if it is to be more than empty locution, would seem to demand that special mode of existence or unscattered life which is described by the idea of eternal simultaneity. Whilst the matter is not quite so clear when one turns to the very difficult question of perfection, there is at least a **prima facie** case that a being which possesses all consistent positive attributes all at once, rather than acquiring these developmentally, is the "greatest conceivable being".

Is it reasonable to conclude that the classical concept of eternity is consistent with classical metaphysics as a whole? I am sure that this is the case if the considered framework is Thomism. From the basic concepts of **ipsum esse** and **actus purus** it is relatively easy to go on to a doctrine of creation and preservation **ex nihilo** by means of which content can be given to the idea of the divine eternity in terms of timeless creative causality. The answer seems to be the same if the doctrine is examined in terms of external consistency, there is nothing in the idea of God's timelessness which negates the reality of time, the signficance of history or the freedom of human persons. I have not however tried to demonstrate that God exists, let alone claim that it can be proven discursively that he must be fulness of being and pure act. The specific argument is certainly questionable at this point.

The reader of this work may perhaps, as with many opponents of classical theism, be left with the impression of an internally consistent but a morally or religiously uninspiring picture of God. There is an

imporant distinction to be observed at this point between religious
adequacy and religious availability. With respect to religious adequacy
Nancy Frankenberry has wisely written: "there the existence of
fundamentally different religious perceptions must be acknowledged.
As there is no known way to resolve disagreements over the character
of authentic religious experience, the task of justifying the religious
adequacy of any particular conception of ultimacy remains a relative
one. The criterion for assessing religious adequacy is precisely what in
each case is assumed to be religiously adequate."[5] That is to say what
counts as an adequate concept of God is inevitably conditioned by
whoever is deciding, so that true objectivity is impossible.
Unfortunately, the question of religious adequacy seems to be a
hidden agenda in many time- eternity discussions.[6] Much more
objective is the question of religious availability. It is this which is
behind Hartshorne's remark:

> A new era in religion may be predicted as soon as men
> grasp the idea that it is just as true that God is the supreme
> benificiary or 'recipient' of achievement ... as that he is the
> supreme benefactor or 'source' of achievement ... There
> has been a secret poison long working in religious thought
> and feeling, the poison of man's wanting to be an ultimate
> recipient of value. Religion then becomes man's self-
> service, not genuinely his service of God. For if God can
> be indebted to no one ... Really it must be ... only the
> creature who is to be served or benefited.[7]

---

[5] N. Frankenberry, "The Emergent Paradigm and Divine Causation", *Process
Studies*, 13, 1983, p.215.

[6] Though it comes out clearly in many process writers, for example, Schubert
Ogden, *Reality*, p.51: "If ... we must conceive of God as nothing other than the
Absolute of classical philosophy, then the reality of God is continually called in
question by the very existence of secular man... Since nothing whatever can make
the least difference to such a God, all our strivings and sufferings also must be
ultimately indifferent ... God's perfection is in every sense statically complete, an
absolute maximum, so we can no more increase him by our best efforts than
diminish him by our worst ... he is, as Camus has charged, the eternal bystander
whose back is turned to the woe of the world."

[7] Hartshorne, *Divine Relativity*, p.58.

What Hartshorne is demanding is a symmetrical relationship between God and man, that each be available to the other. There can be no doubt that an eternal God, as described in this volume, can only exist in an a symmetrical relationship with his creatures. If he is the Creator he gives all and cannot receive anything, neither can a response be evoked in turn by anything his creatures might do, for he is **totum simul existens**. There can be **no** dialogue between such a God and mankind.[8] This of course is a purely objective position and **contra** many opponents its implication for religious adequacy depend upon the separate question of the **moral** nature of such a timeless being. To go further at this point one would have to leave metaphysics and enter into the realm of moral philosophy. Is the timelessness of God compatible with, contradictory to or entailed by the notion of the pure **agape** love of God? To argue for the last position would be a relatively simple matter, but it would not be appropriate here. Rather, the importance of the question of religious availability is that it directs us again to the very concept of God itself. T.V. Morris raises the question: "Are temporalists and atemporalists just differing over the nature of some one being, or over the proper explication of some single concept they both have in common."[9] I would hope at the very least that this book has demonstrated that the God of temporalistic theism and of classical theism are not the same being.

Is God eternal in the sense that I have specified at length? I am not certain. However, whatever the truth of the matter, I do not believe that there have as yet been put forward any intellectual or religious objections sufficient to negate such a conviction.

---

[8] See Garrigou-Lagrange, *God*, vol 2, pp.538, 561; G. Marcel, "Reply to Charles Hartshorne", in *The Philosophy of Gabriel Marcel*, P. Schilpp (ed), La Salle: Open Court, 1984, p.370; Neville, *Creator*, p.98.

[9] Morris, "Perfect", p.19.

BIBLIOGRAPHY

Adams, R.M., "Middle Knowledge and the Problem of Evil", *American Philosophical Quarterly*, 14, 1977, pp.109-117.

Ahern, D.M., "Foreknowledge: Nelson Pike and Newcomb's Problem", *Religious Studies*, 15, 1979, pp.475-490.

Albritton, R., "Present Truth and Future Contingency", *Philosophical Review*, 66, 1957, pp.29-46.

Aldwinckle, R., *Death in the Secular City*, Grand Rapids: Eerdmans, 1972.

Alexander, S., *Space, Time and Deity*, N.Y.: Humanities Press, 2 vols, 1950.

Alston, W.P., "Divine Foreknowledge and Alternative Conceptions of Human Freedom", *International Journal for Philosophy of Religion*, 18, 1985, pp.19-32.

Alston, W.P., "Does God Have Beliefs?", *Religious Studies*, 22, 1986, pp.287-306.

Alston, W.P., "Functionalism and Theological Language", *American Philosophical Quarterly*, 22, 1985, pp.221-230.

Anderson, J.F., *The Cause of Being*, St. Louis: Herder, 1952.

Anderson, J.F., "Creation as Relation", *New Scholasticism*, 24, 1950, pp.263-283.

Anderson, J.F., "The Creative Ubiquity of God", *New Scholasticism*, 25, 1951, pp.139-162.

Anderson, J.F., "Time and the Possibility of An Eternal World", Thomist, 15, 1952, pp.136-161.

Anscombe, G.E.M., "Aristotle and the Sea Battle", *Mind*, n.s., 65, 1956, pp.1-15.

St. Anselm, "'Cur Deus Homo'", in *Anselm of Canterbury*, tr. & ed. J. Hopkins and H. Richardson, London: S.C.M., vol 2, 1976, pp.39-138.

St. Anselm, "'De Casu Diaboli'", in *Anselm of Canterbury*, tr. & ed. J. Hopkins and H. Richardson, London: S.C.M., vol 2, 1976, pp.127-178.

St. Anselm, "The Harmony of the Foreknowledge, The Predestination, And the Grace of God with Free Choice", in *Anselm of Canterbury*, tr. & ed. J. Hopkins and H. Richardson, Toronto: Edwin Mellen, vol 2, 1976.

St. Anselm, "'Monologion'", in *Anselm of Canterbury*, tr. & ed. J. Hopkins and H. Richardson, London: S.C.M., vol 2, 1974.

St. Anselm, *Proslogion*, tr. M.J. Charlesworth, Oxford: Clarendon, 1965.

St. Th. Aquinas, *Summa Contra Gentiles*, Bk 1, tr. A.C. Pegis, N.Y.: Doubleday, 1955; Bk 2, tr. J.F. Anderson, N.Y.: Doubleday, 1956; Bk 3, tr. V.J. Bourke, N.Y.: Doubleday, 1956.

St. Th. Aquinas, *Summa Theologiae*, Oxford: Blackfriars, 1964-1981.

Aristotle, "'De Caelo'", tr. J.L. Stocks, in *The Works of Aristotle*, tr. & ed. W.D. Ross, Oxford: Clarendon, vol 2, 1930.

Aristotle, *Physics*, tr. W.D. Ross, Oxford: Clarendon, 1936.

Armstrong, A.H. (ed), *The Cambridge History of Later Greek and Early Medieval Philosophy*, Cambridge: Cambridge University Press, 1967.

Atkins, P.W., *The Creation*, Oxford: W.H. Freeman, 1981.

St. Augustine, *The City of God*, tr. G.W. Walsh and G. Monahan, in *The Fathers of the Church*, R.J. Deferrari (ed), Washington: Catholic University of America, vol 14, 1951.

St. Augustine, *City of God*, tr. H. Bettenson, Harmondsworth: Penguin, 1972.

St. Augustine, *Confessions*, tr. R.S. Pine-Coffin, Harmondsworth: Penguin, 1961.

St. Augustine, *On Free Choice of the Will*, tr. M. Pontifex, London: Longmans, Green, 1955.

St. Augustine, "On Music", tr. R.C. Taliaferror, N.Y.: in *The Fathers of the Church*, R.J. Deferrari (ed), vol 4, 1947, pp.153-384.

St. Augustine, *On the Psalms*, tr. S. Hegbin and F. Corrigan, London: Longmans, Green, 1960.

St. Augustine, *The Trinity*, tr. S. McKenna, Washington: Catholic University of America, 1963.

Aulen, G., *The Faith of the Christian Church*, London: S.C.M., 1954.

Ayer, A.J., *Probability and Evidence*, London: Macmillan, 1972.

Ayers, R.H., "A Viable Theodicy for Christian Apologetics", *The Modern Schoolman*, 52, 1975, pp.391-403.

Baelz, P., *Prayer and Providence*, London: S.C.M., 1968.

Baillie, D.M., *Faith in God*, London: Faber and Faber, 1964.

Baillie, D.M., *God Was In Christ*, London: Faber, 1961.

Baker, L.R., "Temporal Becoming: The Argument From Physics", *Philosophical Forum*, 6, 1974-175. pp.218-236.

Baltazar, E., "Evolutionary Perspectives and the Divine", in *Traces of God in a Secular Culture*, G.F. McLean (ed), N.Y.: Alba House, 1973, pp.143-165

Barbour, I.G., *Issues in Science and Religion*, N.J.: Prentice-Hall, 1966.

Barnhardt, J.E., *Religion and the Challenge of Philosophy*, Totoura: Littlefield, Adams, 1975.

Barr, J., *Biblical Words for Time*, London: S.C.M., 1969.

Barr, James, *Fundamentalism*, London, S.C.M., 1980.

Barrett, H.M., *Boethius*, Cambridge: Cambridge University Press, 1940.

Barrow, I., "'Lectiones geometricae'", pp.4-15, passim, in *The Concepts of Space and Time*, M. Capek (ed), Dordrecht: Reidel, 1976, pp.203-208.

Barth, K., *Church Dogmatics*, G.W. Bromiley and T.F. Torrance (eds), Edinburgh: T. & T. Clark, 1956-1975.

Barth, K., *The Faith of the Church*, tr. G. Vahanian, London: Collins, 1960.

Barth, K., *The Humanity of God*, tr. J.N. Thomas and T. Wieser, London: Collins, 1961.

Barth, K., *The Knowledge of God and the Service of God*, tr. J.L.M., Haire and I. Henderson, London: Hodder & Stoughton, 1938.

Barth, K., *Romans*, tr. E.C. Hoskyns, Oxford: Oxford University Press, 1933.

Basinger, D., "Human Freedom and Divine Providence", *Religious Studies*, 15, 1979, pp.491-510.

Basinger, D., "Middle Knowledge and Classical Christian Thought", *Religious Studies*, 22, 1986, pp.407-422.

Basinger, D., "Omniscience and deliberation: A response to Reichenbach", *International Journal for Philosophy of Religion*, 20, 1986, pp.169-172.

Baumer, M.R., "The Role of 'Inevitability of Time T' in Aquinas' Solution to the Problem of Future Contingents", *The New Scholasticis Scholasticism*, 53, 1979, pp.147-167.

Baumer, M.R., "Whitehead and Aquinas on the Eternity of God", *The Modern Schoolman*, 62, November 1984, pp.27-41.

Bavinck, H., *The Doctrine of God*, tr. W. Hendriksen, Grand
Rapids: Baker, 1951.
Beauchamp, T.L. (ed), *Philosophical Problems of Causation*, Encino:
Dickenson, 1974.
Berdyaev, N., *The Destiny of Man*, London: Geoffrey Bles, 1954.
Berdyaev, N., *The Meaning of History*, London: Geoffrey Bles,
1936.
Bergson, H., *Time and Free Will*, tr. F.L. Pogson, London: George
Allen and Unwin, 1921.
Berkhof, H., *Christian Faith*, tr. S. Woudstra, Grand Rapids:
Eerdmans, 1979.
Berkhof, L., *Systematic Theology*, Edinburgh: Banner of Truth,
1974.
Berkouwer, G.C., *The Person of Christ*, tr. J. Vriend, Grand Rapids:
Eerdmans, 1954.
Berkouwer, G.C., *The Providence of God*, tr. L. Smedes, Grand
Rapids: Eerdmans, 1952.
Berkouwer, G.C., *Sin*, tr. P.C. Holtrop, Grand Rapids: Eerdmans,
1971.
Bertocci, P.A., *An Introduction to the Philosophy of Religion*, N.Y.:
Prentice-Hall, 1951.
Bertocci, P., *The Person God Is*, London: Allen and Unwin, 1970.
Blake, R.M., "On Mr. Broad's Theory of Time", *Mind*, 34, 1925,
pp.418-435.
Blumenfeld, D., "On The Compossibility of the Divine Attributes",
Philosophical Studies, 34, 1978, pp.91-103.
Blumenthal, H.J. and Markus, R.A. (eds), *Neoplatonism and Early
Christian Thought*, London: Variorum, 1981.
Boethius, *The Consolation of Philosophy*, tr. H.R. James, London:
George Routledge, n.d.
Boethius, *The Theological Tractates and the Consolation of
Philosophy*, tr. and ed. H.F. Stewart, E.K. Rand, S.J. Tester,
Cambridge, Mass: Harvard University Press, 1973.
Boer, S.E. and Lycan, W.G., "Who, me?", *Philosophical Review*,
89, 1980, pp.427-466.
Bohm, D., *Causality and Chance in Modern Physics*, Philadelphia:
University of Pennsylvania Press, 1957.
Bohm, D., *Wholeness and the Implicate Order*, London: Routledge &
Kegan Paul, 1980.

Bondi, R.C., "Immutability", in *A New Dictionary of Christian Theology*, A. Richardson and J. Bowden (eds), London: S.C.M., 1983, p.288.

Bonhoeffer, D., *Christology*, tr. J. Bowden, London: Collins, 1966.

Bonhoeffer, D., *Letters and Papers from Prison*, E. Bethge (ed), London: Collins, 1959.

Born, M., *Einstein's Theory of Relativity*, N.Y.: Dover, 1962.

Bosanquet, B., Value and Destiny of the Individual, London: Macmillan, 1913.

Bowne, B.P., *Metaphysics*, N.Y.: Harper, 1882.

Bowne, B.P., *Studies in Theism*, N.Y.: Phillips and Hunt, 1880.

Bowne, B.P., *Theism*, N.Y.: American Book, 1902.

Boyer, B.L., "Schleiermacher on the Divine Causality", *Religious Studies*, 22, 1986, pp.113-123.

Brabant, F.H., "God and Time", in *Essays on the Trinity and the Incarnation*, A.E.J. Rawlinson (ed), London: Longmans, Green, 1928, pp.323-360.

Brabant, F.H., *Time and Eternity in Christian Thought*, London: Longmans, 1937.

Bradley, F.H., *Appearance and Reality*, Oxford: Clarendon, 1969.

Brand, M., "Simultaneous Causation", in *Time and Cause*, P. Van Inwagen (ed), Dordrecht: Reidel, 1980, pp.137-153.

Brandon, E.P., "What's Become of Becoming", *Philosophia*, 16, 1986, pp.71-77.

Brandon, S.G.F., History, Time and Deity, Manchester: Manchester University Press, 1965.

Brier, B., "An Atemporal View of Causality", *Journal of Critical Analysis*, 4, 1972, pp.8-16.

Bright, L., "Creation: A Philsopher's Point of View", *Downside Review*, 76, 1958, pp.150-160.

Brightman, E.S., "Personalism", in *A History of Philosophical Systems*, V. Ferm (ed), N.Y.: Philosophical Library, 1950, pp.340-352.

Brightman, E.S., *The Problem of God*, N.Y.: Abingdon, 1930.

Brightman, E.S., "A Temporalist View of God", *Journal of Religion*, 12, 1932, pp.544-555.

Britton, B., "Evolution by Blind Chance", *Scottish Journal of Theology*, 39, 3, 1986, pp.341-360.

Broad, C.D., *An Examination of McTaggart's Philosophy*, Cambridge: Cambridge University Press, 1938.

Broad, C.D., "Mr. Dunne's Theory of Time", *Philosophy*, 10, 1935, pp.168-185.

Broad, C.D. and Price, H.H., "The Philosophical Implications of Precognition", *Proceedings of the Aristotelian Society*, Supplementary Volume, 16, 1937, pp.211-245.

Broad, C.D., *Scientific Thought*, London: Routledge and Kegan Paul, 1923.

Broad, C.D., "Time", in *Encyclopedia of Religion and Ethics*, J. Hastings (ed), Edinburgh: T. and T. Clark, vol 12, 1921, pp.334-335.

Brown, P., "St. Thomas' Doctrine of Necessary Being", *Philosophical Review*, 73, 1964, pp.76-90.

Brown, R.F., "Schelling and Dorner on Divine Immutablity", *Journal of the American Academy of Religion*, 53, 1985, pp.237-249.

Bruce, F.F., *Romans*, London: Tyndale, 1963.

Brunner, E., "The Christian Understanding of Time", *Scottish Journal of Theology*, 4, 1951, pp.1-12.

Brunner, E., *Divine-Human Encounter*, tr. A.W. Loos, London: S.C.M., 1944.

Brunner, E., *Dogmatics*, tr. O. Wyen, London: Lutterworth, vol 1-3, 1949-1952.

Buber, M., *Eclipse of God*, N.Y.: Harper, 1952.

Buijs, J.A., "Comments on Maimonides' Negative Theology", *The New Scholasticism*, 49, 1975, pp.87-93

Bultmann, R., *Faith and Existence*, tr. S.M. Ogden, London: Fontana, 1973.

Bultmann, R., *Jesus and the Word*, tr. L.P. Smith and E.H. Lantero, N.Y.: Scribner's, 1958.

Bultmann, R., *Theology of the New Testament*, tr. K. Grobel, London: S.C.M., vol 2, 1951.

Bunge, R., "Physical Time: The Objective and Relational Theories", *Philosophy of Science*, 35, 1968, pp.355-388.

Burnet, J., *Early Greek Philosophy*, London: Black, 1892.

Burns, P., "Questions and Answers On the Attributes of God", *Heythrop Journal*, 27, 1986, pp.171-177.

Burrell, David B., *Aquinas: God and Action*, Notre Dame Indiana: University of Notre Dame Press, 1979.

Burrell, David B., "God's Eternity", *Faith and Philosophy*, 1, 1984, pp.389-406.

Caird, E., *The Evolution of Theology in the Greek Philosophers*, Glasgow: James MacLehose, 2 vols, 1904

Callahan, J.F., *Four Views of Time in Ancient Philosophy*, Cambridge, Mass., Harvard University Press, 1948.

Calvin, J., *Institutes of the Christian Religion*, MacDill: MacDonald, n.d.

Campbell, C.A., *On Selfhood and Goodhood*, London: Allen and Unwin, 1957.

Camfield, F.W., "Man In His Time", *Scottish Journal of Theology*, 3, 1950, pp.127-148.

Capek, M., (ed), The Concepts of Space and Time, *Boston Studies in the Philosophy of Science*, vol 22, Dordrecht: Reidel, 1976.

Capek, M., *The Philosophical Impact of Contemporary Physics*, Princeton: Van Nostrand, 1961.

Capek, M., "Toward a Widening of the Notion of Causality", in *Process Philosophy*, J.R. Sibley and P.A.Y. Gunter (eds), Washington: University Press of America, 1978, pp.79-99.

Carr, W., "The Moment of Experience", *Proceedings of the Aristotelian Society*, 16, 1915-16, pp.1-32.

Castaneda, H.N., "Omniscience and Indexical Reference", *Journal of Philosophy*, 64, 7, April 1967, pp.203-210.

Charlesworth, M.J., *St. Anselm's "Proslogion"*, Oxford: Clarendon, 1965.

Charlton, W., "Review of `Time, Creation and the Continuum'", *Philosophy*, 60, 1985, pp.136-138.

Charnocke, S., *Discourses Upon the Existence and Attributes of God*, London: Henry G. Bohn, vol 1, 1860.

Cherbonnier, E. La B., "The Logic of Biblical Anthropomorphism", *Harvard Theological Review*, 55, July, 1962, pp.188-206.

Cherniss, H.F., "Plato as a Mathematician", in *Selected Papers*, L. Taran (ed), Leiden: Brill, 1977, pp.222-252.

Chernis, H.F., "`Timaeus' 38A-85", in *Selected Papers*, L. Taran (ed), Leiden: Brill, 1977, pp.340-345. Childs, B.S., *Exodus*, London: S.C.M., 1974.

Chisholm, R.M., *Person and Object*, La Salle: Open Court, 1976.

Chisholm, R., "Problems of Identity", in *Identity and Individuation*, M. Munitz (ed), N.Y.: New York University Press, 1971, pp.3-30.

Christian, W.A., "Augustine on the Creation of the World", *Harvard Theological Review*, 46, 1953, pp.1-26.

Chryssides, G.D., "Meaning, Metaphor and Meta-Theology", *Scottish Journal of Theology*, 38, 1985, pp.145-153.

Cheng, Chung-ying, "Greek and Chinese Views on Time and the Timeless", *Philosophy East and West*, 24, 1974, pp.155-158.

Clark, G.H., "The Theory of Time in Plotinus", *The Philosophical Review*, 53, 1944, pp.337-358.

Clarke, W. Norris, "Causality and Time", in *Experience, Existence and the Good*, I.C. Lieb (ed), Carbondale: Southern Illinois University Press, 1961, pp.143-157.

Clement of Alexandria, Stromateis, tr. W. Wilson, *Ante-Nicene Christian Library*, Edinburgh: T. and T. Clark, vol 12, 1882.

Cobb, J.B., *A Christian Natural Theology*, Philadelphia: Westminster, 1966.

Cobb, J.B., "Natural Causality and Divine Action", *Idealistic Studies*, 3, 1973, pp.207-222.

Coburn, R.C., "Professor Malcolm on God", *The Australasian Journal of Philosophy*, 40-41, August 1963, pp.143-162.

Cohen, L.J., "Professor Prior On Thanking Goodness That's Over", *Philosophy*, 24, 1959, pp.360-362.

Cole, G.A., "Towards a New Metaphysics of the Exodus", *Reformed Theological Review*, 42, 1983, pp.75-84.

Collins, J., *God in Modern Philosophy*, London: Routledge and Kegan Paul, 1960.

Collins, J., "God's Eternal Law", *Thomist*, 23, 1960, pp.497-532.

Copleston, F.C., *A History of Philsophy*, vol 2, Medieval Philosophy: Augustine to Scotus, London: Burns, Oates and Washbourne, 1950.

Copleston, F.C., *A History of Philsophy*, vol 3, Ockham to Suarez, London: Burns, Oates and Washbourne, 1952

Cornford, F.D., *Plato's Cosmology*, London: Routledge and Kegan Paul, 1937.

Costa de Beauregard, O., "Time in Relativity Theory: Arguments for a Philosophy of Being", in *The Voices of Time*, J.T. Fraser (ed), N.Y.: George Braziller, 1966, pp.417-433.

Courcelle, P., *Late Latin Writers and Their Greek Sources*, tr. H.E. Wedeck, Cambridge, Mass: Harvard University Press, 1969.

Craig, W.L., "God, Time, and Eternity", *Religious Studies*, 14, 1978, pp.497-503.

Cranfield, C.E.B., *The Epistle To The Romans*, Edinburgh: T. and T. Clark, vol 2, 1975.

Cross, F.L. and Livingstone, E.A., (eds), *The Oxford Dictionary of the Christian Church*, Oxford: Oxford University Press, (2nd ed), 1974.

Cudworth, R., *The True Intellectual System of the Universe*, London: Thomas Tegg, vol 2, 1845. Cullmann, O., *Christ and Time*, tr. F. V. Filson, London: S.C.M., 1951.

Cuppitt, D., "The Christ of Christendom", in *The Myth of God Incarnate*, J. Hick (ed), Philadelphia: Westminster, 1977, pp.133-147.

Cupitt, D., "Mr. Hebblethwaite on the Incarnation", in *Incarnation and Myth: The Debate Continued*, M. Goulder (ed), Grand Rapids: Eerdmans, 1979, pp.43-46.

Curran, R.T., "Whitehead's Notion of the Person and the Saving of the Past", *Scottish Journal of Theology*, 36, 1983, pp.363-385.

Daldy, C.B., "Metaphysics and the Limits of Language", in *Prospect for Metaphysics*, I.T. Ramsey (ed), London: Allen and Unwin, 1961, pp.178-205.

Danto, A.C., "Basic Actions", *American Philosophical Quarterly*, 2, 1965, pp.141-148.

D'Arcy, M., "The Immutability of God", *Proceedings of the American Catholic Philosophical Association*, 41, 1967, pp.19-26.

Darlap, A., "Time", in *Sacramentum Mundi*, K. Rahner (ed), London: Burns and Oates, vol 6, 1970, pp.257-262.

Davenport, S.F., *Immanence and Incarnation*, Cambridge: Cambridge University Press, 1925.

Davidson, D., "Causal Relations", *Journal of Philosophy*, 64, 1967, pp.691-703.

Davies, B., "God, Time and Change", *Clergy Review*, 63, 1978, pp.68-72.

Davies, B., "Impassibility", in *A New Dictionary of Christian Theology*, A. Richardson and J. Bowden (eds), London: S.C.M., 1983, pp.288-289.

Davies, B., *Introduction to the Philosophy of Religion*, Oxford: Oxford University Press, 1982.

Davies, B., "Kenny on God", *Philosophy*, 57, 1982, pp.105-118.

Davis, S.T., "Divine Omniscience and Human Freedom", *Religious Studies*, 15, 1979, pp.303-316.

Delling, G., "'Chronos'", in *Theological Dictionary of the New Testament*, G. Friedrich (ed), tr. G.W. Bromiley, Grand Rapids: Eerdmans, vol 9, 1974, pp.581-593.

Denbigh, K.G., *Three Concepts of Time*, Berlin: Springer-Verlag, 1981.

Dennett, D., "Conditions of Personhood", in *The Identities of Persons*, A.E. Rorty (ed), Berkeley: University of California Press, 1976, pp.175-196.

Dennett, D.C., Elbow Room. *The Varieties of Free Will Worth Wanting*, London: M.I.T. Press, 1984.

Descartes, R., *Philsophical Writings*, tr. and ed. E. Anscombe and P.T. Geach, Edinburgh: Nelson, 1954.

Dewan, L., "St. Thomas and the Possibles", *The New Scholasticism*, 53, 1979, pp.76-85.

Dewart, L., *The Future of Belief*, N.Y.: Herder and Herder, 1966.

Dillistone, F.W., "The Church and Time", *Scottish Journal of Theology*, 6, 1953, pp.156-164.

Dionysius the Areopagite, *On the Divine Names, and the Mystical Theology*, tr. C.E. Rolt, London: S.P.C.K., 1920.

Donceel, J., "Second Thoughts on the Nature of God", *Thought*, 46, 1971, pp.346-370.

Donnelly, J. "`Creatio ex nihilo'", in *Logical Analysis and Contemporary Theism*, J. Donnelly (ed), N.Y.: Fordham University Press, 1972, pp.200-217.

Drury, J., "Personal and Impersonal in Theology", *Theology*, 87, 1984, pp.427-431.

Dummett, M., "Bringing About the Past", *The Philosophical Review*, 73, 1964, pp.338-359.

Dunne, J.W., *An Experiment With Time*, London: Faber and Faber, (5th ed), 1939.

Duthie, C.S., "Providence in The Theology of Karl Barth", in *Providence*, M. Wiles (ed), London: S.P.C.K., 1969, pp.62-76.

Ebeling, G., *The Nature of Faith*, tr. R.C. Smith, Philadelphia: Muhlenberg, 1961.

Eddington, A.S., *Space, Time and Gravitation*, N.Y.: Harper, 1959.

Edwards, J., *Works*, Edinburgh: Banner of Truth, 1974.

Edwards, P., "Introduction to Determinism, Freedom and Moral Responsibility", in *A Modern Introduction to Philosophy*, P. Edwards and A. Pap (eds), N.Y.: Free Press, 1965, pp.2-9.

Edwards, R.B., "The Pagan Dogma of The Absolute Unchangeableness of God", *Religious Studies*, 14, 1978, pp.305-313.

Ehering, D., "Causal Asymmetry", *Journal of Philosophy*, 79, 1982, pp.761-774.

Ehering, D., "Non Simultaneous Causation", *Analysis*, 47, 1987, pp.28-32.

Ehering, D., "Simultaneous Causation and Causal Chains", *Analysis*, 45, 1985, pp.98-102.

Ehrhardt, A., "'Creatio ex Nihilo'", *Studia Theologica*, 4, 1950, pp.13-43.

Einstein, A., "Comment on Meyerson's `La Deductione Relativiste'", in *The Concepts of Space and Time*, M. Capek (ed), Dordrecht: Reidel, 1976, pp.363-367.

Ellis, B., "Has the Universe a Beginning in Time?", *Australian Journal of Philsophy*, 33, 1955, pp.32-37.

Ellul, J., *The Ethics of Freedom*, tr. G.W. Bromiley, Grand Rapids: Eerdmans, 1976.

Emmett, D., "The Concept of Power", *Proceedings of the Aristotelian Society*, 54, 1953-54, pp.1-26.

Emmett, D., *The Nature of Metaphysical Thinking*, London: Macmillan, 1953.

Englebretsen, G., "The Logic of Negative Theology", *The New Scholasticism*, 47, 1973, pp.228-232.

Erlandsen, D.K., "Timelessness, Immutability, and Eschatology", *International Journal for Philosophy of Religion*, 9, 1978, pp.129-145.

Evans, S., "Towards a Chrisian Doctrine of Providence", in *Providence*, M. Wiles (ed), London: S.P.C.K., 1967, pp.88-89.

Ewing, A.C., "Two `Proofs' of God's Existence", *Religious Studies*, 1, 1966, pp.29-45.

Ewing, A.C., *Value and Reality*, London: George Allen and Unwin, 1973.

Factor, R.L., "Newcomb's Paradox and Omniscience", *International Journal for Philosophy of Religion*, 9, 1978, pp.30-40.

Falkenstein, L., "Spaces and Times: A Kantian Response", *Idealistic Studies*, 16, 1986, pp.1-11.

Farley, F., *The Transcendence of God*, Philadelphia: Westminster, 1960.

Farmer, H.H., *The World and God*, London: Collins, 1963.

Farnell, L.R., *The Attributes of God*, Gifford Lectures, Oxford: Clarendon, 1925.

Farrer, A., *Faith and Speculation*, N.Y.: New York University Press, 1967.

Farrer, A., *Finite and Infinite*, Westminster: Dacre, 1943.

Farrer, A., *Freedom of the Will*, N.Y.: Scribner's, 1958.

Felt, J., "Invitation to a Philosophical Revolution", *New Scholasticism*, 45, 1971, pp.87-109.

Ferre, N.F.S., The Christian Understanding of God, N.Y.: Harper, 1951.

Fichte, J.G., *The Science of Knowledge*, tr. A.E. Kroeger, London: Trubner, 1889.

Field, R.W., "The Temporal Dimension of Causal Relationships", *Dialogue*, 26, 1983, pp.17-26.

Field, R.W., "Transmission, Inheritance, and Efficient Caustion", *Process Studies*, 14, 1984, pp.44-46.

Findlay, J.N., "Can God's Existence Be Disproved?", in *New Essays in Philosophical Theology*, A. Flew and A. MacIntyre (eds), N.Y.: Macmillan, 1955, pp.47-56.

Findlay, J.N., "Time and Eternity", *Review of Metaphysics*, 32, 1978, pp.3-14.

Fischer, J.M., "Freedom and Foreknowledge", *The Philosophical Review*, 92, 1983, pp.67-79.

Fischer, J.M., "Ockhamism", *The Philosophical Review*, 94, 1985, pp.81-101.

Fischer, J.M., "Pike's Ockhamism", *Analysis*, 46, 1986, pp.57-63.

Fischer, J.M., "van Inwagen on Freewill", *Philosophical Quarterly*, 36, 1986, pp.252-260.

Fitzgerald, P., "Is the Future Partly Unreal?", *Review of Metaphysics*, 21, 1968, pp.421-446.

Fitzgerald, P., "Relativity Theory and the God of Process Philosophy", *Process Studies*, 2, 1972, pp.251-273.

Fitzgerald, P. "Review of Fate, Logic and Time", *Philosophy of Science*, 38, 1, 1971, pp.122-126.

Fitzgerald, P., "Stump and Kretzmann on Time and Eternity", *Journal of Philosophy*, 82, 1985, pp.260-269.

Fitzgerald, P., "The Truth About Tomorrow's Sea Fight", *Journal of Philosophy*, 66, 1969, pp.307-329.

Flew, A.N. and MacKinnon, D.M., "Creation", in *New Essays In Philosophical Theology*, A. Flew and A. MacIntyre (eds), N.Y.: Macmillan, 1955, pp.170-186. Flew, A., "Divine Omnipotence and Human Freedom", in *New Essays in Philosophical Theology*,

A. Flew and A. MacIntyre (eds), N.Y.: Macmillan, 1955, pp.144-169.

Flew, A., *God and Philosophy*, London: Hutchinson, 1966.

Foerster, W., "`ktidzo'", in *Theological Dictionary of the New Testament*, G. Kittel (ed), tr. G.W. Bromiley, Grand Rapids: Eerdmans, vol 3, 1965, pp.1000-1035.

Flint, T., "The Problem of Divine Freedom", *American Philosophical Quarterly*, 20, 1983, pp.255-264.

Ford, L.S., "An Alternative to `Creatio Ex Nihilo'", *Religious Studies*, 19, 1983, pp.205-214.

Ford, L.S., "Boethius and Whitehead on Time and Eternity", *International Philosophical Quarterly*, 8/1, 1968, pp.38-67.

Ford, L.S., "Can Freedom be Created?", *Horizons*, 4, 1977, pp.183-188.

Ford, Lewis, "The Eternity of God and the Temporality of the World", *Encounter*, 36, 1975, pp.115-122.

Ford, L.S., "The Immutable God and Father Clarke", *New Scholasticism*, 49, 1975, pp.189-199.

Ford, L.S., "Is Process Theism Compatible with Relativity Theory?", *Journal of Religion*, 48, 1968, pp.124-135.

Ford, L.S., *The Lure of God*, Philadelphia: Fortress, 1978.

Ford, L.S., "The Non-Temporality of Whitehead's God", *International Philosophical Quarterly*, 13, 1973, pp.347-376.

Ford, L.S., "The Viability of Whitehead's God for Christian Theology", *Proceedings of the American Catholic Philosophical Association*, 44, 1970, pp.141-151.

Forrest, P., "The Logic of Free Acts and the Power of God", *Notre Dame Journal of Formal Logic*, 27, 1986, pp.20-37.

Fortman, E.J., *The Triune God*, Philadelphia: Westminster, 1972.

Franck, I., "Maimonides and Aquinas On Man's Knowledge of God: A Twentieth Century Perspective", *Review of Metaphysics*, 38, 1985, pp.591-615.

Frank, E., "Time and Eternity", *Review of Metaphysics*, 2, 1948, pp.39-52.

Frank, P., "Is the Future Already Here?", in *The Concepts of Space and Time*, M. Capek (ed), Dordrecht: Reidel, 1976, pp.387-395.

Frankenberry, N., "The Emergent Paradigm and Divine Causation", *Process Sudies*, 13, 1983, pp.202-217.

Frankfurt, H.G., "Freedom and the Concept of a Person", *Journal of Philosophy*, 35, 1957, pp.97-110.

Franklin, R.L., "Necessary Being", *Australasian Journal of Philosophy*, 35, 1957, pp.97-110.

Franks, R., "Passibility and Impassibility", *Encyclopedia of Religion and Ethics*, J. Hastings (ed), N.Y.: Scribers, vol 9, 1924, pp.658-659.

Fraser, J.T., *Of Time, Passion and Knowledge*, N.Y.: Braziller, 1975.

Fredosso, A.J., (ed), *The Existence and Nature of God*, Notre Dame: Notre Dame University Press, 1983.

French, P.A., Uehling, T.E., Wettstein, H.K., (eds), *Mid-Western Studies in Philosophy, 9, 1984: Causation and Causal Theories*, Minneapolis: University of Minnesotta Press, 1984.

Gale, R.M., "Is It Now Now?", *Mind*, 73, No. 289, 1964, pp.97-105.

Gale, R.M., *The Language of Time*, London: Routledge and Kegan Paul, 1968.

Gale, R., "Omniscience-Immutability Arguments", *American Philosophical Quarterly*, 23, 1986, pp.319-335.

Gale, R.M. (ed), *The Philosophy of Time*, N.J.: Humanities Press, 1978.

Galloway, G., *The Philosophy of Relgion*, Edinburgh: T. and T. Clark, 1914.

Garcia, L., "Can There Be a Self-Explanatory Being?", *Southern Journal of Philosophy*, 24, 1986, pp.479-488.

Garrigou-Lagrange, R., *God: His Existence and His Nature*, tr. B. Rose, St. Louis: Herder, vol 1, 1948, vol 2, 1949.

Garrigou-Lagrange, R., *Providence*, St. Louis; Herder, 1937.

Geach, P., "Causality and Creation", *Sophia*, 1, 1962, pp.1-8.

Geach, P., "Causality and Creation: A Note on Mr. Londey's Article", *Sophia*, 1, 1962, pp.27-30.

Geach, P., "The Future", *New Blackfriars*, 54, 1973, pp.208-218.

Geach, P., *God and the Soul*, London: Routledge and Kegan Paul, 1969.

Geach, P., "God's Relation to the World", *Sophia*, 8, 1969, pp.1-9.

Geach, P.T., *Logic Matters*, Berkeley: University of California Press, 1972, pp.295-301.

Geach, P.T., *Providence and Evil*, Cambridge: Cambridge University Press, 1977.

Geach, P.T. and Anscombe, G.E.M., *Three Philosophers*, Oxford: Basil Blackwell, 1961.

Geach, P.T., "What Actually Exists", *Proceedings of the Aristotelian Society*, Supp. Vol. 42, 1968, pp.7-16.

Gerber, R.J., "Causality and Atheism", in *Philosophy and Christian Theology*, G.F., McLean and J.P. Dougherty (eds), Washington: Catholic University of America, 1970, pp.232-240.

Gibson, A.B., "Time and Action", in *Experience, Existence and the Good*, I.C. Lieb (ed), Carbondale: Southern Illinois University Press, 1961, pp.169-177

Gilkey, L., *Maker of Heaven and Earth*, Garden City: Doubleday, 1959.

Gilson, E., *The Elements of Christian Philosophy*, tr. N.Y.: Mentor-Omega, 1960.

Gilson, E., *The Spirit of Medieval Philosophy*, tr. A.H.C., Downes, London: Sheed and Ward, 1936.

Godel, K., "A Remark about the Relationship between Relativity Theory and Idealistic Philosophy", in *Albert Einstein: Philosopher-Scientist*, P.A. Schilpp (ed), N.Y.: Harper, vol 2., 1951, pp.557- 562.

Godfrey-Smith, W., "Beginning and Ceasing to Exist", *Philosophical Studies*, 32, 1977, pp.393-402.

Godfrey-Smith, W., "The Generality of Predictions", *American Philosophical Quarterly*, 15, 1978, pp.15-25

Godfrey-Smith, W., "Special Relativity and the Present", *Philosophical Studies*, 36, 1979, pp.233-244.

Goldman, A.I., "A Causal Theory of Knowing", *Journal of Philosophy*, 64, 1967, pp.357-372.

Gollwitzer, H., *The Existence of God*, London: S.C.M., 1965.

Goodman, N., *The Structure of Appearance*, Dordrecht: Reidel, 3rd ed., 1977.

Gore, C., *The Reconstruction of Belief*, London: Murray, l928.

Goulder, M. (ed), *The Debate Continued: Incarnation and Myth*, Grand Rapids: Eerdmans, 1979.

Goulder, M., "Paradox and Mystification", in *Incarnation and Myth*, M. Goulder (ed), Grand Rapids: Eerdmans, 1979, pp.51-59.

Gowen, J., "God and Timelessness: Everlasting or Eternal?", *Sophia*, 26, 1987, pp.15-29.

Graham, G., "Persons and Time", *Southern Journal of Philosophy*, 15, 1977, pp.309-315.

Graham, K., *Religious Views of Time and History*, unpublished M.A. thesis, La Trobe University, 1983.

Grant, R.M., *The Early Christian Doctrine of God*, Charlottesville: University of Virginia Press, 1966. Green, R. (tr. and ed.), *The Consolation of Philosophy*, Indianapolis: Bobbs Merrill, 1962.

Griffin, D.R., "Bohm and Whitehead on Wholeness, Freedom, Causality, and Time", *Zygon*, 20, 1985, pp.165-191.

Griffin, D.R. (ed), *Physics and the Ultimate Significance of Time*, Albany: S.U.N.Y., 1985.

Griffin, D.R., "Divine Causality, Evil, and Philosophical Theology: A Critique of James Ross", *International Journal for Philosophy of Religion*, 4, 1973, pp.168-186.

Grundbaum, A., "The Meaning of Time", in *Basic Issues in the Philosophy of Time*, E. Freeman and W. Sellars (eds), La Salle: Open Court, 1971, pp.195-228.

Grundbaum, A., *Modern Science and Zeno's Paradoxes*, Middletown: Wesleyan University Press, 1967.

Grundbaum, A., *Philosophical Problems of Space and Time*, Dordrecht: Reidel, 2nd ed., 1973.

Grundbaum, A., "The Status of Temporal Becoming", in *The Philosophy of Time*, R. Gale (ed), N.J.: Humanities, pp.322-354.

Guardini, R., *Freedom, Grace and Destiny*, tr. J. Murray, Westport: Greenwood, 1975.

Guhrt, J., "Time", in *The New International Dictionary of New Testament Theology*, C. Brown (ed), Grand Rapids: Zondervan, vol 3, 1978, pp.826-833.

Gundersdorf Von Jess, W., "Divine Eternity in the Doctrine of St. Augustine", *Augustinian Studies*, 6, 1975, pp.75-96.

Gunn, J.A., *The Problem of Time*, London: Allen and Unwin, 1930.

Gunton, C.E., *Becoming and Being*, Oxford: Oxford University Press, 1978.

Guthrie, W.K.C., *A History of Greek Philosophy, The Early Presocratics and Pythagoreans*, Cambridge: Cambridge University Press, vol 1, 1962.

Guthrie, W.K.C., *A History of Greek Philosophy, The Later Plato and the Academy*, Cambridge: Cambridge University Press, vol 5, 1978.

Gutting, G., "Is Ross's God the God of Religion?", *Journal of Religion*, 77, 1980, p.630.

Haack, S., "On a Theological Argument for Fatalism", *Philsophical Quarterly*, 24, 1974, pp.156-159.

Hallman, J.M., "The Mutability of God: Tertullian to Lactantius", *Theological Studies*, 42, 1981, pp.373-393.

Hamilton, P., *The Living God and the Modern World*, London: Hodder and Stoughton, 1967.

Hanson, A.T., "Two Consciousnesses: The Modern Version of Chalcedon", *Scottish Journal of Theology*, 37, 1984, pp.471-483.

Hardy, A., *The Spiritual Nature of Man*, Oxford: Clarendon, 1980.

Hardy, E.R., (ed), Christology of the Later Fathers, London: S.C.M., 1954.

Harris, E.E., "Time and Eternity", *Review of Metaphysics*, 29, 1976, pp.464-482.

Hartshorne, C., "Absolute Objects and Relative Subjects: A Reply", *Review of Metaphysics*, 14, 1961, pp.174-188.

Hartshorne, C., *Anselm's Discovery*, La Salle: Open Court, 1965.

Hartshorne, C., "Bell's Theorem and Stapp's Revised View of Space-Time", *Process Studies*, 7, 1977, pp.183-191.

Hartshorne, C., *Creative Synthesis and Philosophic Method*, London: S.C.M., 1970.

Hartshorne, C., "The Dipolar Conception of Deity?", *Review of Metaphysics*, 21, 1967, pp.273-289.

Hartshorne, C., *The Divine Relativity*, New Haven: Yale University Press, 1948.

Hartshorne, C., "The Idea of a Worshipful Being", *Southern Journal of Philosophy*, 2, 1964, pp.165-167.

Hartshorne, C., "Marcel on God and Causality", in *The Philosophy of Gabriel Marcel*, P. Schilpp (ed), La Salle: Open Court, 1984, pp.353-366.

Hartshorne, C., "The Meaning of 'Is Going to Be'", *Mind*, 74, 1965, pp.46-58.

Hartshorne, C., "Philosophy and Orthodoxy", *Ethics*, 54, 1944, pp.295-298.

Hartshorne, C., "Whitehead, the Anglo-American-Philosopher-Scientist", *Proceedings of the American Catholic Philosophical Association*, 35, 1961, pp.163-171.

Hartshorne, C. and Reese, W.L., (eds), *Philosophers Speak of God*, Chicago: Chicago University Press, 1953.

Hasker, W., "Concerning the Intelligibility of `God is Timeless'", *The New Scholasticism*, 57, 1983, pp.170-195.

Hasker, W., "Foreknowledge and Necessity", *Faith and Philosophy*, 2, 1985, pp.121-157.

Hatano, S., *Time and Eternity*, tr.I. Suzuki, Ministry of Education, Japan, 1963.

Hazelton, R., *Providence*, London: S.C.M., 1958.

Hazelton, R., "Time, Eternity and History", *Journal of Religion*, 30, 1950, pp.1-12.

Hebblethwaite, B., "Austin Farrer's Concept of Divine Providence", *Theology*, 73, 1970, pp.541-551.

Hebblethwaite, B., "The Logical Coherence of the Doctrine of the Incarnation", in *Incarnation and Myth*, M. Goulder (ed), Grand Rapids: Eerdmans, 1979, pp.60-61.

Hebblethwaite, B., "The Propriety of the Doctrine of the Incarnation as a Way of Interpreting Christ", *Scottish Journal of Theology*, 33, 1980, pp.201-222.

Hebblethwaite, B.L., "Providence and Divine Action", *Religious Studies*, 14, 1978, pp.223-236.

Hebblethwaite, B.L., "Some Reflections on Predestination, Providence and Divine Foreknowledge", *Religious Studies*, 15, 1979, pp.433-448.

Hegel, G.W.F., *Lectures on the Philosophy of Religion*, tr. E.B. Spiers, London: Routledge and Kegan Paul, vol 3, 1962.

Hegel, G.W.F., *The Philosophy of Nature*, tr. and ed. M.J. Petry, London: George Allen and Unwin, vol 1, 1970.

Heidegger, *Being and Time*, tr. J. Macquarrie and E. Robinson, London: S.C.M., 1962.

Heinecken, M.J., *Beginning and End of the World*, Philadelphia: Fortress, 1960.

Helm, P., "Pike on Prior on Action", *Philosophical Studies*, 26, 1974, pp.141-143.

Helm,, P., "Divine Foreknowledge and Facts", *Canadian Journal of Philosophy*, 4, 1974-1975, pp.305-315.

Helm, P., "God and Spacelessness", *Philosophy*, 55, 1980, pp.211-221.

Helm, P., "God and Whatever Comes to Pass", *Religious Studies*, 14, 1978, pp.315-323.

Helm, "Grace and Causation", *Scottish Journal of Theology*, 32, 1979, pp.101-112.

Helm, P., "Omnipotence and Change", *Philosophy*, 51, 1976, pp.454-461.

Helm, P., "Time and Place for God", *Sophia*, 24, 1985, pp.53-55.

Helm, "Timelessness and Foreknowledg", *Mind*, 84, 1975, pp.516-527.

Henderson, H.H., "Knowing Persons and Knowing God", *The Thomist*, 46, 1982, pp.394-422.

Hepburn, R.W., *Christianity and Paradox*, London: Watts, 1958.

Hepburn, R.W., "The Religious Doctrine of Creation", in *The Encyclopedia of Philosophy*, P. Edwards (ed), N.Y.: Macmillan, vol 2, 1967, pp.252-256.

Hepburn, R.W., "Time Transcendence and Some Related Phenomena in the Arts", in *Contemporary British Philosophy*, H.D. Lewis (ed), London: George Allen and Unwin, 1976, pp.152-173.

Heppe, H., *Reformed Dogmatics*, tr. G.T. Thompson, Grand Rapids: Baker, 1978.

Herrera, R.A., "Saint Thomas and Maimonides on the Tetragrammaton: The `Exodus' of Philosophy?", *Modern Schoolman*, 59, 1982, pp.179-193.

Heschel, A., *Man Is Not Alone*, N.Y.: Octagon, 1951.

Heschel, A.J., *The Prophets*, N.Y.: Harper & Row, vol 2, 1975.

Hick, J., "God As Necessary Being", *Journal of Philosophy*, 57, 1960, pp.725-734.

Hick, J., (ed), *The Myth of God Incarnate*, Philadelphia: Westminiser, 1977.

Hick, J., *Philosophy of Religion*, N.J.: Prentice-Hall, 1965.

St. Hilary of Poitiers, *The Trinity*, tr. S. McKenna, in *Fathers of the Church*, N.Y.: The Fathers of the Church, vol 25, 1954.

Hill, W.J., "Does God Know the Future?, Aquinas and Some Moderns", *Theological Studies*, 36, 1975, pp.3-18.

Hill, W.J., "Does the World Make a Difference to God", *The Thomist*, 38, 1974, pp.146-164.

Hinckfuss, I., *The Existence of Space and Time*, Oxford: Clarendon, 1975.

Hintikka, J., *Time and Necessity*, Oxford: Clarendon, 1973.

Hobbes, J., *Leviathan*, London: Dent, 1914.

Hodge, C., *Romans*, London: Banner of Truth, 1972.

Hodges, H.A., *God Beyond Knowledge*, London: Macmillan, 1979.

Hodgson, L., "The Incarnation", in *Essays on the Trinity and the Incarnation*, A.E.J. Rawlinson (ed), London: Longmans, Green, 1928, pp.363-402.

Hoffmann, J. "Pike on Possible Worlds, Divine Foreknowledge, and Human Freedom", *Philosophical Review*, 88, 1979, pp.433-442.

Hollis, M., "Times and Spaces", *Mind*, 76, 1967, pp.524-536.

Holt, D.C., "Timelessness And the Metaphysics of Temporal Existence", *American Philosophical Quarterly*, 18, 1981, pp.149-156.

Hooker, R., *Of the Laws of Ecclesiastical Polity*, London: Dent, 1907.

Hopkins, J. and Richardson, H., (eds), Trinity, *Incarnation and Redemption*, N.Y.: Harper, 1970.

Hosinski, T.E., "Creation and the Origin of the Universe: 1", *Thought*, 48, 1973, pp.213-239.

Hospers, J., *Introduction to Philosophical Analysis*, Englewood Cliffs: Prentice-Hall, 1963.

House, F., "The Barrier of Impassibility", *Theology*, 83, 1980, pp.409-415.

Howe, L.T., "Is the World `Ex Nihilo'", *Sophia*, 7, 197, pp.21-29.

Howe, L.T., "The Necessity of Creation", *International Journal of Religion*, 2, 1971, pp.96-112.

Hoy, R.C., "Becoming and Persons", *Philosophical Studies*, 34, 1978, pp.269-280.

Huby, P.M., "Kant or Cantor? That the Universe, If Real, Must be Finite in Both Space and Time", *Philosophy*, 46, 1971, pp.121-132.

Hudson, W.D., "The Concept of Divine Transcendence", *Religious Studies*, 15, 1969, pp.197-210.

Hudson, W.D., *A Philosophical Approach to Religion*, London: Macmillan, 1974.

Hume, D., *A Treatise of Human Nature*, L.A. Selby-Bigge (ed), Oxford, 1888.

Hyman, A. and Walsh J.J., (eds), *Philosophy in the Middle Ages*, Indianapolis: Hackett, 1973.

Ignatius, "To Polycarp", in *The Epistles of St. Clement of Rome and St. Igantius of Antioch*, tr. J.A. Kleist, London: Longmans, Green, 1946, pp.96-100.

Illingworth, J.R., *Personality: Human and Divine*, London: Macmillan, 1894.

Inge, W.R., *Mysticism in Religion*, Chicago: Chicago University Press, 1948.

Inge, W.R., *The Philosophy of Plotinus*, London: Longmans, Green, vol 1, 1918.

Iseminger, G., "Foreknowledge and necessity: `Summa Theologiae' 1a. 14, 13, 2", *Midwest Studies in Philosophy*, 1, 1976, pp.5-25.

Jacobs, L., "Providence", *Judaism*, 17, 1968, pp.197-202.

Jaeger, W., *The Theology of the Early Greek Philosophers*, tr. E.S. Robinson, Oxford: Clarendon, 1947.

James, W., *The Principles of Psychology*, London: Macmillan, vol 1, 1890.

James, W., *The Varieties of Religious Experience*, London: Collins, 1960.

Jantzen, G., *God's World, God's Body*, London: D.L.T., 1984.

Jantzen, G., "Time, Timelessness", in *A New Dictionary of Christian Theology*, A. Richardson and J. Macquarrie (eds), London: S.C.M., 1983, pp.571-574.

Jantzen, J.F., "Modes of Power and the Divine Relativity", *Encounter*, 36, 1975, pp.379-406.

Jaspers, K., *Philosophical Faith and Revelation*, tr. E.B. Ashton, London: Collins, 1967.

Jenkins, D.E., *The Contradiction of Christianity*, London: S.C.M., 1976.

Jenson, R., *God After God: The God of the Past and the God of the Future, Seen in the Work of Karl Barth*, Indianapolis: Bobbs-Merrill, 1969.

Saint John of Damascus, *The Orthodox Faith*, tr. F.H. Chase, in *The Fathers of the Church*, N.Y.: The Fathers of the Church, vol 37, 1958.

Johnson, C.M., "On Prehending the Past", *Process Studies*, 6, 1976, pp.255-269.

Jones, W.B., "Bell's Theorem, H.P. Stapp, and Process Theism", *Process Studies*, 7, 1977, pp.250-261.

Jones, W.B., "Physics and Metaphysics: Henry Stapp on Time", in *Physics and the Ultimate Significance of Time*, D.R. Griffin (ed), Albany, S.U.N.Y., 1985, pp.278-288.

Jordan, R.D., *The Temple of Eternity: Thomas Traherne's Philosophy of Time*, Port Washington: Kennikal, 1972.

Journet, C., *The Meaning of Grace*, London: Geoffrey Chapman, 1962.

Jowett, B., *The Works of Plato*, Oxford: Oxford University Press, vol 3, 1892.

Kant, I., *Critique of Practical Reason*, tr. and ed. L.W. Back, Chicago: University of Chicago Press, 1949.

Kant, I., *Critique of Pure Reason*, tr. N. Kemp-Smith, London: Macmillan, 1929.

Kapitan, T., "Can God Make Up His Mind?", *International Journal for the Philosophy of Religion*, 15, 1-2, 1984, pp.37-47.

Kattsoff, L.O., "Causality as Dependence", *Methodos*, 15, 1963, pp.17-24.

Kaufman, G., *God the Problem*, Cambrige, Mass: Harvard University Press, 1972.

Kaufmann, W., *Critique of Religion and Philosophy*, Garden City: Doubleday, 1961.

Kelly, A.J., "God: How Near a Relation?", *The Thomist*, 34, 1970, pp.191-229.

Kelly, A.J., "To Know the Mystery: The Theologian in the Presence of the Revealed God", *The Thomist*, 32, 1968, pt. 1., pp.40-66, pt. 2., pp.171-200.

Kelly, J.N.D., *Early Christian Doctrines*, N.Y.: Harper and Row, 1978.

Kelly, M., "St. Thomas and Transuent Causality", *New Scholasticism*, 54, 1980, pp.34-45.

Kemp-Smith, N., *A Commentary to Kant's Critique of Pure Reason*, N.Y.: Humanitites, 1962.

Kenny, A., "Divine Foreknowledge and Human Freedom", in *Aquinas*, A. Kenny (ed), London: Macmillan, 1969, pp.255-271.

Kenny, A., *The God of the Philosophers*, Oxford: Clarendon, 1979.

Kern, W., "God-World Relationship", in *Sacramentum Mundi*, K. Rahner, (ed), London: Burns and Oates, vol 2, 1968, pp.403-406.

Kharmara, E.J., "Eternity and Omniscience", *Philosophical Quarterly*, 24, 1974, pp.204-219.

Kierkegaard, S., *Edifying Discourses*, tr. D.F. and L.M. Swenson, N.Y.: Harper and Row, 1958.

Kierkegaard, S., *Philosophical Fragments*, tr. D.F. Swenson, Princeton: Princeton Universtiy Press, 1936.

King, J.N., "The Experience of God in the Theology of Karl Rahner", *Thought*, 53, 1978, pp.174-202.

King, R.H., *The Meaning of God*, London: S.C.M., 1974.

King-Farlow, J., "`Nothing Greater Can Be Conceived' (Zeno, Anselm and Tillich)", *Sophia*, 21, 1982, pp.19-23.

Kinsbourne, M., "Brain-Based Limitations on Mind", in *Body and Mind*, R.W. Riebner (ed), N.Y.: Academic Press, 1980, pp.155-162.

Kirk, G.S., Raven, J.E., Schofield, M., *The Presocratic Philosophers*, Cambridge: Cambridge University Press, 2nd ed., 1983.

Kleinig, J., "Anthropomorphism", *Tyndale Paper*, 17, 1973, pp.1-28.

Kline, G.L., "'Present', 'Past', and 'Future' as Categorical Terms, and the 'Fallacy of the Actual'", *Review of Metaphysics*, 40, 1986, pp.215-235.

Knasas, John F.X., "Aquinas: Prayer to An Immutable God", *The New Scholasticism*, 57, 1983, pp.196-221.

Kneale, M., "Eternity and Sempiternity", *Proceedings of the Aristotelian Society*, 70, 1969/70, pp.223-238.

Kneale, W., "Time and Eterntiy in Theology", *Proceedings of the Aristotelian Society*, 61, 1960-61, pp.87-108.

Knight, G.A.F., *A Biblical Approach to the Doctrine of the Trinity*, Edinburgh: Oliver and Boyd, n.d.

Kogan, B.S., *Averroes and the Metaphysics of Causation*, Albany: S.U.N.Y., 1985.

Kolakowski, *Religion*, London: Collins, 1982.

Kolb, D.A., "Time and Timelessness in Greek Thought", *Philosophy East and West*, 24, 1974, pp.137-143.

Kondoleon, T.J., "The Immutability of God: Some Recent Challenges", *The New Scholasticism*, 58, 1984, pp.293-315.

Kozak, J.B., "Causality, Time and Eternity", *Communio Viatorum*, 14, 1971, pp.269-278.

Kretzmann, N., "Omniscience and Immutability", *Journal of Philosophy*, 63, 1966, pp.409-421.

Kretzmann, N., "Time Exists - But Hardly, or Obscurely", *Aristotelian Society Supplemenary Volume*, 1, 1976, pp.91-114.

Kung, H., *Does God Exist?*, tr. E. Quinn, London: Collins, 1980.

Kung, H., *On Being a Christian*, tr. E. Quinn, London: Collins, 1976.

Kuyper, L.J., "The Suffering and Repentance of God", *Scottish Journal of Theology*, 22, 1969, pp.257-277.

Kvanvig, J., "Divine Transcendence", *Religious Studies*, 20, 1984, pp.377-387.

327

Lachs, J., "God's Action and Natural Ways", *Idealistic Studies* 3, 1973, pp.223-228.

La Croix, R., "Aquinas on God's Omnipresence and Timelessness", *Philosophy and Phenomenological Research*, 42, 1982, pp.391-399.

La Croix, R., "Augustine on the Simplicity of God", *The New Scholasticism*, 51, 1977, pp.453-469.

La Croix, R., "Omnipotence, Omniscience and Necessity", *Analysis*, 34, 1974, pp.63-64.

La Croix, R., "Omniscience and Divine Determinism", *Religious Studies*, 12, 1976, pp.365-381.

La Croix, R., "Wainwright, Augustine and God's Simplicity", *The New Scholasticism*, 53, 1979, pp.124-127.

La Cugna, C.M., "Re-Conceiving The Trinity As the Mystery of Salvation", *Scottish Journal of Theology*, 38, 1985, pp.1-23.

Lackey, D.P., "A New Disproof of the Compatibility of Foreknowledge and Free Choice", *Religious Studies*, 10, 1974, pp.313-318.

Laird, J., *Mind and Deity*, London: George Allen and Unwin, 1944.

Laird, J., *Theism and Cosmology*, London: George Allen and Unwin, 1940.

Lane, D.A., *The Experience of God - An Invitation to do Theology*, N.Y.: Paulist, 1981.

Langerak, E., "On Foreknowledge and Necessity", *Mid West Studies in Philosophy*, 1, 1976, pp.12-16.

Langford, M.J., *Providence*, London: S.C.M., 1981.

Langford, M.J., "Providence", in *A New Dictionary of Christian Theology*, A. Richardson and J. Macquarrie (eds), London: S.C.M., 1983, pp.478-479.

Laporte, J.M., "Kenosis: Old and New", *The Ecumenist*, 12, 2, 1974, pp.17-21.

Laura, R.S., "The Logic of Creation", *Thomist*, 33, 1969, pp.352-356.

Laura, R.S., "Towards a New Theology of Transcendence", *Sophia*, 25, 1986, pp.30-40.

Leclerc, I., "God And the Issue of Being", *Religious Studies*, 20, 1984, pp.63-78.

Leclerc, I., *Whitehead's Metaphysics*, London: Allen and Unwin, 1958.

Leclercq, J., *The Love of Learning and the Desire for God*, N.Y.: Fordham University Press, 1961.

Lee, Jung Young, *God Suffers for Us: A Systematic Inquiry into a Concept of Divine Passibility*, The Hague: Martinus Nijhoff, 1974.

Legenhausen, G., "Is God a Person?", *Religious Studies*, 22, 196, pp.307-323.

Leibniz, G.W., *Philosophical Papers and Letters*, L.E. Loemker (ed), Dordrecht: Reidel, 1969.

Leibniz, G.W., and Clarke, S., "Discussion on the Nature of Space and Time", in *The Concepts of Space and Time*, M. Capek (ed), Dordrecht: Reidel, 1976, pp.273-288.

Leigh, R.W., "Jesus: the one natured God-man", *Christian Scholar's Review*, 11, 1982, pp.124-137.

Leighton, J.A., *Man and the Cosmos*, N.Y.: Appleton, 1922.

Levine, M.P., "Can We Speak Literally of God?", *Religious Studies*, 21, 1985, pp.53-59.

Levine, M.P., "More On `Does Traditional Theism Entail Pantheism'", *International Journal for the Philosophy of Religion*, 20, 1986, pp.31-35.

Levison, A.B., "Events and Time's Flow", *Mind*, 96, 1987, pp.341-353.

Lewis, C.S., *Mere Christianity*, London: Collins, 1952.

Lewis, C.S., *The Screwtape Letters*, Glasgow: Collins, 1942.

Lewis, Delmas, "Eternity Again: A Reply to Stump and Kretzmann", *International Journal for Philosophy of Religion*, 15, 1984, pp.73-79.

Lewis, Delmas, *God and Time: The Concept of Eternity and the Reality of Tense*, unpublished Ph.D. thesis, University of Wisconsin, 1985.

Lewis, Delmas, "Persons, Morality and Tenselessness", *Philosophy and Phenomenological Research*, 47, 1986, pp.2305-9.

Lewis, Delmas, "Timelessness and Divine Agency", *International Journal for Philosophy of Religion*, 21, 1987, pp.143-159.

Lewis, H.D., *The Elusive Self*, London: Macmillan, 1982.

Litton, E.A., *Introduction To Dogmatic Theology*, London: James Clarke, 1960.

Livingstone, D.W., "Theism and The Rationale of Hume's Skepticism About Causation", *Idealistic Studies*, 15, 1985, pp.151-164.

Locke, J., *An Essay Concerning Human Understanding*, introd. & ed., P. H. Nidditch, Oxford: Clarendon, 1975.

Loemker, L.E. (ed), *Leibniz's Philosophical Papers and Letters*, Dordrecht: Reidel, 1969.

Londey, D., "Causality and Creation: A Note on the Formal Logic of Causal Propositions", *Sophia*, 1, 1962, pp.22-27.

Lonergan, B.J.F., *Grace and Freedom*, J. Patout Burns. (ed), London: Darton, Longman and Todd, 1971.

Lonergan, B., *Insight*, London: Longmans, 1961.

Lonergan, B., "Review of 'De Deo in Operatione Naturae vel Voluntatis Operante'", *Theological Studies*, 7, 1946, pp.602-613.

Lonergan, B., "St. Thomas' Theory of Operation", *Theological Studies*, 3, 1942, pp.375-402.

Lonergan, B., "St. Thomas' Thought on `Gratia Operans'", *Theological Studies*, 3, 1942, pp.533-578.

Long, E.T., "Temporality and Eternity", *International Journal of Philosophy of Religion*, 22, 1987, pp.185-189.

Lossky, V., *In the Image and Likeness of God*, J.H. Erickson and T.E. Bird (eds), St. Vladimir's Seminary Press, 1974.

Lossky, V., *The Vision of God*, tr. A. Moorhouse, London: Faith Press, 1963.

Lotze, H., *Microcosmus*, tr. E. Hamilton and E.E.C. Jones, Edinburgh: T. & T. Clark, vol 2, 1894.

Lotze, H., *Outlines of the Philsophy of Religion*, tr. G.T. Ladd, Boston: Ginn, 1886.

Lovejoy, A.O., *The Great Chain of Being*, Cambrige, Mass: Harvard University Press, 1964.

Lovejoy, A.O., "The Obsolescence of the Eternal", *Philosophical Review*, 18, 1909, pp.479-502.

Lowe, M.F., "Aristotle on the Sea Battle: A Clarification", 40, 1980, pp.55-59.

Lucas, J.R., *A Treatise on Time and Space*, London: Methuen, 1973.

Lucas, J.R., *The Freedom of the Will*, Oxford: Oxford University Press, 1971.

Luhmann, R.S., "The Concept of God: Some Philosophical Considerations", *The Evangelical Quarterly*, 54, 1982, pp.88-104.

Luther, M., *On the Bondage of the Will*, tr. P.S. Watson, London: S.C.M., 1969.

Lyttkens, H., "Religious Experience and Transcendence", *Religious Studies*, 15, 1979, pp.211-220.

Mabbott, J.D., "Our Direct Experience of Time", *Mind*, 60, 1952, pp.153-167.

Macbeth, M., "God's Spacelessness and Timelessness", *Sophia*, 22, 1983, pp.23-32.

MacGregor, G., "The Kenosis", *Anglican Theological Review*, 45, 1963, pp.73-83.

Mackay, D.M., "The Sovereignty of God in the Natural World", *Scottish Journal of Theology*, 21, 1968, pp.13-26.

Mackie, J.L., *The Cement of the Universe*, Oxford: Clarendon, 1974.

Mackie, J.L., *The Miracle of Theism*, Oxford: Clarendon, 1982.

Mackinnon, D.M., "'Substance' in Christology a Cross-Bench View", in *Christ, Faith and History*, S.W. Sykes and J.P. Clayton (eds), Cambridge: Cambridge University Press, 1972, pp.279-300.

Mckintosh, H.R., *The Christian Apprehension of God*, London: S.C.M., 1934.

Mackintosh, H.R., *The Doctrine of the Person of Christ*, Edinburgh: Clark, 1913.

Macmurray, J., *Persons in Relation*, New York: Harper, 1961.

Macquarrie, J., *God-Talk*, London: S.C.M., 1967.

Macquarrie, J., "Kenoticism Reconsidered", *Theology*, 77, 1974, pp.115-124.

Macquarrie, J., *Twentieth Century Religious Thought*, N.Y.: Harper & Row, 1963.

Madden, E.H., "A Third View of Causality", in *Philosophical Problems of Causation*, T.L. Beauchamp (ed), Encino: Dickenson, 1974, pp.178-189.

Maimonides, Moses, *The Guide For The Perplexed*, tr. M. Friedlander, London: Dover, 1904.

Malcolm, M., "Anselms' Ontological Arguments", *The Philosophical Review*, 69, 1960, pp.41-62.

Malkani, G.R., "The Temporal and the Eternal", *Philosophical Quarterly* (India), 30, 1957, pp.11-18.

Mann, W.E., "Simplicity and Immutability in God", *International Philosophical Quarterly*, 23, 1983, pp.267-276.

Marcel, G., "God and Causality", in *Religion and Culture*, W. Leibrecht (ed), N.Y.: Harper, 1959, pp.211-216.

Marcel, G., "Reply to Charles Hartshorne", in *The Philosophy of Gabriel Marcel*, P. Schilpp (ed), La Salle: Open Court, 1984, pp.367-370.

Maritain, J., *Existence and the Existent*, tr. L. Galantiere and G.B. Phelan, N.Y.: Pantheon, 1948.

Marmorstein, A., *The Old Rabbinic Doctrine of God*, London: Oxford University Press, 1927.

Marsh, J., *The Fulness of Time*, London: Nisbet, 1952.

Martin, C.B., *Religious Belief*, Ithaca: Cornell, 1959.

Martin, R., "The Sufficiency Thesis", *Philosophical Studies*, 23, 1972, pp.205-211.

Martin, R.M., "On God and Primordiality", *Review of Metaphysics*, 29, 1976, pp.497-522.

Martin, R.M., "Some Thomistic Properties of Primordiality", *Notre Dame Journal of Formal Logic*, 18, 1977, pp.567-582.

Martineau, R.A.S., "Creation and the Idea of Time", *Hibbert Journal*, 54, 1955, pp.275-280.

Mascall, E.L., "Does God Change? Mutability and Incarnation: A Review Discussion", *The Thomist*, 50, 1986, pp.447-457.

Mascall, E.L., *Existence and Analogy*, Hamden: Archon, 1967.

Mascall, E.L., *He Who Is*, London: Longmans Green, 1943.

Mascall, E.L., *The Openness of Being*, London: Darton, Longman and Todd, 1971.

Mascall, E.L., *Whatever Happened to the Human Mind?*, London: S.P.C.K., 1980.

Mason, D.R., "An Examination of `Worship' as a Key for Re-examining the God Problem", *Journal of Religion*, 55, 1975, pp.76-94.

Mason, D.R., "Can God Be Both Perfect and Free", *Religious Studies*, 18, 1982, pp.191-200.

Matson, W., *The Existence of God*, Ithaca: Cornell University Press, 1965.

Matthews, W.R., *God in Christian Thought and Experience*, London: Nisbet, 1930.

Mavrodes, G.I., "Aristotelian Necessity and Freedom", *Mid West Studies in Philosophy*, 1, 1976, pp.17-21.

Mavrodes, G.I., "Some Puzzles Concerning Omnipotence", *Philosophical Review*, 72, 1962, pp.221-223.

St. Maximus the Confessor, *The Four Centuries of Charity*, tr. P. Sherwood, London: Longmans, Green, 1955.

McArthur R.P.M., "Timelessness and Theological Fatalism", *Logique et Analyse*, 20, 1977, pp.475-490.

McCall, S., "Objective Time Flow", *Philosophy of Science*, 43, 1976, pp.356-362.

McCall, S., "Temporal Flux", *American Philosophical Quarterly*, 3, 1966, pp.270-281.

McConnell, F.J., *Is God Limited?*, London: Williams and Norgate, 1924.

McCord Adams, M., "Is the Existence of God a `Hard Fact'", *Philosophical Review*, 76, 1967, pp.492-503.

McGilvary, E.B., "Time and the Experience of Time", *Philosophical Review*, 23, 1914, pp.121-145.

McGinn, B., "The Development of the Thought of Thomas Aquinas on the Reconciliation of Divine Providence and Contingent Action", *Thomist*, 39, 1975, pp.741-752.

McGrath, P., "Professor Geach and the Future", *New Blackfriars*, 54, 1973, pp.497-504.

McIntyre, J., "Analogy", *Scottish Journal of Theology*, 12, 1959, pp.1-20.

McKenzie, J.S., "Eternity", in *The Encyclopedia of Religion and Ethics*, J. Hastings (ed), Edinburgh: T. & T. Clark, 1912, vol 5, pp.401-405.

McKenzie, J.S., *Lectures on Humanism*, London: Swan Sonneschein, 1907.

McLelland, J., *God The Anonymous*, Cambridge, Mass: Philadelphia Patristic Foundation, 1976.

McLendon, J., "Can There Be Talk About God-and-the-World?", *Harvard Theological Review*, 62, 1969, pp.33-49.

McTaggart, J.M.E., *The Nature of Existence*, Cambridge: Cambridge University Press, vol 2, 1927.

McTaggart, J.M.E., "The Relation of Time and Eternity", *Mind*, 18, 1909, pp.343-362.

McTaggart, J.M.E., "Time", in *The Philosophy of Time*, R.M. Gale (ed), N.J.: Humanities Press, 1978, pp.86-97.

McTighe, T.P., "Eternity and Time in Boethius", in *History of Philosophy in the Making*, L.J. Thro (ed), Washington: Washington University Press, 1982, pp.35-62.

McWilliams, W., "Divine Suffering in Contemporary Theology", *Scottish Journal of Theology*, 33, 1980, pp.35-53.

Mehl, R., *The Condition of the Christian Philosopher*, tr. E. Kushner, London: James Clarke, 1963.

Mehlberg, H., *Time, Causality, and the Quantum Theory*, R.S. Cohen (ed), Dordrecht: Reidel, vol 1 and 2, 1980.

Meijering, E.P., "God Being History", *Studies in Patristic Philosophy*, Amsterdam: North Holland, 1975.

Mellert, R.B., *What is Process Theology?*, N.Y.: Paulist, 1975.

Mellor, D.H., "History Without the Flow of Time", *Neue Zeitschrift fur Systematische Theolgie und Religions Philosophie*, 28, 1986, pp.68-76.

Mellor, D.H., "The Self From Time to Time", *Analysis*, 40, 1980, pp.59-62.

Mellor, D.H., *Real Time*, Cambridge: Cambridge University Press, 1981.

Meynell, H., "The Theology of Hartshorne", *Journal of Theological Studies*, 24, 1973, pp.143-157.

Michalson, G.E., "The Non-Moral Element in Kant's `Moral Proof' of the Existence of God", *Scottish Journal of Theology*, 39, 1986, pp.501-515.

Miller, F., "Aristotle on the Reality of Time", *Archiv fur Geschichte der Philosophie*, 56, 1974, pp.132-155.

Miller, P., "On `Becoming' As a Fifth Dimension", in *Physics and the Ultimate Significance of Time*, D.R. Griffin (ed), Albany: S.U.N.Y., 1985, pp.291-292.

Mohr, R.D., *The Platonic Cosmology*, Leiden: Brill, 1985.

Moltmann, J., "The `Crucified God': God and the Trinity Today", *Concilium*, 6, 1972, pp.26-37.

Moltmann, J., *The Crucified God*, tr. R.A. Wilson and J. Bowden, London: S.C.M., 1974.

Mommsen, T., "St. Augustine and the Christian Idea of Progress", *Journal of the History of Ideas*, 12, 1951, pp.346-374.

Moor, J., "Split Brains and Atomic Persons", *Philosophy of Science*, 49, 1982, pp.91-106.

Moore, W.L., "Schleiermacher as a Calvinist", *Scottish Journal of Theology*, 24, 1971, pp.167-183.

Morreall, J.S., *Analogy and Talking About God*, Washington: University Press of America, 1978.

Morris, T.V., "Creation 'Ex Nihilo': Some Considerations", *International Journal for Philosophy*, 14, 1983, pp.233-239.

Morris, T.V., *The Logic of God Incarnate*, Ithaca: Cornell University Press, 1986.

Morris, T.V., "Perfect Being Theology", *Nous*, 21, 1987, pp.19-30.

Morris, T.V., "Properties, Modalities, and God", *Philosophical Review*, 93, 1984, pp.35-55.

Morris, T.V. and Menzel, C., "Absolute Creation", *American Philsophical Quarterly*, 24, 1986, pp.353-362.

Mouiren, T., *The Creation*, London: Burns and Oates, 1962.

Muller, R.A., "Incarnation, Immutability and the case for classical theism", *Westminster Theological Journal*, 45, 1983, pp.22-40.

Mulligan, R., "Divine Foreknowledge and Freedom: A Problem of Language", *Thomist*, 36, 1972, pp.293-299.

Mundle, C.W.K., "How Specious is the Specious Present?", *Mind*, 63, 1954, pp.26-48.

Mundle, C.W.K., "Time, Consciousness of" in *The Encyclopedia of Philosophy*, P. Edwards (ed), N.Y.:

Macmillan, vol 8, 1967, pp.134-138.

Nagel, T., "Brain Bisection and the Unity of Consciousness", in *Personal Identity*, J. Perry (ed), Berkley: University of California Press, 1975, pp.227-245.

Nash, R.H., *The Concept of God*, Grand Rapids, Zondervan, 1983.

Nelson, H.J., "Time(s), eternity and duration", *International Journal for Philosophy of Religion*, 22, 1987, pp.3-19.

Neville, R.C., "From nothing to being: The notion of creation in Chinese and Western thought", *Philosophy East and West*, 30, 1980, pp.21-34.

Neville, R.C., *God the Creator*, Chicago: University of Chicago Press, 1968.

Newton, I., *Mathematical Principles of Natural Philosophy*, N.Y.: Philosophical Library, 1964.

Newton, I., *Opticks*, Dover, 1952.

Newton-Smith, W.H., *The Structure of Time*, London: Routledge and Kegan Paul, 1980.

Nida, E.A., "The Implications of Contemporary Linguistics for Biblical Scholarship", *Journal of Biblical Literature*, 91, 1972, pp.73-89.

Niebuhr, R., *Faith and History*, London: Nisbet, 1949.

Niebuhr, R., *The Nature and Destiny of Man*, London: Nisbet, vol 2, 1943.

Niermann, E., "Providence", in *Sacramentum Mundi*, K. Rahner (ed), London: Burns and Oates, 1970, vol 5, pp.130-133.

Normore, C., "Future Contingents", in *The Cambridge History of Later Medieval Philosophy*, N. Kretzmann, A. Kenny, J.Pinborg, (eds), Cambridge: Cambridge University Press, 1982, pp.358-381.

Norris, R.A., *God and World in Early Christian Theology*, N.Y.: Seabury, 1965.

Novak, M., *Belief and Unbelief. A Philosophy of Self-Knowledge*, London: Darton, Longman and Todd, 1966.

Nygren, A., *Romans*, tr. C. Rasmussen, Philadelphia: Fortress, 1949.

Oakes, R.A., "Classical theism and Pantheism: A Victory for Process Theism?", *Religious Studies*, 13, 1977, pp.167-173.

Oakes, R.A., "God and Physical Objects", *International Journal for Philosophy of Religion*, 9, 1978, pp.16-29.

Oakes, R.A., "Theism and Pantheism Again", *Sophia*, 24, 1985, pp.30-37.

Oaklander, L.N., "The `Timelessness' of Time", *Philosophy and Phenomenological Research*, 38, 1977, pp.228-233.

O'Brien, T.C., "Appendix I: `Esse', The Proper Effect of God Alone", *Summa Theologiae*, London: Blackfriars, 1975, vol 14, pp.169-175.

Ogden, S.M., "Introduction to 'Faith and Existence'", in *R. Bultmann, Faith and Existence*, tr. S.M. Ogden, London: Fontana, 1973, pp.9-24.

Ogden, S.M., *The Reality of God and Other Essays*, London: S.C.M., 1967.

O'Neill, W., "Time and Eternity in Proclus", *Phronesis*, 7, 1962, pp.161-165.

Origen, *Against Celsus*, tr. F. Crombie, Ante-Nicene Christian Library, Edinburgh: T. and T. Clark, vol 23, 1882.

Origen, `Origenes': Selections from the Commentaries and the Homilies*, tr. R.B. Tollinton, London: S.P.C.K., 1929.

Osborn, E.F., *Clement of Alexandria*, Cambridge: Cambridge University Press, 1957.

Otte, R., "A Defense of Middle Knowlege", *International Journal for Philosophy of Religion*, 21, 1987, pp.161-169.

Otto, R., *The Idea of the Holy*, tr. J.W. Harvey, London: Oxford University Press, 1931.

Owen, G.E.L., "Eleatic Questions", *Classical Quarterly*, 10 (n.s), 1960, pp.84-102.

Owen, G.E.L., "Plato and Parmenides On the Timeless Present", *The Monist*, 50, 1966, pp.317-340.

Owen, H.P., *Concepts of Deity*, London: Macmillan, 1971.

Owen, H.P., *The Christian Knowledge of God*, London: Athlone Press, 1969.

Owen, H.P., "Providence and Science", in *Providence*, M. Wiles (ed), London: S.P.C.K., 1969, pp.77-87.

Owens, J., "`Cause of Necessity' in the `Tertia Via'", *Medieval Studies*, 33, 1971, pp.21-45.

Owens, J., "The Physical World of Parmenides", in *Essays in Honour of Anton Charles Pegis*, J.R. O'Donnell (ed), Toronto: Pontifical Institute of Medieval Studies, 1974, pp.378-395.

Paffard, M., *The Unattended Moment*, London: S.C.M., 1976.

Pailin, D., "Authenticity in the Interpretation of Christianity", in *The Cardinal Meaning*, R. Morgan and M. Pye (eds), The Hague: Mouton, 1973, pp.127-159.

Pailing, D.A., "The Humanity of the Theologian and the Personal Nature of God", *Religious Studies*, 12, 1976, pp.141-158.

Paley, W., *Natural Theology*, Edinburgh: Oliver and Boyd, 1817.

Palmer, H., *Analogy*, London: Macmillan, 1973.

Pannenberg, W., "The Appropriation of the Philosophical Concept of God as a Dogmatic Problem of Early Christian Theology", in *Basic Questions in Theology*, London, S.C.M., vol 2, 1971, pp.119-183.

Pannenberg, W., *Jesus-God and Man*, tr. L.L. Wilckens and D.A. Priebe, Philadelphia: Westminster, 1968.

Park, D., *The Image of Eternity*, Amherst: University of Massachusetts Press, 1980.

Passmore, J., *Philosophical Reasoning*, London: Gerald Duckworth, 1961.

Paterson, R.W.K., "Evil, Omniscience and Omnipotence", *Religious Studies*, 15, 1979, pp.1-23.

Paton, M., "Can God Forget?", *Scottish Journal of Theology*, 35, 1982, pp.385-402.

Peacocke, A.R., "Cosmos and Creation", in *Cosmology, History and Theology*, W. Yourgrau and A.D. Breck (eds), London: Plenum, 1977, pp.365-381.

Peacocke, A.R., *Creation and the World of Science*, Oxford: Clarendon, 1979.

Pearl, L., "The Misuse of Anselm's Formula For God's Perfection", *Religious Studies*, 22, 1986, pp.355-365.

Pegis, A.C., "'Penitus Manet Ignotum'", *Medieval Studies*, 27, 1965, pp.212-226.

Peirce, C.S., *Collected Papers of Charles S. Pierce*, Cambridge: Belknap, vol 5, 1960.

Pelikan, J., "Creation and Causality in the History of Christian Thought", *Pastoral Psychology*, 10, 1960, pp.11-20.

Pelikan, J., "Creation and Causality in the History of Christian Thought", in *Evolution After Darwin, Issues in Evolution*, Sol Tax and C. Callender (eds), Chicago: Chicago University Press, vol 3, 1960, pp.29-40.

Pelikan, J., *The Growth of Medieval Theology (600-1300)*, Chicago: University of Chicago Press, 1978.

Penney, R., "On the dimensionality of the real world", *Journal of Mathematical Physics*, 6, 1965, pp.1607-1611.

Perry, J., "The Problem of the Essential Indexical", *Nous*, 13, 1979, pp.3-21.

Pieper, J., *The Silence of Saint Thomas*, London: Faber and Faber, n.d.

Pierce, T., "Spatio-Temporal Relations In Divine Interactions", *Scottish Journal of Theology*, 35, 1982, pp.1-11.

Pike, N., "Divine Foreknowledge, Human Freedom and Possible Worlds", *Philosophical Review*, 86, 1977, pp.209-216.

Pike, N., *God and Timelessness*, London: Routledge and Kegan Paul, 1970.

Pike, N., "Of God and Freedom, a Rejoinder", *Philsophical Review*, 75, 1966, pp.369-379.

Pinnock, C., "The Need for a Scriptural, and Therefore a Neo-Classical Theism", in *Perspectives On Evangelical Theology*, K.S. Kantzer and S.W. Gundy (eds), Grand Rapids: Baker, 1979, pp.37-42.

Plantinga, A., *Does God Have a Nature?*, Milwaukee: Marquette University Press, 1980.

Plantinga, A., *The Nature of Necessity*, Oxford: Clarendon, 1974.

Plato, "Republic", tr. B. Jowett, *The Works of Plato*, Oxford: Oxford University Press, vol 3, 3rd ed. 1892.

Plato, *The Republic*, tr. F.M. Cornford, Oxford: Clarendon, 1941.

Plato, "Sophist", tr. B. Jowett, *The Works of Plato*, Oxford: Oxford University Press, vol 4, 3rd ed., 1892.

Plato, "'Timaeus'", tr. B. Jowett, *The Works of Plato*, Oxford: Oxford University Press, vol 3, 3rd ed., 1892.

Plecha, J.L., "Tenselessness and the Absolute Present", *Philosophy*, 59, 1984, pp.529-534.

Plotinus, *The Enneads*, tr. S. MacKenna, London: Faber and Faber, 1956.

Plutarch, *Moralia*, 5, tr. F.C. Babbitt, London: Heinemann, 1936.

Poincare, H., "The Measure of Time", *Concepts of Space and Time*, M. Capek (ed), Dordrecht: Reidel, pp.317-327.

Pollard, G.F., "Existential Reactions against Scholasticism", in *Objections to Roman Catholicism*, M. de la Bedoyere (ed), London: Constable, 1964.

Pollard, K.E., "The Impassibility of God", *Scottish Journal of Theology*, 8, 1955, pp.353-364.

Pollard, W.G., *Chance and Providence*, London: Faber and Faber, 1958.

Pontifex, Dom Mark, *Providence and Freedom*, London: Burns and Oates, 1960.

Portalie, R., *A Guide to the Thought of St. Augustine*, tr. R.J. Bastian, Westport: Greenwood, 1975.

Prestige, F.L., *God in Patristic Thought*, London: S.P.C.K., 2nd ed., 1959.

Price, H.H., "Some Considerations About Belief", *Proceedings of the Aristotelian Society*, 35, 1934-35, pp.229-252.

Price, H.H. and Broad, C.D., "The Philosophical Implications of Precognition", *Proceedings of the Aristotelian Society Supplementary Volume*, 16, 1937, pp.211-245.

Pringle-Pattison, S., *The Idea of God in the Light of Recent Philosophy*, N.Y.: Oxford University Press, 1920.

Prior, A.N., "The Formalities of Omniscience", *Philosophy*, 59, 1962, pp.114-129.

Prior, A.N., *Papers on Time and Tense*, Oxford: Clarendon, 1968.

Prior, A.N., *Past, Present and Future*, Oxford: Clarendon, 1967.

Prior, A.N., "Thank Goodness That's Over", *Philosophy*, 34, 1959, pp.12-17.

Prior, A.N., "Time After Time", *Mind*, 67, 1958, pp.244-246.

Proclus, "'Elementa theologia'", E.R. Dodds, Oxford: Clarendon, 1933.

Puccetti, R., "Before Creation", *Sophia*, 3, 1964, pp.24-36.

Puccetti, R., "The Concept of God", *Philosophical Quarterly*, 1964, pp.237-245.

Puccetti, R., *Persons*, London: Macmillan, 1968.

Purtill, R.L., "Foreknowledge and Fatalism", *Religious Studies*, 10, 1974, pp.319-324.
Putman, H., "Time and Physical Geometry", *Journal of Philosophy*, 64, 1967, pp.240-247
Quiller-Couch, A., (ed), *Felicities of Thomas Traherne*, London: Dobell, 1934.
Quine, W.V.O., "Identity, Ostension, and Hypostasis", *Journal of Philosophy*, 47, 1950, pp.621-633.
Quine, W.V.O., *Word and Object*, N.Y.: Wiley, 1960.
Quinn, P.L., "Divine Conservation, Continuous Creation, and Human Action", in *The Existence and Nature of God*, A.J. Fredosso (ed), Notre Dame: Notre Dame University Press, 1983, pp.55-79.
Quinn, P.L., "Divine Conservation and Spinozistic Pantheism", *Religious Studies*, 15, 1979, pp.289-302.
Quinn, P.L., "Divine Foreknowledge and Divine Freedom", *International Journal for the Philosophy of Religion*, 9, 1978, pp.219-240.
Rahner, K., "Grace and freedom", in *Sacramentum Mundi*, K. Rahner (ed), London: Burns and Oates, vol 2, 1968, pp.424-427.
Rahner, K., *Theological Investigations*, Baltimore: Helicon, vol 4, 1966.
Rahner, K. and Rondet, H., "Predestination", in *Sacramentum Mundi*, K. Rahner (ed), London: Burns and Oates, vol 5, 1970, pp.88-91.
Ramberan, O.G., "Omniscience, Foreknowledge and Human Freedom", *Canadian Journal of Philosophy*, 15, 1985, pp.483-488.
Ramsey, I.T., "The Concept of the Eternal", in *The Christian Hope*, G.B. Caird (ed), London: S.P.C.K., 1970, pp.35-48.
Ramsey, P., "A Personal God", in *Prospect for Theology*, E.G. Healey (ed), London: 1966, pp.55-71. Rashdall, H., *Philosophy and Religion*, London: Duckworth, 1909.
Ravicz, M.E., "St. Augustine: Time and Eternity", *Thomist*, 22, 1959, pp.542-554.
Redlon, R.A., "St. Thomas and the Freedom of the Creative Act", *Franciscan Studies*, 20, 1960, pp.1-18.
Rees, W.J., "Continuous States", *Proceedings of the Aristotelian Society*, 58, 1957-58, pp.223-244.

Reichenbach, B.R., *Evil and a Good God*, N.Y.: Fordham University Press, 1982.

Reichenbach, B.R., "Omniscience and Deliberation", *International Journal for Philosophy of Religion*, 16, 1984, pp.225-236.

Reichenbach, H., *Elements of Symbolic Logic*, N.Y.: Macmillan, 1948.

Reichenbach, H., *The Direction of Time*, Berkeley: University of California Pres, 1956.

Reichenbach, H., *The Philosophy of Space and Time*, N.Y.: Dover, 1958.

Reid, T., *Essays on the Intellectual Powers of Man*, A.D. Woozley (ed), London: Macmillan, 1941.

Reitmeister, L., *A Philosophy of Time*, N.Y.: Citadel, 1962.

Relton, H.M., *A Study in Christology*, London: S.P.C.K., 1917.

Relton, H.M., *Studies in Christian Doctrine*, London: Macmillan, 1960.

Rendall, R., *History, Prophecy and God*, London: Paternoster, 1954.

Rescher, N. and Urquhart. A., *Temporal Logic*, Vienna: Springer-Verlag, 1971.

Richard, L., "Kenotic Christology in a New Perspective", *Eglise et Theologie*, 7, 1976, pp.5-39.

Richardson, A., *Christian Apologetics*, London: S.C.M., 1950.

Richardson, R.C., "The `Scandal' of Cartesian Interactionism", *Mind*, 91, 1982, pp.20-37.

Richmond, J., "God, Time and Process Philosophy", *Theology*, 68, 1965, pp.234-241.

Rieser, M., "Causation, Action and Creation", *Journal of Philosophy*, 37, 1940, pp.491-499.

Ritschl, D., "Spring Cleaning", *Interpretation*, 17, 1963, pp.206-209.

Robb, A.A., *The Absolute Relations of Time and Space*, Cambridge: Cambridge University Press, 1921.

Robb, A.A., "The Conical Order of Time-Space", in *The Concepts of Space and Time*, M. Capek (ed), Dordrecht: Reidel, 1976, pp.369-386.

Roberts, R.H., "Karl Barth's Doctrine of Time: Its Nature and Implications", in *Karl Barth*, S.W. Sykes (ed), Oxford: Claredon, 1979, pp.88-146.

Robertson, J.C., "Rahner and Ogden: Man's Knowledge of God", *Harvard Theological Review*, 63, 1970, pp.377-407.

Robinson, C.K., "Biblical Theism and Modern Science", *Journal of Religion*, 43, 1963, pp.118-138.

Robinson, J.A.T., "Book Review, `The Fulness of Time'", *Theology*, 56, 1953, pp.107-109.

Robinson, J.A.T., *Wrestling with Romans*, London: S.C.M., 1979.

Robinson, R., "The Concept of Knowledge", *Mind*, N.S., 80, 1971, pp.17-28.

Rock, J.P., "St. Thomas on Divine Causality", *Philosophical Studies*, 5, 1955, pp.21-43.

Rorty, A.O., "A Literary Postscript: Characters, Persons, Selves, Individuals", in *The Identities of Persons*, A.O. Rorty (ed), Berkeley: University of California Press, 1976, pp.301-323.

Rosenthal, D.M., "The Necessity of Foreknowledge", *Mid West Studies in Philosophy*, 1, 1976, pp.22-255.

Ross, J.F., *Philosophical Theology*, Indianapolis: Hackett, 2nd ed., 1980.

Ross, J.F., "Creation", *Journal of Philosophy*, 77, 1980, pp.614-629.

Ross, J.F., "Creation 2", in *The Existence and Nature of God*, A.J. Fredosso (ed), Notre Dame: Notre Dame University Press, 1983, pp.115-141.

Ross, J.F., *Portraying Analogy*, Cambridge: Cambridge University Press, 1981.

Ross, J.F., "Review of `The God of the Philosophers'", *Journal of Philosophy*, 79, 1982, pp.410-417.

Rowe, W.L., "Augustine on Foreknowledge and Free Will", *Review of Metaphysics*, 18, 1964, pp.356-363.

Royce, J., *The World of the Individual*, N.Y.: Macmillan, 2nd series, 1901.

Runzo, J., "Omniscience and Freedom for Evil", *International Journal for Philosophy of Religion*, 12, 1981, pp.131-147.

Russell, B., *The Analysis of Mind*, London: Allen and Unwin, 1921.

Russell, B., "Foundations of Geometry: Is Position in Space and Time Absolute or Relative?", *Mind*, 10, 1901, pp.293-317.

Russell, B., *Mysticism, Logic and Other Essays*, Harmondsworth: Penguin, 1954.

Russell, B., "On the Experience of Time", *The Monist*, 25, 1915, pp.212-233.

Russell, B., *Our Knowledge of the External World*, London: Allen and Unwin, 1926.

Russell, B., *The Principles of Mathematics*, London: Allen and Unwin, 2nd ed., 1937.

Russell, B., *The Problems of Philosophy*, London, n.d.

Russell, S.H., "I. A. Dorner: A Centenary Appreciation", *Expository Times*, 96, 3, 1985, pp.77-81.

Ryle, G., Dilemmas, Cambridge: Cambridge University Press, 1954.

Saltmarsh, H.F., "Report on Cases of Apparent Precognition", *Proceedings of the Society For Psychical Research*, 42, 1934, pp.49-103.

Sambursky, S., "The Stoic Views of Time", in *The Concepts of Space and Time*, M. Capek (ed), Dordrecht: Reidel, 1976, pp.159-166.

Sanday, W. and Headlam, A.C., *The Epistle To The Romans*, Edinburgh: T. and T. Clark, 1911.

Sasse, H., "'aion, aionios'", in *Theological Dictionary of the New Testament*, G. Kittel (ed), tr. G.W Bromiley, Grand Rapids: Eerdmans, vol 1, 1964, pp.197-209.

Saunders, J.T., "Of God and Freedom", *Philosophical Review*, 75, 1966, pp.219-225.

Sayers, D.L., *The Mind of the Maker*, London: Methuen, 1941.

Sayers, D.L., *Unpopular Opinions*, London: Gollancz, 1946.

Schiffers, N., "Suffering in History", *Concilium*, 6, 1972, pp.38-47.

Schiller, F.C., *Humanism*, London: Macmillan, 1912.

Schilpp, P., (ed), *The Philosophy of Gabriel Marcel*, La Salle: Open Court, 1984.

Schleiermacher, F., *The Christian Faith*, H.R. Mackintosh and J.S. Stewart (eds), Edinburgh: T. and T. Clark, 1960.

Schlesinger, G.N., "Divine Perfection", *Religious Studies*, 21, 1985, pp.147-158.

Schlick, M., "The Four-Dimensional World", in *Problems of Space and Time*, J.J.C. Smart (ed), N.Y.: Macmillan, 1964, pp.292-296.

Schlick, M., *Philosophy of Nature*, N.Y.: Philosophical Library, 1949.

Schmitz, K.L., "Weiss and Creation", *Review of Metaphysics*, 18, 1964, pp.147-169.

Schofield, M., "Did Parmenides Discover Eternity?", *Archiv fur Geschichte der Philosophe*, 52, 1970, pp.113-135.

Schoonenberg, P., *God's World in the Making*, Pittsburgh: Duquesne University Press, 1964.

343

Schoonenberg, P., "Process or History in God", *Louvain Studies*, 4, 1973, pp.303-319.

Schopenhauer, A., "Praedicabilia `A Priori'", from *The World as Will and Idea*, part II, tr. R.B. Haldane and J. Kemp, London: Routledge and Kegan Paul, pp.221-223, in *The Concepts of Space and Time*, M. Capek (ed), Dordrecht: Reidel, 1976, pp.227-230.

Schuster, M.M., "Is the Flow of Time Subjective", *Review of Metaphysics*, 39, 1986, pp.695-714.

Scotus Duns, *God and Creatures, The Quodlibetal Questions*, tr. F. Alluntis and A.B. Wolter, Princeton: Princeton University Press, 1975.

Scotus, Johannes Duns, *Opera Omnia*, L. Dadding (ed), 16 vols, Hildesheim: Goerge Olms Verlagsbuchhandlung, 1969.

Scriven, M., "The Logic of Cause", *Theory and Decision*, 2, 1971, pp.49-66.

Searle, J.R., "Proper Names", *Mind*, 67, 1958, pp.166-173.

Sellars, W., "Metaphysics and the Concept of a Person", in *The Logical Way of Doing Things*, K. Lambert (ed), New Haven: Yale University Press, 1969, pp.219-252.

Sellars, W., "Time and the World Order", in *Minnesota Studies in the Philosophy of Science, Vol 3: Scientific Explanation, Space, and Time*, H. Feigl and G. Maxwell (eds), Minneapolis: University of Minnesota Press, 1962, pp.527-616.

Sharples, R., "Alexander of Aphrodisias, `De Fato'" some parallels", *Classical Quarterly*, 28, 1978, pp.243-266.

Shedd, W.G.T., *Dogmatic Theology*, Nashville, Nelson, vol 1, 1980.

Shepherd, A.P., *The Eternity of Time*, London: Hodder and Stoughton, 1941.

Shepherd, J.J., *Experience, Inference and God*, London: Macmillan, 1975.

Shields, G.W., "Davies, eternity and the cosmological argument", *International Journal for the Philosophy of Religion*, 21, 1987, pp.21-37.

Shields, G.W., "God, Modality and Incoherence", *Encounter*, 44, 1983, pp.29-32.

Schoemaker, S., "Time without change", *The Journal of Philosophy*, 66, 1969.

Shutte, A., "Indwelling, Intersubjectivity and God", *Scottish Journal of Theology*, 32, 1979, pp.201-216.

Sia, S., "On God, Time and Change", *Clergy Review*, 63, 1978, pp.378-387.

Skillen, A., "The Myth of Temporal Division", *Analysis*, 26, 1965, pp.44-47.

Sklar, L., *Space, Time and Spacetime*, Berkeley and Los Angeles: University of California Press, 1974.

Smart, J.J.C., "Causal Theories of Time", *The Monist*, 53, 1969, pp.385-395.

Smart, J.J.C., "The Moving 'Now'", *Australasian Journal of Philosophy*, 31, 1953, pp.184-187.

Smart, J.J.C., (ed), *Problems of Space and Time*, N.Y.: Macmillan, 1964.

Smart, J.J.C., "The River of Time", Mind, 58, 1949, pp.483-494.

Smart, J.J.C., "Spatialising Time", in *The Philosophy of Time*, R.M. Gale (ed), N.J.: Humanities Press, 1978, pp.163-167.

Smart, J.J.C., "Time and Becoming", in *Time and Cause*, P. van Inwagen (ed), Dordrecht: Reidel, 1980, pp.3-16.

Smart, N., "Omnipotence, Evil and Supermen", in *God and Evil: Readings on the Theological Problem of Evil*, N. Pike (ed), New Jersey: Prentice-Hall, 1964, pp.103-112.

Smart, N., "Our Experience of the Ultimate", *Religious Studies*, 20, 1984, pp.19-26.

Smart, N., *Philosophers and Religious Truth*, London: S.C.M., 1969.

Smith, A.D., "God's Death", *Theology*, 80, 1977, pp.262-268.

Smith, J.E., "Existence, the Past, and God", *Review of Metaphysics*, 6, 1952, pp.287-295.

Smith, Q., "The Mind-Independence of Temporal Becoming", *Philosophical Studies*, 47, 1985, pp.109-119.

Smith, T.P., "On the Applicability of a Criterion of Change", *Ratio*, 15, 1973, pp.325-333.

Smulders, P., "Creation", in *Sacramentum Mundi*, K. Rahner (ed), London: Burns and Oates, vol 2, 1968, pp.27-28.

Soelle, D., *Suffering*, London: Darton, Longman and Todd, 1975.

Sontag, F., "Anselm and the Concept of God", *Scottish Journal of Theology*, 35, 1982, pp.213-218.

Sorabji, R., *Necessity, Cause and Blame*, Ithaca: Cornell University Press, 1980.

Sorabji, R., *Time, Creation and the Continuum: Theories in antiquity and the early middle ages*, London: Duckworth, 1984.

Spinoza, B., *Ethics*, tr. W.H. White, London: Oxford University Press, 1910.

Stace, W.T., *Mysticism and Philosophy*, Philadelphia: J.B. Lippincott, 1960.

Stace, W.T. (ed), *The Teachings of the Mystics*, N.Y.: New American Library, 1960.

Stace, W.T., *Time and Eternity*, Princeton: Princeton University Press, 1952.

Stapp, H.P., "Einstein and Process Time", in *Physics and the Ultimate Significance of Time*, D.R. Griffin (ed), Albany: S. U. N. Y., 1985, pp.264-270.

Stein, H., "On Einstein-Minkowski Space-Time", *Journal of Philosophy*, 65, 1968, pp.5-23.

Stein, H., "On the Paradoxical Time-Structures of Godel", *Philosophy of Science*, 37, 1970, pp.589-601.

Steinkraus, W.E., "Time and God", *Philosophical Quarterly* (India), 30, 1958, pp.243-269.

Steven, A.D., "The Freedom of God and Human Freedom", *Scottish Journal of Theology*, 36, 1983, pp.163-180.

Stevenson, J., (ed), *Creeds, Councils and Controversies*, London: S.P.C.K., 1966.

Stiernotte, A.P., *God and Space-time*, N.Y.: Philosophical Library, 1954.

Stocks, J.L., *Time, Cause and Eternity*, London: Macmillan, 1938.

Stokes, W., "Freedom as Perfection: Whitehead, Thomas, and Augustine", *Proceedings of the American Catholic Philosophical Association*, 36, 1962, pp.134-142.

Stokes, W.E., "Whitehead's Challenge to Theistic Realism", *New Scholasticism*, 38, 1964, pp.1-21.

Stoothoff, R.H., "What Actually Exists", *Proceedings of the Aristotelian Society*, Supp. Vol 42, 1968, pp.17-30.

Stout, G.F., *God and Nature*, Cambridge: Cambridge University Press, 1952.

Stump, E., "Petitionary Prayer", *American Philosophical Quarterly*, 16, 2, 1979, pp.81-91.

Stump, E. and Kretzmann, "Eternity", *Journal of Philosophy*, 8, 1981, pp.429-458.

Sturch, R.L., "The Problem of the Divine Eternity", *Religious Studies*, 10, 1974, pp.487-493.

Surin, K. "The Impassibility of God and the Problem of Evil", *Scottish Journal of Theology*, 35, 1982, pp.17-36.

Sutherland, S.R., "God, Time and Eternity", *Proceedings of the Aristotelian Society*, 79, 1978-79, pp.103-121.

Suttor, T., tr and ed., *Summa Theologiae*, London: Blackfriars, vol 11, 1970.

Swinburne, R.G., *The Coherence of Theism*, Oxford: Clarendon, 1977.

Swinburne, R.G., "Conditions for Bitemporality", *Analysis*, 26, 1965, pp.47-50.

Swinburne, R.G., *The Existence of God*, Oxford: Clarendon, 1979.

Swinburne, R.G., *Space and Time*, London: Macmillan, 1968.

Swinburne, R.G., "The Timelessness of God, 1", *Church Quarterly Review*, 166, 1965, pp.323-337.

Swinburne, R.G., "The Timelessness of God, 2", *Church Quarterly Review*, 166, 1965, pp.472-486.

Swinburne, R.G., "Times", *Analysis*, 25, 1965, pp.185-191.

Swinburne, R.G., "Verificationism and Theories of Space-Time", in *Space, Time and Causality*, R.G. Swinburne (ed), Dordrecht: Reidel, 1983, pp.63-76.

Talbott, T.B., "On Divine Foreknowledge and Bringing About the Past", *Philosophy and Phenomenological Research*, 46, 1986, pp.455-469.

Taran, L., *Parmenides*, Princeton: Princeton University Press, 1965.

Taylor, A.E., *Elements of Metaphysics*, London: Methuen, 1903.

Taylor, A.E., "Some Thoughts on `Process and Reality'", *Theology*, 33, 1930, pp.67-80.

Taylor, R., "Causation", in *The Encyclopedia of Philosophy*, P. Edwards (ed), N.Y.: Macmillan, vol 2, 1967, pp.56-66.

Taylor, R., "Deliberation and Foreknowledge", *American Philosophical Quarterly*, 1, 1964, pp.73-80.

Taylor, T., "Determinism", in *The Encyclopedia of Philosophy*, P. Edwards (ed), N.Y.: Macmillan, vol 2, 1967, pp.359-373.

Taylor, R., "Fatalism", *Philosophical Review*, 71, 1962, pp.56-66.

Taylor, R., *Metaphysics*, N.J.: Prentice-Hall, 2nd ed., 1973.

Taylor, R., "The Problem of Future Contingencies", *Philosophical Review*, 66, 1957, pp.1-28.

Taylor, R., "Spatial and Temporal Analogies and the Concept of Identity", *The Journal of Philosophy*, 52, 1955, pp.599-612.

Temple, W., *Christus Veritas*, London: Macmillan, 1954.

Tennant, F.R., *Philosophical Theology*, Cambridge: Cambridge Univerity Press, vol 2, 1930.

Tertullian, *Against Marcion*, tr. P. Holmes, Ante-Nicene Christian Library, Edinburgh: T. and T. Clark, vol 7, 1882.

Teske, R.H., "Omniscience, Omnipotence and Divine Transcendence", *The New Scholasticism*, 53, 1979, pp.277-294.

Teske, T.H., "Properties of God and the Predicaments in `De Trinitae 5'", *Modern Scholasticism*, 59, 1981, pp.1-20.

Thatcher, A., "The Personal God and A God Who Is A Person", *Religious Studies*, 21, 1985, pp.61-73.

Thiel, J.E., "Schleiermacher's Doctrine of Creation and Preservation: Some Epistemological Considerations", *Heythrop Journal*, 22, 1981, pp.32-48.

Thomas, J.H., "The Idea of Creation", *Hibbert Journal*, 50, 1951, pp.153-161.

Thompson, W.R. "Providence", *Thomist*, 5, 1943, pp.229-245.

Tillich, P., *Systematic Theology*, Chicago: University of Chicago Press, vol 1, 1951.

Tomkinson, J.L., "Divine Sempiternity and Atemporality", *Religious Studies*, 18, 1982, pp.177-189.

Torrance, T.F., *The Ground and Grammar of Theology*, Charlottesville: University of Virginia Press, 1980. Torrance, T.F., *Space, Time and Incarnation*, London: Oxford University Press, 1969.

Tracy, T.F., *God, Action and Embodiment*, Grand Rapids: Eerdmans, 1984.

Traherne, T., *Christian Ethics*, C.L. Marks and G.R. Guffrey (eds), Ithaca: Cornell University Press, 1968.

Trethowan, I., *The Absolute and the Atonement*, London: George Allen and Unwin, 1971.

Trethowan, I., "A Changing God", *The Downside Review*, 84, 1966, pp.247-261.

Trethowan, I., *An Essay in Christian Philosophy*, London: Longmans, 1954.

Trethowan, I., "God's Changelessness", *Clergy Review*, 64, 1979, pp.15-21.

Trethowan, I., *Mysticism and Theology*, London: Geoffrey Chapman, 1975.

Trethowan, I., "The Significance of Process Theology", *Religious Studies*, 19, 1983, pp.311-322.

Van Fraasen, B., *An Introduction to the Philosophy of Time and Space*, N.Y.: Random House, 1970.

Van Inwagen, P., *An Essay on Free Will*, Oxford: Clarendon, 1984.

Vaughan, T.D., *The Explication of Divine Eternality: A Philsophical Prolegomenon*, Unpublished B.A. (Hons) thesis, University of Queensland, 1985.

Vendler, Z., "Causal Relations", *Journal of Philosophy*, 64, 1967, pp.704-713.

Verbeke, G., "Some Later Neoplatonic Views on Divine Creation and the Eternity of the World", in *Neoplatonism and Christian Thought*, D.J. O'Meara (ed), Albany, S.U.N.Y., 1982, pp.45-53.

Verdentius, W.J., "Traditional and Personal Elements in Aristotle's Religion", *Phronesis*, 5, 1960, pp.56-70.

Von Hugel, F., Eternal Life, Edinburgh: T. and T. Clark, 1913.

Von Leyden, W., "Time, Number and Eternity in Plato and Aristotle", *Philosophical Quarterly*, 14, 1964, pp.35-52.

Wagers, C.H., "Creation and Providence", *College of The Bible Quarterly*, 38, 1961, pp.36-50.

Wainwright, W.J., "Augustine on God's Simplicity: A Reply", *The New Scholasticism*, 53, 1979, pp.118-123.

Wainwright, W.J., "Worship, Intuitions and Perfect Being Theology", *Nous*, 21, 1987, pp.31-32.

Walker, W.L., *The Spirit and the Incarnation*, Edinburgh: T. and T. Clark, 1901.

Wallace, W.A., "Aquinas on Creation, Science and Matters of Fact", *Thomist*, 38, 1974, pp.485-523.

Wallis, R.T., "Divine omniscience in Plotinus, Proclus and Aquinas", in *Neoplatonism and Early Christian Thought*, H.J. Blumenthal and R.A. Markus (eds), London: Variorum, 1981, pp.223-235.

Wallis,, R.T., *Neoplatonism*, London: Duckworth, 1972.

Walls, J.L., "A Fable of Foreknowledge and Freedom", *Philosophy*, 62, 1987, pp.67-75.

Walls, J.L., "Can God Save Anyone He Will?", *Scottish Journal of Theology*, 38, 1985, pp.155-172.

Ward, J., *The Realm of Ends*, Cambridge: Cambridge University Press, 1912.

Ward, K., *The Concept of God*, Oxford: Blackwell, 1974.

Ward, K., *Fifty Key Words in Philosophy*, London: Lutterworth, 1968.

Ward, Keith, *Holding Fast to God*, London: S.P.C.K., 1982.

Ward, Keith, *Rational Theology and the Creativity of God*, Oxford: Basil Blackwell, 1982.

Ward, M., "The Biblical Doctrine of Providence", in *Providence*, M. Wiles (ed), London: S.P.C.K., 1969, pp.15-34.

Webb, C.C.J., *God and Personality*, London: Allen and Unwin, 1919.

Webb, C.C.J., *Problems in the Relations of God and Man*, London: Nisbet, 1911.

Weiman, H.N., "God is More than We Can Think", *Christendom* 1, 1936, pp.428-441.

Weiman, H.N., "On Using the Word `God'", *Journal of Philosophy*, 30, 1933, pp.399-404.

Weinandy, T.G., "Aquinas and the Incarnational Act: `Become' as a Mixed Relation", *Doctor Communis*, Vatican City, 32, n.d., pp.15-31.

Weiss, H., "An Interpretative Note in a Passage in Plotinus' `On Eternity and Time' (3.7.6)", *Classical Philosophy*, 36, 1941, pp.230-239.

Weiss, P., *Modes of Being*, Carbonale: Southern Illinois University Press, 1958.

Weston, F., *The One Christ*, London: Longmans, Green, 1907.

Westphal, M., "Temporality and Finitism in Hartshorne's Theism", *Review of Metaphysics*, 19, 1966, pp.550-54.

White, M.J. "Causes as Necessary Conditions", in *New Essays on Aristotle*, F.J. Pelletier and J. King-Farlow (eds), Guelph: University of Calgary Press, 1984, pp.157-189.

White, V., *The Fall of a Sparrow: a concept of special divine action*, Exeter: Paternoster, 1985.

White, V.A., "Whitehead, Special Relativity, and Simultaneity", *Process Studies*, 13, 1983, pp.275-285.

Whitehead, A.N., *Process and Reality*, Cambridge: Cambridge University Press, 1929.

Whitehead, A.N., *Science and the Modern World*, Harmondsworth: Penguin, 1926.

Whitney, B.L., "Divine Immutability in Process Philosophy and Contemporary Thomism", *Horizons*, 7, 1980, pp.49-68.

Whitrow, G.J., *A Natural Philosophy of Time*, London: Nelson, 1961.

Whittaker, J., "The Eternity of the Platonic Forms", *Phronesis*, 13, 1968, pp.131-144.

Whittaker, J., *God, Being, Time*, Oslo; In Aedibus Universitetsforlaget, 1971.

Whittaker, J., *Studies in Platonism and Patristic Thought*, London: Variorum, 1984.

Wilcox, J.T., "A Question from Physics for Certain Theists", *Journal of Religion*, 40, 1961, pp.293-300.

Wild, J., "The New Empiricism and Human Time", *Review of Metaphysics*, 7, 1954, pp.537-557.

Wiles, M., "Christianity Without Incarnation", in *The Myth of God Incarnate*, J. Hick (ed), Philadelphia: Westminster, 1977, pp.1-10.

Wiles, M. (ed), *Providence*, London: S.P.C.K., 1969.

Wiles, M., *The Remaking of Christian Doctrine*, London: S.C.M., 1974.

Wiles, M., *Working Papers on Doctrine*, London: S.C.M., 1976.

Wiles, M. and McCabe, H., "The Incarnation: An Exchange", *New Blackfriars*, 58, 1977, pp.542-553.

Wilhelmsen, F.D., "Creation As A Relation in Saint Thomas Aquinas", *Modern Schoolman*, 56, 1979, pp.107-133.

Wilkie, J.S., "The Problem of the Temporal Relation of Cause and Effect", *British Journal for the Philosophy of Science*, 1, 1950, pp.211-229.

Williams, A.H., "The Trinity and Time", *Scottish Journal of Theology*, 39, 1986, pp.65-81.

Williams, D.C., "The Myth of Passage", in *The Philosophy of Time*, R.M. Gale (ed), N.J.: Humanities Press, 1978, pp.98-116.

Williams, D.C., *Problems of Empirical Realism*, Springfield: C.C. Thomas, 1966.

Williams, G., "The Natural Causation of Free-Will", *Zygon*, 3, 1968, pp.72-84.

Williams, R., "'Person' and 'Personality' in Christology", *Downside Review*, 94, 1976, pp.253-260.

Wilson, N.J., "Space, Time and Individuals", *Journal of Philsophy*, 52, 1955, pp.589-598.

Wippel, J.F., *Metaphysical Themes in Thomas Aquinas*, Washington: Catholic University Press, 1984.

Wittgenstein, L., *The Blue Book*, Oxford: Blackwell, 1964.

Wittgenstein, L., *The Brown Book*, Oxford: Blackwell, 1960.

Wolfe, J., "On the Impossibility of An Infinite Past: A Reply to Craig", *International Journal for Philosophy of Religion*, 18, 1985, p.91.

Wolfson, H.A., "Albinus and Plotinus on Divine Attributes", *Harvard Theological Review*, 45, 1952, pp.115-130.

Wolfson, H.A., "Negative attributes in the Church Fathers and the Gnostic Basilides", *Harvard Theological Review*, 50, 1957, pp.145-156.

Wolfson, H.A., *Philo*, Cambridge, Mass: Harvard Uni. Press, vol 1, 1947.

Wolfson, H.A., *The Philosophy of the Church Fathers vol 1: Faith, Trinity, Incarnation*, Cambridge, Mass: Harvard Uni. Press, 1970.

Wolfson, H.A., *The Philosophy of Spinoza*, Cambridge, Mass: Harvard University Press, vol 1, 1934.

Wolterstorff, N., "God Everlasting", in *Contemporary Philosophy of Religion*, S.M. Cahn and D. Shatz (eds) Oxford: Oxford University Press, 1982, pp.77-98.

Woolcombe, K.J., "The Pain of God", *Scottish Journal of Theology*, 20, 1967, pp.129-148.

Wright, J.H., "Divine Knowledge and Human Freedom, The God Who Dialogues", *Theological Studies*, 38, 1977, pp.450-477.

Wright, J.H., "The Eternal Plan of Divine Providence", *Theological Studies*, 27, 1966, pp.27-57.

Wright, J.H., *The Order of the Universe in the Theology of St. Thomas Aquinas*, Rome: Gregorian University, 1957.

Yarnold, G.D., *The Moving Image*, London: Allen and Unwin, 1966.

Yearley, L.H., "St. Thomas Aquinas On Providence and Predestination", *Anglican Theological Review*, 49, 1967, pp.409-423.

Yoncey, P., "Insights on Eternity from a Scientific View of Time", *Christianity Today*, 28, April, 1984, p.26.

Ysaac, W.L., "The Certitude of Providence in St. Thomas", *Modern Schoolman*, 38, 1960-61, pp.305-322.

Zagzebski, L., "Divine Foreknowledge and Human Free Will", *Religious Studies*, 21, 1985, pp.279-298.

Zeis, J., "The Concept of Eternity", *International Journal for Philosophy of Religion*, 16, 1984, pp.61-71.

Zeis, J. and Jacobs, J., "Omnipotence and Concurrence", *International Journal for the Philosophy of Religion*, 14, 1983, pp.17-24.

Zemach, E.M., "Time and Self", *Analysis*, 39, 1979, pp.143-147.

Zwart, P.J., *About Time*, Amsterdam and Oxford: North Holland, 1976.

INDEX

Prior, A.N. 69, 104, 228
process philosophy 115, 120, 286-287, 292, 297, 291, 301
Proclus 24, 34
providence 9, 33, 154, 235, 252, 266, 269-272, 274, 275,
Puccetti, R. 290
Pure Duration 111, 113, 115
Rahner, K. 261
real relation 95, 179-181, 183, 194, 225, 233, 248
reality of time 9, 60, 66, 227, 265, 301
relativity of simultaneity 85, 123-124, 126, 231, 297
Relton, H.M. 109
Rescher, N. 104
revelation 4, 5, 112, 114, 165-166, 187, 285
Richmond, J. 97
Roberts, R.H. 115
Ross, J.F. 146, 231, 260
Royce, J. 99
Russell, B. 72-74, 98, 242
Schleiermacher, F.D. 47, 50, 52-53, 272
Schlick, M. 87
Schopenhauer, A. 59
Scotus, John Duns 43-44, 209, 220
Sellars, W. 77-78, 85, 104
Shoemaker, S. 62-63
Shutte, A. 183
Simultaneity
    relativity of 127
    Stump-Kretzmann 126, 128, 129, 130
sin 152, 262-263, 267
Sklar, L. 59
Smith, Q. 76
Smulders, P. 260
Sorabji, R. 63, 77, 174
Sosa, E. 136
specious present 98-99, 102-104, 122
Steinkraus, W.E. 285
Stout, G.F. 140
Stump, E. 126, 129, 188
Sturch, R.L. 140
Sutherland, S.R. 139, 140